CORNWALL

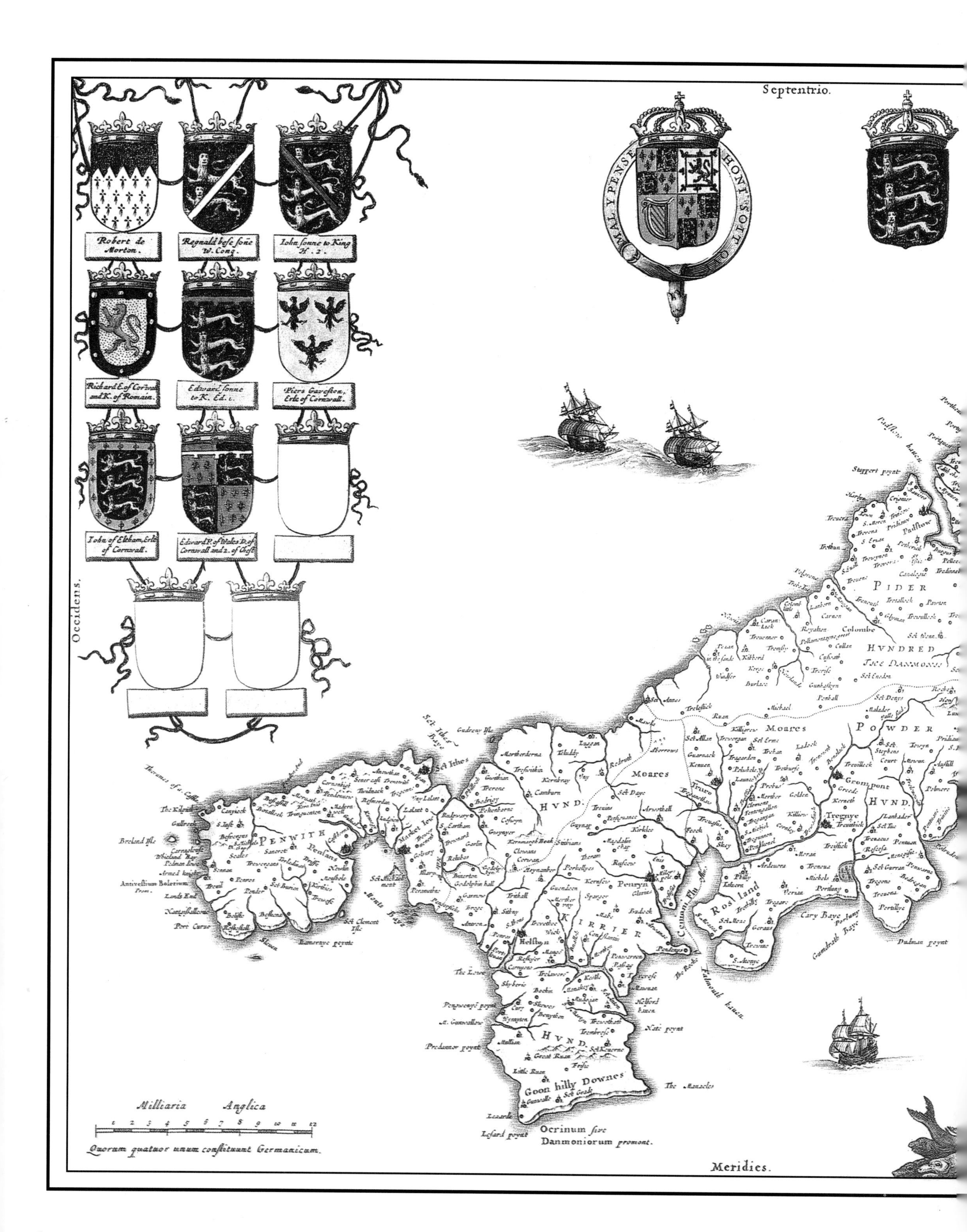
Septentrio.
Occidens.
Meridies.
Robert de Morton.
Ragnald base sonne W. Conq.
John sonne to King H. 2.
Richard E. of Cornwall and K. of Romaen.
Edward sonne to K. Ed. 1.
Piers Gaveston, Erle of Cornwall.
John of Eltham, Erle of Cornwall.
Edward P. of Wales D. of Cornwall and 2. of Chest.
HONI SOIT QUI MAL Y PENSE
PENWITH
KIRRIER
HUND.
PIDER
POWDER
HUND.
HUNDRED
Moares
Ros land
Goon hilly Downes
Ocrinum sive Danmoniorum promont.
Milliaria Anglica
Quorum quatuor unum constituunt Germanicum.

CORNWALL

Philip Payton

Alexander Associates
Fowey Cornwall

To the memory of
Michael Joseph An Gof
and Thomas Flamank
. . . names perpetual, and fame
permanent and immortal.

First Subscribers Edition published
in Great Britain in 1996 by
Alexander Associates
Fowey, Cornwall PL23 1AR. UK.

ISBN 1 899526 60 9

Conceived & Designed by Howard Alexander
Layouts & Typesetting by Martin Frost at
Alexander Associates with Pagemaker 6 on PC's
Reprographics by Input Words & Graphics, Bodmin
Printed and bound by Graficromo SA, Cordoba, Spain

Title page - **Cornwall** from part iv of **J. Blaeu**'s
Theatrum Orbis Terrarum published in 1645.

Foreword

It was exactly ten years ago that I contributed a Foreward to Philip Payton's book *The Cornish Farmer in Australia.* I wrote then that, 'Dr Philip Payton has been doing excellent work with his books, mainly on the mining folk in Australia. Now Dr Payton, with his gift for research and conscientious investigation, is extending his field into other areas'.

There was no way then of telling just how vigorous this extension would be. But now the evidence is before us. Within the last decade Philip Payton has produced a steady stream of books and articles about Cornwall and the Cornish. He has indeed justified the confidence I placed in him when we first met many years ago. I admired his writing, his drive and his enthusiasm, and strongly supported his appointment in 1991 as Director of the Institute of Cornish Studies in succession to my old friend Professor Charles Thomas, our foremost archaeologist.

The Institute is linked to the University of Exeter but is situated in Cornwall. Crucially, it has the backing and financial support of Cornwall County Council, and Philip Payton has become a fine ambassador for Cornwall at home and abroad.

Now Dr Payton has produced an important work which fills a major gap in Cornish literature. For the first time, we have in *Cornwall* a full-length, wide-ranging history that is profusely illustrated and takes account of all the latest writing across the disciplines.

The twelve Chapters encompass the entire Cornish land and people, showing how Cornwall has remained a place apart, and tracing the emigration of Cousin Jacks to North America, Australia and South Africa. Whether of Cornish descent or not, the reader will gain an extraordinarily invaluable insight into our 'little land of Cornwall' and its people.

The subscription list, more than a thousand strong, with subscribers from as far afield as the Falklands and Prince Edward Island, is testament to the enduring fascination of Cornwall. But it also reflects the international reputation that Philip Payton has made for himself. He deserves our congratulation.

A.L.Rowse, Trenarren 1996.

Introduction

We live in an age of anniversaries, forever celebrating this event and that occasion, marking so-called turning points in history, or commemorating triumphs or disasters that have changed the course of human affairs. These days anniversaries follow one another with almost bewildering frequency and rapidity, coming so thick and fast that we have barely recovered from one bout of exuberance or solemnity before it is on to the next. From village hall centenaries to remembering the horrors of global warfare, our diaries are kept full, our emotions taut.

The celebration of Cornishness is curiously fragmented, however, either highly localised in its expression (Padstow's 'Obby 'Oss or Camborne's Trevithick Day) or dependent upon external phenomena such as the success (or otherwise) of Cornwall's rugby football team. The commemoration of the 500th Anniversary of the 1497 Rebellions is, therefore, an event of some significance. Not only is it an opportunity to reflect anew upon those traumatic happenings, but it is a cue for us to consider more widely Cornwall and the Cornish experience.

To complaints that contemporary Cornwall is marginalised as an 'inconvenient periphery', a thorn in the side of planners with grander regional designs that sweep far beyond the Tamar, must be added the fact that Cornwall and the Cornish are so often historiographically 'invisible'. Although we have much 'good' Cornish history, notably in the realms of archaeology and nineteenth-century mining, it is only in the last ten years that scholars have asked serious questions about how Cornish history has been written, and how the Cornish people have been portrayed.

It is only very recently that writers of Cornish history have felt equipped to glance across disciplinary boundaries—to learn from political scientists, anthropologists, geographers, and others—with a view to setting Cornwall and the Cornish in the wider comparative context of European (and ultimately global) ethnic and territorial diversity.

This book, therefore, should be seen both as part of the marking of 1497 and as an attempt to marshall and explain perspectives on the Cornish past—and present. It has been written with the general reader as well as the Cornish specialist in mind, for part of the role of the Institute of Cornish Studies (jointly funded as it is by the University of Exeter and Cornwall County Council) is to bring a considered appreciation of Cornish issues to a wider public.

The late Professor Gwyn A. Williams, whose formidable reputation as remembrancer of the Welsh people will endure for many decades, once wrote that 'A great deal of Welsh history has been Welsh history with the Welsh people left out'. He might as easily have been writing about Cornwall. Until recently, *our* history has been so often the history of Cornwall without the Cornish people, and it is time that *we* offered a corrective.

Philip Payton, Illogan 1996.

Contents

CHAPTER 1
ANCIENT STONES
CORNWALL

Ancient Stones

As we shall see as the story of Cornwall unfolds in this book, this Cornish land is many things to many people, its history so often contradictory and paradoxical. Cornwall is a far-flung half-forgotten remnant of the Celtic world; or maybe it is the limelit stage upon which the global, earth-shattering acts of the Industrial Revolution were first performed. The Cornish are the last of an ancient race, their moribund way of life fast disappearing in response to the homogenising pressures of international Western culture. Or perhaps, like other ethnic groups across the new Europe, the Cornish have at last the self-confidence to express a vibrant separate identity that will ensure their place in the rich regional mosaic of European integration. For outsiders, Cornwall is peace and tranquillity, a haven to which one might retire from the mad rush of modern life; for insiders Cornwall is often poverty and poor housing and a struggle to make ends meet in a low-wage economy.

But behind this fluidity of interpretation there are certainties, and none more so than the bedrock of the land itself. On cliffs and moors, in architecture, in mines and quarries, in the fabric of the landscape, geology is in Cornwall (for even the most casual of observers) a powerful determinant of territorial character and identity. Thus for the contemporary Cornish poet and novelist D.M. Thomas, Cornwall is *The Granite Kingdom*, while for writer James Turner the essential feature of Cornwall is that it is *The Stone Peninsula.*[1] For the romantic fancy of popular fiction, the stones of Cornwall are old, as old as time itself, and this is something with which the scientist will readily concur. The stones of Cornwall *are* old. The oldest rocks are on the Lizard peninsula, a veritable mecca for geologists, but most of Cornwall consists geologically of strongly deformed sediments which were intruded by granites in the late Carboniferous or early Permian periods, about 300 million years ago.

Throughout the preceding Carboniferous and Devonian periods, most of what is now Cornwall lay beneath the sea. In a complex series of geological events sedimentary material was laid down on the seabed while, at the end of the Carboniferous period, the cataclysmic collision of two landmasses—one southern, one northern—threw this material up into a mountain range. The process is known to geologists as the Variscan orogeny, and its consequences for the physical creation of Cornwall have been described recently by Professor Colin Bristow.[2] Briefly, the story is this. Some of the sea-bed caught up in the early phases of this collision was thrust up to the surface to become the Lizard peninsula, known today for its distinctive geological and topographical features. Elsewhere, huge volumes of debris slipped down from the colliding northern landmass and are detected now in the geology of the southern Cornish coast—in the Roseland peninsula and westwards along the southern side of the Helford River towards Mullion. As Professor Bristow has remarked, the geology of these areas has more in common with that of Brittany than any other part of

On windswept Rough Tor, ancient core stones have been weathered into fantastic shapes, to produce a landscape of incredible beauty.

Britain—a fascinating echo of the cultural bonds that were for so long to tie Brittany and Cornwall together, and which in recent years have been re-affirmed in contexts such as inter-Celtic wrestling contests and the twinning of Cornish and Breton towns.

About 10 million years after the Variscan collision had reached its climax (a mere bat of the eyelid in geological time) came the granitic intrusion. A great mass of molten granite welled-up in a line from what is now the Isles of Scilly to Dartmoor so that, in Colin Bristow's phrase, '. . . we may truthfully say that Cornwall is formed of hardened mud buoyed up by granite'.[3] Over the subsequent passage of some 300 million years, erosion has laid bare the granite (the Cornubian batholith, as it is called by geologists), forming the distinctive landscape we know today.

Dartmoor is in Devon (albeit part of the possession of the Duchy of Cornwall) but, running east to west from the River Tamar border which divides Cornwall from the rest of Britain, we encounter first the granite of Kit Hill and Hingston Down near Callington. Further west is Bodmin Moor (or, to give it its historic and more picturesque name, Foweymore), the most extensive of the Cornish moors. Further west still is the granitic intrusion known variously as Blackmore, St Austell Moor, Hensbarrow or today, the china clay country. Beyond Truro, north of the modern road from Penryn to Helston, are the Carnmenellis or Wendron Moors (with the detached mass of Carn Brea overshadowing the mining towns of Camborne and Redruth), and in the far-west in the Land's End peninsula (ancient Belerion) are the moors of West Penwith. Out to sea, amongst what Professor Charles Thomas has so eloquently described as the 'drowned landscape', are the Scillies—the 'Fortunate Isles'.

Cornwall's two 'mountains', Rough Tor and Brown Willy stand proudly over Bodmin Moor.

Other, smaller granitic outcrops of this Cornubian batholith include St Agnes Beacon, Carn Marth near Redruth, Tregonning and Godolphin Hills near Helston, and the exotic island of St Michael's Mount. Each of these intrusions dominates its locality, but the tops of the granite masses become ever lower the further west one travels. Across the border on Dartmoor, High Willhays is some 627m (2039 ft) above sea level. Brown Willy on Bodmin Moor, at 423m (1375 ft) is the highest hill (mountain) in Cornwall. The Isles of Scilly at their highest point are only 51m (166 ft) above the sea. Erosion has capped these Cornish outcrops with often fantastic shapes, from the familiar twin peaks of Rough Tor and the razorback edge of Kilmar Tor, both on Bodmin Moor, to the eerie eminences of the Cheesewring and Carn Kenidjack—the one in East Cornwall, the other in the far west. Here and there the horizontal weathering of outcrops has led to the creation of delicately-balanced rocking or logan stones, the most famous of which is at Treryn Dinas near Land's End. Similarly, strange rock basins—such as those encountered at Carn Brea—have been created as a result of the reaction over very many centuries of acidic rain on granite.

It is not surprising that in earlier times folk seeking explanations for these often weird, and sometimes frightening and forbidding, natural rock formations should have turned to superstition and folklore for their interpretations. In the nineteenth century antiquarians such as Robert Hunt and William Bottrell set about recording the myths and legends of old Cornwall, putting down on paper—often for the first time—stories that then still enjoyed popular currency amongst the ordinary Cornish people.[4] An oral tradition of droll-telling that stretched back across the centuries had perpetuated these stories into modern times, ensuring their preservation but also attesting to the enduring relevance of ancient stones in the cultural make-up of Cornwall.

Typically, natural rock formations were seen to have inherent supernatural powers of their own, or were otherwise the work of giants. A more sinister overlay intimated dark Druidical rites amongst the rock basins, with lurid tales of human sacrifice persisting so strongly that even the Rev William Borlase, the eighteenth-century antiquarian who was in many ways the father of modern Cornish geological and archaeological studies, readily attributed natural monuments to the work of Druids.

Part of ancient 'Belerion'—Kenidjack cliff, west of Carn Kenidjack on the craggy Penwith coastline.

The curious rockpile that is the Cheesewring has attracted various tales, the best known of which is that recorded by Hunt in which the topmost stone turned three times at the sound of a cock crowing. Similar properties were attributed to the cock-crow stone, a rock of 'white marble' (probably quartz) said to lie in Looe harbour, uncovered at low tide. Carn Kenidjack (or Kenidzhek, as Hunt liked to spell it) was the hooting carn, so-called because of its mysterious ability to emit sounds that ranged from a low muttering to a shrill hoot, in reality the effect of winds swirling amongst the rockpiles but in popular imagination evidence of the carn's reputed satanic hauntings.

The bizarre attributes of logan stones attracted much attention. At Nancledra was a logan stone, thought locally to have been created by supernatural power, which would rock like a cradle on the stroke of midnight and was thus known as the twelve-o'clock stone. If placed naked on the stone at exactly that hour, a child suffering from rickets would receive a miracle cure. The alleged healing power of ancient stones was also manifest in the 'crick stone' near Morvah, where to pass between the natural fork in the rock was to find a cure for a bad back. The Giant's Rock near Zennor Churchtown had more sinister powers, for anyone climbing upon it nine times without rocking it would become a witch. Indeed, a widespread belief was that 'Touch a Logan stone nine times at midnight, and any woman will become a witch'.[5]

Hunt wrote of the Treryn logan stone that 'A more sublime spot could not have been chosen by the Bardic priesthood for any ordeal connected with their worship', and that '. . . every kind of mischief which can befall man or beast was once brewed by the St Levan witches'.[6] Madgy Figgy, one of the most celebrated witches of St Levan and St Buryan, was said to have her own chair in the cliffs nearby, formed miraculously in stone amongst the rockpiles, where she commanded the spirits of the storm. At Trewa, on the downs between Nancledra and Zennor, was also the 'Witches' Rock', where all the witches of Penwith '. . . assembled at midnight to carry on their

The Cheesewring is a curious rockpile as seen on page 2. Stowe's Hill, near the Cheesewring is a fine example of the way rocky eminences called 'tors' are left standing above the moor's surface.

St. Michael's Mount has inspired much literature over the centuries. John Milton's *Lycidas* contains a vision of the island:

> 'Where the great vision of the guarded Mount
> Looks towards Namancos and Bayona's hold . . .'

and in 1810, Joseph Farrington wrote that 'the castle is in all respects in such harmony with the rock upon which it stands, as almost seems a natural part of it'.

Dedicated to St. Michael, the island off Marazion, has a traditional Cornish name 'Carrack looz en cooz' meaning the 'grey rock in the wood' which suggests that the Mount was once located within a forest.

wicked deeds', although, curiously, 'Any one touching this rock nine times at midnight was insured against bad luck'.[7]

Amongst the many giant legends collected by the nineteenth-century antiquarians are those of the giants of St Michael's Mount. Perhaps more than any other rock formation in Cornwall, the Mount invites the theory that it was the work of giants. One tale insists that it was built by the giant Cormoran and his wife Cormelian. An interesting detail here is that the small greenstone Chapel Rock that lies between the Mount and the shore at Marazion is said to have dropped from Cormelian's apron as she carried the building materials to and fro. On Trencrom Hill (or Trecobben, as it was sometimes known) lived another family of giants, and their pastime was to engage in energetic games with their neighbours on St Michael's Mount. As Hunt observed, 'In several parts of Cornwall there are evidences that these Titans were a sportive race. Huge rocks are preserved to show where they played at trap-ball, hurling, and other athletic games'.[8]

The giants of Trencrom and the Mount specialised in the game of 'bob-buttons'. The Mount was the 'bob', on which flat slabs of granite were placed to act as buttons, and Trencrom Hill was the 'mit' from which the throw was made. The rocky debris surrounding both outcrops today shows the intensity with which the giants played. In another story, the huge mass of granite boulders strewn near Castle-an-Dinas (in West Penwith), were pieces of rock that had been carried by a local giant to protect himself against his enemies, those giants of Trencrom. In yet another, the giant Bolster—who would in one stride span the distance from St Agnes Beacon to Carn Brea—force his luckless wife to pick up rocks from the country surrounding St Agnes and then carry them in her apron to the summit of the Beacon.

Thus folklore conveniently explained the origins of geological features, noting (or inventing) their *raisons d'être* and accounting for the profusion (or otherwise) of rocks and boulders in the Cornish landscape. In so doing, the imagery of ancient stones became essential ingredients in representations of Cornwall, a trend re-emphasised in modern times when the Romantic movement effectively rehabilitated the wild grandeur of moor and mountain in literary appreciation (for example, Wordsworth's Lake District, or Scott's Highlands and Borders). In this century the evocation of Cornish rocks has been *de rigeur* for any writer attempting a depiction or analysis of Cornwall. The poets D.M.Thomas and Peter Redgrove have penned, respectively, their "Logan-Stone' and 'Minerals of Cornwall, Stones of Cornwall', while Dr A.L. Rowse writes of the timelessness of 'Helman Tor': 'Kingdoms are lost and empires fall,/ States decay. But this remains'.[9] For John Heath-Stubbs:

> This is a hideous and wicked country,
> Sloping to hateful sunsets and the end of time,
> Hollow with mine-shafts, naked with granite, fanatic
> With sorrow. Abortions of the past
> Hop through these bogs; black-faced, the villagers
> Remember burnings by the hewn stones.[10].

A St. Piran's flag, symbolising the white tin on the black rock, and now recognised as the Cornish Flag, flies above the dressed granite of Redruth's clock tower.

Denys Val Baker's *A View from Land's End* returns time and again to the relationship between geology, landscape and the creative impulse.[11] Gerald Priestland has emphasised 'The metaphysical dimension of Penwith . . .', with its '. . . cheesewrings and citadels of weathered moorstone'.[12] Ithell Colquhoun's *The Living Stones of Cornwall*, written in the mid-1950s, exemplifies this *genre*:

> The life of a region depends ultimately on its geologic substratum, for this sets up a chain-reaction which passes, determining their character, in turn through its streams and wells, its vegetation and the animal life that feeds on this, and finally through the type of human being attracted to live there. In a profound sense also the structure of its rocks gives rise to the psychic life of the land.[13]

As Colquhoun adds, 'Stones that whisper, stones that dance, that play on pipe or fiddle, that tremble at cock-crow, that eat and drink, stones that march as an army—these unhewn slabs of granite hold the secret of the country's inner life'.[14] Today, this approach is echoed in the New Age movement, not least in the periodical *Meyn Mamvro* (Cornish for, 'stones of the mother land') which sees in the ancient stones a thread of continuity linking modern Cornwall to earliest times.

This geological heritage has prompted the powerful explanatory phenomenon of myth and legend, transformed in modern times into literary evocation and into spiritual and psychic meaning, but in more practical ways it has also powerfully influenced the material culture of Cornwall. For example, granite moorstone, the rocky debris that still litters much of moorland Cornwall, has for centuries been used for a multiplicity of domestic and monumental purposes—from constructing churches to setting-up the ubiquitous Cornish hedges—and quarried granite has been much sought after for private and public building in Cornwall and in Britain as a whole. Major granite-quarrying areas have included St Breward and Cheesewring on Bodmin Moor, Luxulyan in mid-Cornwall, and the Penryn-Constantine district in the west.

Although Nicklaus Pevsner decided that in the realms of architecture 'Cornwall possesses little of the highest aesthetic quality',[15] a distinctive and self-respecting, if modest, tradition can be detected in Cornish building, related in Frank and Veronica Chesher's book *The Cornishman's House*.[16] And while much is plain and simple, as the hardness of the rock dictates, even Cornish granite has on occasions been the subject of detailed and painstaking attention by craftsmen, especially in church architecture. As John Betjeman wrote, 'Only a Cornishman would have the endurance to carve intractable granite as he has done at St Mary Magdalene, Launceston and Probus towers'.[17] In the eighteenth and nineteenth centuries, granite lent itself especially well to the Georgian and neo-classical buildings that were then emerging. Early Cornish public buildings of note constructed of dressed granite included the town halls at Lostwithiel (1740) and Fowey (1790), the Market (1827) and Assize Court (1838) at Bodmin, Redruth Clock Tower (1828), and St Just-in-Penwith Market House (1840).

The architecture of much of Cornwall has a granite face but other Cornish stone has also been important as building material. From Polyphant in the parish of Lewannick, near Launceston, comes the distinctive grey picrite known as Polyphant stone, used in the construction of Launceston's medieval castle and in many churches in East Cornwall, and in mid-Cornwall is the buff-coloured elvan called Pentewan stone—most noted for its use in the construction of the facade of the eighteenth-century Antony House near Torpoint. From Catacleuse on the north coast, near Trevose, comes the famous Catacleuse stone which was used in churches for fonts, tomb chests and arcades, the raw material for the enigmatic 'Master of Endellion' who was responsible for much of the ecclesiastical stone carving in North Cornwall in the mid-fifteenth century. At St Neot and, even more famously at Delabole, near Camelford, slates have been quarried since medieval times for use as floor flags, sills, chests and cisterns as well as the traditional 'helling' (roofing) slates. Dressed slate ('Cornish marble') has been used for monumental purposes, from the extraordinary slate figure memorials of the late sixteenth and early seventeenth centuries (the surviving sixty or so examples of which were so painstakingly recorded by the late Alice Bizley[18]) to the work of the noted Neville Northey Burnard whose efforts included the Richard Lander memorial in Truro and the carving of John Wesley at Trewint.[19]

Easily accessible rock at or just below the surface has been thus of crucial significance to the economy and character of Cornwall, contributing much to its wealth and material culture. Deep below the surface, the geological heritage is perhaps of even greater importance, for those events of 300 million years ago which threw up the land of Cornwall have also accounted for the remarkable inventory of minerals which has played such an important role in Cornish economic history. The intense heat of the intruding molten granite had sweated out metals and minerals from both the granite itself and the rocks it invaded, leading to the veined deposits (lodes) discovered in the granite outcrops and their metamorphic aureoles—those adjacent rocks changed in character by heat and pressure. Foremost amongst the metamorphic rocks of these aureoles is 'killas' the Cornish word for clay-slate, which has also been used as a building material.

The principal metals of Cornwall are copper and tin, and their deposits are distributed along and beside the granitic backbone, almost literally from Land's End to the Tamar. In the far west are the districts of St Just-in-Penwith, St Ives and Marazion. In the Central Mining District and its hinterlands are Camborne-Redruth, Gwennap, St Agnes-Perranporth, and Wendron. In mid-Cornwall is St Austell, and in the east are the Liskeard-St Cleer and Callington-Gunnislake districts. Silver-lead has been discovered and exploited in areas such as East Wheal Rose (near the village of Newlyn East in mid-Cornwall) and in East Cornwall at Menheniot and Herodsfoot. Although often overlooked or under-estimated by commentators, iron

The dazzling white slopes of a china clay pit in mid-Cornwall, with pyramidal tips in the background. The industry has been a mixed blessing, bringing both prosperity and environmental conflict.

deposits have been appreciable and important, as at the Great Perran Iron Lode (near Perranporth) and the Restormel Royal Iron Mine (near Lostwithiel). Uranium (pitchblende) has been discovered at Wheal Trenwith, near St Ives, and at South Terras near St Stephen-in-Brannel in mid-Cornwall. Amongst other metals exploited in Cornwall have been manganese at Altarnun on Bodmin Moor, wolfram on Goss Moor, and antimony near Port Quin on the north coast.

China clay is yet another important component of the Cornish geological inheritance, dominating as it does today the daily life and economy of Trewoon, Treviscoe, Bugle, Stenalees, St Dennis and a score of other villages to the north of St Austell. Over the last 300 million years the granite of the Hensbarrow upland has been exposed to the elements. Rainwater soaked into the granite and over those millions of years was circulated convectively by the residual heat of the rocks (a function of their radioactivity), leading to a significant decomposition of the granite into kaolin or china clay. This process was accelerated by periods of intense earthquake activity, when old faults created during the Variscan orogeny were reactivated to form new cracks through which water might be further circulated and the phenomenon of 'kaolinisation' thus extended. The explorations and discoveries of William Cookworthy in the mid-eighteenth century led to the speedy development of these hitherto long-dormant china clay deposits, spawning a new form of Cornish extractive industry and prompting in turn the creation of distinctive clay communities. Alan Kent's recent novel, simply entitled *Clay*,[20] evokes much of the atmosphere of this singular part of Cornwall, and the poetry of the late Jack Clemo (the blind and deaf poet of the clay country) conveys the harsh, paradoxical, puritancial beauty of the china clay environment:

> Yes, I might well grow tired
> Of slighting flowers all day long,
> Of making my song
> Of the mud in the kiln, of the wired
> Poles of the clay dump; . . .
> Is there a flower that thrills
> Like frayed rope? Is there grass
> That cools like gravel, and are there streams
> Which murmur as clay-silt does that Christ redeems?[21]

NATIVE COPPER
This was a common secondary copper mineral which formed in the upper parts of the lodes. Particularly good examples came from the Gwennap mines. This arborescent growth may be from Wheal Unity or Wheal Virgin. Such was the quality of Wheal Virgin native copper that it was locally called "virgin copper".

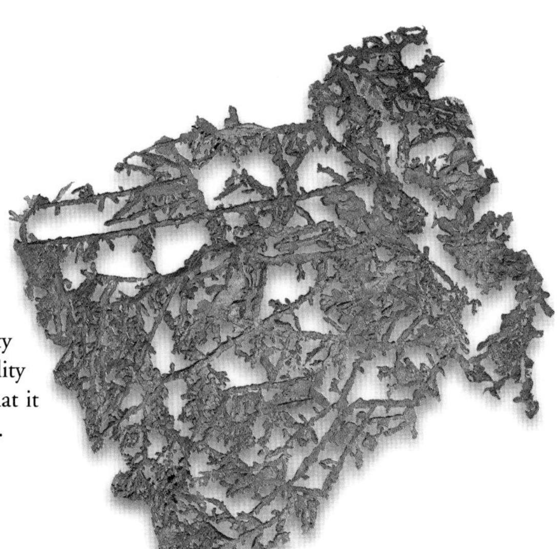

CERUSSITE (carbonate of lead)
A secondary lead mineral which was found in beautiful straw-like crystals at Pentireglaze Mine, St Endellion. So delicate were the crystals that, to prevent injury, single specimens destined for a collection at Trevince, Gwennap, were carried in a wicker basket slung on a pole resting on the shoulders of two men, a distance of over 30 miles (*Mining Journal*, 30 Jan. 1858).

OLIVENITE (arsenate of copper)
This specimen from Philip Rashleigh's collection is said to be from Tincroft, but it is most likely to be from one of the Gwennap mines, such as Wheal Gorland or Wheal Unity, which were noted for the superlative quality of their copper arsenates.

CASSITERITE (oxide of tin)
Cassiterite is the only important tin-bearing mineral. Because it is an oxide it is stable and does not break down chemically into secondary minerals as happens with primary copper minerals which are sulphides. Shiny black crystals of cassiterite were commonly called 'diamond tin'. This specimen is from one of the St Agnes mines.

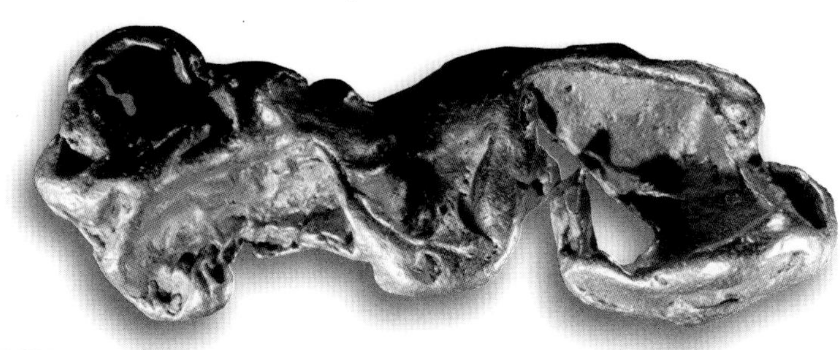

NATIVE GOLD
Most of the alluvial tin deposits contained small amounts of gold, usually of sand-grain size or smaller, and rarely larger than a split-pea. This nugget, 59mm long and weighing nearly 2 ounces, is the largest known from Cornwall. It was recovered in January 1808 from the Carnon Stream Tin Works, Perranarworthal, and was obtained by Philip Rashleigh (1729-1811), most of whose collection is now at the Royal Cornwall Museum, Truro.

CHALCOPYRITE (sulphide of copper)
An unusual variety known as 'blistered copper'. Fine specimens came from various mines around St Agnes and Camborne. This specimen may have come from Dolcoath Mine, Camborne.

CASSITERITE (oxide of tin)
A remarkable group of diamond tin on yellow topaz from Wheal Trevaunance, St Agnes. Philip Rashleigh illustrated this specimen in Volume 1, Plate 5 of his *Specimens of British Minerals,* 1797.

GALENA (sulphide of lead)
An unusual specimen of galena crystals which have replaced pyromorphite (phosphate of lead) but retained the prismatic form of the latter. This rare pseudomorph, locally called 'blue lead', was discovered at Wheal Hope, Perranzabuloe, in 1822. Normally, pyromorphite is an alteration product after galena.

CASSITERITE (oxide of tin)
A particularly fine specimen of 'diamond tin' from Wheal Trevaunance, St Agnes, from Philip Rashleigh's collection. It brings to mind the old Cornish saying *stên sen Agnes yû'n gwella stên en Kernow* (St Agnes tin is the best tin in Cornwall).

OLIVENITE (arsenate of copper)
Olivenite varies in colour from very pale green to near black. These dark crystals on quartz came from Wheal Gorland

> '. . . once without peer.
> For colours the rarest of very rich ore, And beautiful minerals valued yet more'.

(W.Frances, *History of Gwennap,* 1845)

CASSITERITE (oxide of tin)
Crystals of cassiterite take many forms. These long brownish crystals from Dolcoath Mine, Camborne, are known as 'sparable tin' from their likeness to a sparrow's bill. Cassiterite varies in colour from white (almost unknown in Cornwall) to black: the deeper the colour the greater the iron content, though always minute. Cassiterite contains about 78 per cent tin.

KAOLINITE (a complex aluminium silicate)
Kaolinite or china clay is a decomposition product of feldspars in granite. In this specimen the clay has replaced a cubic mineral, probably fluorite. It was discovered when a large specimen, from Rostowrack China-stone Quarry, St Dennis, was broken open. The kaolinite is surrounded by quartz, partly of the dark smoky variety.

OLIVENITE (arsenate of copper)
This specimen from Wheal Gorland, Gwennap, was loaned by Philip Rashleigh to James Sowerby (1757-1822) who illustrated it on Plate 170 of his *British Minerals* (5 Vols. 1804-1817).

CHALCOPYRITE (sulphide of copper and iron)
Because it contains nearly as much iron (30.5 per cent) as copper (34.5 per cent), chalcopyrite at great depth was not always economic to mine. Normally it is a brassy yellow colour, but these crystals from the Rashleigh collection are thinly coated with zinc blende. The group sits on quartz crystal. The specimen is from one of the St Agnes mines.

CHALCOCITE (enriched sulphide of copper)
One of the most important economic copper minerals which formed in lodes in the zone of secondary enrichment below the water-table. It contains about 79 per cent copper, more than double that found in the primary mineral chalcopyrite. In Cornwall it was popularly called 'redruthite'. This specimen came from Cook's Kitchen Nine, Illogan.

CUPRITE (oxide of copper)
Small but distinct ruby-coloured octahedral crystals of cuprite from Gwennap, probably Wheal Gorland or near mine. The mineral was frequently associated with native copper and other secondary coppers in the upper parts of the lodes.

As if all this were not enough, mineralogists present us with yet another distinctive aspect of this extraordinary geological inheritance.[22] For them the ancient stones that excite their attentions are not the rocky outcrops, nor even the mineral wealth of tin and copper and china clay, but rather the startling diversity and beauty of Cornish mineral specimens that exist in astonishing mineral suites below ground. Of scientific as well as aesthetic importance, many of these specimens are extremely rare, and all are eminently collectable. Bassetite, for example, consists of small yellowish-brown crystal plates and comes from the Basset mines in Illogan, where it was first recognised in 1915. Bright grey bournonite comes from localities such as Wheal Boys in St Endellion and Herodsfoot, near Liskeard, while pale-green Liskeardite is from Marke Valley mine on the edge of Caradon Hill, again near Liskeard. Specimens of siderite, pyromorphite, olivenite, chalcosine, cassiterite, malachite, baryte and hundreds of other striking and often rare minerals grace priceless Cornish collections such as those in the Camborne School of Mines, the Rashleigh collection at the Royal Cornwall Museum in Truro, and the recently re-opened Royal Cornwall Geological Society museum in Penzance. Indeed, the 440 species of minerals identified in Cornwall thus far represent a startling 15% of the entire world total.

The tradition of mineral collecting is a venerable and respected one in Cornwall, and an appreciation of this fact is essential to our understanding of the significance of ancient stones in representations of Cornwall.[23] The Rev William Borlase (1695-1772) was the first Cornishman to form an extensive mineral collection, his enthusiasm for mineralogy informing much of his *Natural History of Cornwall*, published in 1758, an indication of the importance to him of geological complexity as an explanation for much that was 'Cornish'. Fascinated as he was by the supposed Druidic associations of rockpiles and rock basins, he was also extremely careful to assemble specimens of Cornish minerals. Borlase sent many of his best specimens to the Ashmolean Museum in Oxford, as well as to the Royal Society in London and to Leyden University, but sadly very few items from his collection have survived. His *Natural History*, however, remains of inestimable importance to students of Cornwall and, although it is not as well known as William Pryce's *Mineralogia Cornubiensis* of 1778, it is a classic volume and a model of its type.

Philip Rashleigh (1729-1811) of Menabilly, near Fowey, was perhaps the most famous Cornish collector but members of the celebrated Fox family (the Cornish Quakers) in the first half of the nineteenth century are also known to have been keen collectors. Others included John Hawkins (1761-1841), the mineral dealer and bookseller Joseph Tregoning (1762-1841), the Penzance banker Joseph Carne (1782-1858), the Williams family of Scorrier and Caerhays (mining magnates who made their wealth in the Gwennap copper mines), the antiquarian and folklorist Robert Hunt (1807-1887), and the aristocratic Sir John St Aubyn (1758-1839). Two especially interesting characters were John Lavin (c1794-1856) and Richard Talling (1820-1883). Lavin was a mineral dealer who also sold maps, stationery and guides from his grandly-named 'Lavin's Museum', the extraordinary Egyptian revivalist style house that still stands in Chapel Street, Penzance. Richard Talling operated from his 'Fancy Repository' (a shop selling gifts and trinkets) in Fore Street, Lostwithiel, and established an enviable reputation that has lasted to our own time as a shrewd and perceptive acquirer of outstanding mineral specimens—particularly from the East Cornwall mines.[24]

In Penzance, Egyptian House's eccentricity is testament to the life of the mineral dealer John Lavin (c1794-1856).

St. Cleer Church is dedicated to *Sanctus Clarus* or St. Clair, who was said to have been a 'martyr of chastity', murdered by the plotting of 'an impious and lewd lady of quality'. The tower itself is one of the finest examples of fifteenth century church architecture in Cornwall.

The establishment of the Royal Cornwall Geological Society in 1814 marked the significance of this mineralogical tradition and its value to Cornwall (it is the second oldest geological society in the United Kingdom) but it also demonstrated the wider comparative importance of Cornwall in which some of the earliest developments in the science of geology involved aspects of Cornish geology or scientists who were themselves Cornish. Sir Humphry Davy, leading Cornishman of his age, delivered lectures of world-wide significance to the Royal Institution in 1805, to be followed by the publications of H.T. de la Beche in 1839 and William Henwood in 1843. Later, they in turn were followed by the writings of J.H. Collins (1840-1916) and W.A.E. Ussher (1849-1920) in which significant advances in the geological understanding of Cornwall were made. Today, Cornwall continues to command the attention of geologists, often still on the world stage, and a telling fact is that Cornwall has more hard-rock (granite and related) Sites of Special Scientific Interest (a governmental designation of important localities) than any other county in Britain.[25]

The distinctive geology of Cornwall, together with the distinguished place that Cornwall and Cornish people have enjoyed in the global development of the science of geology, has ensured that those ancient stones remain central to an understanding of our Cornish land. However, as intimated above, in historic times ancient stones have not remained inert memorials to the forces that first created the physical entity of Cornwall but have become materials in the hands of men and women. In the modern era this process is not difficult to chart, and we may point to any number of startling examples of human handiwork in which the raw materials of Cornish rock have been crafted into enduring memorials of Cornish history. The fifteenth century, for example, witnessed that great spate of ecclesiastical building activity, bequeathing to us those grand and so typically Cornish church towers of the order of Morwenstow, St Cleer, Constantine, Linkinhorne, and Lanlivery. Later, in the period of energetic industrial expansion in the eighteenth and nineteenth centuries were created not only those impressive public buildings but also the engine-houses, Methodist chapels, lighthouses, harbour-arms, railway viaducts, workhouses, and honest rows of workers' cottages which were in stone the everyday icons of modern Cornish life.

However, the crafting of ancient stones by men and women in the more distant past is for us a more impenetrable and mysterious process, elucidated but slowly by the cautious and painstakingly meticulous methods of our contemporary archaeologists. Standing stones, hut circles, stone circles and the like, mark in often dramatic fashion the activities of our distant forebears. In earlier centuries, without the rational deliberations of scientists to train their thoughts, ordinary folk saw in these monuments the work of giants or of Divine retribution and, as in their explanations for 'hooting carns' and 'cock-crow stones', wove stories (fanciful to us but all too convincing for them) to interpret their provenance. Again, we are indebted to the inquisitive antiquarianism of Hunt, Bottrell and others who recorded before it was lost, the oral tradition of story-telling as explanation. And again we see the significance of ancient stones in our reconstructions of the Cornish past. 'And shall these mute stones speak?' asks Professor Charles Thomas of the inscribed stones of the early Christian era, but he might have asked the same question of a much earlier and much broader range of Cornish monuments. The fact is that the existence of quoits and circles and standing stones spoke volumes to our ancestors, as recorded folklore attests, and still has much to say to many of us today.

Remains of Stone-Age henges can be found at Castilly, near Lanivet, at Castlewich, near Callington, and on the slopes of Hawks Tor on Bodmin Moor where the Stripple Stones form a circle enclosed within a single ditch and bank.[26] More impressive are the megalithic chamber tombs, built in the late Stone-Age/early Bronze Age c.4000 years ago, the so-called portal dolmens more popularly known as 'Penwith' tombs, cromlechs or quoits. Although often seen as distinctive they share features with similar structures in Brittany, Wales and Ireland. As their name suggests, they are found principally in West Penwith although the perhaps finest example is Trethevy Quoit at St Cleer, on the southern edge of Bodmin Moor. Lesquite or Lanivet Quoit lies some three miles south of Bodmin, the Pawton or Giant's Quoit is on St Breock Downs, near Wadebridge, while two miles south of Camborne is Caerwynnen Quoit (also known as the Giant's Frying Pan). In West Penwith itself are the quoits at Lanyon (halfway between Penzance and Morvah), Zennor (south-east of Zennor Churchtown), Chun (near St Just), and Mulfra (near Zennor). Today their distinctive appearance is characterised by the upright slabs of rock (usually granite) surmounted by a giant capstone, but when originally constructed these tombs would have been covered with earth. It is possible that two other well-known Cornish monuments, the Men-an-tol near Morvah and the Tolvan Stone near Gweek, may represent the residual remains of once similar tombs. According to Hunt, scrofulous children passed naked through the Men-an-tol three times, and then drawn on the grass three times against the sun, would be cured of their disease.

Together with these quoits, the other archetypal early stone monuments of Cornwall are the menhirs (or standing stones) and stone circles. The menhirs are numerous (there are said to be 90 positively identified standing stones in West Penwith alone) and consist largely of rough-hewn or unhewn moorstone, erected vertically (probably as gravestones or memorials) during the Bronze-Age. The tallest known in modern times (and now alas destroyed) was the Maern Pearn in Constantine, which stood some 7.4m (24ft) high. Other surviving menhirs of note include the Pipers (two standing stones near the Boleigh stone circle), the Blind Fiddler or Tregonebris Stone halfway between Land's End and Penzance, the Old Man of Gugh (situated on the island of Gugh in the Scillies), and the Tremenheere Longstone near St Keverne on the Lizard peninsula. In the village of Roche in mid-Cornwall stands the impressive Longstone, relocated in 1970 from its original site on Longstone Downs (near St Austell) when the expansion of china clay quarrying necessitated its removal.

Of all the ancient stones of Cornwall, none is more redolent of the relationship between folklore and archaeology than the Bronze-Age (or late Stone-Age) stone circles. Altogether there are over twenty such circles in Cornwall, almost all on Bodmin Moor or West Penwith and all (with the exception of a remarkable quartz circle at Duloe) made of granite. Their purpose remains conjectural, although there is general agreement that they were probably used for religious rituals. In folklore, they are seen usually as people petrified in stone for Sabbath-breaking, typically for hurling (the Cornish ball game) or dancing. The most famous are the Merry Maidens at Boleigh (also known as the Dawns Men, the Cornish for 'Dancing Stones') on the coast road between Penzance and Lands End, and the Hurlers near Minions on Bodmin Moor. The Merry Maidens were, according to legend, turned to stone for dancing, as were the nearby Pipers who provided the music for their indiscretion. The Hurlers consists of the remains of three

Men-an-tol, one of Cornwall's most enduring symbols, retains its ancient magic. Its varied interpretations—curer of rickets and scrofula, fertility enhancer and astronomical marker—all contribute to its on-going mystery.

large circles. They occupy an impressive moorland site, close to both the Cheesewring and Trethevy Quoit and another stone circle on Craddock Moor, and are near an array of other significant archaeological sites ranging from hut circles and the well-known Rillaton barrow to more modern remains of tin and copper mining and mineral railways. Also of note is the circle at Boscawen-un (the Nine Maidens), again between Penzance and Lands End, and the circle at Tregeseal, near St Just-in-Penwith, known variously as the Dancing Stones, Merry Maidens and Nine Maidens. Another Nine Maidens (or Virgin Sisters) stands near Wendron, and there is a further Nine Maidens in St Columb Major. As Hunt observed:

> In many parts of Cornwall, we find, more or less perfect circles of stones, which the learned ascribe to the Druids. Tradition, and the common people, who have faith in all that their fathers have taught them, tell us another tale. These stones are everlasting marks of Divine displeasure, being maidens or men, who were changed into stone for some wicked profanation of the Sabbath-day.[27]

Although Hunt did not say so, one reason why the Sabbath-breaking explanation was so widespread and remembered with such intensity when he

Trethevy Quoit in mid-winter — snow settling on the capstone of this massive neolithic chamber.

was recording in the mid-nineteenth century, was that the Methodists in their transformation of modern Cornwall were, amongst other things, determined to eradicate the frivolities of hurling and dancing. Like all missionaries, they were not averse to co-opting existing beliefs in pursuit of their modernising agenda. Ancient stones and the modernity of Cornish Methodism might seem unlikely allies but in the history of Cornwall such paradoxes are commonplace.

A further paradox, which we shall investigate in greater depth in subsequent chapters, is the co-option by the Cornish-Celtic revivalists in this century of these Stone-Age and Bronze-Age monuments as Celtic stones. Although the origins of the Celts in Cornwall remains problematic, the ancient stones pre-date by centuries if not millennia the first folk we may with some confidence label as 'Celts'. This, however, has not dimmed the enthusiasm of many Celtic revivalists. We may forgive Robert Hunt for supposing that 'The spirit of the Celts, possibly the spirits of yet older people, dwell amidst those rocks' and that in the Cornish landscape 'Nothing but what the Briton planted remains, and if tales tell true, it is probable long years must pass before the Englishman can banish the Celtic powers who here hold sovereign sway'.[28] More recent work perpetuates these ambiguities, however, as in John Sharkey's *Celtic Mysteries*, published in 1975, where (despite a captioned aside which admits the pre-Celtic provenance of Cornish portal dolmens) an arresting photograph of Lanyon Quoit is used to illustrate a discussion of 'Celtic' religion.[29] In the same book the Men-an-tol receives similar treatment, as does Chun Quoit.

James Turner is also drawn to 'stark Celtic stones' but his approach is not so much revivalist as mystical, echoing the thrust of *Meyn Mamvro*, a theme investigated in Evan Hadingham's *Circles and Standing Stones*[30] and made explicit in the writings of Janet and Colin Bord. In considering the ancient stones of Cornwall (and Britain and Ireland) they believe that 'Our twentieth-century logic cannot explain their significance. Our only real illumination is the glimmer of folklore, legend and "race memory" '.[31]

> When the archaeologist and psychic researcher T.C. Lethbridge attempted to find the date of the construction of the Merry Maidens stone circle near Lamorna in Cornwall, he took his dowsing pendulum in one hand and placed the other upon one of the stones. Immediately he received a strong tingling sensation like an electric shock, while his pendulum gyrated in a nearly horizontal position, and the huge, heavy stone felt as if it were rocking wildly . . . photographs have occasionally shown inexplicable light radiations emanating from the stones.[32]

As ever, the mystic possibilities of such ancient stones appeal to the poet, evidenced for example in the verse of a native Cornish writer, the late Anne Treneer, who tells the story of the 'Nine Maidens':

> Oh misty sprites, and bodies cold
> Of greying stones, what have you told
> The wailing winds, that still they cry
> Your sorrows to the passer-by?
> 'We who lived and danced in the sun
> Into the dark went one by one
> As you shall when your day is done'.[33]

The near perfect symmetry of the Merry Maidens stone circle makes it one of the most famous and most visited megalithic sites in Britain. The Merry Maidens, so folk-lore has it, were turned to stone for dancing on the Sabbath. Nearby are to be found the Pipers, the guilty musicians.

The sense of despair inherent in these stones, of the inevitabilty and finality of death, is not only melancholy but intimates malevolence, a theme pursued by other Cornish writers. In his 'The Stone that Liked Company', A.L. Rowse skillfully recounts the story of a longstone, implicated by local folklore in human sacrifices of long-ago, which terrorises the life of a young lad ('the menacing rythyms of those monolithic steps') and finally takes it: 'They found him in the grey light of a morning moon: an old moon, a rind of a moon upon its back in the west, which turned the whole landscape into death's kingdom and lit his face with a strange glimmer there where it lay at the stone's foot'.[34] Similarly, in Mary Williams' short-story 'The Dark Land' we learn the fate of Julie '. . . sucked deep into the womb of that awful place . . . another victim, prey of those forces, the elemental evil which had survived with the stone from primeval times . . .'.[35]

However, just as the tradition of Cornish antiquarianism has led modern enthusiasts into the realms of Celtic revivalism, spirituality and mysticism, so it has prompted a scientific archaeology in which, like Cornish geology, Cornwall has proved not only an incomparable resource but also a laboratory in which great strides in archaeological knowledge have been made.[36] William Borlase himself was an early part of this process. In addition to his *The Natural History of Cornwall*, noted above, was his *Observations on the Antiquities of Cornwall*, published in 1754, his *Observations on the Ancient and Present State of the Islands of Scilly* of 1758, and his *Antiquities, Historical and Monumental, of the County of Cornwall* which appeared in 1769. His *Parochial History of Cornwall* was never finished. Borlase was also a practical archaeologist and engaged in a number of excavations, especially on the Isles of Scilly, and his descriptions of the digs give us the first real accounts of what might be called modern archaeological excavation in Cornwall. His illustrations in his various books are a further clue to his interests and activities, and range from drawings of the Men-an-tol and stone circles to sketches of pottery from Bronze-Age graves.

Professor Malcolm Todd has drawn attention to the hitherto little-known Richard Thomas, a tramway engineer from Falmouth who in the first half of the nineteenth century undertook a tremendous amount of field observation, much of it recorded in fifty-five articles in the *West Briton* newspaper between 1850 and 1852 in which he discussed no fewer than 490 barrows and 180 various earthworks. Later, in 1885 the Society of Antiquaries published the Rev W.C.Lukis' *The Stone Monuments of the British Isles, Cornwall* (the first in a projected series of regional surveys, the rest of which never appeared). Lukis had been assisted in his Cornish work by .C.Borlase, a descendent of the famous William Borlase, who in 1872 published his own *Naenia Cornubiae* which described his field-work and excavations. George Bonsor carried out important field-work in the Scillies at the end of the century but its full value was not recognised until Hugh O'Neil Hencken undertook his own survey of Cornish archaeology in the early 1930s.

Today Hencken is celebrated as the scholar who advanced Cornish archaeology from nineteenth-century antiquarianism to the sophistication of twentieth-century science. His *The Archaeology of Cornwall and Scilly* appeared in 1932, and was followed shortly by the foundation of the West Cornwall Field Club in 1935. In the same decade C.A. Ralegh Radford undertook his famous excavations at Tintagel and Castle Dore and, after the hiatus of the Second World War, the momentum was restored through the revival of the West Cornwall Field Club in 1947-48 and the work of Lady Aileen Fox. Her important synthesis, *South West England 3,500BC-AD600*, appeared in 1964, while in 1961 the West Cornwall Field Club had reinvented itself as the Cornwall Archaeological Society.

Thereafter, there was much progress, a lot of it published in the society's own journal *Cornish Archaeology*. Paul Ashbee emerged as the 'hero of Scillonian archaeology' (as Charles Thomas dubbed him), leading to his *Ancient Scilly* in 1974, while Professor Charles Thomas himself rapidly became the dominating, inspiring figure of Cornish archaeology. His *Exploration of a Drowned Landscape*, published in 1985, and his more recent *And Shall These Mute Stones Speak?* (which appeared in 1994) are two of the most important Cornish books to have been written since the Second World War.[37] They are complemented by Professor Todd's powerful synthesis *The South West to AD 1000*, which appeared in 1987, and by the many specialist publications of the Cornwall Archaeological Unit under the distinguished leadership of Nicholas Johnson (notably *Bodmin Moor*, published in 1994).[38]

The Cornwall Archaeological Unit itself grew out of the Cornwall Committee for Rescue Archaeology, becoming a statutory body under the aegis of Cornwall County Council and attesting to the politicisation of archaeology as a branch of the conservation movement. For Nicholas Johnson the value of such conservation lay in educating children (and others) in the inherent significance of ancient stones in the cultural heritage of Cornwall and the Cornish: 'Without this education there would seem to be little point in preserving monuments to be viewed merely as irrelevant curiosities in the twenty first century'.[39] It is difficult to disagree with his conclusion, and the point he makes might be further extended to include much else that comprises the diverse field of Cornish Studies.

Notes & References (Chapter 1).

1. D.M.Thomas (ed.), *The Granite Kingdom: Poems of Cornwall*, Bradford Barton, Truro, 1970; James Turner, *The Stone Peninsula: Scenes from the Cornish Landscape*, William Kimber, London, 1975

2. Colin Bristow, 'Wealth from the Ground: Geology and Extractive Industries', in Philip Payton (ed.), *Cornwall Since the War: The Contemporary History of a European Region*, Dyllansow Truran/Institute of Cornish Studies, Redruth, 1993.

3. Bristow, 1993, p.102.

4. Robert Hunt, *Popular Romances of the West of England*, 1865; William Bottrell, *Traditions and Hearthside Stories of West Cornwall*, 3 Vols., 1870-1880.

5. Hunt, 1865, p.321.

6. Hunt, 1865, pp.329-330.

7. Hunt, 1865, p.328.

8. Hunt, 1865, p.51.

9. D.M.Thomas, 'Logan-stone', in Peter Redgrove (ed.), *Cornwall in Verse*, Penguin, London, 1982, p.52; Peter Redgrove, 'Minerals of Cornwall, Stones of Cornwall', in Thomas, 1970, pp.56-57; A.L.Rowse, 'Helman Tor', in A.L.Rowse (ed.), *A Life: Collected Poems*, William Blackwood, Edinburgh, 1981, p.306.

10. John Heath-Stubbs, 'The Mermaid oat Zennor', in Thomas, 1970, p.27.

11. Denys Val Baker, *A View from Land's End: Writers against a Cornish Backdrop*, William Kimber, London, 1982.

12. Gerald and Sylvia Priestland, *West of Hayle River*, Wildwood House, London, 1980, p.12 & p.25.

13. Ithell Colquhoun, *The Living Stones of Cornwall*, Peter Owen, London, 1957, p.46.

14. Colqhhoun, 1957, p.53.

15. Nicklaus Pevsner, *The Buildings of England: Cornwall*, Penguin, London, 1951, p.11.

16. Frank and Veronica Chesher, *The Cornishman's House*, Bradford Barton, Truro, 1968.

17. John Betjeman, *Cornwall: A Shell Guide*, Faber & Faber, London, 1964, p.9.

18. Alice Bizeley, *The Slate Figures of Cornwall*, published privately, 1965.

19. Mary Martin, *A Wayward Genius: Neville Northey Burnard - Cornish Sculptor 1818-78*, Lodenek Press, Padstow, 1978.

20. Alan Kent, *Clay*, Amigo Books, Launceston, 1991.

21. Jack Clemo, 'Sufficiency', in Thomas, 1970, p.58.

22. See P.G.Embrey and R.F.Symes, *Minerals of Cornwall and Devon*, British Museum, London, 1987, pp.79-126.

23. Embrey and Symes, 1987, pp.61-78.

24. Embrey and Symes, 1987, pp.61-78.

25. Bristow, 1993, p.98.

26. A still-useful guide to 'ancient stones' is *Antiquities of the Cornish Countryside*, Tor Mark Press, Truro, nd c.1970; more recent publications include Nicholas Johnson and Peter Rose, *Cornwall's Archaeological Heritage*, Twelveheads Press, Truro, 1990; Craig Weatherhill, *Belerion: Ancient Sites of Land's End*, Alison Hodge, Penzance, 1981; Craig Weatherhill, *Cornovia: Ancient Sites of Cornwall and Scilly*, Alison Hodge, Penzance, 1985.

27. Hunt, 1865, p.177.

28. Hunt, 1865, p.216.

29. John Sharkey, *Celtic Mysteries: The Ancient Religion*, Thames and Hudson, London, 1975, p.40.

30. Evan Hadingham, *Circles and Standing Stones*, William Heinemann, London, 1975.

31. Janet and Colin Bord, *The Secret Country: More Mysterious Britain*, Paladin, 1978, dustcover notes.

32. Janet and Colin Bord, *Mysterious Britain*, Paladin, 1974, p.3.

33. Anne Treneer, 'Nine Maidens: Bosullow Common', in Muriel Hawkey, *A Cornish Chorus*, Westaway Books, London, 1948, pp.96-97.

34. A.L.Rowse, 'The Stone That Liked Company', in A.L.Rowse, *Westcountry Stories*, Macmillan, London, 1945.

35. Mary Williams, 'The Dark Land', in Mary Williams, *The Dark Land: A Book of Cornish Ghost Stories*, William Kimber, London, 1975.

36. See Malcolm Todd, *The South West to AD 1000*, Longman, London, 1987.

37. Charles Thomas, *Exploration of a Drowned Landscape: Archaeology and History of the Isles of Scilly*, Batsford, London, 1985; Charles Thomas, *And Shall These Mute Stones Speak? Post-Roman Inscriptions in Western Britain*, University of Wales Press, 1994.

38. Nicholas Johnson and Peter Rose, *Bodmin Moor: An Archaeological Survey, Volume 1: The Human Landscape to c1800*, English Heritage et al, London, 1994.

39. Nicholas Johnson, 'The Historic Heritage: Present and Future Attitudes', *Cornish Archaeology*, No.25, 1986.

CHAPTER 2
Ancient People
CORNWALL

Ancient People

Although ancient stones loom large in the imagery of Cornwall and Cornishness, the early Stone-Age and Bronze-Age folk who made their lives amongst the moorstone and outcrops, and who fashioned the quoits and circles, are for the most part anonymous. Of course, we shall never know their names because they lived long before the emergence of written records—they were in that sense quite literally prehistoric—and their few bodily remains have lain hidden from view across the centuries in contrast to their monuments which have been so starkly and profoundly visible. It is no surprise, then, that we should be so preoccupied with those extraordinarily huge slabs of granite and yet forget the invisible ancient people who erected them.

However, modern archaeology has discovered skeletal remains (if not always in Cornwall, then in contemporaneous parts of southern Britain), lifting these ancient people from their obscurity and shedding at least some light upon their lives and physical characteristics. Thus, as Aileen Fox remarked, the Neolithic (new Stone-Age) people who arrived in Cornwall in the fourth and third millennia BC '. . . were of small stature, lightly boned and neatly built, with delicately fashioned hands and feet . . . they had long thin faces . .'.[1] The later, Bronze-Age people were, in turn, '. . . a race of powerfully built, short, ugly men and women, with round heads and prominent brow ridges'.[2] This knowledge, however, has not rehabilitated these early folk or increased their prominence in our estimation of the pageant of Cornish history. Indeed, the more we know of them the more many observers would wish to stress their 'prehistoric' attributes, categorising them as mere precursors as though their place in the historical scheme of things was to await patiently the dawn of civilization.

Ruth Manning-Sanders, for example, while claiming to observe the persistence of 'prehistoric' physical traits in the features and build of certain twentieth-century Cornish men and women, was keen to place these ancient people in a prehistoric milieu far removed from civilization. Thus '. . . in the mining-district around St Just there are short-legged, knobby-faced, squat people, who might be the first cousins to the Buccas themselves'.[3] The unflattering physical description intimates an early place in the Evolutionary chain (compare the contemporary use in British society of the word Neanderthal as a pejorative adjective) while the fascinating allusion to Buccas (Cornish imps) reveals a deeper and more significant insight into the role that ancient people have come to play in our view of Cornish history.

The status of these ancient people as not only prehistoric but also pre-civilization has been confirmed, or at least emphasised, by the Celtic revival in Cornwall in this century. In the revivalist construction of history, Cornwall, its people and their civilization are essentially 'Celtic'. And so, just as early monuments have had to become 'Celtic stones' to fit this view, so those people who inhabited Cornwall before the coming of the Celts are allowed their place in Cornish history as at best 'pre-Celts', 'proto-Celts' or possibly 'Celtiberians'. Curiously, the revivalist view reflects the more long-established perspective of Cornish folklore itself where, echoing Manning-Sander's Buccas, stories of spriggans and piskies co-exist tellingly with legends of 'inferior races'. Here again these 'inferior races'—the ancient people—pre-date the mainstream of 'Celtic civilization', surviving into it as bizarre anachronisms.

These myths of inferior races are clearly folk-memories of ancient people conquered or subjugated by 'superior' newcomers. For example, Robert Hunt recorded in the last century that 'There is a tradition that the Lizard people were formerly a very inferior race. In fact, it is said that they went on all fours, till the crew of a foreign vessel, wrecked on the coast, settled among them, and improved the race . . .'.[4] To this, as Venetia Newell has observed, is added the wider explanation in British folkloric studies which suggests that the Buccas, spriggans, piskies, brownies, goblins and other assorted little people are the same defeated primitives, perhaps banished to impenetrable moors and forests and so rarely and only fleetingly glimpsed. As she remarks, it is suggested '. . . that the little people of British tradition are the defunct or assimilated prehistoric and early peoples of these islands, changed by folk imagination into diminutive inhabitants of an imaginary and often subterranean world'. She admits a particular Cornish variant of this tradition, so that '. . . folk tales about piskeys and spriggans . . . may seem to derive from memories among the Cornish Celts about predecessors of a different race . . .' but considers this fanciful, concluding that '. . . all that can sensibly be said is that Cornwall was inhabited before the Celts arrived . . .'.[5]

Charles Thomas, however, has taken the tradition more seriously. In a paper published as long ago as 1952 he considered that in Cornwall the little people were Neolithic survivors of Bronze Age intrusion:

> To the Bronze Age immigrants, seeping into Cornwall in search of metal, or perhaps *lebensraum*, the smaller fur-clad natives with their untidy secretive lives and their strange tongue must have been objects of contempt. These surely became the 'small people' of Penwith, the 'inferior race' of the Lizard peninsula, and the 'men of the hills' of the Wendron region.[6]

In the same paper Charles Thomas suggested the wider applicability of Cornish folklore as an insight into the behaviour and beliefs of Cornwall's ancient people. The tradition of Crying the Neck, for example, was seen as a ritualistic survival of a Neolithic sacrifice to the corn-spirit. Preserved and observed today by the Federation of Old Cornwall Societies, in the nineteenth century Crying the Neck was still an integral part of Cornish popular culture. In 1861, J.O. Halliwell noted in his *Rambles in West Cornwall* that at the harvest's end 'When the reapers have cut the last handful, they shout and wave their hands, a custom which goes by the name of crying the neck'.[7] The ritual was also noted by other nineteenth-century observers including Robert Hunt, Sir J.G. Frazer and the Rev R.S. Hawker of Morwenstow, and its survival into this century was chronicled by A.K. Hamilton Jenkin, Lady C.C. Vyvyan and various correspondents in the journal *Old Cornwall.* Crying the Neck was still marked at Towednack and at Gweek in the inter-War period, and in the post-War years was observed at Corva Farm, St Ives, in 1950, and in 1951 at Gwarthandrea, Mawgan-in-Meneage, where the following ritual was recorded:

> First Harvester: 'I have'n. I have'n. I have'n'.
> Second Harvester:'What have ee? What have ee? What have ee?'
> First Harvester: 'The neck! The neck! The neck!'
> All: 'Hooray!'.[8]

Crying the Neck—An ancient tradition is re-enacted every year at harvest time.

Since then, Crying the Neck has become institutionalised within the calendar of Old Cornwall Society events, a revived tradition which links contemporary Cornwall with Neolithic times, a ritual whose origins may lie in Eastern Europe and the Mediterranean. Also of Neolithic provenance, perhaps, is the 'No Man's Land' of Cornish topography where parcels of land were left unused, a territorial taboo signifying a sacrifice to Bucca. Charles Thomas recalled that one-such No Man's Land was near Bolenowe, south of Camborne, and that John Harris (the nineteenth-century miner-poet) wrote in his *Autobiography* that when he was about five (i.e. c1825) he became lost at nightfall in the wild croft country near his home. When found, he was sobbing that 'There is nobody here but I and the buckaw (sic)'. As Charles Thomas mused, 'Harris was born on Bolenowe Carn . . . If his buckaw-haunted croft was not actually No Man's Land, it cannot have been more than a few hundred yards from it'.[9]

Primitive well-worship and sacrifice by fire, both attested in Cornish lore, may also have their origins in the Neolithic period. In the subsequent Bronze Age such behaviour was no doubt perpetuated, made more complex in the conflict between newcomers and natives (with the emergence of the 'little people' myths) and in perhaps new beliefs in river-spirits and sea-gods. The latter may well be reflected in Hunt's eerie tale of an incident at night on Porthtowan beach when a voice was heard calling three times from the sea, 'The hour is come, but not the man'.[10] A black figure, like a man, appeared on the hill-top, pausing briefly before rushing down the incline and across the sands, to be lost in the sea. Hunt noted that the story appeared in various forms 'all around the Cornish coast', and we may add that it is also known in Wales. The interpretation is simple; that the sea-god, which provides and sustains life, demands perpetual sacrifice—a permanent and inevitable toll, the burden and obligation of fishing and sea-faring communities who will always lose from amongst their number those called to appease the sea-god.

This imperative may also inform Cornish mermaid stories, such as those of Seaton (near Looe), Padstow, Lamorna and, most famously, Zennor. In the latter, the Mermaid of Zennor (portrayed to this day in Zennor church on a bench-end, complete with mirror and comb) enticed the churchwarden's son, Matthew Trewhella, to live with her beneath the waves. A sort of corollary is Tom Bawcock's Eve (23 December) at Mousehole, which celebrates the courage, good luck and blessing from the sea of Tom Bawcock who, in the most appalling storm conditions, put out in his fishing boat and returned with a huge catch to break the famine that had gripped his village. The traditional Cornish fare, star-gazy pie (with the fishes' head staring-up disconcertingly from the dish), is said to commemorate Tom Bawcock's stupendous feat.

A bench end at Zennor Parish Church has carved upon it the image of a Mermaid, with whom Mathey Trewhella fell in love. In her hands she holds the intriguing symbols of a mirror and a comb.

The further close scrutiny of Cornish folklore may yet tell us more about the beliefs and behaviour of our distant forbears, or will at least throw up new hypotheses which may be considered alongside the wider comparative material of British and European folkloric studies. There are potentially rich pickings here for the anthropologist with an historical (or rather prehistorical) turn of mind. However, for the moment, to penetrate further into the lives of Cornwall's ancient people we must turn again to the surer evidence of archaeology, the study of the past through the material remains that have been left behind.[11]

The so-called Stone-Age may be divided conveniently into its three constituent periods, the Paleolithic, Mesolithic and Neolithic. The Paleolithic stretches back to the earliest days of human existence, the classic Stone-Age of popular fancy with its 'ape men' and 'cave women'. The Mesolithic, the era of 'hunters and gatherers', is dated with rather more precision from c8000 to c4000BC. The Neolithic, the era of the 'first farmers' and the builders of the megalithic portal dolmens or Penwith chamber tombs, dates from c4000/3500BC to the relatively recent 2500BC. In comparison with these Stone-Age eras, the Bronze Age seems altogether more recent and shorter—dating as it does from c2500 to about 600BC.

In Cornwall there are but scant remains from the Paleolithic era, and indeed until recently many archaeologists believed that Cornwall was uninhabited until the Mesolithic. However, recent finds and the reassessment of earlier evidence has led to the view that there was at the very least sporadic human activity in Cornwall in the Paleolithic era. In the Council for British Archaeology's gazetter of Paleolithic finds, published in 1968, only two finds in Cornwall were recorded—both handaxes, one from the Lizard and the other from near St Buryan.[12] Since then, new discoveries have been added to the list. A paleolithic implement was found at Polcoverack on the Lizard, a small chert handaxe was located at Lanhydrock, and another handaxe unearthed at Trewardreva, Constantine, was given to the Royal Cornwall Museum. Further handaxes of varying descriptions have subsequently been found on the Lizard peninsula and at Looe. Rescue archaeology work near Stithians Reservoir uncovered a large bladelet, and re-examination of a hitherto overlooked flint collection in the Royal Cornwall Museum identified an implement known as a penknife point.[13]

Star-gazey Pie, with the pilchards' heads looking skywards, is made for good reason: it was better to cook the fish whole, to enable the rich oil to drain back into the meat. The pie is most associated with the story of the Mousehole fisherman, Tom Bawcock, who saved his village from starvation. A fish-feast in memory of Tom is held every year on the night before Christmas Eve.

However, despite these recent finds, the paucity of Paleolithic remains, even when compared to neighbouring Devon and Somerset, is noteworthy. It may be that human activity in Cornwall in that period was indeed slight, or it is possible that erosion or the rise in sea-level at the end of the Ice Age may simply have obliterated or obscured Cornish sites. Certainly, since the end of the last Ice Age (approximately 10,000 years ago) the Cornish land-

Gwithian Towans, now a popular surfing location, is an important settlement site, stretching back to pre-history.

scape has undergone considerable change. For example, the sea level at that time was 37m (120ft) lower than it is today, with the coast in places up to four miles beyond the current shoreline. But as the climate warmed and the ice-cap melted, the seas rose, engulfing the lowland areas and creating the deeply intrusive, sunken tidal estuaries such as the Fal, Fowey and Tamar. Encroaching sand dunes (towans) advanced inland, a process that was still apparent as late as the Medieval period when coastal sites such as Gwithian and St Enodoc were threatened or overwhelmed.

Although Professor Charles Thomas' painstaking archaeological detective work has undone the theory that the inundation of the Scillies was part of this immediate post-Ice Age melt-down,[14] the submergence having occurred in much more recent time (with Scilly still essentially a unitary block until perhaps as late as the eleventh century), there are evidences of submerged forests around the Cornish coast (most famously in Mounts Bay) which even to this day are laid bare when winter storms wash away the sand to reveal roots and stumps. These submergences *do* date back to those post-Ice Age days. And so from earliest times in Cornwall humans have been faced with the evidence of inundations and 'lost' lands. This, of course, is also true of other European and Near Eastern cultures, leading, for example, to tales of Atlantis and, perhaps, to the Biblical memory of Noah's Flood. But in Cornwall the 'lost land' thesis has a peculiarly Cornish persistence, the progressive sea-incursion of the Scillies in historic times perhaps serving to perpetuate a much older folk-memory of inundation.

Professor J. Markale has indicated the importance of submerged towns in Celtic literature and lore (in Cornwall and elsewhere), and has hypothesised a link between these lost lands and the Celtic myth of origins. Indeed, for Markale, an appreciation of this link is fundamental to an understanding of classical Celticity and its Creation Myth: '. . . this myth founded as it is on historical facts forms the last barrier to our understanding of the whole mystique of the Celts'.[15] Be that as it may, Charles Thomas certainly agrees that:

> Particular facets of the Cornwall-and-Scilly 'submerged land' syndrome are found in both Wales and Brittany . . . Still older notions of magical, rarely-visited lands somewhere out in the far Atlantic takes us further afield, to Ireland, where the common Celtic root lies back in prehistory.[16]

Moreover, tales of King Arthur and Tristan and Iseult have become enmeshed in the lost land myth. The connections between Cornwall and the Arthur legend are of ancient provenance, and the Tristan and Iseult story, even in its most complex and literary continental forms, is always rooted in Cornwall. Both, significantly, have become entwined in a Cornish identification of the lost land as the mythical 'Lyonnesse'. Beroul's verse *Tristan* (c1170) has a 'Leonois', identified vaguely as in Brittany or South West Britain, and by the fifteenth century Malory's *Morte d'Arthur* describes Tristan's homeland as 'Lyones' and places it somewhere off the coast of Cornwall. By this time this literary tradition appears to have become wedded firmly to the lost land stories based on those evidences of submerged forests, and in this fusion it is Lyonnesse that becomes *the* lost land beyond Cornwall.

The earliest and best testament to this in its authentic Cornish form is Richard Carew's *Survey of Cornwall* of 1602. Carew, in explaining the geographical context of Cornwall, tells us that '. . . the encroaching sea hath ravined from it the whole country of Lyonnesse . . . and that such a Lyonnesse there was these proofs are yet remaining'. He implies that the

The Isles of Scilly, some twenty eight miles west-south-west of Land's End, are surviving hills of a much larger land area now submerged beneath the waters of the Atlantic.

Loe Pool, near Helston—one of the supposed sites of *The Passing of Arthur*.

name Lyonnesse is an echo of Lethowsow, the Cornish word for the waters between Cornwall and Scilly, and notes that that stretch of sea '. . . carrieth continually an equal depth of forty or sixty fathom (a thing not usual in the sea's proper dominion) . . .'. He also reports that fishermen have drawn-up pieces of doors and windows when operating in those waters, and further cites the fact that '. . . the ancient name of St Michael's Mount was *Caraclowse in cowse*, in English, The Hoar Rock in the Wood, which now is at every flood encompasse by the sea, and yet at some low ebbs roots of mighty trees are descried in the sands about it'.[17] Carew's description was echoed in 1690 by Nicholas Boson (an inhabitant of Newlyn, in Mount's Bay) who confirmed the traditional name of 'Carrack Looes en Cooes' (his spelling) and 'That bodyes and roots of trees lye along the sand . . .'.[18]

Robert Hunt recorded the survival of the Lyonnesse legend into nineteenth-century Cornwall, noting the stories that the Trevelyan family of St Veep and the Vyvyans of Trelowarren were descended from individuals who had fled the inundation on horsesback and arrived on Cornish soil in the nick of time—events depicted on those families' armorial bearings. But the nineteenth century also witnessed the further elaboration of the Lyonnesse myth and its entwining with the Arthurian cycle, this time in the guise of English literary romance from the pen of Alfred Lord Tennyson. For Tennyson in his *The Passing of Arthur*, the Lake into which the sword is thrown is clearly Loe Pool, near Helston (not the Dozmary Pool of alternative Cornish legend), and the place of Arthur's last days is an indeterminate Lyonnesse in the far west: '. . . the sunset bound of Lyonnesse—A land of old upheavan from the abys . . .'.[19] Lyonnesse thus 're-invented' gained new currency in the romantic portrayal of Cornwall that emerged in the latter half of the last century. For Thomas Hardy, for example, Cornwall was sometimes the marginal 'Off Wessex' but was more importantly the far-off land of Lyonnesse:

> When I set out for Lyonnesse,
> A hundred miles away,
> The rime was on the spray,
> And starlight lit my lonesomeness
> When I set out for Lyonnesse
> A hundred miles away.

When I came back from Lyonnesse
With magic in my eyes,
All marked with mute surmise
My radiance rare and fathomless,
When I came back from Lyonnesse
With magic in my eyes![20]

Even in the 1950s the myths of Lyonnesse and Arthur's Avalon so enchanted F.E. Halliday that, in musing on the profusion of Neolithic and early Bronze Age burial sites on the Isles of Scilly, he could recall Celtic

> . . . stories about an island of the dead and a land beyond the sea inhabited only by women, stories that are recalled by the legend of the death of Arthur, who, when mortally wounded in his last great battle in the west, was carried away by queens to the island of Avalon. Can it be, therefore, that the Isles of Scilly really were the islands of the dead? That the bodies of their most illustrious men were rowed across from Penwith to be buried there? Or, like the legend of Lyonesse (sic), are the stories merely the fabrications of later people to account for this mysterious burial ground?[21]

In the 1990s the enduring strength of such myth produced Craig Weatherhill's powerful children's novel, *The Lyonesse Stone*, in which the present-day descendants—Penny and John Trevelyan—of the Trevelyan who

Dozmary Pool, in the heart of Bodmin Moor, is reputed to be bottomless.

escaped the deluge are haunted by the legend and transported back to 'the hidden realms of West Cornwall'.[22]

However, the Lyonnesse of Tennyson and Hardy, or indeed of Craig Weatherhill, is a literary construct many steps removed from the more prosaic facts of practical archaeology, and once more we must return to that surer evidence to continue our story of ancient people. What is certain that, following the end of the Ice-Age and the rising of the sea level, there were rapid changes in climate. This, in turn, affected flora and fauna and from about 8000BC the cold grassland that had characterised Cornwall gave way to new vegetation. Oak and hazel, elm and lime, had developed by 6000BC, although the upland areas continued to be grassy and only lightly wooded. Before 6000BC Britain was still connected to the continental mainland, and Cornwall was the hunting ground of semi-nomadic bands. In winter they hunted in the woods and in the summer they followed grazing herds onto the higher grasslands. They collected nuts and fruits from trees, fished in the seas, and gathered shellfish and other foods from along the shoreline. They made shelters from hides, arrowheads from flints, and fish-spears from bones. They knew how to make clothes and nets and bags. From about 4000-3500BC these Mesolithic hunter-gatherers became more sophisticated and more efficient in the exploitation of their environment. As well as burning woodland to flush out game, they began the partial domestication of animals and started to grow pasture.

There is relatively little evidence remaining from the Mesolithic period in Cornwall, although a comprehensive study by Peter Berridge and Alison Roberts has drawn attention to the advances in 'Cornish Mesolithic studies' made since the 1970s by the Cornwall Archaeological Society and has marshalled together our knowledge of the period thus far.[23] There is some evidence of raw materials and Mesolithic technology, notably the high quality black flint used in tool manufacture in an early Mesolithic site at Dozmary Pool on Bodmin Moor. This flint apparently came from Beer Head in Devon, itself evidence of communications, trade and mobility in this period. Various microliths (for example, arrowtips) have been found at Mesolithic sites in Cornwall (as at Trevose Head), as have other artefacts such as scrapers, burins (chisel-like tools for working bone and antler), types of piercing and bladed tools, occasional axes and adzes, choppers and picks, and implements mades from pebbles.

In the West Penwith area the activities of J.G. Marden in the years before the First World War did much to locate Mesolithic sites, although unfortunately many of his finds have now been lost. Similarly, the work of R.J. Noall in St Ives and Zennor has largely been lost. In contrast, on the other side of the Hayle River, in the neighbourhood of Godrevy Point and Gwithian which Professor Thomas has made so much his own,[24] there is rich Mesolithic material which has been made the subject of systematic archaeological study in the years since the Second World War. The richness of the sites here no doubt reflect the exploitation by a Mesolithic population of what was for them an especially advantageous estuarine environment well-endowed with natural resources. Further east, between Perranporth and Newquay at Penhale Point and Kelsey Head, some evidence of Mesolithic activity has also been detected. But, after Gwithian, the only other major north coast site is that at Trevose Head. Trevose was the object of much nineteenth-century antiquarian activity, the main value of which was to point up the locality as a suitable case for treatment for present-day archaeologists. However, the only systematic fieldwork there in recent years has been that undertaken by Nicholas Johnson. In the same area as Trevose are other sites such as Pentire, Constantine Bay, and Harlyn Bay, while further north still at Bude quantities of Mesolithic microliths have been collected.

On the South Coast the Lizard peninsula is an area of particular interest. The early work of the Lizard Field Club identified traces of Mesolithic activity at Poldowrian, Croft Pascoe and Windmill Lane, all of which (as Berridge and Roberts emphasise) have proved to be important sites. In 1979 a major research effort, the Lizard Project, concentrated on these sites. As a result Poldowrian has been identified as a base camp, occupied during the autumn and winter, while Windmill Farm on Predannack Moor is thought to be a similar site. North of the Helford River, in the area of Gweek and Constantine, fieldwalking by Hilary Shaw has uncovered Mesolithic traces but east of the Lizard little has been found, except at Maker in the far south-east. The granite uplands are potentially richer sources of Mesolithic remains. The best known location is Dozmary on Bodmin Moor, the first area in Cornwall where Mesolithic material was systematically evaluated (by G.J. Wainwright).[25] However, although there had been work at Dozmary as early as the 1860s, and although the efforts of Wainwright have subsequently been built upon by other scholars, there is still much to be learnt about the site. The same is true of other locations on Bodmin Moor, and indeed of Carnmenellis and the St Austell granite, while there is still uncertainty as to whether the Scillies were occupied at all during this period.

Of course, given the relative paucity of material beyond microliths and pebbles, it is difficult to comment upon the daily lives of the ancient people in Cornwall during the Mesolithic period, except to generalise about the seasonal cycles of hunter-gatherer societies. Certainly, there is little we can say about their social or political organisation, although Malcolm Todd considers that in general material cultural terms '. . . the available evidence gives general support to this notion of the South West as a distinct territory, at least in the late Mesolithic'.[26] In contrast, however, the subsequent Neolithic period gives us the startling evidence of the portal dolmens—Trethevy Quoit, Chun Quoit, Lanyon Quoit, and the rest—which points to

Chun Quoit—an impressive example of a Neolithic portal dolmen.

An aerial view of Chun Castle, a magnificent Iron Age fort, with Chun Quoit tucked away in the bottom left.

Carn Brea, home to an Iron Age hill camp, forms the backdrop to the ruinous mining landscape: symbol at once of Cornwall's ancient and more recent past. Development of both sites is highly contested.

an increasingly organised society. The erection of these megaliths would have required well-organised and well-controlled labour forces of sizeable proportions, while the quoits themselves would have served as foci for ritualistic purposes and may have been important in both reflecting and enhancing a sense of territory and community. The portal dolmens are in that sense 'political' monuments, and are an insight into the nature, organisation and culture of the Neolithic society that had by then emerged.

Hugh Hencken's work in the 1930s dealt with the Neolithic in Cornwall but, in R.J. Mercer's estimation, was largely a typological examination of lithic (stone) material on the lines of models employed elsewhere. Thus Hencken had some difficulty in addressing Cornish differences as well as integrating consideration of the portal dolmens into a wider assessment of Neolithic life:

> Not for the last time was it found impossible to deal with Cornwall as part of the Southern English *continuum* of neolithic development. Not for the last time were megalithic tombs dealt with as an entirely separate issue which, despite their palpable substance, floated insubstantially above mundane concerns of period and culture.[27]

The Neolithic period, therefore, has attracted considerable attention from Cornish archaeologists in the years since 1945. There have been four major reviews of the era—that by Ralegh Radford in 1962, Vincent Megaw's in 1963, Paul Ashbee in 1970, and R.J. Mercer's exhaustive synthesis of 1986.[28] The Cornwall Archaeological Society, meanwhile, had taken up the challenge of Cornish Neolithic studies: 'Starting at Sperris Quoit in 1964, a funerary site, via the settlement at Gwithian and the henge at Castilly, leading to the fortress at Carn Brea, the Society's excavation record is enviable'. In addition, '. . . its synthetical involvement with the subject has been prodigious'.[29] Combining this flair for excavation and synthesis, for practical and theoretical archaeology, the Society was thus able to shed considerable light on the lives (and deaths) of ancient people in Neolithic Cornwall.

The domestication of animals became increasingly prevalent in the early Neolithic, with new farming techniques leading to the cultivation of land and the harvesting of crops. Hunter-gatherers had become the first farmers. Populations were no longer nomadic and so required the territorial and community affirmation provided by the portal dolmens. They also needed to consider questions of land control and ownership, and, as assets became more complex (and more valuable) and as populations grew, so defence became a major consideration. Tribal delineations became important, and tribal centres emerged to dominate and control comparatively large sections of Cornwall. Helman Tor in mid-Cornwall was one such site, as were possibly Trencrom, Rough Tor and Carn Galver, but better known and incomparably more impressive is Carn Brea where a series of massive ramparts enclose and defend some 18.62 hectares (46 acres).

Some 750 arrowheads have been found at Carn Brea which, together with evidences of burnings and breachings of the ramparts, suggests warfare of a fairly traumatic nature and tells us that inter-tribal competition in Neolithic Cornwall could be violent. Today Carn Brea, with its dominating castle and monunument, remains one of the great icons of Cornwall and Cornishness, although there are fierce disagreements as to whether it should be managed minimally as a conservation area or developed more ambitiously as a leisure amenity with a large car-park and perhaps other facilities. Carn Brea remains a contested site.

Reflecting this new sophistication in land use and political organisation, an extensive trading system was developed in the Neolithic period. Pottery and artefact remains are an important clue to this activity, especially the telltale axe heads made of Gabbro rock which indicate that the Lizard peninsula was an important focus of axe production. There is evidence of quarrying elsewhere in Cornwall, with Cornish stones and axes turning up far afield—at Hambledon Hill in north-east Dorset and elsewhere in Wessex, and even in Essex and perhaps Yorkshire. Similarly, artefacts from outside Cornwall were imported. The black flints from Beer continued to find their way westwards. More intriguing are jade axes, thought to be of Breton origin, which turned up in Cornwall, together with other axes from North Wales and the Lake District. No farming settlements have been discovered in Cornwall thus far but remains at Carn Brea suggest that houses generally were rectangular in shape. Well-defined field boundaries were also appearing during this period, the Neolithic farmers using stones and boulders cleared from the land to build walls to keep animals in or out.

The portal dolmens, as chamber tombs or as monuments with wider ritual significance, are also a clue to religious life. So too are the henges—Castlewich, Castilly and the Stripple Stones—which are clearly not defensive

Ballowall Barrow, near St Just, is a complex chamber tomb. It was constructed in a number of phases and forms a spectacular site (and sight) above the ocean.

and must, therefore, have had ritual functions. Even more intriguing are the so-called entrance graves. In West Cornwall about twenty of these entrance graves can be distinguished from other megalithic tombs. The most important archaeological investigation has been that of a kerbed cairn at Bosiliack, Madron, where a partial cremation was found placed in a coarse ware pot. The most spectacularly-sited entrance grave, with its cliff-top setting, is Ballowall at Carn Gluze, near St Just-in-Penwith, which was discovered by Borlase in the 1870s after it had lain hidden beneath mine spoil for decades. But it is in the Isles of Scilly that the entrance graves are at their most majestic, not merely as individuals but in their profusion. In all, some 50 tombs survive in the islands (many others will have been lost to farming or in the inundations). More than half are to be found in three cemeteries—one each on St Mary's, Samson and Gugh—with small clusters on Bryher, St Martin's, Tresco and the evocatively-named Little Arthur.

Professor Malcolm Todd considers that the Neolithic and early Bronze Age Scillonian entrance graves are the most remarkable group of burial monuments in Europe and yet, despite the efforts of Paul Ashbee, they remain only partially investigated. In construction and style, the Scillonian entrance graves are all very similar. In essence they consist of a circular cairn with a massively-built kerb, containing a regular chamber which opens from the edge of the cairn. Most are between 6m (20 feet) and 18m (60 feet) in diameter. This uniformity of style is echoed in some of the West Penwith structures but is to be found nowhere else in Britain. Most of the Scillonian entrance graves are now empty (making further work by archæologists extremely problematic) but one that was found largely intact was Knackyboy Carn on St Martin's.

Knackyboy Carn contained eight urns, which had probably once held cremated remains, and around the urns was a deposit of ash, charcoal, cremated bones, several fragments of pottery, a number of beads and and a bronze fragment. All this was overlain by further urns, and it has been estimated that from all the fragments of pottery some twenty-two urns could be reconstructed—evidence of a major burial place. At Obadiah's Barrow on Gugh, the unburnt remains of a Neolithic skeleton were found, together with subsequent secondary internments in cremation urns, indicating a sequence of burials. At Bant's Carn on Halangy Down, St Mary's, pottery recovered during the 1970 restoration of the site revealed decorative elements such as combing, finger-marking, corded ornament, and grooves.

Taken together, the evidence of the Scillonian entrance graves suggests the continuance of the tradition of collective burial on the Scillies long after it had ceased on the mainland. The graves stand amidst the remains of Neolithic field-systems, an eerie juxtaposition for the modern observer but testament to the close links between life and death, farming and funerary, in the society of those Neolithic ancient people.

However, even as the Scillonians were perpetuating their practice of collective burial, newly-emergent Beaker people, named after their distinctive pottery, were arriving in Cornwall in the late Neolithic/early Bronze Age era. They practised individual interment and were responsible for many of the early menhirs (standing stones), especially in West Cornwall. At Try in Gulval parish, for example, a handled beaker was found buried in a small cist a metre (3ft) away from the base of a menhir, together with burnt and unburnt human fragments. Cremated human remains from this period have also been discovered in the vicinity of standing stones at Tresvennack, in the

Bant's Carn on St Mary's is a beautifully preserved burial chamber in a superb location.

parish of Paul, at Trelew, Tregiffian and Pridden in St Buryan, at Trenuggo in Sancreed, and at Kerrow in Zennor. The few known settlements of the Beaker arrivals in Cornwall are coastal: Praa Sands on Mount's Bay, where a long-necked beaker was recovered, and at Gwithian and Harlyn Bay on the north coast.

The Beaker people were the precursors of the Bronze-Age proper in Cornwall, a period that has been reviewed in detail by Patricia M. Christie but is also the subject of an especially useful summary by Nicholas Johnson and Peter Rose in their *Cornwall's Archaeological Heritage*.[30] They make the important point that although the introduction of metalworking was a significant development (and thus marks for us the beginning of the Bronze Age) in fact it was not until as late as 1400BC that bronze was in everyday use for tools and weapons. Before then bronze—an alloy of tin and lead with copper—was a precious commodity used only for display and prestige, a rare resource controlled by an elite. The real cultural movement from one era to another occurred much earlier, in the late Neolithic when the Beaker intrusion brought important changes in funerary practices and when the appearance of the henges marked the beginnings of a new tradition of ceremonial monuments which stretched throughout the early Bronze Age.

In the earliest days of this period (before 2000BC) prestige items were more likely to be made of gold and copper, rather than bronze. Four impressive gold lunulae (crescendic collars) have been discovered in Cornwall; two at Harlyn, one at Cargurra in St Juliot, and one at Gwithian. Their style is essentially Irish but the gold is Cornish, suggesting close cultural and trading contacts with Ireland. Similar lunulae have been found at Guingamp and Dinard in Brittany, indicating that the Armorican peninsula—modern-day Brittany—was also part of this cultural and trading zone. At Rillaton barrow in the parish of Linkinhorne on Bodmin Moor, human remains have been discovered along with beads, pottery, glass and other items, together with a remarkably fine gold cup some 90mm (3.5 inches) high. The story has it that the cup became lost after discovery and turned up years later in use by King George V as a receptacle for his collar studs! Happily, the Rillaton cup is now safely in the British Museum. Apart from its intrinsic beauty and craftsmanship, the cup is of interest because of its stylistic echo of Aegean metalwork of the period. It resembles similar finds that have been made at the important Greek site of Mycenae, and here the suggestion is of cultural and trading links with the eastern Mediterranean, although archaeologists caution against making too much of this alleged connection. Nevertheless, it is a humbling experience when visiting Bronze Age sites in Cornwall to reflect that the Bronze Age was also the time of Mycenae and Troy, of the Aechaen Greeks and Agamemnon, Achilles, Hector and Helen ('the face that launched a thousand ships'), the era recorded by Homer in *The Illiad* and Aeschylus in his *Oresteian Trilogy.* However tenuous the link might be, it is not too fanciful to think of Cornish connections with the Aegean and eastern Mediterranean in the days when

> . . . the strong sons of Atreus,
> Menelaus and Agamemnon, both alike
> Honoured by Zeus with throned and sceptred power,
> Gathered and manned a thousand Argive ships,
> And with the youth of Hellas under arms
> Sailed from these ports to settle scores with Priam.[31]

Three gold lunulae; these moon-shaped pieces were worn around the neck on ceremonial occasions.

This cup, found in Rillaton round barrow, is made of corrugated sheet gold. The cup went missing for a number of years before being found in the dressing room of George V. The cup is housed in the British Museum, but an exact copy may be seen in the Royal Institution of Cornwall Museum in Truro.

An aerial view of Taphouse Ridge round barrow cemetery. This western group is well-preserved. To the east are to be found four more, one of which is almost ploughed out.

For example, a dagger of supposed Mycenaen style has also been found in one of the ten Bronze Age burial barrows at Pelynt, while beads of allegedly eastern Mediterranean provenance have turned up at Carn Creis in West Penwith. There are also links with the near Mediterranean and Atlantic, with Iberia, again emphasising the trading and cultural contacts determined largely by Cornwall's maritime context, jutting out as it does into the Western Approaches at the far south western tip of Britain. Cornwall always was, and still is, a window to a wider world—something to be experienced profoundly at Ballowall on a fine clear summer's evening, standing on that ancient cairn and gazing westwards into the setting sun, with a hint of the Scillies on the horizon and the wide, calm blue sea beckoning enticingly towards Ireland and to Spain. It is not unlike Mount's Bay in Milton's *Lycidas*, 'Where the great Vision of the guarded Mount/Looks towards Namancos and Bayona's hold . . .'.[32] Claims by 'foreigners'—those from the wrong side of the River Tamar—that the Cornish are somehow parochial or inward-looking have always been nonsense.

Other exotic Bronze Age finds have included the Towednack gold horde (consisting of two twisted torcs, four plain bracelets, and three coiled bars of gold), the six Irish-style gold bracelets uncovered at Morvah, and (less exotically) the thirty pieces of copper and smelted tin from Carn Kenidjack. The latter is evidence that even at this early date metals were being worn and refined in Cornwall. Startlingly visible and impressive are burial mounds such as those on the Taphouse ridge in East Cornwall, as are the famous stone circles such as the Merry Maidens and the Hurlers. Notwithstanding lay-line and earth-power theories, these circles are best interpreted as public ritual sites of ceremonial or religious significance. Standing stones, as noted above, sometimes mark burial sites but also appear to have been used widely in other contexts and for other purposes. Some may have been way-markers, and others territorial boundaries. Like the earlier portal dolmens, Bronze Age stones seem also to have been political in that they too may have been important in community and territorial deliniation and affirmation.

Evidence of mutilation on one of the Taphouse barrows.

Three Bronze Age stone circles are to be found near Minions on Bodmin Moor. Known as the Hurlers, the central ring extends in diameter to 43.4m.

Johnson and Rose explain that in Cornwall 'We get our best glimpse of Bronze Age life and death on Bodmin Moor, on the Lizard, and in West Penwith'.[33] In the second millenium BC locations such as Rough Tor and Stowe's Pound on Bodmin Moor became densely settled, and the foundations of hundreds of round stone huts and hedge banks have been found dating from this era. Some of these remains represent permanent settlements, lived in all year round, but others seem to have had only occasional use—perhaps during the summer grazing of stock on upland pastures. These settlements often exist in association with stone circles, standing stones, and burial cairns and barrows, the most complete (and astonishing) example of which today is the landscape around Minions on the southern edge of Bodmin Moor. Here cheek-by-jowl are the Hurlers, Stowe's Pound, Rillaton barrow, the Pipers (two standing stones), a stone row, and the circle on Craddock Moor, together with inumerable hut and field remains. In lowland areas individual barrows (such as those at Cubert Common or Veryan Beacon) which exist now in isolation, must once have been surrounded by round hut settlements that have since been obliterated by modern agriculture. The corollary is that the upland landscape around Rough Tor (for example), with its large curvilinear boulder-enclosed fields and tracks leading from one farmstead to another, is some 3000 years old.

Towards the middle of the Bronze-Age there seems to have developed a more systematic use of the landscape. Substantial stone boundaries appeared on Bodmin Moor, and the network of small, regular arable fields found today in West Penwith has developed from the basic layout devised in those times. Excavations of Bronze Age fields buried by sand at Gwithian have revealed scratch marks made in the sub soil by hook-shaped ploughs as well as spade marks in those areas the ploughs could not reach. Although it is on the uplands today that we see much of the remains of the Bronze-Age, by the first millennium BC the moorland areas had been largely given over to seasonal grazing, with the lowlands increasingly opened-up for permanent settlement and farming. The ritual monuments had been long-since abandoned as these ancient people of Cornwall settled into a more domestic and predictable existence, not far removed from the cycles of small-farming observable in Cornwall almost down to our own time.

Notes & References (Chapter 2).

1. Aileen Fox, *South West England 3500BC-AD600*, Thames and Hudson, London, 1964, repub. David and Charles, Newton Abbot, 1973, p.31.

2. Fox, 1973, p.63.

3. Ruth Manning-Sanders, *The West of England*, Batsford, London, 1949, p.42.

4. Robert Hunt, *Popular Romances of the West of England*, 1865, p. 451.

5. Venetia J. Newell, 'Introduction', in Tony Deane and Tony Shaw, *The Folklore of Cornwall*, Batsford, London, 1975, p.18-19.

6. Charles Thomas, *Studies in Cornish Folklore No. 2: The Sacrifice*, Institute of Archaeology, University of London, 1952, pp.52-53.

7. J.O.Halliwell, *Rambles in West Cornwall*, 1861, cited in Thomas, 1952, p.9.

8. *Cornishman*, 6 September 1951, cited in Thomas, 1952, p.11.

9. Thomas, 1952, p.19.

10. Robert Hunt, *Popular Romances of the West of England*, 1865, p.366.

11. Here the best sources are: Fox, 1973; John Barnatt, *Prehistoric Cornwall: The Ceremonial Monuments*, Turnstone Press, Wellingborough, 1982; *Cornish Archaeology*, No. 25, 1986; Malcolm Todd, *The South West to AD1000*, Longman, London, 1987; Nicholas Johnson and Peter Rose, *Cornwall's Archaeological Heritage*, Twelveheads Press, Truro, 1990; Nicholas Johnson and Peter Rose, *Bodmin Moor: An Archaeological Survey, Vol. 1: The Human Landscape to c1800*, English Heritage, London, 1994.

12. D.A. Roe, *Gazeteer of British Lower and Middle Paleolithic Sites*, Council for British Archaeology, London, 1968.

13. There is a useful summary of the Paleolithic period in Cornwall in Peter Berridge and Alison Roberts, 'The Mesolithic Period in Cornwall', *Cornish Archaeology*, No 25, 1986.

14. Charles Thomas, *Exploration of a Drowned Landscape: Archaeology and History of the Isles of Scilly*, Batsford, London, 1985.

15. J. Markale, *Celtic Civilization*, Gordon & Cremonesi, London, 1978, p.36.

16. Thomas, 1985, p.275.

17. Richard Carew, *The Survey of Cornwall, 1602,* ed. F.E. Halliday, Melrose, London, 1953, p.83.

18. In his *Duchess of Cornwall's Progress*, cited in Thomas, 1985, p.281.

19. Cited in Thomas, 1985, p.273.

20. See D.M. Thomas, *The Granite Kingdom: Poems of Cornwall*, Bradford Barton, Truro, 1970, p.96.

21. F.E. Halliday, *A History of Cornwall*, Duckworth, London, 1959, p.29.

22. Craig Weatherhill, *The Lyonesse Stone*, Tabb House, Padstow, 1991.

23. Berridge & Roberts, 1986.

24. See Charles Thomas, *Gwithian: Ten Years Work (1949-1958)*, Camborne, 1958.

25. G.J. Wainwright, 'Three Microlithic Industries from South West England and their Affinities', *Proceedings of the Prehistorical Society*, No. 26, 1960.

26. Todd, 1987, p.66.

27. R.J. Mercer, 'The Neolithic in Cornwall', in *Cornish Archaeology*, No. 25, 1986.

28. Ralegh Radford, 'The Neolithic in South West England', *Cornish Archaeology*, No. 1, 1962; Vincent Megaw, 'The Neolithic in South West England: A Reply and some Further Comments', *Cornish Archaeology*, No. 2, 1963; Paul Ashbee, ' Problems of the Neolithic and Bronze Age in Cornwall', *Cornish Archaeology*, No 9., 1970; Mercer, 1986.

29. Mercer, 1986.

30. Patricia M. Christie, 'Cornwall in the Bronze Age', *Cornish Archaeology*, No. 25, 1986; Johnson and Rose, 1991.

31. Aeschylus, *The Oresteian Trilogy*, trans. Philip Vellacott, Penguin, London, 1956, p.43.

32. John Milton, *Lycidas*, cited in A.L. Rowse, *A Cornish Anthology*, Macmillan, London, 1968, p.12.

33. Johnson and Rose, 1990, p.5.

CHAPTER 3

The Mystery of the Celts

CORNWALL

The Mystery of the Celts

For many modern observers, not least the Celtic revivalists of this century, it is with the dawn of the Iron Age that Cornwall begins to emerge from the murk of prehistory into the flowering and eventual full-glare of Celtic civilization. There are, however, as we have seen already, problems with this view. To begin with, the organisational and constructional feats of the Neolithic and Bronze-Age eras, once understood, are not easily relegated to the margins of an irrelevant prehistoric pre-civilization. Thus our inclination to continue to stress their 'primitive' attributes is not only unfair and erroneous but dishonest.

But the alternative (should we wish to insist that the root source of all that is 'Cornish' is 'Celtic') is simply to co-opt Neolithic and Bronze-Age monuments as 'Celtic' (or more cautiously, 'pre-Celtic') and by implication to suggest that the ancient peoples of those periods were themselves 'proto-Celtic'. This is in fact, as we have seen in earlier chapters, a device that has indeed been adopted by many writers. It is tempting to dismiss such licence as merely the stretching of historical fact but, even leaving aside the powerful ideological motives of the revivalists in wishing to locate the Cornish identity in a Celtic origin, there is for us the additional complication that archaeologists, historians, linguists and anthroplogists cannot themselves agree a definitive answer to the question 'who were (and are) the Celts?'.

The problem is multi-dimensional. It is not merely a question of ethnogenesis (when did the Celts emerge, where did they come from?) but is also one of meaning. As Anne Ross has explained, the terms 'Celt' and 'Celtic' have different connotations for different scholars.[1] For linguists, Celtic is an exclusively linguistic term, referring in the modern period to Cornish, Welsh, Breton, Irish, Scottish Gaelic and Manx but also acknowledging the existence in earlier times of now extinct tongues (for example, Gaulish) as well as postulating a notional common Celtic root language. As Miles Dillon explained, 'By Celts I mean people who spoke a Celtic dialect . . . This is not an infallible statement of known truth; it is merely an agreed use of the term upon which linguists insist'.[2] However, just as speakers of Celtic languages are thus 'Celts', so by further extension the territories that these peoples inhabit become 'Celtic lands', and here already the exclusivity and clarity of linguistic definition becomes open to doubt and confusion.

Inherent within these extensions, convenient as they may be, is the inference that a strictly linguistic definition of Celt and Celtic is unduly restrictive. But this realisation is itself problematic and has led some observers, in wishing to identify Celtic peoples, to stray into the arid, spurious and potentially dangerous arena of racial theories. The idea that there is (or was) a model 'Celtic type' is absurd (vide the widely different literary descriptions of the Celts, ranging from tall, fair and blonde to short, swarthy and dark) and has been dismissed from the earliest days of serious Celtic Studies in British and Irish universities. This has not, however, prevented some Pan-Celtic enthusiasts from proclaiming, for example, the '. . . close racial relationship between the Irish and the Scots', or the common racial origin of the Cornish and Bretons, or that '. . . the people of Scotland are . . . one racial whole'.[3] It is not surprising therefore, that some contemporary writers on Pan-Celtic themes should find it necessary to offer disclaimers to the effect that the Celts of whom they write are defined by language rather than race. But even this throws up some unusual results. For example, Peter Berresford Ellis' determined advocacy of a strictly linguistic criterion has led him to suggest that if the Cornish do not fully revive their language, then they shall cease at some (unspecified) point in the future to be Celtic. Equally, he has spent much time agonising over the status of Galicia (in Spain) and Galician claims to be Celtic. Discounting the increasing tendency of many Galicians to self-define as Celtic as merely a latter-day invention of identity, Berresford Ellis has decided that because no Celtic language has been spoken in Galicia in modern times, '. . . in no way could the Galician claim meet the linguistic criterion'.[4]

This simplistic conclusion conveniently ignores the whole issue of identity creation and contestation. Elsewhere, Rosemary McKechnie has written provocatively of 'Becoming Celtic in Corsica',[5] while Anthony D. Smith has argued that the insistence on language as the essential marker of national identity is '. . . a gross simplification and misunderstanding of both ancient and modern periods of ethnic community'.[6] It also begs the question—where did the linguistic criterion come from in the first place? The answer is that 'Celtic' as a linguistic term was invented in the sixteenth century by George Buchanan, and was given wider currency in the following century by Edward Lluyd in his comparative studies of the Celtic languages (including Cornish).[7] This, in turn, informed the scholarly construction of Celtic Studies and helped, as we have seen, to mould the ideological perspectives of Pan-Celticism as the latter emerged in the nineteenth and twentieth centuries. Although, as their surnames attest, Buchanan (Scots) and Lluyd (Welsh) were of Celtic provenance, many of the subsequent discussions of 'Celticity' were by Continental (especially German) and English commentators, leading modern observers such as Nick Merriman and Malcolm Chapman to argue in recent years that the notions of Celt and Celtic are essentially a romantic portrayal of 'Otherness' by outsiders.[8] This is a view that will be examined again in later chapters but it is important to note its significance here because it reinforces our central point, that there is no scholarly consensus when it comes to discussion of the Celts.

Indeed, Colin Renfrew has identified eight different (and more or less mutually exclusive) uses of the term 'Celtic' by different writers, and has himself offered a revolutionary re-assessment of early Celtic prehistory by claiming that Celtic languages were installed in Britain by 4500BC and in Ireland by 4000BC— a startling assertion which places the origins of Celtic Britain (and thus Celtic Cornwall) in the earliest days of the Neolithic era and attempts to destroy forever the 'Iron Age equals Emergence of the Celts' equation.[9] However, whilst few would accept Renfrew's theories, his intervention does point to the controversy and disagreement that exists amongst archaeologists in their use of the terms Celt and Celtic. Anne Ross notes that some archaeologists use Celtic in an ethnological sense to describe an integrated socio-cultural life-style, an approach which emphasises artifacts and language as well as art-forms, beliefs, territorial and tribal organisation, and collective identity as expressed in myth or story-telling. Others, however, take a more strictly limited definition, preferring to concentrate only on material culture revealed by excavation.

Recently, the debate amongst archaeologists has taken a more aggressive turn, as those who embrace the Celticity— as-romantic-portrayal-of-otherness thesis, question the whole validity of 'Celt' and 'Celtic' in the realms of practical archaeology, a view that has itself provoked fierce reaction. Professor Vincent and Dr Ruth Megaw objected when a conference of senior archaeologists at Southampton in 1992 was allegedly '. . . preoccupied with the idea that prehistoric Celts did not exist', a preoccupation which, in the Megaws' view, reflected an unhealthy political correctness in modern British, or rather, English archaeological thinking: 'To deny the existence of prehistoric Celts because others have manipulated their image is to deny a possible past and to present a form of archaeological and political correctness which is both wrong-headed and potentially dangerous'.[10]

For those who enjoy debate between competing scholars, this is heady stuff. However, for the rest seeking tangible evidence and explanations of the emergence of the Celts and their impact in Cornwall, we are thus far none the wiser. Perhaps, despite all the scholarly controversy of the 1980s and 1990s, we can do no better than to return to the firm but balanced summary offered by Professor Barry Cunliffe back in 1979:

> The Celts were the inhabitants of Europe in the pre-Roman period, occupying a vast territory stretching from the Pyrenees to the Rhine and from Ireland to Romania. They were barbarian in the classical sense of the word, energetic, quick-tempered, and 'war-mad'; but their craftsmen created a brilliant art style and by the first century BC a truly urban society had begun to to develop in many areas. It was against these people that the Roman armies moved in the first centuries BC and AD, leaving only a Celtic fringe in Scotland, Ireland, Wales, and Brittany to survive unconquered. When the Roman world collapsed in the fifth century AD, the Celts once more emerged from the obscurity of their windswept Atlantic regions. Populations moved from Ireland to Britain and from Cornwall to Brittany, while individuals —chiefly monks— carried the ideals of Irish monasticism deep into Europe. Politically and culturally the western Celts have been persecuted and subjugated; today their cry for the recognition of their separate identity is becoming louder . . . the study of Celtic achievement in all its diversity acquaints us with a people too often dismissed as barbaric, too long neglected and misunderstood—a whole civilization, multi-faceted but with an underlying unity.[11]

In other words, academic distinctions between linguistic, archaeological and other criteria are just that; academic. Behind the facade of scholarly objection lies a rich world ripe for interdisciplinary attention, a coherent culture which in modern times may have undergone re-invention (as a romantic portrayal of 'otherness', or at the hands of Celtic Revivalists) but which is nevertheless tangible in its own right. Although in classical times the Celts were then also Other-defined (the Greeks called them *Keltoi*), the fact that these classical observers felt able to generalise about this far-flung collection of barbarian tribes suggests that the Celts exhibited at least some common, unifying charactersistics. Indeed, Anne Ross insists that on occasions these barbarians *did* self-define as 'Celts',[12] while Professor Cunliffe adds that 'The word *Celt* may have been the name of a particularly powerful tribe or even a ruling household, or it may have been a generic term by which the disparate groups of central and western Europe distinguished themselves from their more distant neighbours'.[13]

Be that as it may, Barry Cunliffe also insists that it is '. . . clear that it was within this Late Bronze-Age complex of barbarian Europe that the Celts had their origins'.[14] As far as Britain is concerned, Richard Muir agrees that the Beaker people *may* have introduced an early form of Celtic speech (although he thinks it 'highly improbable'[15]) and considers that the Celtic settlement and acculturation of Britain was probably a drawn-out affair, perhaps beginning early in the first millenium BC and continuing through to historical times with the well-documented Belgic invasion of what is now South East England. Lloyd and Jennifer Laing, however, while recognising the difficulties of appealing to linguistic, archaeological or wider ethnological criteria, are more cautious in their analysis of the origins of Celtic Britain.[16] Like Professor Cunliffe, they look to the Late Bronze-Age for the emergence of the Celts. In particular, like other archaeologists, they point to the legacy of the so-called Urnfielders, the immediate cultural ancestors of the Celts.

The Urnfielders have acquired their prosaic name as a result of their practice of burying their dead in urns in flat cemetries. Around 1200-700 BC these Urnfielders spread out from their Eastern European homeland to penetrate central and western parts of the continent. It is thought that they spoke an early Celtic dialect, and that they exhibited other proto-Celtic characteristics such as a predeliction for the construction of hillforts and the use of iron for weapons and artifacts (a skill that they had learned from contacts in the Caucasus). Lloyd and Jennifer Laing have suggested that Urnfield immigrants would have introduced a primitive form of Celtic language into Bronze-Age Britain, and that the cultural delineation of the Late Bronze-Age would have influenced the territorial sub-divisions of subsequent periods (for example, the geographical distribution of 'Trevisker' pottery in the Late Bronze-Age coincides more or less with the territorial extent of the later Dumnonia). Anne Ross agrees and considers that '. . . it is legitimate . . . to speak of these people as proto-Celts'.[17] The Laings, though, are more circumspect, insisting that the 'Use of a primitive dialect is, however, hardly sufficient for us to speak of 'Bronze Age Celts' in Britain, as some have done'.[18]

Rather, 'Celtic Iron Age Britain begins at Llyn Fawr',[19] an allusion to the discovery of the mid-seventh century BC 'Lyn Fawr hoard' in Glamorganshire in 1910-11. This find shed new light on the shadowy divide between the Bronze and Iron-Ages in Britain. In addition to the typical Bronze Age items, the hoard included some items made of iron and others which, though crafted in Bronze, were reminscent of artifacts from Halstatt —the so-called birthplace of Celtic culture. Thus, according to the Laings, the immigrants or traders who brought their belongings to Llyn Fawr were 'undoubtably Celts'. So where or what was this Halstatt that had lent these newcomers their impeccable Celtic credentials?

Briefly, Halstatt is a village in the Salzhammergut in Austria, the generally accepted scene of the first stage of 'Celtic development'. Excavations there have revealed both cemetries and salt mines (salt and iron provided wealth in early Celtic society), the centre of a vibrant and expanding culture. By the sixth century BC Halstatt power had moved from its upper Austrian confines to penetrate other parts of central and western Europe, (Anne Ross suggests that there is evidence of Halstatt influence in North

East Scotland as early as 600 BC), establishing the first wave of Celtic cultural and economic importance in continental Europe as a whole. The second wave is known as La Tene, and is named after a site on Lake Neuchatel in Switzerland where excavations in 1906-17 discovered iron weapons and artifacts, woodwork, and remains of human skeletons. The progression from Halstatt to La Tene was characterised by change of burial rite, notably the interment of society's elite in two-wheeled chariots with weapons, armour and other items necessary for the after-life. Such practices suggest a warrior society with a strong economic base (in farming), an inference confirmed in classical writings, which by the fifth century BC were already describing what was, from their perspective, a flambouyant but flawed life-style. Although their boastful and quarrelsome characterstics were criticised, the La Tene Celts were technologically advanced. They came to dominate much of Europe and their culture was well-established by the first century BC.

The Celtic influence in Cornwall has been of enduring significance, most notably in the Cornish language which developed eventually from the Celtic dialect spoken in the peninsula, and has given us the vast majority of Cornish placenames, many surnames, and a vernacular which survived until modern times. And yet the early evidence of Iron Age Cornwall is of continuity rather than upheaval, of evolution not revolution, suggesting an era of gradual cultural and technological change rather than a sudden break due to mass migration or invasion.[20] It seems likely that iron deposits found in Cornwall (for example, at Trevelgue, near Newquay, a promontory fort located close to natural iron bands in the cliff) were exploited at an early date. But the adoption of iron was predated by other significant innovations which heralded the dawn of a new era, especially the distinctly new forms of pottery that had emerged in the Late Bronze-Age. And yet, other typically Iron-Age or typically Celtic features, such as the construction of hillforts and defended settlements, do not appear generally in Cornwall until as late as the fourth century BC.

By the first few centuries BC the inhabitants of Cornwall, Scilly, and what is now Devon, and the western part of Somerset, a geographical community of perhaps some twenty to forty thousand individuals, had coalesced into the territorial/tribal grouping known to classical writers as the Dumnonii — a name that would endure into the Roman and post-Roman eras and feature large in the early history of these islands. Although in the territory of the Dumnonii there are few massive fortifications of the type that characterise Wessex or parts of Wales, the construction of hillforts was nevertheless typical of the Dumnonii. In Cornwall alone there are over eighty, evidence perhaps of a warrior society in which power and wealth were guarded jealously. The longevity of some of these forts is impressive, with evidence of occupation and re-occupation through the Iron Age and into the Roman and post-Roman periods.

Two of the most impressive of these hillforts, situated at extreme opposite ends of Cornwall, are Chun Castle and Warbstow Bury. Chun is rare amongst Cornish Iron Age fortifications because its ramparts are made of stone which, viewed in the clear light of West Penwith, lends it an almost Mediterranean ambience that is somehow reminiscent of Mycenae. Although there is no equivalent of the Lion Gate, the staggered entrance through the double-walled ramparts is impressive and, more than anywhere else in Cornwall today, gives the inquisitive and sensitive visitor a feel for those long-departed days of Celtic warrior chieftains. In the eighteenth century the

inner rampart stood as much as 4.5m (15 ft) high but during the last century much of the stone was removed for local building projects, such as Madron Workhouse and the new north pier at Penzance harbour. A similar fort at nearby Caer Bran, where the inner rampart is severely degraded, seems to have suffered similar damage at some point in its history. Nonetheless, both Chun and Caer Bran remain awesome sites (and sights). From Chun on a clear day, the sea is visible on three sides and there are commanding views across Penwith. Nearby is Chun Quoit, dating from the Neolithic period, and all around are hundreds of acres of prehistoric fields and the remains of round houses.

The pillars that mark the entrance to Chun Castle somehow retain a sense of former inhabitants.

On the horizon sit the ancient ramparts of Warbstow Bury in North Cornwall.

The oval hill fort of Warbstow Bury is one of Cornwall's most important defensive structures. The large mound in the centre is known locally as 'The Giant's Grave' or 'King Arthur's Tomb'.

The primary occupation of Chun Castle was during the Iron Age, from the third to first centuries BC, with evidence of later re-occupation during the Roman and post-Roman eras. The same appears to be true of Warbstow Bury, situated in north-east Cornwall where it dominates the heights above the River Ottery, the strategically important tributary of the Tamar. Warbstow is amongst the largest of the Cornish Iron Age hillforts, with a complicated series of ramparts and ditches which seems to have been altered and re-arranged over time. Nicholas Johnson and Peter Rose describe Warbstow Bury as an important chieftain's stronghold,[21] and there can be no doubting its former strategic importance as a centre of military and political power in that part of Cornwall.

Other Iron Age hillforts whose geographic locations intimate strategic importance are Castle-an-Dinas, near St Columb Major, Castle Canyke, at Bodmin, and Castle Dore near Fowey. Castle-an-Dinas (not to be confused with the site of identical name in West Penwith) is a particularly large hillfort, dominating the Goss Moor area and guarding east-west and north-south routes that pass close by. Situated in the heart of mid-Cornwall, Castle-an-Dinas has a special place in Cornish lore, identified in historical times as a centre of royal power, an assertion made in the Cornish late medieval miracle play *Beunans Meriasek* (the *Life of St Meriasek*, of which

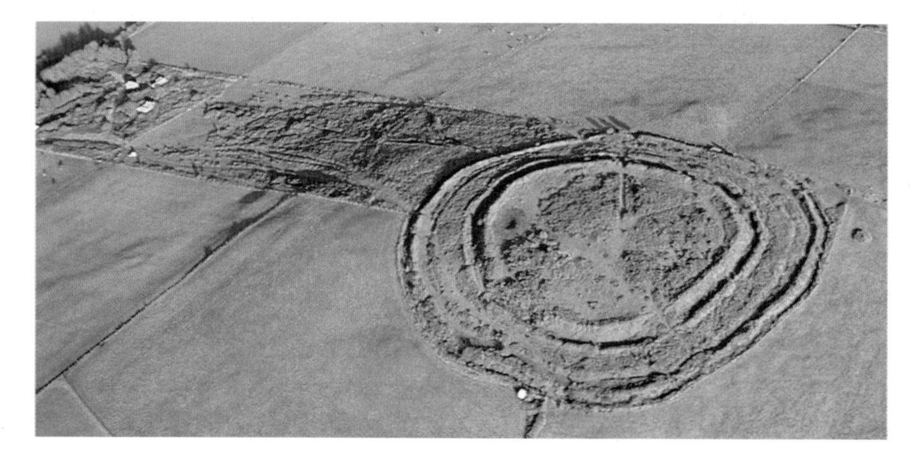
Interwoven into the tales of King Arthur is the hill fort of Castle-an-Dinas in Mid-Cornwall. The formidable earth ramparts set up in the Iron Age make for a striking feature of the landscape above Goss Moor.

Castle Dore is a well-preserved hill fort near Golant. Legend suggests that this sixth-century site was occupied by local royalty; one of whom may well have been King Mark.

more in later chapters) where the fort is claimed as a dwelling place of the Duke of Cornwall.[22] In Baring-Gould's fanciful *A Book of the West* of 1899, this royal status is translated to the other Castle-an-Dinas in West Penwith: '. . . this was a royal dinas. Not only had it the requisite double wall, but also the *drecht gialnai*, or dyke of the hostages. Every king retained about him pledges from the under-chiefs that they would be faithful'.[23]

Be that as it may, to return to the strictly strategic issues, the impressive eminence of Castle Canyke overlooks the important trading and communication route between the Camel and Fowey estuaries. Castle Dore likewise keeps watch over the River Fowey, and is yet another well-preserved hillfort with an impressive set of ramparts. Ralegh Radford's excavations in the 1930s confirmed that these ramparts had been strengthened during the first century BC, and that both within the fort and outside near the entrance had been many round houses. To this list of strategic hillforts one might add Cadsonbury, overlooking the River Lynher in south-east Cornwall, Resugga Castle, guarding the confluence of the Fal and St Stephens rivers, Helsbury, overlooking the Camel, and St Dennis (now incorporated into the churchyard) which looks across Goss Moor to Castle-an-Dinas. There is also Gear, to the south of the Helford River, and of course the other Castle-an-Dinas in West Penwith.

The promontory forts or 'cliff castles' are the other form of defended site that characterise the Iron Age in Cornwall. They exist on both north and south coasts, often dramatic in their situation and making excellent use of strategic and easily defensible positions. As Henrietta Quinnell has noted, although these forts seem inconvenient to modern eyes, they served their purpose well and occur wherever the coastal geography allows in Britain, Ireland and Brittany.[24] Often, however, the promontory forts have been seen as a specifically Cornish phenomenon, with the suggestion that they represent the intrusion of maritime immigrants, perhaps from Brittany. One suggestion, indeed, is that the forts may be the work of the Veneti, a formidable Breton seafaring people whose naval power was finally crushed by the Romans. However, although the connections between Brittany and Cornwall are ancient and complex, the theory does not now enjoy general currency amongst archaeologists. Malcolm Todd concludes that there is no direct evidence to link the promontory forts with Breton influence, and Henrietta Quinnell remarks that, as some of these forts were occupied from early in the Iron Age to well into the post-Roman era, the chronological range is so vast that we should envisage different types of occupancy at different times during that span.[25]

Trevelgue, near Newquay, and Maen Castle, near Sennen, were both occupied in the earlier Iron-Age, and evidence at Trevelgue suggests a long (but interrupted) occupancy from early in the Iron-Age until as late as the sixth century AD. At both Trevelgue and Maen Castle, excavation has

Trevelgue, near Newquay, a promontory fort in a spectacular setting.

This aerial photograph of the Dodman Point, near Gorran, clearly shows the huge earth rampart, known locally as the 'Balk' or the 'Hack and Cast'.

yielded considerable quantities of pottery from different eras, from the earlier Iron Age to the post-Roman. Trevelgue is generally recognised as the most heavily defended prehistoric site in Cornwall, the headland cut off by a series of seven ramparts. It is thought that iron from local deposits was smelted on-site, which may have added to the relative self-sufficiency of the fort community.

Again, it is possible to list some of the most impressive and significant of these Cornish cliff castles. On the south coast, at the extreme south-eastern tip of Cornwall, is Rame Head—a distinctive and familiar shape for all seafarers hugging the Cornish coast or making for Plymouth Sound. Today the most prominent feature on Rame Head is the tiny fourteenth century chapel (dedicated, like so many other high places in Cornwall and the Celtic lands, to St Michael) but there is also evidence of a deep Iron Age defensive ditch across the neck, together with traces of a rampart. Further along the Cornish coast, at the western extremity of St Austell Bay and near the present-day fishing village of Gorran Haven, is Dodman Point. The expansion of Elizabethan 'Bulwarks' during the Spanish scare may have enhanced the single massive bank which forms the promontory fort here, but even in Iron Age times the Dodman must have been the largest cliff castle in Cornwall. Situated strategically halfway along the Cornish coast, jutting out into the Channel, Dodman fort could have kept a close eye on all passing maritime traffic.

Not surprisingly, such a vast edifice as the Dodman cliff castle has found its way into Cornish lore. Robert Hunt informs us that 'Marvellous as it may seem, tradition assures us that this was the work of a giant, and that he performed the task in a single night. This fortification has long been known as *Thica Vosa,* or the Hack and Cast'. Apparently, the giant was the

The medieval chapel dedicated to St. Michael is found on the conical Iron age cliff castle at Rame Head. The Cornish poet Charles Causley in 'Ramhead and Dodman' alludes to the old saying 'When Ramhead and Dodman meet', meaning 'never'. The two headlands are twenty-five miles apart.

The astonishing promontory fort of Treryn Dinas stands sentinel over the beach at Porthcurno.

scourge of the neighbourhood but one day he fell ill. A local doctor bravely answered the giant's plea for help. The doctor's advice was that the giant should be bled, and when the giant was sufficiently weakened by the loss of blood, the doctor kicked him over the edge of the cliff to his death. As Hunt has it, 'The well-known promontory of The Dead Man, or Dodman, is so called from the dead giant'.[26]

Still on the south coast, but in the far west of the Penwith peninsula, is the famous promontory fort of Treryn Dinas. Perhaps better-known for its folklore than for its archaeology (something for which we may blame Robert Hunt), it is nonetheless an intensely impressive site. It exists in one of the most spectacular stretches of coastline in Cornwall. Four huge ramparts and ditches seal off the entire headland, with a further bank and ditch at the headland's extremity. Inevitably, perhaps, Hunt has a giant's story to relate about Treryn Dinas. As he put it:

> Treryn Castle, an ancient British fortress, the Cyclopean walls of which, and its outer earthwork, can still be traced, was the dwelling place of a famous giant and his wife. I have heard it said that he gave his name to this place, but that is, of course, doubtful.[27]

Interestingly, in an echo of the Dodman tale, the giant was stabbed and kicked over the cliff, into to the sea. This time, however, the mortal blow was performed by another giant, the secret lover of the Treryn giant's wife 'The guilty pair took possession of Treryn Castle, and, we are told, lived happily for many years'.

Confusingly, on the north coast of West Penwith is the similarly named Trereen Dinas, situated at Gurnard's Head between Pendeen and Zennor. Here, three stone ramparts across the neck of the headland create the fort, and a number of house platforms have also been identified. However, the jewell of the north coast, perhaps even surpassing Trevelgue, is further east at The Rumps, near St Minver. Excavated as recently as 1963-67, The Rumps was occupied between the fourth century BC and the first century AD. The four ramparts represent two phases of fortification, the latter of which was the most elaborate. Round houses have been excavated at the site, revealing pottery, bones and other domestic items.

The Rumps, perhaps Cornwall's finest Iron Age cliff castle

The extensive remains of courtyard houses at Carn Euny.

Less spectacular than either the hillforts or 'cliff castles', but in their own way equally remarkable, are the so-called rounds or enclosed settlements which seem to have multiplied in the late first millenium BC. They were hardly known or understood before 1958 but subsequently have been demonstrated to be typifying features of the Iron Age Cornish landscape. Generally, these rounds are small farmsteads or hamlets surrounded by a single rampart, and are situated on spurs or hillsides close to good farming country. In 1966 Charles Thomas suggested that there might be some 750 rounds in Cornwall and Devon, but more recent examination has shown that this is likely to be a conservative estimate. Several rounds have been excavated, at locations such as Threemilestone near Truro, Trevisker at St Eval, Goldherring in Sancreed parish, and Castle Gotha near St Austell.

Perhaps better known to the lay observer are the so-called courtyard houses, at least two of which are so popular with the visiting public that they might almost be called tourist attractions! One of these, Chysauster, is of late construction and properly belongs to the Roman era. Others, however, are earlier, including the well-preserved Carn Euny in the parish of Sancreed. Porthmeor is also well-kown, and another Penwith site of note is Bosullow. In all, there are said to be some sixty examples of courtyard houses in Cornwall, each one constructed after about 200BC. The Carn Euny site consists of at least three interlocking courtyard houses but is especially famous for its *fogou* or underground chamber. Another *fogou* of note is that at Halligye, south of the Helford River. These stone-built subterranean tunnels have excited much comment, and popular explanations for their existence range from religious ritual to hiding-place. However, the favoured archaeological theory today is that they may have been sophisticated underground storage tunnels or larders, evidence of the production and preservation of a sizeable agricultural surplus in later Iron Age Cornwall. From this perspective, as Malcolm Todd explains, 'Although they are a striking response to peculiar local needs, *fogous* are thus firmly to be accommodated within the framework of the wider Celtic Iron Age economy'.[28]

The interior of Carn Euny *fogou*. From the Cornish word for cave, *fogous* have been variously interpreted as hiding places, cold storages for food, or ritual structures.

As has been noted already, prehistoric cultures are often characterised by their funerary practices. In Iron Age Cornwall, burial was in cemetries of pit-graves or stone cists, with corpses placed on their side in a crouched position, usually aligned north-south. Although archaeologists complain that little is found in these cemetries other than skeletons and the odd brooch, in fact Cornwall is one of the few areas in Britain to have produced Iron Age cemetries. Important burial sites have been excavated at Trelan Bahow on the Lizard peninsula and at Trevone on the north coast (at both of which La Tene-style brooches have been found), and in a startling excavation at Harlyn on the north Cornish coast in 1900-5, 130 inhumations were revealed. This discovery has entered Cornish lore, an indication that folk consciousness and popular folk culture can be of recent origin. The fount of myth and story-telling does not have to be lost in the mists of time. Jack Clemo's poem *In Harlyn Museum* articulates the compelling horror-fascination that the idea of Harlyn has had for many Cornish people:

When I last stood here
My childish eyes were wide, fear-clouded,
Vaguely mocked by the skulls and bones
Lodged in their neat glass cases.
A tide within me groped among stones,
A chilly friction whispered:
'Ancestors, Celts, before Julius Caesar
Sent his legions towards the Tamar.
Something called death, and then,
After a long spell, something dug up
From Harlyn strand'. I preferred it
To ball games and sand-castles on the beach.[29]

Mention of Julius Caesar, like earlier references above to Roman and post-Roman evidences, reminds us that the later Iron Age in Cornwall was not only on the eve of the Roman invasion of Britain but occurred against the backdrop of the ever-widening compass of Roman power in Western Europe. Tales of Phœnicians and Carthaginians making their way from the Mediterranean to trade for Cornish tin, like claims of Mycenaen contacts in the Bronze Age, are routinely repeated but not attested in hard fact. And yet, speculation that classical allusions to the Cassiterides (the Tin Isles) refer to Cornwall or the Scillies is commonplace, deserving of a mention in even the most cautious and sober of archaeological surveys. There is, however, no documentary evidence until the first century BC when one Publius Crassus, a Roman official, visited the Cassiderites and recorded his findings. He decided that the tin was readily accessible and the natives friendly, and he actively set about recommending the development of this trading route.

Corroborating evidence is provided by Diodorus who records that the inhabitants of the peninsula of Belerion were remarkably civilized, due to their routine trading contacts with other parts. He noted that these natives not only extracted the tin but ground it down and then smelted the ore into ingots. These ingots were then taken to the island of Ictis, a maritime trading post from which the export of tin would be organised. Again, there has been much speculation as to where this Ictis might be. The long-held assumption that it could be St Michael's Mount is now generally discredited, as is the more recent suggestion of Mount Batten on the Plymouth side of the Tamar. An intriguing thought is that Ictis might in fact be St George's

St. George's (Looe) Island—is this the legendary Ictis?

(Looe) Island, just off the coast of south-east Cornwall, which even in the seventeenth century could still be reached on foot from the mainland. Whatever the case, the reality is that increasing trade and contact with the Mediterranean in the later Iron Age foreshadowed the growing interest and eventual intervention of Rome.[30]

Although much that is routinely celebrated as 'Celtic Cornwall'—the Saints, Celtic crosses, miracle plays, holy wells, and so on—are from later eras, it is the Iron Age that without caveat first establishes Cornwall as a Celtic land and provides the inspiration and point of origin for those who would champion Cornwall first and foremost as a Celtic nation. This is a process located in the debate noted earlier in this chapter, and to which we will return again later in the book.

For the moment, however, we should remember that notions of Cornish Celticity emerge first in antiquarian guise in the last century, especially in its latter half, where enthusiasts such as Robert Hunt related 'the "inner life" of the Cornish people' to 'the peculiarities of any Celtic race',[31] tracing contemporary beliefs and observances through popular folklore to those Iron Age communities who first created those 'cliff castles' and hillforts. Later, at the end of the nineteenth century and into this, this antiquarian background helped give content and inspiration to a new Celtic Revival in Cornwall, which sought not only to re-emphasise Cornish roots as essentially Celtic but in effect to recreate Celtic Cornwall in the closing century of this millenium. Thus, for example, in 1971 James Whetter was able to write his *The Celtic Background of Kernow*, a volume which ranged from Iron Age promontory forts to the political nationalism of the post-Second World War era '. . . dedicated to the preservation, enhancement of the Celtic character of the land and its people'.[32] Elsewhere he could add that:

> The Cornish are proud of their Celtic origins, their history, their heritage, their plot of land and the imprint their ancestors made upon it. Through neglect . . . the modern Cornishman frequently has little knowledge of his Celtic past, the struggles of his race in early historic and pre-historic times, their long centuries of independence, their first effloresecence.[33]

His conclusion was that, 'After long centuries of submergence, the Cornish are at last rediscovering their Celtic identity'.[34]

Notes & References (Chapter 3)

1. Anne Ross, *Pagan Celtic Britain*, Cardinal, London, 1974, p33.

2. Miles Dillon, unpub. lecture 'The Coming of the Celts', cited in Colin Renfrew, *Archaeology and Language: The Puzzle of Indo-European Origins*, Jonathan Cape, London, 1987, p.225.

3. Ronald MacDonald Douglas, 'The Scottish Brits', in Cathal O'Luain, *For A Celtic Future*, Celtic League, Dublin, 1983, pp.50-51.

4. Peter Berresford Ellis, *The Celtic Dawn: A History of Pan Celticism*, Constable, London, 1993, p.25.

5. Rosemary McKechnie, 'Becoming Celtic in Corsica', in Sharon Macdonald (ed.), *Inside European Identities*, Berg, Oxford, 1993.

6. Anthony D.Smith, *The Ethnic Origin of Nations*, Blackwell, Oxford, 1986, p.181.

7. John Collis, unpub. lecture 'George Buchanan and the Celts of Britain', 10th International Congress of Celtic Studies, University of Edinburgh, 1995.

8. Nick Merriman, 'Value and Motivation in Prehistory: The Evidence for "Celtic Spirit"', in Ian Hodder (ed.), *The Archaeology of Contextual Meanings*, Cambridge University Press, Cambridge 1987; Malcolm Chapman, *The Celts: The Construction of a Myth*, Macmillan, London, 1992.

9. Renfrew, 1987, especially chapter 9. 'Ethnogenesis: Who Were the Celts?'.

10. Vincent Megaw and Ruth Megaw, 'The Prehistoric Celts: Identity and Contextuality', in Martin Kuna and Natalie Venclova, *Whither Archaeology?*, Institute of Archaeology, Prague, 1995, p.241.

11. Barry Cunliffe, *The Celtic World*, Bodley Head, London, 1979, p.7.

12. Ross, 1974, p.33 & p.37.

13. Cunliffe, 1979, p.15.

14. Cunliffe, 1979, p.15.

15. Richard Muir, *Reading the Celtic Landscapes*, Guild Publishing, London, 1985, p.33.

16. Lloyd Laing and Jennifer Laing, *The Origins of Britain*, Granada, London, 1982; Lloyd Laing, *Celtic Britain*, Routledge, London, 1979.

17. Ross, 1974, p.34.

18. Laing and Laing, 1982, pp.242-243.

19. Laing and Laing, 1982, p.243.

20. Excellent summaries of the Iron Age in Cornwall appear in Henrietta Quinnell, 'Cornwall During the Iron Age and Roman Period', *Cornish Archaeology*, 25, 1986; Malcolm Todd, *The South West to AD 1000*, Longman, London, 1987; Nicholas Johnson and Peter Rose, *Cornwall's Archaeological Heritage*, Twelveheads, Truro, 1990.

21. Johnson & Rose, 1990, p.47.

22. Myrna Combellack, *The Camborne Play: A Verse Translation of Beunans Meriasek*, Dyllansow Truran, Redruth, 1988, pp.96-98.

23. S. Baring-Gould, *A Book of the West: Cornwall*, London, 1899, repub. Wildwood, London, 1981, p.49.

24. Quinnell, 1986.

25. Quinnell, 1986; Todd, 1987, p.163.

26. Robert Hunt, *Popular Romances of the West of England*, 1865, p.59.

27. Hunt, 1965, p.21.

28. Todd, 1987, p.175.

29. Jack Clemo, 'In Harlyn Museum', *Cornish Review*, Summer 1973.

30. Todd, 1987, p.188.

31. Hunt, 1865, p.380.

32. James Whetter, *The Celtic Background of Kernow*, MK Publications, St Austell, 1971, p.12.

33. James Whetter, *A Celtic Tommorrow*, MK Publications, St Austell, 1973, p.9.

34. Whetter, 1973, p.1.

CHAPTER 4

From Dumnonia to Cornubia

CORNWALL

From Dumnonia to Cornubia

If it is in the Iron Age that Cornwall acquires that 'Celtic identity' which we recognise today, then it is in the succeeding era—as we move from prehistoric to historic times—that Cornwall begins to develop the territorial identity which marks it out geo-politically as the land apart. But, as we have seen in earlier chapters, characterising Cornwall is never that simple, and as ever there are difficulties and paradoxes. To begin with, the modern territorial identity emerges out of a wider geographical construct—Dumnonia—while the defining act of setting the River Tamar as the Cornish border was a function of English intrusion in the tenth century. And yet, there is also a suggestion that Cornwall was long before that time an administrative subdivision (*pagus*) of the Roman canton of Dumnonia. However, (in a further paradox) if we are to acknowledge the Romans as the first to establish Cornwall as an administrative-political unit, then we must also admit that in other respects Roman influence west of the Tamar was in fact minimal.

Even so, we are constrained by historical convention to speak of pre-Roman, Roman and post-Roman Cornwall, a relatively harmless convenience if we can agree what we mean by these terms but altogether more misleading (and dangerous) should we infer that Cornwall was somehow an exemplar of Roman Britain. 'Roman Britain' is an inherently misleading concept, implying as it does a homogenous political and cultural Romanisation of the entire island. Worse still is the idea of a 'Roman Britain' that gives way to an 'Anglo-Saxon England', a view of early history that leaves little room for consideration of indigenous continuity (not least in Cornwall), encourages the erroneous equation of *Britain* with *England*, and reduces the *British* (and thus *Cornish*) experience to a succession of invasions—Celts, Romans, Anglo-Saxons, Vikings, Normans. This is the approach of the so-called National Curriculum, the staple diet of schoolchildren in Cornwall as much as it is in Sussex or Hampshire, one which leaves pupils in many Cornish schools with little idea of the reality and issues of early Cornish history. We can only agree with Professor Charles Thomas when he expresses:

> . . . sorrow and annoyance . . . at the undue extension of words like 'England, English' or a philosophy of a taught *British* past underlying such book-titles as *Everyday Life in Roman and Anglo-Saxon Times*, *Roman Britain and the English Settlements*, or *Roman Britain to Saxon England*. There *are* still others of us, west of Offa's Dyke and the river Tamar, and north of Hadrian's Wall . . . .[1]

In fact, there is still remarkably little evidence for the Roman conquest of South West Britain, and the popular assumption of a relentless westerly thrust following the arrival of the Legions in Britain in AD43 is probably flawed.[2] A fort was established at *Isca Dumnoniorum* (Exeter) in cAD55, the base of the Second Augustan Legion, and it was from there that Roman rule was exercised and Roman power extended in the far West. As far as Cornwall is concerned, there are few clues to the extent of this rule and power. The only tangible evidence of military intrusion is the Roman fort at Nanstallon, near Bodmin, constructed cAD55-60 and excavated in the early 1970s by Aileen Fox and the late Professor W.L.D. 'Bill' Ravenhill. Situated in the middle of Cornwall near the Fowey-Camel trade and communication route, Nanstallon was probably a forward operating-base and was strategically well-placed for the Roman presence to be felt. However, the Legion at Exeter was withdrawn cAD75 and, with no Roman town west of *Isca Dumnoniorum*, Cornwall (as Ian Soulsby puts it) '. . . settled down to four centuries of only nominal Roman rule'.[3]

Cornwall was part of the *Civitas Dumnoniorum*, the canton of Dumnonia, with its administrative centre in Exeter. The Dumnonii themselves were a tribal grouping that had emerged during the Iron Age, and their name may mean or be derived from their reputation as 'Worshippers of the God *Dumnonos*'.[4] Their territory included modern Cornwall, Devon (the name comes from the word Dumnonia), the western parts of Somerset and perhaps the fringes of Dorset. The Romans formalised this tribal territory into their administrative region of *Civitas Dumnoniorum* although, as suggested above, there is evidence to indicate that Cornwall may have been a *pagus* in its own right.[5] Both Charles Thomas and Malcolm Todd have pointed to the seventh or eighth century Ravenna *Cosmography* wherein is a reference to *Purocoronavis*, almost certainly a corruption of *Durocornovium*—'fort or walled settlement of the Cornovii'. Thomas concludes '. . . that in late Roman, and putatively in early Roman times, the lands west of the Tamar were those of the Cornovii; that this later formed a pagus of the canton of the Dumnonii . . .'.[6] Todd adds that 'This is the earliest mention of a people who presumably formed a sect of the Dumnonii and who in a later period gave their name to Cornwall (Kernow)'.[7] Certainly, they were sufficiently established for their territory (Cornwall) to be recorded as 'Cornubia' by cAD700. The root *corn* means a horn (probably a reference to the Cornish peninsula), a prefix which has given us both Kernow and Cornwall (the latter including the Anglo-Saxon suffix *wealas*, foreigner, the same word as in Wales and Welsh).

Intriguingly, the tribal name Cornovii (or Cornavii) occurs elsewhere in Britain at this time, in the north-west of what is today the English Midlands and in the far north of Scotland in what is now Caithness (there were also Dumnonii or Damnonii in west-central Scotland). This may reflect nothing more than the cultural and linguistic affinities between the various Celtic groups that inhabited Britain, although John Morris in his controversial *The Age of Arthur* postulates an ingenious theory which has the (Midlands) Cornovii as a fifth-century military unit surviving from the then deteriorating Roman administration. Britain was under pressure from both Irish settlement and Saxon invasion, and Morris suggests that the Cornovii were re-deployed from their Midlands base to Dumnonia where their task was to contain and control the Irish arrival.[8] Although there is indeed evidence of Irish settlement in post-Roman Dumnonia, the Morris thesis is not widely accepted by archaeologists and early historians, and we may safely conclude that the Cornovii located west of the Tamar were an indigenous people quite separate from their namesakes in the Midlands and Caithness.

To return to the sparse evidence of Roman activity in Cornwall, mention should be made of Carvossa, a large enclosed site near Probus where much imported Roman pottery has been found, datable to the mid and later first

The extensive and remarkably well-preserved courtyard house settlement at Chysauster. This late Iron Age /Romano-British village consists of nine dwellings, most of which have a terraced garden plot attached.

century AD and comparable with that uncovered at Exeter. A similar site, again suggesting wealth, status and strategic importance as well as Roman interest or influence, is Carloggas in St Mawgan-in-Pydar where Roman and Gaulish artefacts have been located. The commonest type of settlement, however, was the more modest enclosed homestead or round, first established in the later Iron Age and existing in profusion by the Roman period—a fact attested in contemporary place-names in the tell-tale elements *car*, *caer*, *ker*, and *gear*. They are especially thick on the ground in west and central Cornwall but they do exist right up to the Tamar, with a smaller number in west and north Devon. These are, however, the dwellings of the native Cornish and are only 'Roman' in the sense that they were constructed during the period of Roman rule. The best known example is that at Trethurgy (late Roman period), near St Austell, which has been subject to exhaustive investigation by archaeologists. Also typical of Cornwall and the indigenous Cornish were the courtyard houses, again first emerging in the Iron Age but developing in the Roman period to the form in which they survive today. Carn Euny, founded as early as the fifth century BC, was at its zenith in the fourth century AD. Chysauster, near Castle-an-Dinas in West Penwith, is the best-preserved courtyard house complex in Cornwall. It is dated from the second to fourth centuries AD.

Common sense (and classical allusion) tells us that the Romans would have been interested in Cornwall for trading purposes, not least the traffic in tin and perhaps also silver and gold. Near St Enodoc church in North Cornwall a wide range of late Roman metalwork and pottery has been uncovered, suggesting that there may have been an important harbour nearby on the Camel estuary. There is no real evidence for the existence of Roman roads in Cornwall, except for a milestone of Gordian III found *in situ* at Gwennap Pit, near Redruth, and four road-maintenance record stones

St Enodoc church, on the Camel Estuary, an important landfall for travellers in early times. The slate gravestone of the poet Sir John Betjeman (1906-84) can be seen in the churchyard.

(also popularly called milestones)—one at Breage, another at St Hilary and two at Tintagel. One of the Tintagel stones (dated AD251-3) was located at Trethevy, and the other (dated AD250 and inscribed with the name of the Emperor Caesar Gaius Valerius Licinius) was found in 1889 in Tintagel churchyard where it was serving as a lych post. Tin ingots of supposedly Roman provenance have been located at a number of sites, including Trethurgy and Chûn Castle, and Cornish tin production for Roman Imperial needs was especially important from the second century when the Iberian silver mines were in decline. The widespread use of pewter table ware and tin-based alloys in Roman coins ensured continuing demand for Cornish tin in the later Empire.

Malcolm Todd has observed that *Civitas Dumnoniorum* was one of the least Romanised regions in Roman-controlled Britain, and Henrietta Quinnell notes that if we compare Cornwall to, say, Sussex (with its Fishbourne Palace and Bignor Villa) then Cornish Dumnonia seems impoverished indeed.[9] There are no mosaics, no baths, no theatres. Holcombe Villa in East Devon lies at the western extremity of the Romano-British villa country of southern Britain, and further west there is nothing similar of note except for the recognisably Roman villa that has been uncovered at Magor in Illogan. This is surely a classic case of an exception proving the rule, for its very existence in this unlikely spot reminds us forcibly that nothing comparable has been located anywhere else west of Holcombe. The suggestion is that Magor may have been the retirement home of a former Dumnonian official who had served in the western part of the canton;[10] it is intriguing to speculate that even in those days Cornwall evoked nostalgia and was seen as an attractive place in which to retire!

But if Dumnonia appears impoverished in comparison with other parts, it must also be admitted that it was probably socially more stable than many other areas during the period of Roman rule. The life-style no doubt continued much as before, with local rule devolved to indigenous tribal chieftains, and with steady progress made in areas such as tin production, agriculture and the manufacture of metalwork. As Johnson and Rose conclude, 'Cornwall was still, despite 350 years of Roman bureaucracy, essentially Celtic in character'.[11] However, by the time that the last Roman Legions were withdrawn from Britain in AD410 to reinforce the Empire's heartland, a new sense of insecurity and uncertainty was already leading in Cornwall to the reoccupation of old Iron Age strongholds. Dumnonia was to survive the departure of the Legions but it was to become much altered by Irish settlement and the arrival of Christianity. Mass migration to Brittany was to be a further social upheaval, as was the increasing intrusion of the English, the latter leading to the final collapse of Dumnonia and the territorial definition of modern Cornwall.[12] Within this period of change, from the early fifth to the mid-tenth centuries, Cornwall emerges ever more clearly as a distinct culture zone with an identity and experience that we can with increasing confidence label 'Cornish'. Indeed, as David Dumville has remarked:

> A potentially unfortunate tendency of the last generation's work, on the history of Britain's South-west peninsula in the earliest phase of the middle ages, has been the frequent treatment of the whole region as a single unit. 'The Kingdom of Dumnonia' can hardly be defined thus from any contemporary sources. And by the time when, in the ninth century, Anglo-Saxon sources speak of *Cornwalas* or *Westwalas,* Latin texts refer to *Cornubia,* and the Old Welsh form *Cerniu* is found, the names Dumnonia and the Dumnonii have passed from view save through the Old English derivatives *Defnascir* and *Defnas,* '(the territory of) the people of Devon'.[13]

Indeed, there is no real evidence as to how the Roman canton transformed itself into the petty kingdom of Dumnonia in the first place. We can surmise that it was part of the general fragmentation of power in post-Roman Britain and that, although Exeter may have remained its titular capital, other centres of competing importance (for example, Tintagel) may have emerged at an early stage. Similarly, a network of chieftains or petty sub-kingdoms may have emerged, with the reality of political and military power in Dumnonia shaped by the shifting balance of alliances between these rulers. Again, there is much to recommend the view that Cornwall as an entity emerged from this process, with Peter Berresford Ellis insisting that '. . . Dumnonia did not incorporate Cornwall as is popularly thought . . . Cornwall was already a separate kingdom in the time of Gildas'[14] (Gildas was the author of the cAD560 *De Excidio et Conquestu Britanniae*—On the Ruin and Conquest of Britain). Ellis, however, is rather over-egging his cake, looking for clearly defined boundaries (constitutional as well as territorial) of political power which really are a function of the organised (modern) state and not appropriate to the shifting sands of the so-called Dark Ages. We are on safer ground when we envisage a shifting balance of alliances between petty rulers against the ill-defined background of Dumnonia and the emerging entity of Cornwall. In the final analysis, of course, Dumnonia (or at least its remnant) becomes Cornwall.

It is difficult to construct king-lists for Dumnonia or the emerging Cornwall.[15] In the fifth century there is the legendary Cynan (or Conan) Meriadoc, the supposed leader of the first emigrations to Armorica. Three generations from Cynan is Tudwal. Cynfawr son of Tudwal is Cunomorus ('Hound of the Sea'), who may be the Cunomorus identified on the so-called Tristan stone near Fowey. This reads DRVSTANVS HIC IACIT/CUNOMORI FILIVS—here lies Drustanus, son of Cunomorus. 'Drustanus' has been equated with 'Tristan' and Cunomorus is commonly identified with the sixth century ruler Marcus Cunomorus ('King Mark') whose fortress is said to be the nearby Castle Dore. But there is also a British ruler of the same name in sixth-century Armorica, and this raises two further points. First of all, the emigration to Armorica led to the creation of a new Dumnonia in the north and north-west of Brittany. Contemporary sources do not always distinguish between these two territories of the same name (so that a Breton ruler may in fact turn out to be Cornish, or *vice versa*), and it is also possible that on occasions the same ruler may have held sway in both kingdoms—not unlike the twin-kingdom of Dalriada that emerged in north-eastern Ireland and western Scotland. Secondly, the Armorican connection highlights the twin Breton and Cornish claims to the legend of Tristan and Iseult in which, indeed, King Mark plays a central role.

Carved on this pillar of stone near Fowey is the inscription DRVSTANVS HIC IACIT / CUNOMORI FILIVS—(Drustanus, lies here, son of Cunomorus). Drustanus has been equated with Tristan of the Tristan and Iseult story.

The tale of the tragic lovers, Tristan and Iseult, is known throughout European literature and in many guises but its Cornish credentials are strong.[16] In its later versions it becomes entangled in the Arthurian cycles and the Quest for the Holy Grail, but in its earlier forms its association with Cornwall is clear. In the twelfth-century poem by the Anglo-Norman Beroul, for instance, King Mark's seat of power is said to be 'Lancien' and the nearby church is the monastery of St Sampson. Lancien has been identified (by Ralegh Radford) with Lantyan, which to this day is a farm near Castle Dore, while there is of course a church of St Sampson at nearby Golant (though see Charles Thomas' alternative below).[17] Tristan (Trystan, Tristram) was (and is) a common name in Cornwall, and Iseult (Esyld) is decidedly Cornish. Professor Kenneth Jackson suggests that it comes from the root British 'Adsiltia'—'She-who-must-be-gazed-upon'—an equivalent of the Latin 'Miranda' and, one might add, distinctly resonant of Helen of Troy in *her* great tale of Greek tragedy.[18]

The Tristan and Iseult story itself has many versions, 're-invented' in modern times by Swinburne, Tennyson, Wagner and others. In its simplest form, Tristan is the nephew (not son) of King Mark. Tristan is sent to Ireland as ambassador to seek the hand of Iseult, the Queen's daughter, for Mark. The princess and her maid Brangwayn journey from Ireland to Cornwall. The Queen has given Brangwayn a magic love-potion which must be given to Iseult and Mark on their wedding night to bind them in eternal love. By mistake (design, in some versions) the love-potion is drunk instead by Iseult and Tristan, with the inevitable result. Tristan is Iseult's true love, but she must marry Mark. Tristan and Iseult resort to various deceptions to give expression to their love but eventually Tristan leaves Cornwall to fight for King Hywel of Brittany. In Brittany he meets, falls in love with and marries another Iseult (Iseult of the White Hands). The first Iseult, however, begs him to return to Cornwall. Tristan obeys, and as he is playing his harp before her he is slain by an angry and jealous King Mark who has uncovered the truth of the liaison.

In some versions of the story Tristan's death is not mentioned, and indeed, in a contemporary re-telling Donald R. Rawe has King Arthur intervening in the triangle. He finds in favour of Tristan and Iseult (who live happily ever after) by resorting to a device suggested by the wizard Merlin. Tristan and Mark are told they may share Iseult, one having her when there are leaves on the tree and the other claiming her when the trees are leafless. Mark immediately choses the leafless option (for then the nights are longer) but Iseult reminds him that the holly, ivy, laurel and yew never lose their leaves, so she will always be Tristan's.[19] Wagner, in his version, as one might expect, choses the more drawn-out ending in which Tristan lies dying in Brittany. He sends to Cornwall for the first Iseult. If she is in the ship when it returns, it is to fly a white flag (or, in some versions, hoist a white sail); if not the flag is to be black. The flag is white but, in a fit of jealousy, Iseult of the White Hands tells Tristan that it is black. He promptly dies, as does the first Iseult when she comes ashore and discovers what has happened. A.L. Rowse tells the amusing story of when Matthew Arnold, the nineteenth-century poet—Cornish on his mother's side—who had written a poetic version of Tristan and Iseult, went to see Wagner's opera in Munich. Arnold commented, 'I may say that I have managed the story much better than Wagner. The second act is interminable, without any action'.[20]

King Mark may have received lavish attention in the realms of literature but in history he remains a shadowy figure. The first Dumnonian king that we can name with confidence as an historical character is Constantine, a mid sixth-century king who has been identified as Custennin, son of our King Mark. Constantine's life also seems to have been one of violence and betrayal, and Gildas in his *De Excidio* condemns him as the '. . . tyrant whelp of the filthy lioness of Dumnonia'.[21] Even when Constantine gives up the throne and retires to a monastery, he maintains a life-style of murder and corruption as he organises the liquidation of his opponents.

Constantine's son is Erbin, and Erbin's son is Geraint. This is not the famous Geraint who met his end at the Battle of Llongborth (Langport, Somerset?) but an ancestoral predecessor, possibly the 'Geraint rac deheu'—Geraint for the South—mentioned in the list of British heroes in the Welsh (actually, southern Scottish) *Gododdin* poem. These heroes were warriors mustered cAD600 to fight against the Northumbrian English. One wonders what was the dynastic relationship between this Geraint and Bledericus, *dux Cornubiae* (duke of Cornwall), who was reported killed at a British interception of Ethelfrith of Northumbria in the early seventh century. The better-known Geraint is clearly an historical figure, who in cAD705 was the recipient of a long letter from Aldhelm, the West Saxon first bishop of

Sherborne, who addresses him diplomatically as 'Geruntius, King of Dumnonia'.[22] Geraint was in fact the Cornish king of what was then left of Dumnonia, and we are told that he died trying to defend his territory from the encroaching English kingdom of Wessex. As the Welsh poet Llywarch Hen put it:

> In Llongborth was Geraint slain:
> Heroes of the land of Dumnonia,
> Before they were slaughtered, they slew,
> Under the thigh of Geraint, swift chargers,
> Long their legs, wheat their fodder,
> Red, swooping like the milk-white eagles.[23]

Later kings are again shadowy, as in the 'Dumnarth rex Cerniu' (Dumgarth, king of Cornwall), whose drowning is recorded in the *Annales Cambriae* (Welsh Annals) for the year AD875. Dumgarth is identified with Doniert whose ninth-century memorial stone is situated near St Cleer and reads in its Latin inscription DONIERT ROGAVIT PRO ANIMA—Doniert has asked (prayers?) for (his?) soul. One must imagine that Doniert was drowned in the nearby River Fowey, which after torrential rain rushes through the

Snow accentuates the beautiful knotwork upon King Doniert's Stone, near St. Cleer. King Doniert is said to have drowned in the nearby River Fowey c.AD875.

nearby white water rapids of Golitha Falls with fierce intensity. If Doniert was indeed king of Cornwall, it is not clear how much of Cornwall he actually ruled or to whom, if anyone, he owed allegiance. Less than one hundred years later Athelstan, king of the English kingdom of Wessex and now lord of all Britain, held a great court in Exeter in AD928. Amongst the attendees was probably the 'Huwal, king of the West Welsh'[24] mentioned in the *Anglo-Saxon Chronicle*. Huwel (Hywel) is generally recognised as the last in the line of independent (or semi-independent) Cornish (Dumnonian) kings, although there is in Penzance an inscribed cross dated cAD1000 which reads proudly: REGIS + RICATI CRUX - the cross of King Ricatus. In the far west of Cornwall, then, less than a century before the Norman conquest, there was a semblance, an echo, an assertion of Cornish kingly independence.

Imperfect as it may be, and reliant all too often upon legend and literary embroidery, the attempted construction of a king-list reaffirms the fragmented nature of power in post-Roman Dumnonia (what exactly *was* the extent of rule of a Mark or Constantine, let alone a Geraint, Doniert, Hywel or Ricatus?), and suggests again that shifting pattern of alliance of petty kings. Archaeological evidence paints the same picture. Charles Thomas has postulated that the Cornish Hundreds may represent early territorial divisions, perhaps based on military muster districts. The Cornish word for Hundred is in fact *keverang*, cognate with Welsh *cyfranc* (meeting, armed encounter) and Breton *coufranc* (muster, dispute).[25] In the far west of Cornwall were the Hundreds of Penwith and Kerrier, names that survive today as local government Districts. In mid-Cornwall were Pydar and Powder, and in the south-east were the twin Hundreds of East and West (Wivelshire). North Cornwall beyond the Camel was the Hundred of Trigg, later sub-divided into the constituent Hundreds of Trigg, Lesnewth and Stratton.

Even more intriguing, perhaps, are the earthwork survivals that suggest territorial subdivision in the post-Roman period. The Bolster Bank near St Agnes originally ran for some two miles (the rampart is still partly visible between Trevaunance Cove and Chapel Coombe) and enclosed both St Agnes Head and St Agnes Beacon. It has been dated to the fifth or sixth century, shortly after the departure of the Legions but long before the English made their presence felt in the far West. Craig Weatherhill suggests that the word Bolster comes from the Cornish '*both-lester*' (an upturned boat), although of course the name is linked in folklore with the local giant Bolster.[26] In south-east Cornwall is the more dramatic Giant's Hedge which stretched originally from the head of the Lerryn River (a creek of the Fowey) to West Looe, enclosing a large tract of land between the Fowey and Looe rivers. Again, this is dated to the post-Roman period and is strongly suggestive of the territorial extent of a petty kingdom. It is not clear where its capital might have been, although one possibility is Hall Rings, an earthwork fort near Pelynt. Impressive sections of the Giant's Hedge are still visible north of Lanreath, and the old folk-rhyme is still remembered:

> One day, the Devil, having nothing to do
> Built a great hedge from Lerryn to Looe.[27]

For the casual visitor, infinitely more spectacular than either the Giant's Hedge or the Bolster Bank is Tintagel Castle, situated dramatically on the north-east coast of Cornwall. For the casual visitor, Tintagel is a difficult site to interpret. To begin with, the visible remains are clearly medieval (most

A classic view of Tintagel, but what is the association with King Arthur?

dating from Earl Richard's constructions in the thirteenth century, although some reflect Reginald of Cornwall's activities in the twelfth). Tintagel, thus interpreted, is merely part of the great castle-building phase of the high Middle Ages. However, our visitor is left with nagging doubts. Why did they go to the trouble and expense of constructing a castle in such a difficult, remote and strategically irrelevant location? And what about the supposed link with King Arthur, and how does this fit with suggestions of a pre-medieval Celtic foundation at Tintagel?

Intriguingly, the answer to all three questions may be bound up with the status and role of Tintagel in post-Roman times. Ralegh Radford's conclusion that the Celtic foundation at Tintagel was monastic has been increasingly challenged by post-War scholarship. The evidence simply does not fit and is not corroborated by other sources detailing monastic and religious activity in Cornwall. Rather the suggestion now is that Tintagel in Dumnonian times was a cliff fortress, probably a major seat of royal power, perhaps even the *Durocornovium* of the Ravenna *Cosmogrophy*.[28] This, amongst other things, would help to explain the persistent importance of Tintagel in Cornish and wider European lore. In some versions of the Tristan and Iseult story, for example, it is Tintagel rather than Castle Dore that is the seat of King Mark. In Geoffrey of Monmouth's *History of the King's of Britain* Tintagel is the seat of Gorlois, Duke of Cornwall, and thus the place of Arthur's conception. This is mirrored in Malory's *Morte d'Arthur* ('It befell in the days of Uther Pendragon, when he was king of all England, and so reigned, that there was a mighty duke in Cornwall that held war against him long time. And the duke was called the Duke of Tintagel'),[29] and the Tintagel-Arthurian nexus has been repeated and embellished over time to the extent that in Tintagel today there is even a 'King Arthur's Car-park'!

But if we can look for a moment behind the facade of modern commercialism, nineteenth-century pre-Raphaelitism and high medieval European romance, we can see how the notion of Arthur—a great leader destined to drive the English from the Isles of Britain—could be linked in the Celtic (Cornish, Welsh, Breton) imagination with a far-famed seat of royal power at Tintagel. We can also begin to understand how the Anglo-Norman Earls of Cornwall, anxious to confirm their legitimacy in Cornwall, could have decided upon the politically important but strategically irrelevant site of Tintagel for the construction of their castle, the visible symbol of their power and authority. Such sources of legitimacy were important to the medieval mind. In 1278 Edward I visited the alleged grave of Arthur at Glastonbury in Somerset, arranging for the remains to be re-entombed forthwith in front of the high altar, and subsequently using his claim to Arthurian descent as an act of policy. He justified his attacks on Wales and his claim to Scottish overlordship on the basis of the rights of King Arthur to the whole island of Britain.[30] Later, Henry Tudor used his Welsh-Arthurian connections as a claim to the throne. Tintagel, then, must be interpreted in this light, a seat of royal power in post-Roman times and a potent symbol for those who chose to exercise political power in Cornwall, a fact echoed in the late fifteenth-century Cornish miracle play *Beunans Meriasek* in which the Duke of Cornwall explains that he has a '. . . castle sound /Which is named Tintagel,/ Where my chief dwelling is found'.[31]

As noted earlier, inscribed stones are also a clue to rulers and petty kingdoms in this post-Roman period. In addition to those stones discussed above, others of note include the Men Scryfa ('writing stone') on the moors of West Penwith, a fifth to seventh-century standing-stone inscribed RIALOBRANI CUNOVALI FILI—Rialobran son of Cunoval. When it is pointed out that Rialobran and Cunoval are Latinised Cornish names meaning, respectively, Royal Raven and (probably) Famous Chieftain, then we begin to appreciate that this is a memorial to a dynasty which must have exercised power and enjoyed considerable status in this part of Cornwall in the post-Roman era. Indeed, taken together, the many inscribed stones that typify Cornwall in this period are an important documentary source in their own right. Malcolm Todd notes the existence of over forty of these stones, overwhelmingly in Cornwall but with a few in Devon, one in Somerset, and a curious group of five marooned at Wareham in Dorset. Elizabeth Okasha,

Men Scryfa, the Writing Stone.

however, has counted and exhaustively documented seventy-nine such stones in Cornwall and Devon (again, overwhelmingly in the former) and notes that they are '. . . of considerable importance in view of the paucity of other evidence concerning the history of the area'.[32] Charles Thomas goes further. He notes that conventional written sources for the period are difficult to interpret and have been discussed almost to exhaustion. The inscribed stones, therefore, should be seen as prime documents in their own right and, in Professor Thomas' estimation, are the single most important written source for fifth to seventh-century western British history.

Charles Thomas has put this to the test in his impressive study, *And Shall These Mute Stones Speak? Post-Roman Inscriptions in Western Britain*.[33] The other major concentration of inscribed stones in Britain is in south-west Wales (Dyfed, or post-Roman Demetia), and Thomas undertakes a comparative examination of these two kingdoms, Dumnonia and Demetia. As Heather James has commented in her review of the Thomas book, 'Few can match his range'.[34] The major thrust of Charles Thomas' thesis is that the inscribed stones can be used collectively as an historical document to reconstruct Irish settlement in south-west Wales, the foundation of the kingdom of Demetia, the adoption of Christianity, the establishment of the small Irish kingdom of Brycheiniog, and (most importantly, from our perspective) the settlement of Demetian notables of Irish descent in Dumnonian Cornwall. It was this settlement, Thomas argues, that facilitated the wider dissemination of Christian beliefs. Far from being the 'Land of Saints' of popular fancy, Cornwall was largely pagan until the sixth century. The inscribed stones help chart the conversion of Cornwall to Christianity, and their very existence points-up the importance of written (and thus spoken) Latin to the spread of Christian teachings.

In terms of historical chronology, Charles Thomas shows that the earliest inscribed stones in Dumnonia and Demetia are those written in Ogham, the curious Irish stroke alphabet. Later inscriptions are bi-lingual, in Latin as well as Ogham, and later still are the familiar *hic iacit* ('here lies') inscriptions in Latin only. In Cornwall, interesting examples of bi-lingual inscriptions occur at St Kew and Lewannick. At the former a stone in the church is inscribed in Latin as IVSTI ('of Justus'), a name repeated in Ogham. At Lewannick there are two stones, one in the churchyard and the other inside the church. The latter commemorates one Ulcagnus, and the churchyard stone is in memory of Igenavus. Although obviously Latinised, the great majority of personal names that appear on the inscribed stones of Dumnonia are Celtic. Some can be specifically identified as being either Irish (Q-Celtic) or Cornish(P-Celtic). Several more are genuinely Latin names, although it must be said that the process of attributing linguistic provenance to early names is fraught with difficulties. In Cornwall, only two are certainly English (Alseld and Aelwyneys) and they both appear on the same stone at Lanteglos-by-Camelford where, unusually, the inscription is in English and reads approximately 'Alseld and Genered wrought this memorial for Aelwyneys' soul and for their own'. Given the context, Genered may also be an English name, while the stone itself is probably as late as the eleventh century.[35]

If the inscribed stones can give us an insight into the arrival and cultural impact of newcomers of Irish and later, English descent, they are of course silent on the other and at least as important social movement, the emigration to Armorica. At one level the scale and impact of this emigration is plain for all to see. Placenames across Brittany echo those of Cornwall, as do the multiplicity of Saints' dedications and the shared Cornish-Breton Saints' *Lives*; while the Cornish and Breton languages were indistinguishable until the eighth century and remained close into modern times. In the north and north-west of Brittany lay the province or kingdom of Dumnonia, while in the south was Cornouaille (in Breton, *Kerneo* or *Kernev*), indisputable evidence of the extensive influence of South West Britain in their creation. Even today, the French language does not distinguish between Cornouaille in Britain and Cornouaille in Brittany. Bretons continued to routinely visit and even settle in Cornwall until the Reformation (and even then contacts were not entirely broken), while Cornwall's St Michael's Mount has an almost uncanny counterpart (if not quite a mirror-image) in Mont St Michel on the marches of Brittany and Normandy. Such was the impact of this emigration that by the mid sixth century north-western Gaul was no longer Armorica but Britannia or Brittany—in Cornish *Breten Vyghan*—Little Britain. Although the principal focus of this emigration was Brittany, it should not be forgotten that there was a parallel emigration to what is now Galicia in northern Spain, so that, for example, there was by AD570 a Galician bishopric *ecclesia Britonesis* of which one Mailoc (a Celtic name) was bishop.

However, although there is much circumstantial evidence for this Armorican and Galician emigration, there is little in the way of historical documentation. Gildas infers that the emigration was flight in the face of the English advance in the later fifth century, after the legendary battle at Mount Badon. However, Dumnonia, from which the bulk of the emigration must have occurred, did not feel the intrusion of the English for several centuries yet. Similarly, suggestions of departure in response to Irish colonisation are not sufficiently convincing to account for what, from some areas, may have been a wholesale exodus. It may be that we should not look for a single explanation but a blend of factors that contributed to a general sense of unease in the post-Roman era, a fear of impending dislocation or even disintegration. However, the Byzantine historian Procopios, a contemporary of Gildas, relates that the emigration was conducted with the full co-operation of the Franks in Gaul, a strategy to settle and develop hitherto sparsely populated areas. This suggests an orderly and well-planned emigration, not unlike those to the 'New World' from Europe in modern times, in which would-be colonists were as much motivated by the prospect of better opportunities abroad as they were by a desire to escape shortcomings at home. And just as Cornish emigrants in Australia in the nineteenth century chose names such as Redruth and Truro for their new settlements, so their ancestral kinfolk in Armorica decided upon Dumnonia and Kerneo.

Contemporary British scholarship is sceptical of the insistence in legend, such as that of Conan Meriadoc, that the Armorican emigration was underway by the fourth century and, taking its cue from Gildas and Procopios, places its origins in the later fifth century. However, recent work in Brittany by Gwenael Le Duc and others has raised startling new suggestions, not least that the emigration was in progress as early as AD300.[36] This movement, it is argued, was indeed a planned colonisation to settle sparsely populated lands. But it was implemented long before the departure of the Legions and, therefore, enjoyed Roman sanction. From this perspective, British immigrants were already in full possession of the Armorican peninsula by AD500. If this is the case, then, curiously, the claims of Geoffrey of Monmouth, much discounted by modern scholarship, begin to have a glimmer of authenticity. Although we may still object that he has hi-jacked the historically-attested activities of one Magnus Maximus elsewhere in fourth-century Gaul to give content and colour to his account of the British colonisation of Armorica, his insistence that the emigration was a fourth-century phenomenon no longer seems unreasonable. According to Geoffrey, however, the colonisation was not the result of co-operative planning but of war. The soldiers of Magnus Maximus conquered Armorica and then brought out civilians to settle the new territories. Thus:

> Without more ado they drew up their lines of battle and marched on Rennes, taking it the same day. The savagery of the Britons was well known, as was the number of men they had killed. The townsfolk sped at full speed . . . . In this way he created a second Britain, which he gave to Conanus Meriadiadocus . . . [who] decided to find wives for his troops, so that heirs might be born from them who should hold the land for ever. To prevent any mixture of blood with the Gauls he ordered women to come from the island of Britain and to be married to his men. With this end in view, he sent messages to Britain, to Dionotus, Duke of Cornwall, who had succeded his brother Caradocus in the kingship of Britain, telling him to take personal charge of the business.[37]

Le Duc's suggestion that the Armorican emigration was, after all, an early phenomenon is attractive; but more difficult is his assertion that these settlers were Christians 'with a difference'.[38] As we have seen already, it is now thought that Christianity came relatively late to Cornwall, with Cornwall remaining largely pagan until the sixth century. As Charles Thomas remarks, '"Early Christian Cornwall" and "The Land of Saints" are resounding names but, until the second half of the sixth century, devoid of true meaning'.[39] This is a message that has been slow to sink in in Cornwall, our view of early Christianity in Cornwall coloured not only by the impressive hagiography of the high middle ages but, in our own time, the efforts of Celtic Revivalists whose imperatives are reflected, in Cornwall, in the scholarship of Canon Doble and more widely in the *Saints, Seaways and Settlements* of E.G. Bowen or the more popular *Celtic Inheritance* by Peter Berresford Ellis.[40] Although the Armorican debate must remain unresolved, it is time to look more closely at Cornwall and the coming of Christianity.

Early contacts with Gaul—and perhaps also Ireland—may be responsible for the first introductions of Christianity into Cornwall, and an apparently fifth century memorial to one CUNAIDE, discovered at Carnsew near Hayle, is possibly our first evidence. As in earlier times, and like the Camel further along the north coast, the Hayle estuary was an important point of contact and communication with the outside, for trade but also for cultural exchange. Other early indications of Christian influence are the chi-rho monograms inscribed on slabs. There is one at Phillack church, again near Hayle, and others are at St Erth, South Hill, and St Endellion. However, as Charles Thomas has suggested, it is not until well into the sixth century that Christianity begins to make important inroads in Cornwall, facilitated by contacts with Demetia in south-west Wales. It may be, as Ian Soulsby notes, that many of the Welsh church dedications in Cornwall—St Breock, St Teath, St Mabyn, St Endellion, St Issey, and so on—represent the important influence from Wales, rather than the founding activities of those saints themselves.[41] However, in the seventh-century *Vita Sancti Samsonis* the Life of St Samson of Dol in Brittany we have an intriguing insight into the activities of one Welsh (Demetian) monastic missionary who was active in Cornwall in the early days of Cornish Christianity.

Samson arrived from Wales via the Camel estuary, perhaps somewhere near the old Roman landfall at St Enodoc, on his way to Brittany. The ancient Fowey-Camel route, already long-established by Samson's day, has been popularised in recent times as 'The Saints Way', and Samson does indeed travel the route as he makes his way down to Fowey for his departure to Brittany. However, it is no fleeting visit, and he stays in Cornwall long enough to provide us with important glimpses of missionary activity. For example, we learn of the existence of a monastery at a place called Docco (ancient Landochou, in St Kew) and we discover, too, that before leaving for Brittany Samson founds a second monastery. Traditionally, this has been identified as either Golant or (less likely) South Hill, both dedicated to St Sampson (or Samson), but Charles Thomas rejects both in favour of Fowey itself. Immediately behind the church at Fowey is Place, the seat of the Treffry family, and Thomas notes that in 1841 JosephThomasTreffry discovered 'a great number of bodies' on his grounds—for Thomas, this is evidence of Samson's monastery, the ancient Langorthou.[42]

Samson's *Vita* also demonstrates the extent of pagan belief in Cornwall. He confronts idol worshippers whom he encounters on his travels but is only able to persuade them of the error of their ways, and to convert them to Christianity, by performing a miracle healing. He also wins trust and support by ridding the locals of a dreadful serpent that was inhabiting a cave near Fowey (the cave is still there). This intimation of contact and conflict between Christians and the pagan population indicates that conversion was a slow process, and it may be remembered in the folk tales of the legendary 'King Teudar', the pagan tyrant who expended much energy in the eradication of Christian missionaries from his territories in West Cornwall.[43]

Place, at Fowey, the site of JosephThomas Treffry's remarkable discovery in 1841.

St Piran's Cross, in Perranzabuloe, a reminder of Cornwall's Patron Saint.

The reference to monasteries in Samson's *Vita* is evidence that such establishments existed in sixth-century Cornwall, as they did in Wales and Ireland, but generally they were almost certainly small, introverted, ascetic communities, with only the larger foundations having a cultural or educational role in the wider community. Missionary work, then, would have been limited, perhaps further retarding the spread of Christianity. Monastic sites are identifiable by the *Lan* prefix (comparable to the Welsh *Llan*) in placenames. This prefix is found all across Cornwall (with a few examples in Devon) and, although *lan* means an enclosure and has occasional secular use, it normally signifies a holy enclosure. Many are recognisable today, as in Lanlivery, Lanivet and Landewednack (although some apparent examples, such as Lanteglos or Lanseaton, may be the result of a confused later substitution of *Lan* for *Nan*, a valley), while others have lost the prefix with the passage of time. Charles Henderson, for example, noted that Constantine was Langostenton until the late sixteenth century.[44] These holy enclosures are also associated with the raised churchyards characteristic of many Cornish sites, notably at Lewannick, South Petherwin, Sancreed and St Buryan.

By the ninth century the pre-eminent monastery in Cornwall was clearly St Germans. A tenth-century text refers to Lannaled, the 'famed and universally known place, where the relics of Bishop Germanus are preserved',[45] and this helps to explain why St Germans (Lannaled) was chosen as the seat of the Cornish See constructed by Aethelred in the tenth century. By the tenth century, however, the monastery of St Petroc at Bodmin was also prominent, the focus of St Petroc's cult having moved there from its earlier locations at Padstow and nearby Little Petherick. The *Domesday Book* lists several Cornish religious houses, all but one dedicated to Celtic saints, and they are St Germans, St Petroc, St Piran, St Carantoc, St Achebran (Keverne), St Buryan and St Neot. Others we can add include St Michael's Mount, St Goran, Constantine, Lammana (Looe Island), and St Anthony-in-Roseland. Celtic crosses, popularly supposed to date from as early as the sixth century, are properly the product of the middle ages. Early examples include St Piran's Cross in the dunes at Perranzabuloe, dated to before AD960, and a splendid tenth-century example in Sancreed churchyard which has the maker's name RUNHO carved at the bottom of the shaft. Christianity was by this time well-entrenched in Cornwall, with the pagan worship of natural springs now long-since transformed into the veneration of holy wells (such as those at St Clether or Dupath), with the more prominent secular houses acquiring their own chapels, and with even minor groups of settlements (such as at Mawgan Porth, or Merther Uny in Wendron) having their own burial grounds.

Sancreed Cross, a splendid example of Cornwall's many Celtic crosses.

Today much energy is expended in debating the relative merits of St Piran, St Petroc and St Michael as Patron Saints of Cornwall (each has a good case, it seems, and this author—for no good reason other than personal prejudice—prefers St Piran). This is not only part of a contemporary concern to acquire or confirm the symbols and attributes consistent with 'national status', itself a consequence of the Cornish-Celtic Revival which focused renewed attention on Cornish hagiography, but reflects an earlier Age of Hagiography which in medieval Europe spawned a multiplicity of Saints' Lives. Many Cornish churches still sport their Celtic dedications, and Catherine Rachel John's comprehensive and highly-readable *The Saints of Cornwall* makes these lives easily accessible to the modern reader.[46]

We learn, for example, that Cury (a parish on the Lizard) is a form of the name Corentin, and that St Corentin (whose feast day is 12 December) was the first bishop of Quimper, the chief town of Cornouaille in Brittany. St Ia

Like Wales, Brittany and Ireland, Cornwall is rich in holy well sites. Here, the venerable well-housing is tucked behind the Chapel at St Clether.

is patron of St Ives (Porth Ia, in Cornish) and, it is said, came to Cornwall from Ireland, probably with a group led by St Gwinear. And just as St Piran is supposed to have drifted from Ireland to Cornwall on a mill-stone, so St Ia came across on a giant leaf. St Mewan, whose parish in Cornwall adjoins St Austell, is also commemorated at St Meen in eastern Brittany, while St Mawes (near Falmouth) is remembered in Brittany at Ile Maudez and Lanmodez. St Uny (or Euny), a brother of St Ia and St Erth, is another of St Gwinear's Irish missionaries, and is recalled at Uny Lelant and Merther Uny as well as being patron of Redruth. Brigid of Kildare has no surviving dedications in Cornwall (Morvah is apparently dedicated to St Bridget of Sweden) but is remembered across the Devon border at Bridestowe. St Winwaloe is patron of Gunwalloe and Landewednack on the Lizard peninsula, Tremaine (and formerly Poundstock) in North Cornwall, and St Winnolls in south east Cornwall. In his Breton guise he is St Gwenole, founder of the great monastery of Landevennec in Cornouaille.

It is these Lives, told and retold across the centuries, and rediscovered and re-invented both in earlier times and today, that gives Cornwall its reputation as the 'Land of Saints'. 'There are more Saints in Cornwall than there are in Heaven', so runs the old saying, and the late Rev Canon Miles Brown's *Hymn to the Cornish Saints* says it all:

All these Cornish shores are holy,
Here the Saints in prayer did dwell,
Raising font and altar lowly
Preaching far with staff and bell -
Piran, Petroc, Paul Aurelian,
Euny, Samson, Winwaloe.

If all this has the air of a Celtic 'Golden Age', with Cornwall—in the midst and mist of the Celtic Sea—the centre of a Celtic Church and wider Celtic World, then this is to forget that just as Christianity was consolidating its grip in Cornwall in this apparently very 'Cornish' fashion, so the English intruders were at last making themselves felt in Cornish life. It is tempting to portray the expansion of Anglo-Saxon England into South West Britain as a remorseless, relentless westerly thrust, a deadly power struggle between the two rival states of Dumnonia and Wessex. However, as has been argued already, we should see power structures in those times as loose, sometimes even incoherent, and the English penetration of the South West peninsula must be considered a piecemeal process taking centuries of consolidation. At times there would have been fierce tussles over land ownership, and occasionally British resistance (such as that in Dorset cAD600) would have stopped the English in their tracks. At other times, as in parts of Dorset and North Devon, the native British population may simply have been left untouched, and in still other areas the Armorican emigrations may have left large tracts deserted (accounting, perhaps, for the almost total absence of Celtic placenames in modern Devon) into which the newcomers could move with ease.

However, it would be foolish to deny that there was a geo-political aspect to all this. The fateful battle of Durham (Deorham) Down near Bristol in AD577 drove an English wedge between the British populations of Wales and the South West, a strategic disaster which the British themselves recognised. According to the *Anglo-Saxon Chronicle*, the defeated leader who was slain at Durham was Condidan. Condidan has been identified with Cyndylan, son of Cyndrowen, king of Powys, who is celebrated in the *Death Song of Cyndylan*, attributed to Llywarch Hen. As Professor Markale observes, in this poem Cyndylan's death '. . . has all the proportions of a national disaster, and the poem it inspired is one of the most powerful and evocative in all Welsh literature':[47]

The hall of Cyndylan is dark tonight
without fire, without light,
and what a silence surrounds it!
The hall of Cyndylan is dark-panelled,
it shelters no laughing company now.

Similarly, British tales of Arthur, the great war-leader, both report and yearn for strategic action against the expanding English, and although Arthur is killed, there is the belief that one day he will return to drive out the intruders. Such sentiment, a desire for concerted, co-operative strategic action, is also expressed in the remarkable *Armes Prydein* (the Prophecy of Britain), written cAD930, probably at St David's, which foretells that the

Welsh together with their Celtic cousins in Cornwall, Brittany, Ireland, and the Old North (Cumbria and southern Scotland), together with the Norsemen of Dublin, will expel the English from Britain and reclaim the whole kingdom '. . . from Manaw Gododdin to Brittany, from Dyfed to Thanet'.[48] However, it was not to be.

In geo-political terms, it is also possible to see that, as Dumnonia begins to collapse, so the English start to press home their advantage. In AD682 it was reported that Centwine had driven the British as far as the sea (probably north-east Cornwall), and placename evidence suggests that the English may have already crossed into and settled that part of North Cornwall lying above the River Ottery. The Ottery seems to have acquired significance as an ethnic and linguistic border, and if Warbstow Bury was re-occupied at this time it would have provided a powerful buffer fortress. As an even cursory glance at an Ordnance Survey map will show, to the south of the Ottery the names are overwhelmingly Celtic and typical of Cornwall—Trevillion, Tremaine, Hendra, and so on—while to the north they are English or hybrid Celtic-English and reminiscent of those found in adjoining North Devon: Canworthy, Pattacott, Billacott. In AD710 Gerient was defeated by Ine, King of Wessex, leading to limited English settlement between the Tamar and Lynher rivers (attested by the admixture of Cornish and English placenames in that area) but in AD722 a combined Cornish and Danish force defeated the English at 'Hehil', probably the strategically important Camel estuary. In AD753 Cuthred launched a new campaign against what we may now call Cornwall (rather than the remnant of Dumnonia), and in AD815 Egbert is said to have harried Cornwall from east to west. In AD838 a combined force of Cornish and Vikings was defeated at the great battle of Hingston Down, near Callington. Soon after, the Cornish bishop Kenestec was compelled to acknowledge the superiority of Canterbury.

The final subjugation of Cornwall, however, was left to Athelstan who in AD936 set the River Tamar as the border between Cornwall and England, rather as he had set the Wye as the boundary between England and Wales. The remaining Cornish were evicted from Exeter and perhaps the rest of Devon (William of Malmesbury comments unpleasantly that Exeter was 'cleansed of its defilement by wiping out that filthy race').[49] In effect, Athelstan had created the modern geo-political entity of Cornwall. He had guaranteed its territorial and ethnic integrity (attacks from east of the Tamar would now be a thing of the past) but the price was satellite status as an appendage of the emergent English state. There was a certain ambiguity in this status, as indeed there is today, being neither separate nor incorporated. However, Athelstan's settlement represented a considerable accommodation of the Cornish. In AD944 his successor, Edmund, styled himself 'King of the English and ruler of this province of the Britons',[50] an indication of how that accommodation was understood at the time. In ecclesiastical terms, the so-called *Bodmin Gospels* (liturgical texts containing the Gospels appointed to be read at Mass throughout the year) indicate that by cAD900 the rite followed in Cornwall was Roman rather than Celtic but Athelstan was careful to ensure that the Cornish Bishop, Conan, was made an auxiliary bishop under the Bishop of Crediton. In AD994, in a further act of accommodation, Aethelred created an independent Cornish diocese, with the historically significant St Germans as its seat. However, this independence was lost in 1046 when Cornwall was re-incorporated into Crediton, perhaps a reaction to the uneasiness after Edward's coronation in 1043 or a symptom of the consolidating power of Godwine Earl of Wessex.

The twin towers of St Germans Church show the historical importance of this site.

Whatever the case, Cornwall on the eve of the Norman Conquest had been transformed from the western heartland of the long-disintegrating Dumnonia to a recognisable geo-political entity accommodated within the consolidating English state. Territorially and ethnically secure, it was this accommodation that allowed Cornwall to survive as a recognisably distinct region into the middle ages and which led, for example, to the development of an extensive literature in the Cornish language and to the further constitutional accommodation inherent in the Duchy of Cornwall and the Stannary system.

Notes & References (Chapter 4).

1. Charles Thomas, *And Shall These Mute Stones Speak? Post-Roman Inscriptions in Western Britain*, University of Wales Press, Cardiff, 1994, p.xvii.

2. Malcolm Todd, *The South West to AD 1000*, Longman, London, 1987, p.189 and p.200. For good accounts of general archaeological evidences of the period under discussion see Henrietta Quinnell, 'Cornwall During the Iron Age and Roman Period', and Ann Preston-Jones and Peter Rose, 'Medieval Cornwall', both in *Cornish Archaeology*, No.25, 1986; see also Nicholas Johnson and Peter Rose, *Cornwall's Archaeological Heritage*, Twelveheads Press, Truro, 1990.

3. Ian Soulsby, *A History of Cornwall*, Phillimore, Chichester, 1986, p.20.

4. Charles Thomas, *The Importance of Being Cornish in Cornwall*, Institute of Cornish Studies, Redruth, 1973, p.4.

5. Thomas, 1973, p.5.

6. Thomas, 1973, p.5.

7. Todd, 1987, p.203.

8. John Morris, *The Age of Arthur: A History of the British Isles from 350-360*, Weidenfeld and Nicolson, London, 1973.

9. Todd, 1987, p.216; Quinnell, 1986.

10. Todd, 1987, p.222 (citing the opinion of Charles Thomas).

11. Johnson and Rose, 1990, p.10.

12. For a general overview of the history of post-Roman Dumnonia, see Susan M. Pearce, *The Kingdom of Dumnonia: Studies in History and Tradition in South West Britain*, Lodenek Press, Padstow, 1978.

13. David Dumville, 'General Editor's Foreword', in Lynette Olson, *Early Monasteries in Cornwall: Studies in Celtic History XI*, Boydell Press, Woodbridge, 1989, pp.ix-x.

14. Peter Berresford Ellis, *Celt and Saxon: The Struggle for Britain AD410-937*, Constable, London, 1993, p.69.

15. Todd, 1987, pp.236-237.

16. Good overviews of the literary development of the Tristan and Iseult legend are provided in Michael Stapleton (ed.), *The Cambridge Guide to English Literature*, Cambridge University Press, Cambridge, 1983, pp.891-892, and Margaret Drabble (ed.), *The Oxford Companion to English Literature*, Oxford University Press, Oxford, 1985, pp.998-999.

17. C.A. Ralegh Radford, 'Romance and reality in Cornwall', in Geoffrey Ashe (ed.), *The Quest for Arthur's Britain*, Paladin, St Albans, 1971, pp.70-77.

18. cited in Charles Thomas, *Celtic Britain*, Thames and Hudson, London, 1986, p.70.

19. Donald R. Rawe, *Traditional Cornish Stories and Rhymes*, Lodenek Press, Padstow, 1971, pp.9-10.

20. A.L. Rowse, *Matthew Arnold: Poet and Prophet*, Thames and Hudson, London, 1976, p.200.

21. Todd, 1987, p.237.

22. Thomas, 1986, p.67.

23. Todd, 1987, p.237.

24. Michael Wood, *In Search of the Dark Ages*, BBC, London, 1981, p.135.

25. Thomas, 1986, p.68.

26. Craig Weatherhill, *Cornovia: Ancient Sites of Cornwall and Scilly*, Alison Hodge, Penzance, 1985, p.42.

27. Weatherhill, 1985, p.32.

28. Thomas, 1986, p.75.

29. Michael Senior (ed.), *Sir Thomas Malory's Tales of King Arthur*, Guild Publishing, London, 1980, p.29.

30. C.A. Ralegh Radford, 'Glastonbury Abbey', in Ash (ed.), 1971, pp.109-110.

31. Myrna Combellack, *The Camborne Play: A Verse Translation of Beunans Meriasek*, Dyllansow Truran, Redruth, 1988, pp.96-98.

32. Elisabeth Okasha, *Corpus of Early Christian Inscribed Stones of South West Britain*, Leicester University Press, Leicester, 1993, Preface.

33. Thomas, 1994.

34. Heather James, Review of Thomas, 1994, in *The Welsh History Review*, Vol.17, No.4, December 1995.

35. Okasha, 1993, p.47 and pp.141-145.

36. Gwenael Le Duc, 'The Colonization of Brittany from Britain: New Approaches and Questions', unpub. paper delivered at the 10th International Congress of Celtic Studies, University of Edinburgh, July 1995.

37. Geoffrey of Monmouth, *The History of the Kings of Britain*, ed. & trans, Lewis Thorpe, Guild Publishing, London, 1982, pp.140-141.

38. Le Duc, 1995.

39. Thomas, 1994, p.324.

40. G.H. Doble, *The Saints of Cornwall*, Parts 1-5, Dean and Chapter of Truro, Truro, 1960-70; E.G. Bowen, *Saints, Seaways and Settlements in the Celtic Lands*, University of Wales Press, Cardiff, 1977; Peter Berresford Ellis, *Celtic Inheritance*, Muller, London, 1985.

41. Soulsby, 1986, p.30.

42. Thomas, 1994, p.232.

43. W.H. Pascoe, *Teudar: A King of Cornwall*, Dyllansow Truran, Redruth, 1985.

44. Charles Henderson, *A History of the Parish of Constantine in Cornwall*, Royal Institution of Cornwall, Truro, 1937, p43.

45. Todd, 1987, p.247.

46. Catherine Rachel John, *The Saints of Cornwall*, Lodenek Press/ Dyllansow Truran, Padstow/Redruth, 1981.

47. J. Markale, *Celtic Civilization*, Gordon and Cremonesi, London, 1978, p.183.

48. Janet Davies, *The Welsh Language*, University of Wales Press, Cardiff, 1993, p.14.

49. W. Stubbs (ed. & trans.), William of Malmesbury's *Gesta Regum*, Royal Society, London, 1887, p.89.

50. Todd, 1987, p.289.

CHAPTER 5

Anglia et Cornubia

CORNWALL

Anglia et Cornubia

'People are back on the historian's agenda'.[1] This was Professor R.R Davies' message when he delivered his Presidential address to the Royal Historical Society in November 1993. In the 1980s Steven Ellis had criticised '. . . the inadequacy of Anglo-centric presentations of British history . . .',[2] a view echoed in Professor Hugh Kearney's insistence '. . . that it is only by adopting a "Britannic" approach that historians can make sense of the particular segment in which they may be primarily interested, whether it be "England", "Ireland", "Scotland", "Wales", Cornwall or the Isle of Man'.[3] But in 1993 Professor Davies went further. He suggested that not only should our new-found concern to give balanced attention to all the constituent peoples of these islands be seen as part of a wider appreciation of the significance of ethnicity in human behaviour, but also there was a:

> . . . growing recognition that the centrality that academic historians have so long given to the unitary nation state as the natural, inevitable and indeed desirable unit of human power and political organisation is itself a reflection of the intellectual climate in which modern academic historiography was forged in the nineteenth century.[4]

Put simply, Professor Davies' point was that until recently we have seen the creation of the modern nation-state (the United Kingdom, France, Italy, and so on) as the inevitable and desirable outcome of the historical process, and our reading and writing of history itself has, therefore, been conducted in that light. Of late, however, dramatic events on the world stage (for example, the collapse of the Soviet empire) have combined with a general air of uncertainty in the conduct of human affairs to remind us very forcibly that '. . . our historical gaze could be shifted from the state and its institutions . . .' towards '. . . other solidarities and collectivities . . .', some of which '. . . seemed to have as great, if not occasionally greater depth and historical resilience than did the nation state'.[5] Cornwall, we might suggest, is one of these solidarities, an entity which in at least some of its imagined constructions pre-dates not only the emergence of the English state but also the arrival of the English themselves. But here there is a paradox, for, as Professor Davies reminds us, despite the deep-seated Celtic tendency to regard the English as the Johnny-come-lately interlopers in these islands, the English nation-state was in fact one of the first to emerge. Thus:

> Nowhere arguably are these issues of more historical and contemporary significance than in the British Isles. Nowhere in medieval Europe was the potential of a nation state realised at an earlier date than in England, where the *gens Anglorum* and *regnum Anglie* came early to be regarded as co-terminus; nowhere were the institutions of an effective state power developed so precociously.[6]

One effect of this early emergence of the institutions of the English state was to marginalise the histories of the other peoples of the British Isles, either by ignoring them altogether or by co-opting them as subsidiarities of the central English theme. The task of the contemporary historian, therefore, is to un-package this, partly (as Kearney has done) by emphasising the essentially Britannic character of our collective experience but also (as Davies advocates) by concentrating on the separate identities of the constituent peoples. As both R.R. Davies and Professor Anthony D. Smith agree, while Nationalism as the ideology that underpins the modern nation-state may be a recent construct, ethnic identities and communities (which Smith calls *ethnie*) pre-date the modern world.[7] The early emergence of the English nation-state, therefore, should not blind us to the existence of other *ethnie* in the British Isles (or indeed to differences and divisions within England itself),[8] and amongst those *ethnie* that emerged as proto-nations in the medieval period were the Cornish.

The relationship between England and Cornwall, *Anglia et Cornubia* as medieval documents sometimes had it,[9] was complex and has yet to be teased-out fully. But everywhere there are hints and clues, and the new perspectives drawn recently by Alan Kent intimate a unique relationship that was close but where Cornish distinctiveness was important, and where, paradoxically, behind the power-nexus of superior and subservient, coloniser and colonised, was an English respect of (and indeed), reliance upon Cornish attributes.[10] Of course, this echoes the institution of the Duchy of Cornwall, founded in this period for the maintenance of the Heir Apparent to the English throne, an institution which bound Cornwall tightly into the needs and imperatives of the English state and yet at precisely the same moment was a powerful mechanism of constitutional accommodation which allowed Cornwall a considerable degree of political autonomy. Cornwall was bound closely to the English state but in an important sense was not an integral part of it.

For the observant traveller today there are still echoes of this union without integration. In gift and book shops at castles, museums and cathedrals across England may be obtained those facsimile (sic) copies of *Magna Carta*, headed at the top, left and right, by the separate Arms of England and Cornwall. More profoundly, on State occasions when the Royal Standard flies above Buckingham Palace, incorporating as it does the heraldic devices of the Union, adjacently across the road at Buckingham Gate (the offices of the Duchy of Cornwall), flies the Duchy flag of fifteen gold bezants on a black background. For the student of constitutional niceties, it may also be observed that today in contrast to every English and Welsh county the High Sheriff of Cornwall is appointed by the Duke of Cornwall and not the Crown.

To trace the origin of this special relationship we should go back to the tenth-century Athelstan settlement, discussed in Chapter Four, in which both the territorial limits and constitutional existence of Cornwall were defined by Athelstan's emerging English state. But at a more symbolic (and ideological) level the Arthurian legend is equally important, for it served both as a mechanism by which the Cornish 'remembered who they were' and as a device by which the expanding medieval English state attempted its 'British project' (of which more shortly). Historically, there may or may not have been an Arthur (a war-leader, rather than a 'King'), and he may or may not have had a particular association with Cornwall and South West Britain. Of course, much of what we might call Celtic Britain has its Arthurian associations—Lowland Scotland and Cumbria as much as Wales and Cornwall, or even Somerset and Brittany— with various writers claiming periodically to have discovered the true story,[11] but the many attempts at historical reconstruction are for our purposes irrelevant or at least unimportant. The contested facts of Arthur's existence and where he lived and ruled and fought, are far less significant than the actual fact that the Cornish claimed him as theirs'. As Ralegh Radford put it, 'Arthur, the past and future king: this was the belief of the Bretons and Cornish, attested as early as the beginning of the twelfth century and certainly far older than that'.[12]

When the Canons of Laon visited Cornwall in 1113, they were assured that Arthur was not dead but would come again. They were shown several sites of supposed Arthurian connection but were involved in a disturbance at Bodmin Priory when it was suggested at great offence to the Cornish that in fact Arthur might not be alive.[13] The enduring strength of this Arthurian belief in Cornwall is indicated in a fifteenth-century vernacular poem in the *Red Book of Bath*:

> But for he skaped that batell y-wys
> Breton and Cornysh sayeth thus
> That he lyveth yet, pardi,
> And schall come and be a kyng aye.[14]

Later still, in his *Survey of Cornwall* of 1602, Richard Carew also alluded to the longevity and popularity of the Arthurian tradition. Upon the River Camel, near Camelford he said, was 'the last dismal battle' between 'the noble King Arthur' and his 'treacherous nephew Mordred'. Significantly, he

How many people have wondered whether Excalibur lies in its depths? Dozmary Pool, on Bodmin Moor, offers no answers.

added that 'For testimony whereof, the old folk thereabouts will show you a stone bearing Arthur's name, though now depraved to *Atry* . . .'.[15] Carew was referring to the spot known to this day as Slaughter Bridge, a name as evocative as any can be of some dimly-remembered conflict of long ago, and—as Carew attests—it was claimed as the site of Arthur's last struggle, the Battle of Camlann, long before it was co-opted by modern Arthurian romance. There is indeed an inscribed stone at Slaughter Bridge, still known as Arthur's Grave, although it is actually a fifth or sixth-century bi-lingual Ogham/Latin memorial to one LATINUS.

Camelford the placename is also, of course, redolent of Camelot, the legendary court and castle of King Arthur, and has the geographical advantage of being near Tintagel. Other Arthurian associations of apparent long-standing include Bossiney Mound (again near Tintagel), a presumably Bronze Age monument which is nonetheless supposed to conceal Arthur's Round Table, and Castle-an-Dinas in mid-Cornwall (with its royal connotations) which is said to have served as Arthur's hunting lodge.[16] King Arthur's Hall, a mysterious rectangular earthwork deep on Bodmin Moor, near St Breward, is of unknown provenance. Dozmary Pool, also in the heart of Bodmin Moor, is one of the sites associated with the Passing of Arthur and the Lady of the Lake, where, as Arthur lay mortally wounded, Sir Bedivere was persuaded finally to throw the mighty sword Excalibur into the expanse of water. Although Tennyson preferred the alternative site at Loe Pool, near Helston, his evocation of Arthur's passing sits well in the desolate brooding remoteness of Dozmary:

> So flash'd and fell the brand Excalibur:
> But ere he dipt the surface, rose an arm
> Clothed in white samite, mystic, wonderful,
> And caught him by the hilt, and brandish'd him
> Three times, and drew him under in the mere.[17]

Thanks to Tennyson and others, the legend of Arthur has also become entangled with that of Lyonnesse (as we saw in Chapter Two), to the extent that the Scillies have even been suggested as Avalon, Arthur's final resting place. There is also a link with Tristan and Iseult. The most famous association, however, as discussed in Chapter Four, is with Tintagel, the medieval castle built on an earlier site of royal significance in an apparent attempt to secure the legitimacy of Anglo-Norman rule in Cornwall. This is, perhaps, an early and peculiarly Cornish fragment of England's 'British project', the strategy by which the English state sought to establish the legitimacy of its expansion into 'Celtic Britain'.

The link between Arthur and Tintagel was first suggested by Geoffrey of Monmouth in his *History of the Kings of Britain*, a brilliant piece of propaganda which would not only serve generations of English kings in justifying their adventures in Wales, Scotland and Ireland, but which in its Cornish context fused the political significance of Tintagel the place with the powerful folk-belief that Arthur was not dead but would come again. In a sense, Geoffrey was shameless in his manipulation of Cornish sentiment. At the same time as securing the political legitimacy of Tintagel, he could pen those inflammatory lines in the *Prophecies of Merlin* which foresaw that 'The race that is oppressed shall prevail in the end, for it will resist the savagery of the invaders. The Boar of Cornwall [Arthur] shall bring relief from these invaders, for it will trample their necks beneath its feet'.[18] In other words, as

Geoffrey and his Anglo-Norman clients saw it, the triumph of the English state, the success of its British project, would also represent the triumph of Arthur. Paradoxically, although the English were the invaders, the success of England's British project would in a very real sense be the restoration of Britain. As Professor Christopher Brooke has observed, Geoffrey:

> . . . succeeded in flattering the Celts . . . and flattering the Normans by revealing Arthur in all essentials an Anglo-Norman king. In the midst of the book are some very strange prophecies, put into the mouth of the magician Merlin. It is not clear whether these forecast a wonderful Celtic revival, or the building up of a great British empire by Norman kings to come. The ambiguity is clearly deliberate . . . There is no doubt that the English kings, in the long run, were the gainers.[19]

Geoffrey Ashe has provided a sensitive and perceptive assessment of this process. When the Cornish, Welsh and Breton bards invented and elaborated their legendary Arthur, between the sixth and twelfth centuries, '. . . they were expressing what Gandhi was to express long afterwards, however differently: the un-subdued spirit of a race conquered by the English'. However, in the wake of Geoffrey of Monmouth's co-option of Arthur, 'The Plantaganet kings of England annexed him and claimed Arthurian succession'. Later still, the chaos of the Wars of the Roses prompted '. . . Malory's resurrection of the Arthurian Kingdom, as the model for a degenerate England', while 'The Tudors found vitality enough in the Return [of Arthur] to exploit it as propaganda . . . [20].

The Tudors, indeed, with their alleged Welshness, their Celticity, their Arthurianism, their centralist control of England, their grip on Wales and Cornwall, their designs on Scotland and Ireland, their adventures abroad, represented the apogee of the British project. With the death of Elizabeth, their mantle was assumed by James I and VI who decreed that 'the divided name of England and Scotland' be discontinued in favour of 'Great Britain'.[21] Despite the interregnum and the brief dictatorship of Cromwell, 'God's Englishman', when the 'British project' was cast aside in favour of a decidedly English military evangelism, the Act of Union in 1707 ushered in a new Britishness (described recently by Linda Colley) nurtured through war, religion, trade and imperial expansion.[22] This was the 'British project' celebrated by James Thomson (1700-1748):

> When Britain first, at Heaven's command,
> Arose from out the azure main,
> This was the charter of the land,
> And guardian angels sung this strain.
> 'Rule Britannia, rule the waves;
> Britons never will be slaves'.[23]

The place of Cornwall in this British project is important. It is rooted, as we have seen, in the earliest days of Arthur and Tintagel. But, as we shall see in later chapters, it displays its significance in the Elizabethan era—the Cornish sea-dogs and the confrontation with Spain—in the Civil War, where popular sentiment as 'true Brittaines' was for the King, in the days of Admiral Boscawen and his 'little Cornish navy', and later in the era of Victorian High Imperialism where the Cornish as 'Ancient Britons' assumed their rightful place (sic) as proto-Anglo-Saxons and progenitors of Britain's greatness.

But to return to the medieval focus of this chapter, the co-option of the Arthurian tradition by the British project was matched (like the Europeanisation of Tristan and Iseult) by its adoption by Continental romancers who wove tales of Arthur as medieval sovereign. Here stories of kingship and chivalry, of courtly love and the Holy Grail, produced a further 'Vision of Albion', a Continental view of these islands in which Cornwall's distinctive place in the 'Matter of Britain' was made plain. It is no coincidence that most European languages have their own word for Cornwall (but never for Hampshire or Rutland), as though it were a Scotland or a Wales, so that Cornwall's status is not merely of British but rather wider European significance. Colin Wilson was right when he observed that this was 'Arthur's real conquest—the conquest of the European imagination'.[24]

And behind the fantasy and illusion of the Arthurian tradition, politically significant as it may have been, was (as we have noted already) the reality of the institution of the Duchy of Cornwall. It was the Duchy which formalised the relationship between *Anglia et Cornubia*, both effecting and accommodating Cornwall's constitutional position within the state. The Duchy grew out of the earlier Earldom of Cornwall, which was itself a singular institution and appears to have been created as an accommodating successor to the earlier line of Cornish chieftain kings. At the time of the Norman Conquest what we might term the pre-Norman Earldom was held by one Cadoc (or Condor), a native Cornishman, but he was soon replaced, albeit briefly, by Count Brian of Brittany. Brian, however, took part in a failed baronial *coup* against King William in 1075, and was in turn replaced by Robert, Count of Mortain.

The Domesday Book records the extent of Robert of Mortain's influence in Cornwall, with 277 of the 350 Cornish manors being held directly in his hands. Tellingly, only 67 (poorer) Cornish manors were held by Anglo-Saxons, while a number was in the hands of a sprinkling of Bretons and Flemings. Just as the Normans had established themselves as the new elite in England, so in Cornwall the English, the recent conquerors, were themselves dislodged. Cleverly, the Normans were able to dissociate themselves from those recent conquerors, and in so doing secure the legitimacy of their own conquest. Professor Markale discerns a link between the Norman conquest, the Breton presence, the renewed accommodation of Cornwall, and Arthur:

> In fact, it is agreed that about one third of William's army at Hastings was made up of Breton nobility and foot soldiers. Many of them received land in Devon and Cornwall, just retribution it seemed for Saxon oppression . . . and a means not only of recovering their estates but of tightening the links between Britain and the continent. It was during this time, when the Bretons dreamt of rebuilding the old Britain, that the Arthurian myth came into being, and came to be seen as a kind of religious history for a people who had never accepted their own defeat.[25]

In securing Cornwall, Robert of Mortain dispossessed the religious houses of St Kew and St Neot and was responsible for the construction of castles at Launceston (then the Cornish capital) and Trematon, strongholds which secured the two important *entrees* (one overland, the other maritime) into Cornwall from England. Launceston—Castle Terrible as it was known when

The ruins of Robert of Mortain's eleventh-century castle look over the town of Launceston (pronounced 'Lanson').

used later as a gaol—towered over the Tamar and guarded the strategic crossing point at Polson Bridge. Even today the hurrying motorist, rushing along the A30 from Exeter, cannot fail to notice the dominating presence of Launceston's twelfth-century shell keep and thirteenth-century round tower. More discreet but of equal strategic importance was Trematon Castle, near Saltash, keeping watch over the confluence of the Tamar and Lynher rivers in this south-eastern corner of Cornwall.

Robert, Count of Mortain, as *de facto* Earl of Cornwall, had established the characteristics of Norman rule in Cornwall but this apparent order was threatened when the death of Henry I in 1135 plunged the realm into civil war between Stephen and Matilda. Illegal or 'adulterine' castles, notably at Truro, appeared, evidence that in Cornwall as elsewhere, there was disturbance and uncertainty. Stephen appointed Count Alan of Brittany (the Breton connection yet again) to administer Cornwall and he in turn was replaced, following Stephen's death in 1154, by one Richard—uncle of Henry II—as Earl of Cornwall. The Earldom as an institution was by now clearly established, and its constitutional and political significance was underscored by the fact that the title and lands were as a rule given to a member of the Royal Family. An interesting aside is that when in c1173 Earl Reginald granted freedoms and privileges to the burgesses of Truro, he addressed them '. . . the barons of Cornwall, and all men both Cornish and English'.[26]

This significance was mirrored in the career of Richard, second son of King John, who in 1225 was granted the rights of the Cornish tin-works and two years later became Earl of Cornwall. It seems that Richard used this status to secure the purely honorary but prestigious (and, therefore, politically useful) title of 'King of the Romans'. He was thus elected in 1257 and was crowned at Aix-la-Chappelle (Aachen), ancient capital of the Holy Roman Empire. Richard was also careful to perpetuate the Tintagel connection, adding substantially to the castle's fortifications (much of what one sees today is his work). His son Edmund, who succeeded him as Earl of Cornwall, was equally conscious of his status and its possibilities. He modernised Restormal Castle, Launceston by then having given way to Lostwithiel as administrative capital of Cornwall, and in Lostwithiel itself he built the so-called Duchy Palace. This once-extensive building accommodated the Shire Hall, the Exchequer of the Earldom (later Duchy), and the Coinage Hall, together with the Stannary Gaol. The latter was notorious, its reputation on a par with that of Devon's Stannary Gaol at Lydford Castle:

> Lydford Law,
> Where first they hang and draw
> And hold the trial after.[27]

Edmund, however, was the last Earl to reside in Cornwall. He died in 1299 without an heir, the Earldom passing first to Edward I and then to Edward II, who gave it to his favourite Piers Gaveston. However, Gaveston was executed in 1312 and thereafter the Earldom languished until Edward III re-invented it in March 1337 as the Duchy of Cornwall. Edward III had decided that the Duchy lands should be used as the source of revenue for the Heir Apparent (at that time, the seven-year old Black Prince), and that the Heir should always be the Duke of Cornwall. This was an important, defining moment in the relationship between Cornwall and the English state, perhaps as significant as the Athelstan settlement. The Heir Apparent was already always the Prince of Wales, and so the creation of the Duchy of Cornwall emphasised the historic bonds of Cornwall (West Wales, as it was still often known) and Wales as well as constructing a new constitutional link between the two. It also demonstrated how important it was for the English state to successfully accommodate its Celtic peripheries. The Principality of Wales (created in 1307), like the Duchy of Cornwall, evidenced separate status and smacked of semi-autonomy.

In crafting this accommodation, Edward III was fully aware that he was building the Duchy of Cornwall, not only upon the Earldom but upon a much earlier line of indigenous Cornish rulers. He saw that he was advancing '. . . our most dear first begotten Edward . . . to be Duke of Cornwall, over which awhile ago Dukes for a long time successively presided as chief rulers'.[28] In that sense, as a device to secure legitimacy, the creation of the Duchy of Cornwall was the constitutional equivalent to the exploitation of Tintagel the place and Arthur the legend. However, a further significance of its creation was that it established a unique relationship between Cornwall and the English Crown, not only binding Cornwall to the state at its source but prompting the financial dependence of the Heir Apparent upon his Duchy.

The Charters of 1337 and 1338 defined in detail the constitutional status of the Duchy and set the powers and privileges of the Duke. Today, when it is possible to point to the distinct and quite separate activities of the Cornwall County Council (the local government authority which administers the territorial entity of Cornwall) and the Duchy of Cornwall (an essentially commercial organisation which manages the Duke's land holdings in Cornwall and elsewhere), it is customary to emphasise the difference between the County and the Duchy. A.L. Rowse complains of '. . . the popular confusion between the Duchy and the county of Cornwall', while Crispin Gill, explaining that the Duke of Cornwall owns more land out of Cornwall than within, emphasises that 'His Duchy is not the county and the county is not the

Duchy'.[29] In the fourteenth century, however, there was no such distinction. As Richard Pearse has argued,

> Under the ancient earldom Cornwall had been to a considerable extent independent, enjoying privileges in the shape of a measure of autonomy and freedom from direct interference by the central government in many of its affairs. This sense of autonomy and separateness was now strengthened. From 1337, when Prince Edward was seven years old, until he died in 1376 the only forms of government known to Cornwall were, at first, that of his household and, later, of his council.[30]

Julian Cornwall has also observed that Cornwall was then 'A Celtic survival not yet assimilated into the English nation . . .', and that an 'illusion of autonomy' was furnished by 'The administrative structure of the Duchy [which] constituted in effect a miniature government complete with a hierarchy of officials . . .'.[31] The best and most complete survey of the constitutional condition of the Duchy of Cornwall, however, was that undertaken by the Duchy itself in 1855-57 when, in response to a legal dispute over foreshore rights, it sought to establish the origins and extent of the Duchy's authority. This study concluded that:

> . . . the three Duchy Charters are sufficient in themselves to vest in the Dukes of Cornwall, not only the government of Cornwall, but the entire territorial dominion in and over the county which had previously been invested in the Crown . . . not only all the territorial possessions of the Crown in Cornwall, but every prerogative right and source of revenue.[32]

Moreover, the Duchy insisted that 'the Duke was quasi-sovereign within his Duchy':

> '. . . from earliest times Cornwall was distinct from the Kingdom of England, and under separate government . . . Cornwall, like Wales, was at the time of the Conquest, and was subsequently treated in many respects, as distinct from England'.[33]

To this constitutional semi-autonomy was added the strong influence that the Duchy exercised over Cornish society and economy, often with results that acted to further differentiate Cornwall. As John Hatcher observed of the Duchy in this period, 'Much of what is significant . . . provides a contrast with the general experience of English medieval history'.[34] In addition to the original seventeen Duchy manors (formerly part of the Earldom) owned directly by the Duchy, the castles of Tintagel, Launceston, Trematon and Restormal, together with the boroughs of Launceston, Lostwithiel, Tintagel, Helston, Camelford, Grampound, Liskeard and Saltash, were under the control of the Duke, as were the shrievalty and havenership of Cornwall, the County and Hundred courts, feodary, and (as we shall see) the entire Stannary system. To this was added a whole array of feudal duties deriving from the Duke's position as a great Lord; all of this managed from the Duchy capital at Lostwithiel.

As A.L. Rowse has pointed out, most of the *Antiqua Maneria*, the original seventeen Duchy manors, were situated in East Cornwall. Only Helston-in-

Kerrier was in the far west, and the further east towards the Tamar one travelled, the greater the concentration of Duchy manors: Moresk, Tewington, Tywarnhaile, Restormal, Tybesta, Penketh, Penlyne, Penmayne, Rillaton, Helston-in-Trigg, Tintagel, Talskedy, Liskeard, Trematon, Calstock, and Stoke Climsland. Moreover, several of the place-names have English elements (such as the Saxon '*ton*'), and Dr Rowse has suggested that this eastern predominance and the evidence of early English influence may reflect the enduring impact of the Athelstan settlement. As he puts it, 'Something of the status of conquest remained . . .'.[35] To these original manors were added the *Forinseca Manora*, those outside Cornwall, and the *Annexata Manoria*, properties both within and outside Cornwall which were later added by Act of Parliament. By the time of the Civil War, there were seventy-eight Duchy manors all told.

In its Cornish context, however, the term 'manor' should be used with caution. As Ian Soulsby has noted, at the time of Domesday there were few manors in Cornwall in the English sense. Those that are listed are for the most part bureaucratic creations, artificial administrative conveniences drawing together the scattering of otherwise diverse settlements in particular geographic areas.[36] Moreover, John Hatcher has argued that the Duchy of Cornwall manors '. . . differed so markedly from the structure of manors in other parts . . .'[37] that they had little in common with the classic English manor and ought not really to be called 'manorial' at all. There was, for example, no exploitation of demenses, the absence of demense farming indicating that lands were entirely in the hands of Duchy tenants. Equally significantly, there was no trace of the open-field, strip-system of agriculture (so typical of English manors) on any of the Duchy properties—a reflection of the predominant form of land settlement that the Duchy had inherited, where the population tended to be scattered in small hamlets rather than grouped in 'nucleated' villages such as those that characterised much of lowland England.

We know that in some parts of Cornwall, probably as a result of pressure on land use and maybe again as a function of English influence (especially in the new towns that had emerged), there was some strip farming, for example around Truro, Penryn and notably Helston (where the Cornish word *gweal*, a field, is prominant in place-names and indicates the presence of the strip system), a fact indicated in the seventeenth-century so-called *Lanhydrock Atlas*. At the Forrabury stitches near Boscastle in North Cornwall, such strips survived in use into the nineteenth century. However, the Cornish landscape was essentially as that characterised by W.G.V. Balchin in his memorable description:

> This is the Celtic under-writing. Small settlements of only two or three farmhouses and labourers' cottages, carrying Celtic names are common at cross-roads. In some will be found the parish church, but often this stands alone, with only the rectory or vicarage nearby. Between the hamlets stretches open farmland of mixed pasture and arable, in which the fields are characteristically small irregular-shaped enclosures bounded by massive granite or slate-walled hedges. Set down in this chequer-board pattern of fields, at remarkably regular intervals, are isolated farms, joined to each other by narrow and often tunnel-like lanes where trees and bushes grow on top of monumental hedgebanks.[38]

For some observers, this scattered isolation accounts for the alleged 'individualism' and 'independence' of the Cornish, but probably more important was the influence of the tenancy system operated by the Duchy of Cornwall. Instead of the familiar categories of free, villein, or cottar (typical of the English manorial system), the Duchy operated tenancies that were free, conventionary, or villein. Most Duchy land, in fact, was held in conventionary tenure. This was not the classic hereditary (and bonded) security of tenure with attendant rights and obligations, but instead a seven-year lease at a free-market rent with only negligible services and no renewal as a right. Those tenants who were free had very few obligations, and only a minority of tenants were villeins bound to their land. Moreover, the number of villeins declined—although, paradoxically, villeinships remained longer in Cornwall than elsewhere—as the Duchy pursued a policy of not renewing them when for various reasons they had lapsed.

The result of all this was that, in medieval Cornwall, a class of independent and potentially mobile peasants was created, a precursor of the independently-minded small tenant farmer that came to typify Cornwall in later centuries. And, just as the Duchy of Cornwall had served to create the independent small farmer, so its political and economic power served to inhibit the emergence of a strong and influential (and potentially rival) gentry. There were no great independent landowners, and in 1602 in his *Survey of Cornwall* Richard Carew could note wryly that '. . . so noblemen I may deliver in a word, that Cornwall at this present enjoyeth the residence of none at all' while 'The Cornish gentlemen can better vaunt of their pedigree than their livelihood . . .'. [39] The influence of the Duchy was all-pervading in medieval Cornwall.

In economic terms, although the long-term effect may have been to drain-off surplus wealth with little return, in the medieval period the activities of the Duchy and its predecessor the Earldom served to encourage commercial diversification. The Domesday survey had revealed the relative poverty of Cornwall at the end of the eleventh century. In contrast to later centuries, over twenty percent of the population were serfs or slaves (compared to the average of nine percent for England), while a third of Cornish parishes was worth £1 or less. The more prosperous and probably heavier-populated areas were those in the far north-east, in the Tamar Valley, and the coastal strip of south-east Cornwall — significantly, perhaps, those areas of English settlement or interest in which the Anglo-Norman Earldom would develop many of its estates. The southern estuaries were, of course, well-placed geographically to participate in maritime trade on both sides of the Channel. Fowey, especially, together with Looe, Penryn and Tregony (to which the Fal was navigable in those days) were thus developed. Saltash, on the Tamar, was granted its charter as early as 1190:

> Saltash was a Borough Town,
> When Plymouth was a Furzy Down.

Between the twelfth and fourteenth centuries there was general economic and population growth in Cornwall, leading amongst other things to the settlement of upland areas on Bodmin Moor. The Black Death reached Cornwall in 1349 (with a second outbreak in 1360), checking this expansion and leading to the abandonment of many of these moorland hamlets. However, the relative diversification that the Cornish economy had by then achieved, cushioned Cornwall from the worst effects of the Black Death, and

In 1724, Daniel Defoe wrote that he liked Looe with its 'very beautiful and stately stone bridge' but thought it wrong that the West and East boroughs sent two MPs each to Parliament, which was 'as much as the city of London chooses'. Always an important maritime and fishing centre, Looe now attracts thousands of tourists to its narrow winding streets.

Fowey has been an important maritime centre since the Medieval period . In Tudor times, the harbour prospered and the 'Fowey Galants' achieved innumerable successes in their actions against 'foreign' shipping.

indeed created the conditions for the rapid decline of peasant servility. The Hundred Years War proved an important stimulus to renewed growth, in particular bringing prosperity and prominence to the southern ports such as Saltash, Looe and Fowey. The ports of South West Britain had promised seventy ships of 100 tons and more, and there is no doubt that there were more than a few Cornish-built and Cornish-manned vessels in the great fleet that defeated the French at Sluys in 1340. By the middle of the fifteenth century, as the Hundred Years War dragged to a close, Cornish ports had become increasingly important in providing Naval logistics: Fowey was by then supplying nineteen transport ships, Saltash six, Landulph five, Truro and Penryn two each, Mevagissey one, Penzance four, and Marazion two.

Moreover, by the first half of the fifteenth century, cloth exports from Cornish ports had increased ten-fold. The Cornish economy featured shipping (Cornish exports were often carried by Cornishmen in Cornish ships), shipbuilding, fishing, quarrying, textile manufacture, and tin-mining and tin-streaming, all of which stimulated agriculture by providing a market for it. Mixed farming predominated, with upland pasturing during the summer months, and the principal arable crops being wheat, oats, rye and barley. As we have seen, the general settlement pattern in Cornwall was of scattered hamlets and isolated church-towns, a pattern mirrored in other Celtic countries where, Richard Muir argues, the thinly spread resources and the thin acidic soils did not lend themselves to close settlement. Thus the '. . . various attempts to seed the countryside with feudal villages scorned the traditions of settlement that were deeply rooted in Celtic societies and were doomed to failure'.[40]

In Cornwall, the attempts to create such nucleated villages were largely confined to the small area of substantial English settlement north of the Ottery (where the linguistically-hybrid Kilkhampton is a good example of a nucleated village built around the core of an earlier Cornish hamlet) and the strategically-placed centres of English influence elsewhere in Cornwall where the English suffix '*ton*' is found appended to existing Cornish place-names. Balchin considered that in the medieval period, even when there were strong economic motives for the establishment of speculative market towns, 'The Cornish never took kindly to town-life', [41] while Charles Henderson considered that such towns which did exist were highly artificial creations which the Cornish did not trust.

Certainly, towns came late to Cornwall (there are few what we might call 'urban features' observable before the mid-twelfth century—Launceston was the only town important enough to have a wall and gate), and in the tax assessments of 1327 (as well as later in the fifteenth century) many of the inhabitants of Cornish towns were foreigners—Dutch, Irish, Flemings, French, English, Bretons. At Penryn in 1327 half the burgesses were foreigners. At Tregony they were more than half, and at Grampound they predominated. Even today, Cornish surnames can be a clue to this intrusion. 'Flamank', for example, is from Fleming. The provenance of 'England' is obvious: Dr James Whetter tells us that even in anglicised north-eastern Cornwall, foreigners in the towns were given such surnames as 'Anglicus' or 'Le Engleys'.

However, whilst towns were clearly in one sense an alien intrusion, in other respects their creation might also be considered a natural response to the stimuli noted by Balchin. The maritime dimension, as we have seen already, was important in the development of ports such as Saltash, Fowey and Looe, and of fishing communities such as Polperro and Mevagissey, while the presence of religious communities was important in towns such as Penryn and Bodmin. The Earldom was an early stimulus to the creation of borough towns, Earl Richard granting charters to Bossiney, Tintagel, Camelford, West Looe, Bodmin, Launceston, Liskeard, and Lostwithiel. Some towns (for example, Mitchell and Wadebridge) grew-up along the spinal communication routes; others—such as Week St Mary and Tregony—served as centres for their rural hinterlands.

By the late medieval period the Cornish economy had achieved a considerable diversity, not least through the exploitation of Cornwall's maritime opportunities and as a result of the activities of the Earldom and Duchy. However, even at that date tin mining was emerging as a central feature of the Cornish economy, the relative mobility of the Cornish population facilitating its development, a hint of both the relative de-diversification of the Cornish economy and the predominance of mining that would characterise later centuries. Of course, as we have seen in earlier chapters, the search for tin (and other metals) goes back into the depths of prehistoric Cornwall. By Roman times Cornish tin was an export commodity of considerable importance. In the medieval period its importance grew apace. The arrival of the Black Death in 1349 was a temporary blow (by 1351 tin production had fallen by 80%) but output had recovered by the 1380s. By then the focus of tin production had begun to move from East Cornwall (where moorland tin-streaming predominated) to more westerly districts where new open-cut and (increasingly) underground mining was developed. Water-power was harnessed to crush the extracted ore, and the tin was smelted in so-called blowing houses—the place-name Blowinghouse survives in several parts of Cornwall, most famously at the western end of Redruth.

The importance of the tin industry was reflected in the significance of the Stannaries, an institution (or series of linked institutions) which became an integral part of the Duchy organisation and which, like the Duchy, was a powerful mechanism of constitutional accommodation. The Stannaries appear to have emerged from the ancient customary rights and privileges enjoyed by the tinners of Cornwall (and Devon), similar to the ancient free mining status enjoyed by miners in areas as diverse as the Mendips in Somerset, the Forest of Dean, the Derbyshire Peak district, and Alston Moor in the North of England, not to mention comparable areas on the continent in France, the Low Countries and Germany. Professor Robert Pennington, the leading authority on the Stannaries, considers that Stannary Law evolved from three sources—Cornish, Anglo-Saxon and Norman—with 'Cornish customary law . . . being kept alive from generation to generation . . .'.[42] However, the Stannary system, as it evolved in the medieval period, went much further than mere 'free mining' to provide Cornwall with what Dr John Rowe has observed '. . . might almost be termed territorial semi-independence . . .', the Stannary Parliament operating in a manner that (as G.R. Lewis wrote) '. . . scarcely differed from that at the House of Commons . . . ' in London.[43]

The relationship between the Duchy and the Stannaries was both constitutional and economic. As the Duke was quasi-sovereign in his Duchy, and as the Duchy was under the terms of its Charters the source of governmental legitimacy within Cornwall, it was only right and proper that the legal and political powers of the Stannary Courts and Parliament should be subject to the authority of the Duchy. Of equal significance, however, was tin coinage, a tax payable on smelted tin which had been imposed by the Crown in the late eleventh century. When the Duchy of Cornwall was created in 1337, tin coinage became part of the income of the Duchy and thus the Heir Apparent, gave the tin industry a special place in the relationship between *Anglia et Cornubia.*

The first attempt at describing the nature and constitutional status of the Stannaries had occurred in 1198, and this was followed in 1201 by the first Charter of the Stannaries which arose from '. . . the desire of the Cornish tinners to be separated from those of Devon . . .'[44] (there was already a traditional distinction, perhaps hostility, between the two). The Charter of 1201 established the four mining districts—or Stannaries—in which Stannary Law might operate: Foweymore (modern Bodmin Moor), Blackmore (the Hensbarrow downs above St Austell), Tywarnhaile (the area around Truro and St Agnes), and Penwith-with-Kerrier in the far-west. There was, however, no attempt to decide where the boundaries of these Stannaries might lie. This sometimes caused confusion for the Stannary Courts which operated in each of these Stannaries (they did not always know how far their jurisdiction might extend, and in practice there was much over-lapping) but it also led to the argument that, as the whole of Cornwall was apparently metaliferous, the jurisdiction of Stannary Law and the Stannary Parliament could if needs be be considered to encompass all Cornwall. Thus the legislative semi-independence of the Stannary Parliament was also a Cornish semi-independence, a point emphasised by the Duchy of Cornwall itself when in 1857 it argued that the Duchy, Stannaries and County were in territorial terms co-terminous: '. . . the Stannary unquestionably extended over the whole County, it is manifest that the term Duchy was used in an equally extensive sense'.[45]

In 1305 Edward I in two separate Charters (one for Cornwall, one for Devon) defined the privileges enjoyed by the tinners. Most important of these was that tinners were not to be brought before ordinary courts (except for the most serious of charges) but were to be tried in Stannary Courts (irrespective of whether the suit was to do with mining) before a jury consisting of tinners—for a mining suit—or half tinners and half 'foreigners' for a non-mining suit. The Charters also offered a liberal interpretation of the right of 'bounding', under which a tinner might establish a tin bound (an area of ground that he was to work) on certain types of land, and gave the tinner exceptions from local taxation and imposts. Like the Duchy tenancies, one effect of the Stannary Charters was to create a class of independent workers, living and toiling according to their own rules, capable of enacting their own laws independently of Westminster, answerable only to their own kind, and jealous of their rights and privileges. As we shall see in Chapter Six, it was an apparent threat to these rights and privileges that, amongst other things, precipitated the Cornish rebellions of 1497, when Cornwall attempted its first resistance to the encroaching influence of a Tudor state that threatened to disturb the balance of constitutional accommodation.

We may also speculate that, in the longer term, the independent working practices of the Cornish tinner under Stannary Law led to the eventual emergence of the famous tribute and tutwork forms of employment in which part of the entrepreneurial function was performed by the miner himself—the miner bidding for the area or 'pitch' that he was to work, providing his own equipment and materials, and being paid according to the value of the ore won (tribute) or the amount of ground mined (tutwork). Thus, as well as being a significant element of Cornwall's constitutional accommodation and an important source of revenue for the Heir Apparent, the Stannary system had an important impact at the societal level. The independent tinner, like the independent tenant farmer, would play a prominent role in the development of Cornwall's characteristics in the centuries that lay ahead. Again, the conclusion must be that the Duchy's influence was indeed all-pervasive in medieval Cornwall.

To look beyond the bounds of Cornwall for a moment, it was significant that in the same year that Edward III had created his seven-year old son Duke of Cornwall, he had also advanced his claim to the crown of France. Here, then, was a monarch anxious to consolidate, enhance and expand his territories, accommodating his Celtic peripheries at home while precipitating continental adventure abroad. The young Duke of Cornwall, the Black Prince, was to play an important role in both these objectives. In 1346 he was at Crécy, one of the great English victories of the Hundred Years War, and in 1354 he held court at Restormel before returning to France where he was at the triumph of Poitiers, when the French were again routed. By 1363 the Black Prince was back in his Duchy at Restormel, hero of England but also specifically of Cornwall. The Black Prince died in 1376, to be followed by Edward III's death in 1377. For a while, the French gained the upper-hand (Fowey was burnt in 1378) but the conflict drifted towards a truce (although Looe was sacked in 1405 by the French and Spanish, when nineteen fishing boats were destroyed), the Hundred Years War not being renewed with any vigour until the accession of Henry V in 1413.

If the prominence of the Black Prince at Crécy and Poitiers had given a Cornish perspective to those battles (as those who welcomed him at Restormel may well have believed), then equally Cornish and as significant, was the presence of those Cornish archers who had contributed in no small measure to the English victories. Although the archers of the Hundred Years War are popularly described as Welsh, the Cornish—then often still known as the West Welsh, and speaking a tongue that must have sounded very

Crowning a hill overlooking the River Fowey is Restormel. It was built in the twelfth-century and was the castle of the Black Prince. Its defences were last tested in the Civil War.

much like Welsh to the un-discerning ear—were a sizeable and distinct contingent.

At Agincourt, Henry V's great battle of 1415, the Cornish archers reached their apogee. Michael Drayton (1563-1631), author of the narrative poem *The Battaile of Agincourt,* reported that the Cornish fought at Agincourt under a banner depicting two Cornish wrestlers. Richard Carew in his *Survey of Cornwall* (1602) waxed lyrical about the Cornish proficiency at archery and, in what Alan Kent has called a 'remarkable proof of the Cornish connection'[46] with Agincourt, Carew not only alluded to the victories at Crécy, Poitiers and Agincourt (and Flodden) but even borrowed Shakespeare's phrase 'which I doubt not' from Henry V's famous Harfleur speech. All this, Carew explained, was '. . . to give you [the reader] some taste of the Cornishmen's former sufficiency that way . . . they would pierce any armour', a point emphasised again in his personal recollections of Master Robert Arundell, son of Sir John Arundell of Trerice, who '. . . could shoot twelve score, with his right hand, with his left, and from behind his head' and '. . . Robert Bone of Antony [who] shot at a little bird sitting upon his cow's back, and killed it, the bird (I mean) not the cow . . .'.[47] Of the Cornish who fought at Agincourt, (as F.E. Halliday put it) 'Sir John Cornwall and Sir John Trelawny lived to feast their neighbours on the anniversary of St Crispin's Day, but the body of Sir John Colshull was brought home to rest in Duloe church . . .'.[48] Over the south gate at Launceston was a portrait of Henry V with a couplet:

> He that will do aught for mee
> Let him love well Sir John Tirlawnee.[49]

Alan Kent has also drawn attention to the way in which the Cornish are depicted (albeit fleetingly) in Shakespeare's *Henry V.* In the play there is a famous scene when the English, Irish, Scots and Welsh captains all meet together, a dramatic tactic employed by Shakespeare to emphasise their unity in the English army and their service to the English Crown. As Kent observes, for the Irish, Scots and Welsh, '. . . 'service' is the operative word, for in rank, in dramatic importance, and in linguistic competence, they are comical second-order citizens'.[50] However, the Cornish are treated rather differently, exemplified in the scene where Henry V, disguised as a common soldier, tours the camp on the eve of battle. He is challenged by Pistol, one of the ancients of the English army, who demands 'What is thy name?'. The disguised Henry replies with the appropriate pun 'Harry Le Roy'. Pistol misses the joke but recognises that it is not a normal English name, it is an 'other'. So he responds, 'Le Roy! a Cornish name: art thou of Cornish crew?' It is significant that Pistol imagines that a foreign-sounding name not immediately recognisable is probably Cornish, and equally telling is the use of crew—a word that suggests not comic second-order subservience but familiarity, fondness, respect, perhaps a reputation for working efficiently as a team.

The Cornish at Agincourt, then, were an 'other', an identifiably different group apparently working well on their own as a team, exuding a confidence and competence that demanded respect. In this light, it is significant that three years later Sir John Arundell of Lanherne contracted with the King's uncle, the Duke of Exeter, to supply 364 Cornish men-at-arms and 770 Cornish archers for further service in France. Although Henry V died in 1422, his continental empire thereafter gradually lost, that the Cornish remained a distinct and recognisable element of subsequent English armies is evidenced in one contemporary (but certainly not respectful) comment on the huge army of some 44,000-strong assembled in 1544 for Henry VIII's adventure on the continent:

> So many depraved, brutish soldiers from all nations under the sun—Welsh, English, Cornish, Irish, Manx, Scots, Spaniards, Gascons, Portingals [Portuguese], Italians, Albanians, Greeks, Turks, Tartars, Almains, Germans, Burgundians, Flemings, who had come there . . . to have a good time under the king of England, who by nature was too hospitable to foreigners.[51]

It is worth adding, however, that at the famous Field of Cloth-of-Gold extravaganza in France in 1520, when Henry VIII aimed to impress the French, amongst the demonstrations was a display of Cornish wrestling.

If, as Alan Kent avers, the relationship between *Anglia et Cornubia* had a special quality, distinct from that between England and its other Celtic peripheries, then this perhaps explains the trouble John Trevisa took to defend his Cornishness while trying at the same time to embrace Englishness, behaviour we observe later in Richard Carew, and in our own time in Sir Arthur Quiller Couch and, indeed, A.L. Rowse who in 1944 confessed to 'Not being English, alas—except by conviction—but hopelessly Cornish'.[52] John Trevisa, the subject of a recent biography by Professor D.C. Fowler, was born of lesser-gentry stock in c1340, possibly at Crocadan in St Mellion but more likely in St Enoder.[53] He spent some years at the Oxford colleges of Exeter and Queen's before becoming chaplain at Berkeley Castle in Gloucestershire. In 1385, at a time when the English language was growing in status (as opposed to French), Trevisa noted that forty years earlier two Cornish-born Oxford schoolmasters, John of Cornwall (probably from St Germans, said to be a speaker of Welsh, i.e. probably Cornish) and Richard Pencrich, were responsible for initiating the practice of requiring schoolboys to translate their Latin texts into English rather than French. Trevisa evidently approved of this trend. He himself translated a number of important Latin works into English, and advocated that there should be an English-language version of the Bible.

Perhaps even more telling than his enthusiasm for English (and there is no evidence of his speaking or writing, let alone supporting, Cornish) is the muddle he got into when describing the status of his native Cornwall. Although irritably dismissive of those who claimed that Cornwall was not part of England, he was nonetheless adamant that Cornwall was one of the chief parts of Britain. However, Cornwall could not be part of Wales because they were separated by the sea. Equally, it could not be part of Scotland because they were separated by great distance. Thus, Cornwall must be part of England! In translating Ranulf Higden's *Polychronicon* from Latin into English, Trevisa had difficulty in dealing with Higden's assertion that there were thirty-six shires in England apart from Cornwall (*praeter Cornubia*). Higden's point, of course, was that while Cornwall might formally be a part of England it also enjoyed a distinctive and separate status. As L.C.J. Orchard has astutely observed, 'It may be thought ironic that Higden's phraseology should be challenged by a Cornishman, one, moreover, who asserted the important place of Cornwall within Britain'.[54]

Dr Mark Stoyle has added recently, 'Yet Trevisa protested too much, and as he himself must have known very well, there were many respects in which Cornwall differed greatly from its eastern neighbours'.[55] We might further observe that Trevisa's certainties and uncertainties tell us much about the ambivalence and difficulties experienced by a medieval Cornishman conscious of his identity but owing his scholarly *raison d'être* to England and the English ecclesiastical and literary establishment. One also wonders what went through the mind of Robert Tresilian, a Cornishman born near St Buryan and, like John Trevisa, educated at Exeter College (they may even have been contemporaries), who in 1381 played a prominent role in suppressing the Peasants' Revolt. Appointed Lord Chief Justice, it was Tresilian who sentenced John of Northampton to languish imprisoned in distant Tintagel Castle, far from harm's way. Tresilian himself came to a sticky end, being executed at Tyburn in 1388.

The other side of the coin to Trevisa, however, and indeed in marked contrast to the apparent order of the Duchy administration, was what A.L. Rowse has called the mood of 'feudal anarchy' that prevailed in much of medieval Cornwall. As John Hatcher has written, 'Cornwall was a remote and somewhat forbidding county to most Englishmen in the middle ages', citing the view of Bishop John de Grandisson who in 1327 exclaimed that Cornwall was '. . . not only the ends of the earth but the very ends of the ends thereof'.[56] A few years later, in 1342, the Archdeacon of Cornwall resigned, confessing himself unable to communicate with the Cornish—this was not only a question of language, because '. . . the folk of these parts are quite extraordinary, being of a rebellious temper, and obdurate in the face of attempts to teach and correct'.[57] The disorder of the reign of Stephen and Matilda has been noted already but more interesting, perhaps, are the Wars of the Roses where, as Hugh Kearney wrote, 'During the late fifteenth century, Scotland, Ireland and Wales were left largely to their own devices and even smaller communities such as the Isle of Man and Cornwall . . . enjoyed a good deal of independence'.[58] Whether characteristic of the whole of medieval Cornwall or not, the feudal anarchy of the late fifteenth century was crucial in mobilising an independence of action which, with the end of the Wars of the Roses, made Tudor attempts to whip Cornwall into line even more difficult than they might otherwise have been. In a sense, the Cornish rebellions of 1497 were as much the culmination of a period of lawless independence as they were resistance to the Tudor regime.

The Cornish were to a degree 'beyond the Pale', like the feuding society of Gaelic Ireland, or the turbulent Highlands and Borders of Scotland. In the anarchic reign of Edward II there had been almost open war between Fowey and the Cinque Ports of South East England. The king did what he could to prevent the Cinque Ports (over which theoretically he had some control) from molesting ships from Lostwithiel, Fowey and Polruan. But he had little success and the Gallants of Fowey responded by attacking Rye and Winchelsea. In the Wars of the Roses, the Fowey seafarers were equally active, blatantly attacking Norman, Breton, Spanish, even Plymothian shipping. A Breton fleet retaliated in 1457 by attacking Fowey, an event that has passed into Cornish lore as a result of the spirited defence mounted by Elizabeth, the wife of Thomas Treffry (then absent from the town), who was reputed to have poured molten lead over would-be intruders at Place. On his return to Fowey, Thomas Treffry (a descendent of the John Treffry who had been knighted by the Black Prince at Crécy) decided that further fortification of Place was in order. The Gallants, meanwhile, had responded by building towers at either end of the harbour mouth and suspending a great chain in between.

This feudal anarchy also encompassed the often unrestrained feuding between (the often impecunious) lesser-gentry, again especially during the Wars of the Roses. The Bodrugans, a medieval Cornish knightly family, have been recently the subject of an astonishingly painstaking study by Dr James Whetter, almost certainly the most detailed research on medieval Cornwall from original sources since L.E.Elliott Binn's rather impenetrable history of 1955.[59] Although Whetter agrees that the lawlessness and rebelliousness of the Bodrugans were symptomatic of Cornish families of the time, he complains that the infamous 'Henry Bodrugan has had a bad press from modern historians', while admitting that 'On the face of it the case against him is overwhelming'.[60]

In 1450, for example, Henry Bodrugan was alleged to have led an assault on the house of Lawrence Trewonall of Lamorran. Shortly afterwards he was accused of attacking the house of Robert Wolvedon in Probus. In 1461 he assaulted one Thomas Tregarthen, who held land at Gorran, and in 1465 he ambushed Richard Tomyow at Lostwithiel. In the late 1460s he was in trouble for harassing a husbandman, one Nicholas of Sticker, and in May 1471 he robbed the house of William Carnsew of Trecarne. In the same month he encouraged a raid on the house of John Trelawney at Woolston in Poundstock. He was also accused of attacking the house of James Trefusis in Lamorran, and of breaking into the houses of John Penpons at Truro and Helston, of Otes Philips at Polwhele in St Clement, and that of John Arundel at Tolverne. Ships belonging to him, including the *Barbarye* of Fowey and the *Mary Bodrugan*, were implicated in piracy, and he also robbed a vessel at Feock. And so the list goes on.

However, apart from the general lawlessness of the era, James Whetter points to the relative weakness of the Duchy of Cornwall at the time (it was unable to play its usual ameliorating role), while also emphasising that much of this conflict was actually political. Henry Bodrugan was Cornwall's chief

Place, at Fowey, defended bravely by Elizabeth Treffry against a fierce Breton assault in 1457.

Cotehele House—site of the celebrated occasion on which Richard Edgcumbe was chased through his own woods by the conscientious Henry Bodrugan.

supporter of Edward IV, the Yorkist, who after the Battle of Tewkesbury in 1471 was in the ascendancy. However, most of the Cornish gentry were loyal to the Lancastrian cause; hence the enmity that Bodrugan engendered. Cornwall was in fact the scene of the last Lancastrian revolt, in September 1473 when the Earl of Oxford seized St Michael's Mount and was besieged by Henry Bodrugan. Edward IV did nothing to improve his popularity in Cornwall when in 1474 he decided to punish the 'Gallants' for their lawlessness, imprisoning the burgesses of Fowey, Polruan and Bodinnick, one of whom he executed.

Important Cornish gentry such as Sir Thomas Arundell, Richard Edgcumbe and John Treffry plotted for the Lancastrian cause (at Bodmin they proclaimed Henry Tudor king, even before his return from Brittany) and drew the ire of Henry Bodrugan. Another story to have entered Cornish lore is that of the famous chase along the wooded Cornish bank of the Tamar at Cotehele, when Richard Edgcumbe (the pursued) threw his hat into the river to deceive his pursuer (Henry Bodrugan) into thinking that he had escaped (or perished) by jumping into the water. Cotehele was the principal residence of the Edgcumbes until Mount Edgcumbe was built in the late sixteenth century; a small chapel in the grounds commemorates Richard's escape from Henry. For his pains in harassing his Lancastrian opponents, Henry Bodrugan was rewarded by Richard III with the manors of Trelawne and Tywardreath. However, in 1485 Henry Tudor had landed at

Milford Haven (where John Treffry was there to meet him, and was knighted on the spot), and at the Battle of Bosworth Field in August of that year Richard III was killed and Henry Tudor became Henry VII.

The feudal anarchy of medieval, especially late medieval, Cornwall may well have been a measure of Cornish independence of action at a time when the influence of the 'centre' had waned and the mechanisms of accommodation had faltered. A more distinctive badge of 'difference', however, was the Cornish language. Although, as we have seen, for men such as John Trevisa (or John of Cornwall and Richard Pencrich) English was the language of the future, it is notable that they pursued their careers outside of Cornwall. Within Cornwall, the Cornish language remained an important vehicle of communication and culture, not only amongst the common folk but in religious scholarship too. Early English settlement in the far north-east had first brought the English language to Cornwall, and thereafter the presence of foreigners in the emerging towns, together with the international contacts of major ports such as Fowey, would have caused further intrusion. However, much of this international contact was actually with Brittany (the Breton and Cornish languages were mutually intelligible in this period), while the ports and towns of medieval Cornwall were (to use a modern phrase) multicultural communities where Cornish, Latin, French and English would have co-existed with a smattering of other European languages such as Breton, Flemish and Irish.

Cornish itself is one of the three modern languages of the Brythonic group of Celtic tongues. The other two are Breton (to which Cornish is especially close, a result of the Armorican settlement) and Welsh; more distant are the modern Goidelic group of Celtic languages comprising Irish, Scots Gaelic and Manx. Dr Ken George has asked the difficult question, 'How many people spoke Cornish traditionally?'[61] and has come up with some ingenious answers. He estimates, for example, that in 1200 Cornish was spoken over the greater part of Cornwall (about 93% of the land mass). The population of Cornwall was then approximately 35,000, and the number of Cornish speakers would have been in the order of 30,000. By 1300 the linguistic border had slipped further west, with Cornish being spoken in about 73% of Cornwall. However, as the population had expanded, there were now probably some 38,000 Cornish speakers. By 1500, argues George, the language had fallen back to the Fowey-Camel line in mid-Cornwall. Nevertheless, this meant that Cornish was still spoken in 54% of the territory of Cornwall, probably by some 33,000 people (out of a total population of about 69,000). Moreover, George adds that in 1500 the area in which 'practically everyone spoke Cornish' was still some 48% of Cornwall. In other words, even as the medieval period drew to a close, Cornish was overwhelmingly the dominant language of the western half of Cornwall.

Ken George's demographic history of Cornish is persuasive and convincing. However, recently Dr N.J.A.Williams has criticised the general assumption that the experience of Cornish was an ever-westerly retreat in the face of relentless pressure from English. He insists instead that 'There is good evidence that until the Reformation, i.e. the middle of the sixteenth century, Cornish was probably spoken as far as the Tamar'. Considering that 'It is a common error of Anglophones to believe that the Celtic languages have always been in retreat',[62] Williams goes on to argue that after the Norman Conquest there was a resurgence of Cornish at the expense of English. Amongst other things, says Dr Williams, the Breton influence in post-

Conquest Cornwall was a significant factor in the renewed expansion of Cornish. The inference is that if indeed Cornish was spoken up to the Tamar until as recently as the 1550s, then there would have been many more speakers than the numbers estimated by Ken George. Moreover, if Williams is right, then the impact of the Tudor Reformation on the Cornish language was even more sudden and devastating than had been thought hitherto, for Williams agrees that Cornish had retreated to the Fowey-Camel line by the late sixteenth century.

Be that as it may, we have considerable evidence of the Cornish language surviving from the medieval period.[63] There are even a few survivals from Old Cornish, the form of the language spoken from the ninth to the thirteenth century. These are glosses, scribbled notes on Latin texts, the most substantial of which is that in the so-called *Bodmin Gospels* where the names of freed slaves are recorded. There is also the *Old Cornish Vocabulary*, an English-Latin vocabulary of cAD1000 to which was added about a hundred years later a Cornish translation. In all some 961 Cornish words are recorded, ranging from celestial bodies, through Church and craft occupations, to plants and animals. A final Old Cornish survival dates from 1265 and is a single sentence in an account of the founding of the church of St Thomas at Glasney, Penryn. The story explains that St Thomas had appeared in a dream to the Bishop of Exeter, telling him to establish a church at Polsethow in Penryn. Thus was fulfilled the ancient prophecy, 'In Polsethow ywhylyr anethow'. 'Anethow' has two meanings, dwellings and marvels, and so here we have a nice pun: 'In Polsethow shall be seen dwellings (or marvels)'.

It is through the activities of the Church, indeed, that we have received many of our insights into the Cornish language in the middle ages. For example, we learn that when Bishop John de Grandisson preached in the far-western parish of St Buryan in 1328 or 1329, his sermon had to be translated by an interpreter for the benefit of the monoglot Cornish population. In 1339 one J.Polmarke was appointed to preach in the Cornish language at St Merryn, near Padstow. In 1354-55 de Grandisson appointed two penitentiaries for Cornwall—one in Truro for those who spoke only Cornish, and one at Bodmin for those who spoke Cornish and English. As late as 1538 the Bishop of Exeter decreed that the Epistle or Gospel of the Day might be read in Cornish in those parishes where English was not understood, and in 1560 it was directed by the Bishop that those who had no English might be taught the Catechism in Cornish. The tenacity of the Cornish language in mid-Cornwall well into the sixteenth century is attested by a court case in 1587 where an interpreter had to be provided for certain Gorran Haven fishermen who knew no English.[64] Similarly, in the neighbouring parish of St Ewe in 1595 the inhabitants were shown to be bi-lingual. In 1542 Andrew Borde summed-up the state of the Cornish language: 'In Cornwall is two speches; the one is naughty Englyshe, and the other Cornyshe speche. And there be many men and women the which cannot speake one word of Englyshe, but all Cornyshe'.[65]

An early piece of written Cornish surviving from the Middle Cornish period is forty-one lines of verse, dated to c1400, penned on the back of a charter relating to the parish of St Stephen-in-Brannel. However, this is a mere fragment compared to the extensive body of material that comprises the Middle Cornish *Passion Poem* and 'Miracle Plays', the earliest of which is the *Ordinalia*, written towards the end of the fourteenth century. The *Ordinalia* appears to have been composed at Glasney College, the collegiate church at Penryn which emerged as a centre of religious scholarship in the Cornish language.[66] An enormous work comprising three separate plays, the *Ordinalia* took three days to perform, the normal venue being the open-air *'plen-an-gwarry'* or playing place. Today there are two well-known and well-preserved playing places, one at St Just-in-Penwith and the other at the Perran (or Piran) Round, near Perranporth. However, archaeological evidence has indicated the presence of many more such sites across Cornwall, while place-names such as Plain-an-gwarry (for example, at Redruth and Marazion) and Playing Place (near Truro) are further clues.

The *Ordinalia* is, of course, a religious cycle. The first play commences with the creation of the world and the placing by God within it of Adam. However, Adam falls and it is not until the conclusion of the third play that, through the triumph of Christ, Adam is at last restored to Heaven:

arluth ker bynyges os	Dear Lord, ever blessed be,
a syv ioy gynef gothfos	joy it brings to us to see
an denses the thos th'en nef	man brought to heaven again,
an tas dev dre'n spyrys sans	The Father and Holy Ghost
the'n beys danvonas sylwyans	redeemed a world that was lost
a huhon map dev a seyf	On high the Son will remain.[67]

There is a close relationship between the *Ordinalia* and the *Passion Poem*, one seeming to have borrowed from the other, and Professor Brian Murdoch suggests that the *Passion Poem* is the older of the two. There is also some connection between the *Ordinalia* and a later play, *Gwreans an Bys* (the Creation of the World). Although the manuscript for the latter has survived

Penryn, the medieval focus of literary scholarship in the Cornish language.

Perran Round, near Perranporth, Cornwall's best preserved example of a medieval *plen-an-gwarry.*

as a copy made in 1611 by William Jordan of Helston, *Gwreans an Bys* is pre-Reformation in style and has been dated to c1530-40. There are strong echoes of one of the *Ordinalia* plays, the *Origio Mundi*, and again the theme is strictly religious:

Gallas Lucifer, droke preve, Mes an Nef tha dewolgowe. Ha lemyn un y lea ef Me a vyn heb falladowe Un dean formya In valy Ebron devery, Rag collenwall aredy An le may teth anotha.	Gone is Lucifer the snake, out of heaven to dark hell. Now, without fail I shall make, to take and fill his place well, a new-formed man in the Valley of Hebron. And the man shall fill, anon, the place from which he was banned.[68]

But *Gwreans an Bys* is its own play and has distinctive features, such as the death of Cain at the hands of the character Lamech. This Lamech is depicted as an unsavoury womaniser:

Moy es vn wreag thym yma Thom pleasure rag gwyll ganssy. Ha sure me ew an kensa Bythqwath whath a ve dew wreag.	Not just one wife - I have more to give great pleasure to me. I'm the first - of that I'm sure - to marry two wives at once.
Han mowyssye lower plenty Yma thym; nyngens dentye. Me as kyef pan vydnaf ve; Ny sparyaf anothans y, Malbew onyn a vo teag.	And I have girls a-plenty, they're never over-dainty! I pick them when it suits me. Damned if I'll keep off them, see, especially pretty ones![69]

More intriguing still is the play *Beunans Meriasek* (the Life of St Meriasek). Although written c1500, and thus predating *Gwreans an Bys*, *Beunans Meriasek* is quite different in many respects. It is at one level a subversive document, perhaps even a political commentary on the position in which Cornwall found itself in the late medieval, early modern period as the Tudor state developed. It is best seen, therefore, in the light of the Cornish reaction to the intrusions of the Tudor state and the aftermath of the Cornish rebellions of 1497, and is discussed in Chapter Six.

Of course, the Miracle Plays, as well as emphasising the significance and extent of the Cornish language in the medieval period, also highlight the importance of religion and the Church. For example, by the sixteenth century pre-Reformation Bodmin had a priory, a friary, a parish church (in which was kept the Reliquary of St Petroc), five chapels, two hospitals, and two leper hospitals. Many of Bodmin's forty guilds were religious or charitable associations. Scores of Celtic crosses, many of them reminiscent of the High Crosses of Ireland, with their wheel-heads and carved 'Celtic' interlacing, were erected all across Cornwall. Thankfully, many of these have survived and can be found today in churchyards and by the roadside.[70] Holy wells continued to be tended and venerated (as they are today), with well-houses erected at locations such as St Cleer and Dupath. Some 700 chapels

Casket containing the remains of St Petroc is displayed at Bodmin Parish Church.

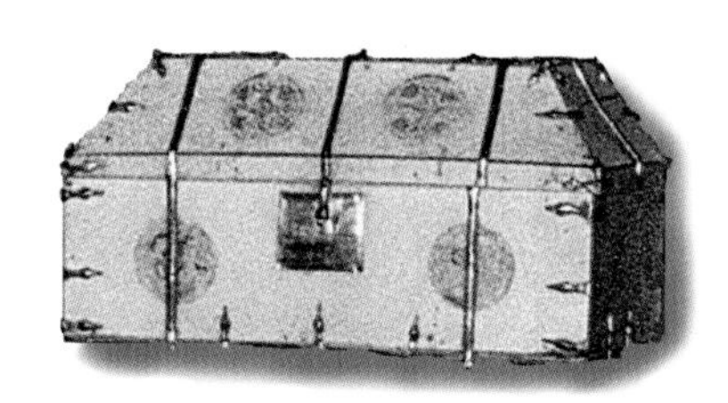

Strong Breton architectural overtones can be observed in this holy well at Dupath, near Callington.

Atop Roche Rock sits a ruined medieval chapel dedicated to St Michael. The mysterious Rock has been used as a location for numerous films.

were erected during the medieval period, although only a handful survive today—notably Henry Trecarrel's in Lezant, and the stupendous 'hermit's chapel' of St Michael on Roche Rock.

Religious pilgrimage was taken seriously, with pilgrims not only visiting the holy sites of Cornwall (for example St Piran's Oratory in the sands at Perranzabuloe) but venturing (when gaps in the warfare allowed) to Santiago de Compostela in northern Spain. A number of Cornish churches were in fact dedicated to St James, including Jacobstowe, Antony and Kilkhampton. Saints' days continued to be important events and Nicholas Roscarrock, the seventeenth-century Cornish Catholic and hagiographer, tells us that on St Piran's Day (March 5th) the Saints relics would be carried from one parish to another. Many of these Saints retained their particular associations—Cadoc with intestinal worms, Meriasek with ague, Nonn with lunatics, Sancreed with pigs—and devotees with particular complaints or desires might appeal directly for their intervention. In the later medieval period, as Professor Nicholas Orme has observed, 'Cornish people remained sufficiently conscious of Celtic hagiography to invent new Celtic saints . . . where parishes seemed to be (but were not) named after them'.[71] Thus we learn of a St Keynwynus at Kenwyn in 1342, a St Ludewanus at Ludgvan in 1319, St Morvetha at Morvah in 1390, and St Tallanus at Talland in 1452—each of them quite spurious!

But this desire to associate placenames and church dedications with supposed Celtic Saints was part of a wider late medieval enthusiasm amongst the Cornish for their churches. In the fifteenth century many churches were rebuilt with the characteristic three-stage Cornish tower and acquired what Richard Muir has called their '. . . instantly recognisable Cornish identity'.[72] Norman fonts, barrel roofs, and rood-screens and rood-lofts were generally retained, contributing to that particular Cornish atmosphere. Although the often severe rebuilding of Cornish churches in Victorian times has left some like scraped-clean barns, many retain their medieval ambience, not least those that were affected by the Anglo-Catholic revival in this century and have become (once again) religious icons of Celtic-Catholic Cornwall. The interior of Blisland church, a favourite of Sir John Betjeman, typifies this *genre*. In late medieval times, however, the epitome of this Cornish enthusiasm for their churches was the installation of a series of glorious stained-glass windows in the early sixteenth century in St Neot church. The earliest of the windows, the finest and the least restored, is the so-called Creation Window at the east end of the south aisle. Other windows portray a variety of other themes, from the Noah story to the Life of St Neot himself.

Intriguingly, as Morwenna Jenkin and Dr Joanna Mattingly have shown, Breton craftsmen had a particular part to play in this late medieval, pre-Reformation enhancement of Cornish churches.[73] At North Petherwin in 1523-24, for example, 'brytons' were paid £58 on completion of the timber rood-loft, and at Bodmin in 1529-30 two unnamed 'Bretouns' were contracted to set up seats and dismantle the organ. There is some evidence that the presence of Bretons in Cornwall (or indeed the experiences of Cornish pilgrims in Brittany, such as those who attended the pardon at Lantregar—probably Treguier—in 1537) influenced Cornish ecclesiastical architecture. The spire of Lostwithiel church was probably built to a Breton design in the early fourteenth century, and the well-house at Dupath has a decidedly Breton flavour. However, there was no reason for the Cornish to slavishly copy Breton example, and local fashion derived a distinctive style that became characteristic of Cornwall and West Devon.

The Breton connection, however, reflects a recurring theme in this chapter: the influence of the Bretons in medieval Cornwall. As we have seen, the Conquest reaffirmed the historical links between Cornwall and Brittany, and religious pilgimage and growing cross-Channel trade ensured their perpetuation throughout this period. Although the Hundred Years War and the Wars of the Roses led to conflict and lawlessness on the high seas, with sometimes Cornishman pitted against Breton, the links remained remarkably close. This was partly because Brittany had been able to retain much of its independence (the Treaty of Union with France was not until 1532) and was keen to retain cordial relations, as far as was possible, with the English state. Many Bretons actually settled in Cornwall, and the extent to which they became ingrained in Cornish society is reflected even today in Cornish surnames of Breton origin such as Harvey, Tangye and Britton. Breton settlers were to be found in the west of Cornwall, where the Cornish language (so similar to their own) was strongest, in parishes such as St Ives, Towednack, Zennor and Lelant. In Constantine there were still nine Breton families resident as late as 1558. But there were also numerous Bretons in the east in maritime areas

The interior of Blisland church, much loved by Sir John Betjeman, conveys all the atmosphere of a medieval Cornish church.

The impressive church of St Neot, with it's incomparable stained glass windows.

such as Fowey, Polruan and East Looe; in the Hundreds of Trigg and West Wivel some seventy nine Bretons were registered in the mid-sixteenth century.

However, the intimacy (and legitimacy) of these Cornish-Breton contacts became difficult to sustain as the English and French states intruded further into the affairs of their peripheries in the sixteenth century. When there was war between France and England in the 1540s, Bretons in Cornwall faced with expulsion declared that they 'would rather die than go hence'.[74] And the Reformation served to make matters worse, traumatising Cornwall and, eventually, making Protestant Cornwall and Catholic Brittany mutually antagonistic. In a sense, this loss of intimacy between Cornwall and Brittany was symptomatic of the wider changes that were wrought in Cornwall (and in the relationship between *Anglia et Cornubia*) by the intrusion of the Tudor state, the subject of our next chapter.

Notes & References (Chapter 5).

1. R.R. Davies, 'The Peoples of Britain and Ireland, 1100-1400: Identities', in *Transactions of the Royal Historical Society*, sixth series, Vol.IV, Royal Historical Society, London, 1994, p.1.

2. Steven Ellis, 'Not Mere English: The British Perspective 1400-1650', *History Today*, December 1988.

3. Hugh Kearney, *The British Isles: A History of Four Nations*, Cambridge University Press, Cambridge, 1989, p.1.

4. Davies, 1994, p.1.

5. Davies, 1994, p.1.

6. Davies, 1994, p.18.

7. See John Hutchinson, *Modern Nationalism*, Fontana, London, 1994, p.26.

8. We ought not, for example, to forget the distinction between North and South within England; see Helen M.Jewell, *The North-South Divide: The Origins of Northern Consciousness in England*, Manchester University Press, Manchester, 1994.

9. Henry Jenner, *A Handbook of the Cornish Language*, David Nutt, London, 1904, p.xii; The Duchy of Cornwall, *Preliminary Statement Showing the Grounds on which is founded the Rights of the Duchy of Cornwall to the Tidal Estuaries, Foreshore, and Under-Sea Minerals within and around The Coast of the County of Cornwall*, Duchy of Cornwall, London, 1855, p.9.

10. Alan Kent, 'Art Thou of Cornish Crew? Shakespeare, Henry V and Cornish Identity', in Philip Payton (ed.), *Cornish Studies: Four*, University of Exeter Press, Exeter, 1996.

11. For example, see Graham Phillips and Martin Keatman, *King Arthur: The True Story*, Century, London, 1992.

12. C.A. Ralegh Radford, 'Glastonbury Abbey', in Geoffrey Ashe (ed.), *The Quest for Arthur's Britain*, Paladin, London, 1971, p.97.

13. F.E.Halliday, *A History of Cornwall*, Duckworth, London, 1959, p.82.

14. Radford, 1971, p.97.

15. Richard Carew, *The Survey of Cornwall*, ed. F.E.Halliday, Melrose, London, 1953, p.193.

16. A useful catalogue of 'Arthurian sites' in Cornwall is contained in Brenda Duxbury and Michael Williams, *King Arthur Country in Cornwall*, Bossiney Books, St Teath, 1979; see also R.J.Hutchings, *The King Arthur Illustrated Guide*, Dyllansow Truran, Redruth, 1983.

17. Cited in D.M. Thomas (ed.), *The Granite Kingdom: Poems of Cornwall*, Bradford Barton, Truro, 1970, p.24.

18. Geoffrey of Monmouth, *The History of the Kings of Britain*, ed. & trans. Lewis Thorpe, Guild Publishing, London, 1982, p.171.

19. Christopher Brooke, *The Saxon and Norman Kings*, Book Club Associates, London, 1978, p.185.

20. Geoffrey Ashe, *Camelot and the Vision of Albion*, Heinemann, London, 1971, pp.210-212.

21. R.R.Davies, 'The Peoples of Britain and Ireland, 1100-1400: II: Names, Boundaries and Regnal Solidarities', in *Transactions of the Royal Historical Society*, Sixth Series, V, Royal Historical Society/Cambridge University Press, Cambridge, 1995, p.4.

22. Linda Colley, *Britons: Forging the Nation, 1707-1837*, Pimlico, London, 1992.

23. Jon Stallworthy (ed.), *the Oxford Book of War Poetry*, Book Club Associates, London, 1995, p.66.

24. Colin Wilson, 'The Search for the Real Arthur', in Duxbury & Williams, 1979, p.100.

25. J. Markale, *Celtic Civilization*, Gordon & Cremonesi, London, 1978, p.210.

26. Cited in Ian Soulsby, *A History of Cornwall*, Phillimore, Chichester, 1986, p.52.

27. John Rowe, *The Hard-Rock Men: Cornish Immigrants and the North American Mining Frontier*, University of Liverpool Press, Liverpool, 1974, p.13.

28. The Duchy of Cornwall, *The Tidal Estuaries, Foreshore, and Under-Sea Minerals within and around The Coast of the County of Cornwall*, Duchy of Cornwall, London, 1857, p.58 (quoting Charter Roll 11, Edward III, n55), Appendix L.

29. A.L.Rowse, *The Little Land of Cornwall*, Alan Sutton, Gloucester, 1986, p.40; Crispin Gill (ed.), *The Duchy of Cornwall*, David and Charles, Newton Abbot, 1987, p.14.

30. Richard Pearse, *The Land Beside the Celtic Sea: Aspects of Cornwall's Past*, Dyllansow Truran, Redruth, 1983, p.51.

31. Julian Cornwall, *Revolt of the Peasantry 1549*, Routledge, London, 1977, p.42.

32. The Duchy of Cornwall, 1855, p.9.

33. The Duchy of Cornwall, 1855, pp.3, 7, 14.

34. John Hatcher, *Rural Economy and Society in the Duchy of Cornwall 1300-1500*, Cambridge University Press, Cambridge, 1970, p.258.

35. Rowse, 1986, p.41.

36. Soulsby, 1986, p.36.

37. Hatcher, 1970, p.52.

38. W.G.V.Balchin, *The Cornish Landscape*, Hodder and Stoughton, London, 1983, pp23-24.

39. Carew (Halliday), 1953, pp.135-136.

40. Richard Muir, *Reading the Celtic Landscapes*, Guild Publishing, London, 1988, p.88.

41. Balchin, 1983, p.120.

42. Robert R. Pennington, *Stannary Law: A History of the Mining Law of Cornwall and Devon*, David and Charles, Newton Abbot, 1973, p.13.

43. John Rowe, *Cornwall in the Age of the Industrial Revolution*, Liverpool University Press, Liverpool, 1953, repub. Cornish Hillside, St Austell, 1993, p.13; G.R.Lewis, *The Stannaries: A Study of Medieval Tin Miners of Cornwall and Devon*, 1908, repub. Bradford Barton, Truro, 1965, p.127.

44. Lewis, 1908 & 1965, p.39.

45. Duchy of Cornwall, 1857, Part II, Supplementary Appendix, p.16.

46. Kent, 1996.

47. Carew (Halliday), 1953, pp.145-147.

48. Halliday, 1959, p.148.

49. A.L.Rowse, *A Cornish Anthology*, Macmillan, London, 1969, p.114.

50. Kent, 1996.

51. cited in Ian Roy, 'Towards the Standing Army 1485-1660', in David Chandler (ed.), *The Oxford Illustrated History of the British Army*, Oxford University Press, Oxford, 1994, p.30.

52. A.L.Rowse, *The English Spirit: Essays in History and Literature*, Macmillan, London, (2nd ed.) 1945, pv.

53. D.C. Fowler, *John Trevisa*, Washington University Press, Washington DC, 1996.

54. *Old Cornwall*, Vol.VIII, No.5, Autumn 1975.

55. Mark Stoyle, '"Pagans or Paragons?": Images of the Cornish during the English Civil War', *The English Historical Review*, Vol.CXI, No.441, April 1996.

56. Hatcher, 1970, p.1.

57. Hatcher, 1970, p.2.

58. Kearney, 1989, p.105.

59. L.E. Elliott Binns, *Medieval Cornwall*, Methuen, London, 1955.

60. James Whetter, *The Bodrugans: A Study of a Cornish Medieval Knightly Family*, Lyfrow Trelyspen, St Austell, 1995, p.135.

61. Ken George, 'How Many People Spoke Cornish Traditionally?', *Cornish Studies*, 14, 1986.

62. N.J.A.Williams, *Cornish Today*, Kernewek dre Lyther, Sutton Coldfield, 1995, pp.77-80.

63. an excellent overview of the Cornish language in this period is provided in Crysten Fydge, *The Life of Cornish*, Dyllansow Truran, Redruth, 1982; see also Peter Berresford Ellis, *the Story of the Cornish Language*, Tor Mark Press, Truro, 1970, and Peter Berresford Ellis, *The Cornish Language and Its Literature*, Routledge, London, 1974.

64. James Whetter, *The History of Gorran Haven, Part 1: 0-1800 AD*, Lyfrow Trelyspen, St Austell, 1991, p.11 and pp.15-16.

65. cited in Fudge, 1982, p.25.

66. James Whetter, *The History of Glasney College*, Tabb House, Padstow, 1988.

67. Brian Murdoch, *Cornish Literature*, Brewer, Cambridge, 1993, p.73; for an excellent study of the *Ordinalia* see, Jane A.Bakere, *The Cornish Ordinalia: A Critical Study*, University of Wales Press, Cardiff, 1980.

68. Murdoch, 1993, pp.79-80.

69. Murdoch, 1993, p.87.

70. For example, see Laura Rowe, *Granite Crosses of West Cornwall*, Bradford Barton, Truro, 1973, and Andrew Langdon, *Stone Crosses in North Cornwall*, Federation of Old Cornwall Societies, 1992.

71. Nicholas Orme (ed.), *Nicholas Roscarrock's Lives of the Saints: Cornwall and Devon*, Devon and Cornwall Record Society, Exeter, 1993, p.35.

72. Richard Muir, 1985, p.91.

73. Joanna Mattingly, 'A Note on Cornish-Breton Links', *Institute of Cornish Studies Associates' Newsletter*, 2nd series, No.4, May 1995.

74. Soulsby, 1986, p.55.

CHAPTER 6

'We Utterly Refuse This New English

CORNWALL

'We utterly refuse ... this new English'

Returning from the safety of still-independent Brittany, landing in Wales, and proclaiming his Welshness and his descent from Arthur, Henry Tudor fought at Bosworth Field in 1485 under the standard of the Welsh dragon and with Cornishmen at his side. As we saw in Chapter Five, Cornwall was generally Lancastrian in sympathy (despite the exploits of Henry Bodrugan), and Henry Tudor had already been declared Henry VII at Bodmin. And there was an older history of Cornish service to the Lancastrian cause; John Trevelyan had been a household official at Henry VI's court, and for his pains had drawn the ire of Henry's critics:

> The Cornish chough oft with his train [deceit]
> Hath made our eagle [the king] blind.[1]

And yet, in little over a decade, the Cornwall that had rallied to Henry Tudor's cause was in open revolt and posing what was perhaps the most significant political-military threat to his regime. What had happened in those intervening years? In one sense, very little, for the lawless independence that had characterised Cornwall during the Wars of the Roses continued into Henry VII's reign. From that perspective, the two Cornish rebellions of 1497 were part of an established pattern of behaviour, albeit at a more serious and more organised level. But if Cornish behaviour had altered little, the regime established by Henry VII heralded what historians have called 'the Tudor revolution in government',[2] and in Cornwall its impact was felt early on. From this second perspective, Cornwall and the Tudors were on an inevitable collision course, the Cornish habit of independent action (enshrined as it was constitutionally in the Duchy and the Stannaries) increasingly at odds with the demands of Tudor centralism.

This conflict, and its 'inevitability', has a certain poignancy—not just because the Cornish had in the main supported the Tudors but because the Tudor claim to Celtic-Arthurian legitimacy that had wooed the Cornish and Welsh was in fact the paradoxical British project which disguised the centralising, expansionist designs of the English state behind the rhetoric of Arthur-returned and Britain-regained. For Cornwall, it took just a decade for the reality to strike home. As A. L. Rowse has written:

> From being a far-away, insignificant corner of the land, sunk in its dream of its Celtic past, with its own inner life of legends and superstitions and fears, its memories of Arthur and Mark and Tristan, lapped in religion and the cult of the saints, it was forced in the course of the Elizabethan age into the front-line of the great sea- struggle with Spain. Inevitably the small backward-looking society struggled against the process: the Rebellions of 1497 and 1549 were to Cornwall what the '15 and '45 were to the Highlands.[3]

According to Dr Rowse, Tudor England was '. . . the most taut and vigorous national society in Europe',[4] driven by the twin imperatives of centralism and expansion. The Tudors moved swiftly to strengthen their personal power and their instruments of government, a process which involved both military and political action against their peripheries (Cornwall, Wales, Ireland, the North and the Borders) together with a more systematic and controlled system of taxation and, eventually, the Reformation. This was part of the broader

> . . . expansion of that society, both by the state and by individual enterprise, first into the margins of backward societies at home—Cornwall, Wales, the Borders, with the sweep of a sickle on the map; into Ireland, where the process involved conquest and colonisation; then across the oceans, to our first contacts with Russia, the Canadian North . . . the colonisation of North America.[5]

However, Christopher Haigh and other 'revisionist' historians have downplayed the impact of Henry Tudor's victory at Bosworth Field in 1485, arguing that Henry VII and indeed Henry VIII ruled in much the same manner as their predecessors Edward IV and Richard III—managing their territories through alliances with local elites.[6] According to these revisionists, there was no major shift in the style of government until as late as the 1530s. It was only then, it is argued, that Parliament began to legislate on a whole range of new issues, including price controls and a plan to introduce a state-wide system of poor relief. It was only with the re-organisation of the administration of Wales (the Act of Union of 1536) and the English regions, together with the enforcement of the Reformation, that 'the Tudor revolution in government' was really underway. However, there is an admission that, once this revolution was in progress, the Tudor state '. . . had arrogated to itself the power to determine, in theory, a range of issues from the nature of salvation to the price of beef, on a scale so far unprecedented'.[7] There is also the admission that this process had already overreached itself by the 1550s (the third Cornish rebellion was in 1549), with the second half of the sixteenth century given over to consolidation rather than further 'revolution'.

Moreover, it must be said that Haigh's analysis seems unduly Anglocentric (or rather London-centric), for not only does it ignore (or at least underestimate) the impact and consequences of early Tudor intervention in Cornwall, but also it fails to appreciate the considerable upheaval in the North of England in the 1480s. Helen Jewell provides a corrective when she indicates that Henry's victory was '. . . followed immediately by a southern offensive [against the North]. . . when Henry defeated Richard at Bosworth in 1485 a dangerous northern independence was averted'.[8] Nonetheless, there were Northern risings in 1486, 1487 and 1489. In an ironic anticipation of Cornwall's rebellion in 1497, in 1489 Yorkshire rose when the people of that county refused to pay taxes in support of intervention in Brittany. The Tudor response was to engineer the political isolation of the old Northern families (usually by wooing other local gentry direct into Crown service) and to tighten the institutional grip on the North. The Council of the North had its origins in Richard of Gloucester's lieutenancy of the North from 1482, instituted as a means of copying the management of the Welsh borders by the Council of the Marches and the Prince of Wales. The lieutenancy continued in various guises until formalised as the king's Council in the North Parts in 1530.[9]

Tremodrett (spelt today with the double 't'), the scene of the raid in 1490 on the tin-works of Peter Edgcumbe, an act of lawlessness typical of the unrest that characterised late fifteenth-century Cornwall.

This unrest in the North was mirrored in Cornwall.[10] Cornish ships engaged in open piracy, as in 1486 when two Hamburg ships, the *Grasinius* and the *Marie* were seized off the coast of Cornwall, taken into Fowey and then plundered. In the same year the *Anne* of Fowey captured a Breton ship bound for Ireland with a valuable cargo of wheat, wine, salt, and mercury. In the 1490s disturbances in Cornwall were commonplace, the local lesser gentry often implicated in robberies and burglaries which on occasions involved armed bands several hundred strong. The tin-works of Peter Edgcumbe at Tremodret on Goss Moor, for example, were attacked in 1490 by a band of forty men under the leadership of three gentlemen, John Roche, Peter Roche and Walter Tripkimyn. They stole twenty-eight feet of black tin to the value of fourteen marks. Three years later they were back, carrying off seventeen feet of black tin worth £20 6s 8d.

On 10 July 1492 a band of 200 men led by a yeoman and five tinners attacked the Franciscan friary at Bodmin, apparently in a dispute over tin-rights. In 1493 Stephen Tregasow, gentleman, with two yeomen and a 'holy-water clerk' (one Philip Wallshe of Probus) were accused of stealing six silver chalices worth £40, belonging to the parishioners of Lanreath. John and Oliver Calwodeley, with a band of supporters, attacked John Tresythney and John Butler at Padstow on Thursday after Michaelmas 1495 and carried them off to Blisland, where they were held for four days. Even more extraordinary, twenty-six complaints were made against Roger Whalley, a yeoman of Park, near Egloshayle, for offences against his neighbours. These included driving off their cattle, killing their sheep, refusing to pay tithes, and assaulting John Trenowith (Whalley beat Trenowith's wife and shot at his windows)! All these incidents are evidence of a continuing unrest in Cornwall, and it is significant that amongst the names of those implicated in the risings of 1497 are Calwodeley, Tresythney and Roger Whalley.

As in the North of England, the Tudors wooed elements of the local gentry, a task made easier given that many of the Cornish gentry had in any case supported the Lancastrian side. Richard Edgcumbe of Cotehele,

Although no longer the Cornish capital in anything but name, Bodmin retains a quiet dignity. In earlier times the town was an important focus of Cornish resistance to the intrusions of the Tudor State.

knighted after Bosworth Field, at last got his revenge against Henry Bodrugan. A writ for Bodrugan's arrest was issued in February 1487 and, in a strange echo of Edgcumbe's dramatic escape from Bodrugan on the banks of the Tamar, Richard Edgcumbe chased Henry Bodrugan from his home (Bodrugan) near Gorran to a spot on the cliffs between Gorran Haven and Mevagissey. According to the story, Henry leapt from the cliff at this point (the location is still called Bodrugan's Leap), landing on a small grassy island whence a waiting boat took him into exile abroad.

Richard Edgcumbe was rewarded for his loyal services with a diplomatic career which saw him undertake important missions to Ireland, Scotland and Brittany. He negotiated a seven-year peace with the Scots, and in Ireland extracted from the Earl of Kildare and the Irish Lords an oath of allegiance to Henry VII. In February 1489, as the French pressed home their attacks against the Bretons, Edgcumbe was in Brittany to negotiate a treaty. He was successful, promising English support for Brittany against the French, the price of which was English control over Breton foreign policy and the marriage of Anne, Duchess of Brittany. Edgcumbe himself died abroad, and was buried at Morlaix in September 1489. Henry VII had, of course, spent the greater part of his earlier life in Brittany. His support for the Bretons may have reflected a genuine sympathy (bolstered by his Celtic-Arthurian pretensions) but it also fitted his expansionist objectives. It is interesting, and with the benefit of hindsight, ironic, that a Cornishman, Peter Edgcumbe, should have played such a major role in the diplomatic construction of the Tudor's 'British project'. It does, however, tell us something more about the relationship between *Anglia et Cornubia*.

Henry VII, indeed, continued to play the 'Cornish card'. When his first son was born in 1486, he named him Arthur—destined, of course, (if fate were kind) to become in the fullness of time *King Arthur*, but from the very moment of his birth, Duke of Cornwall. A skilful diplomatic coup, conducted by another Cornishman, Sir Richard Nanfan, in 1489 secured the betrothal of the young Arthur to the infant Katherine of Aragon. In 1489 Nanfan was Sheriff of Cornwall, and in the preceding year he had been granted the Cornish manors of Blisland, Carnanton and Helstonbury. Arthur and Katherine were married in 1501, when they were sixteen and fifteen respectively, but in the following year Arthur died. Prospects for a new Arthurian era were dashed but, in a further triumph of diplomatic and legal creativity, the second-born son Henry (later Henry VIII) was instead betrothed to Katherine and also became Duke of Cornwall.

Meanwhile, and in a further echo of the pacification of the North, Henry VII had used the institution of the Duchy of Cornwall as a means of rewarding and thus winning the further loyalty of his supporters. Sir Richard Willoughby became Receiver of the Duchy. Sir John Halliwell became Steward, and John Upcote became captain of Tintagel Castle and bailiff of the manor of Helston. James Bonython was made Surveyor of Customs in Cornwall and Devon. William Treffry was made Controller of the tin coinage of the Stannaries of Cornwall and Devon, and was appointed Keeper of the Stannary Gaol at Lostwithiel. He also became an usher of the King's Chamber and was given the lucrative position of Surveyor of Customs within the City of London. (A. L. Rowse notes that William Treffry was a kind, generous and conscientious man. He died without children of his own and, as well as providing for his nephews, left money for the poor of Fowey and neighbourhood, horses for his menservants, and dowers for his maidservants).

The decade after Bosworth Field then, had witnessed within Cornwall a continuing lawless independence. But Henry VII had worked hard to accommodate the Cornish; using the Duchy of Cornwall to reward his supporters, co-opting the Cornish gentry in his 'British project' and other diplomatic endeavours, even naming the new Duke of Cornwall *Arthur*. However, the wooing of the gentry seems not to have won the affection of the lower orders of society. In Wales, the cultural gulf between an increasingly Anglicised gentry and the general populace did not occur until after 1660,[11] but in Cornwall the process is likely to have begun much earlier.

This was evidenced in the life of John Trevisa (glimpsed in Chapter 5), and in the intimate connection between Henry VII and his supporters such as Richard Edgcumbe, Richard Nanfan and William Treffry. The diary of William Carnsew of Bokelly, near St Kew, compiled in the 1570s, reveals a country gentleman steeped in the daily life of his native heath, but it also illuminates a politically-aware and well-informed observer of events on the wider stage. As well as following closely the intense debate between the religious factions of the time, Carnsew took a keen interest in international affairs, looking out beyond Cornwall to England and Europe. All manner of rumours reached him in his North Cornwall fastness, and he recorded them dutifully (in English) in his diary—penning in the margin 'A lie' if subsequently they were shown to be untrue. Thus:

> The Turk hath summoned Vienna, in Austria. *A lie* ... The Saracens took Cadiz in Spain in January, as I heard. *A lie* ... The King of Spain loseth in Barbary daily . . . It was told me in March that the great Turk was dead, and that Lord John d'Austria is said to be in Flanders . . . and he was in Paris also . . . .[12]

This 'man of the world' ambience was reflected even more strongly in Richard Carew's *Survey of Cornwall* of 1602, where Carew proudly exhibited his Cornishness and yet also wrote *about* the Cornish as any modern 'Englishman' of the Renaissance might, writing both literally and culturally from the margins of Cornwall and Cornish society. By the time of Carnsew and Carew, there was already an emerging gulf between gentry and people (Carew's knowledge of the Cornish language was virtually non-existent), and we may speculate that even in the early Tudor period this process was underway. Certainly, the urbanity of a Carnsew or a Carew contrasts strongly with the reputation enjoyed by the ordinary Cornish folk. When the Venetian Ambassador to Castille was in Cornwall for a week in 1506, he wrote that 'We are in a very wild place which no human being ever visits, in the midst of a most barbarous race, so different in language and custom from Londoners and the rest of England that they are as unintelligible to these last as to the Venetians'.[13]

And, as we have seen, there was considerable popular unrest in Cornwall in this period; much of which seems to have been focused on the tin industry. In 1586 one observer was to describe the Cornish tinners as 'so rough and mutinous a multitude, 10,000 or 12,000 the most strong men in England',[14] and in the 1480s and 1490s their standard of living was in decline. The annual yield of tin had fallen from 1,600 thousand-weight in 1400 to 800 thousand-weight in 1455, and did not rise much above 1,000 until 1496. This decline may have reflected the political dislocation of significant parts of the fifteenth century but more likely it represented the exhaustion of easily accessed tin-streams at a time when new technologies were not fully applied in the exploitation of more difficult deposits.

Be that as it may, the tinners were not happy. And, accustomed as they were to the independence and freedom of action lent by their presumed economic importance and the institutions of the Stannaries, they reacted angrily when in 1495-96 the Council of Prince Arthur, Duke of Cornwall, announced new, stricter rules governing the recording of tin bounds and blowing houses and the marking of tin ingots. As Professor Pennington has observed, '. . . such rules appealed little to the conservative and independent Cornish spirit'.[15] Indeed, the new regulations were generally ignored, an affront to the authority of the Duke which led to Henry VII's angry confiscation of the Stannary charters and thus the suspension of Stannary government in Cornwall. The historic accommodation of Cornwall was apparently breaking down. The stage was set for confrontation.[16]

St Keverne on the Lizard peninsula, the crucible of rebellion in 1497 and 15548-49. Michael Joseph *An Gof*,'The Smith', who hailed from St Keverne might usefully be compared to Scotland's William Wallace—he was the 'Cornish Braveheart'.

The real precipitating factor in this confrontation, however, was not the stifling of Stannary independence but new taxes to finance a war against Scotland. The Scots were supporting the claims of Perkin Warbeck, a pretender to the English throne, and were raiding all along the Border. In January 1497, Parliament voted heavy taxes to pay for Henry's planned reprisals. In Cornwall, four commissioners were appointed to assess the taxes: John Arundell, Richard Flamank, John Trevenor and Thomas Erisey. Immediately, the people began to complain about the new taxes. As the contemporary observer Francis Bacon put it:

> For no sooner began the subsidy to be levied in Cornwall, but the people there began to grudge and murmur. The Cornish being a race of men stout of stomach, mighty of body and limb, and that lived hardly in a barren country, and many of them could for a need live under ground that were Tinners.[17]

The first explicit talk of resistance was in the remote parish of St Keverne on the Lizard peninsula. Although not a traditional tin mining district, it was in the Cornish-speaking heartland and, perhaps significantly, it was within the sphere of Sir John Oby, Provost of Glasney College, who was notorious for his zealous behaviour as tax collector and could be expected to enforce the new tax levy with enthusiasm. Whatever the case, the St Keverne folk found a popular and outspoken leader in Michael Joseph *An Gof* ('The Smith'), the local blacksmith who has given his name to the first—or 'An Gof'— Cornish rebellion of 1497.

Thereafter, resentment spread rapidly throughout Cornwall, with the notion of resistance finding ready support amongst the yeomen and lesser gentry. In the far-west, John Trevysall of Madron and William Antron (whose mother was a sister of the anti-Lancastrian Henry Bodrugan) came forward as leaders. So too did John Rosewarne of Rosewarne (near Camborne), and in mid-Cornwall there was Ralph Retallack of St Columb, Richard Borlase of St Wenn, and Thomas Polgrene of Polgrene. In the east, on the border with England, were John Allen and William Ham of Stoke Climsland. In Bodmin, Thomas Flamank, a clever and persuasive lawyer, emerged as the intellectual leader of the rebellion. His father was none other than Richard Flamank of Boscarne, one of the recently-appointed tax commissioners, and his father-in-law was a Justice of the Peace, John Trelawny. Nonetheless, Thomas Flamank took a firm stand, arguing that it was illegal to tax the Cornish for the defence of the Border against Scotland. That defence was properly the responsibility of the people who lived there—

as it had been since time immemorial.

The king's historian, Polydore Virgil, gives us a contemporary view of the circumstances that led to the rising. As he explained in his *Anglica Historia*:

> For the men of Cornwall, who live in a part of the island as small in area as it is poor in resources, began to complain that they could not carry the burden of taxation imposed for the Scottish war. First, they accused the king, grumbling at the cruelty and malice of counsellors: then they began to get completely out of hand, threatening the authors of this great oppression with death, and daring to seek them out for punishment.[18]

The suggestion of economic depression and poverty conveyed by Virgil is further elaborated in his description of the popular response to the posturings of Michael Joseph *An Gof* and Thomas Flamank:

> While the people were thus in a ferment, two men out of the scum of the people, namely Thomas Flammock (sic), a lawyer, and Michael Joseph, a blacksmith, two bold rascals, put themselves at the head of the rising. When they saw that the mob was aroused they kept shouting that it was a scandalous crime that the king in order to make a small expedition against the Scots, should burden the wretched men of Cornwall, who either cultivated a barren soil, or with difficulty sought a living by digging tin . . . .[19]

Armed, as Bacon put it, '. . . with bows and arrows and bills, and such other weapons of rude and country people',[20] the impromptu Cornish army of tinners, yeomen and lesser gentry marched across the Tamar. Resisting the temptation to loot and slaughter, they made their way without violence to Wells in Somerset where they were joined by an important recruit, James, Lord Audley, a malcontent disappointed that he had been passed over by the king in the distribution of his royal favours. With Audley at their head, the Cornish marched on to Salisbury, and from there to Winchester, and out across Hampshire and Surrey, deep into the heart of southern England. Thus far they had met no resistance, the determination and speed of their expedition having perhaps caught Henry VII by surprise (engrossed as he was in the Scottish problem). However, Henry had raised a well-equipped army of 8,000 strong under the command of Lord Daubeney, earmarked for action against the Scots. He decided to keep this powerful force in London, to await the arrival of the Cornish.

On 13 June 1497 Lord Daubeney's army, fresh and well-provisioned and now swollen to perhaps some 10,000 men, took up position on Hounslow Heath. The next day the Cornish were at Guildford where, upon Gill Hill, the first action of the An Gof rebellion took place. It seems to have been a light skirmish, resulting in the capture of two Cornish spearmen who were brought before Daubeney. Daubeney deployed his army in order of battle on St George's Field, to protect London, while the Cornish moved into Sussex. The King, meanwhile, had been joined by the nobility of the surrounding counties, increasing his forces to some 25,000 men, a safe numerical superiority over the estimated 15,000 Cornish. The Cornish ventured into Kent, in the forlorn hope that the notoriously rebellious men of Kent might join them (shades of Wat Tyler and Jack Cade), and on 16 June they encamped upon Blackheath—overlooking London and directly threatening the English military and political establishment at its heart in Greenwich Palace. This was the moment of crisis for Henry VII, probably the most dangerous day of his reign, but already there were signs that the rebels' resolve was weakening, with individuals slipping away in the hope of escape or pardon.

Although Michael Joseph *An Gof* tried his best to boost morale in the Cornish camp, many of the rebels stole away overnight, so that in the morning only some eight to ten thousand remained upon the heath. The next night both sides prepared for battle, and the Cornish placed the few guns they had, together with archers, at Deptford Strand to intercept the passage of the river. This strategy 'wrought wonders' during the following morning, according to one contemporary observer, the reputation of Cornish archery from the days of Agincourt no doubt striking apprehension if not outright fear in the King's army. But, as elsewhere on the battlefield, the rebel leaders had not planned in detail or provided support in depth. In his contemporary account, though probably exaggerating the King's losses, Bacon noted that 'On the King's part there died, about 300, most of them shot with arrows, which were reported to be of the length of a tailor's yard, so strong and mighty a bow the Cornishmen were said to draw',[21]but the reality was that the Cornish were unable to exploit this one military advantage. With no support for the archers, the bridge at Deptford was quickly taken.

Daubeney charged onto the heath at the head of his men, so rapidly that he found himself alone amongst the rebels. Curiously, the Cornish left him unharmed, a strange deference or hesitancy overtaking them which may have reflected the numbness of battle or perhaps the dread realisation that already all was lost, a paralysis similar to that which overcame the Young Pretender at Culloden Moor in 1746. As one contemporary account put it, '. . . whether it were for fear or for hope of favour, they let him go at liberty without any hurt or detriment'.[22] Regaining his ranks, Daubeney pressed home the advantage. Poorly led without an adequate battle plan, and with no artillery and no cavalry, the Cornish were soon put to flight. Bacon thought that some 2,000 rebels were slain in the rout but A. L. Rowse's estimates are lighter. He considers that some 200 Cornish were killed, while Henry VII's losses were few beyond the eight (not 300) killed by the archers at Deptford Strand.

Audley and Flamank were captured on the battlefield, and *An Gof* was taken as he fled to the Friar's Church in Greenwich. Henry VII rode to Blackheath, where he dubbed a score or more knights for their services, and in the afternoon he passed into the City. Soon after there followed '. . . riding behind a yeoman of the guard, the Smith [*An Gof*], being clad in a jacket of white and green of the King's colours and held as good countenance and spake as boldly to the people as he had been at his liberty'.[23] On 26 June *An Gof* and Flamank were sentenced in the White Hall at Westminster. On the following day, 27 June 1497, they were drawn on hurdles from the Tower to Tyburn where, in accordance with the barbaric treatment meted out to common traitors in those days, they were hanged, drawn and quartered (Audley, as a peer, was spared this and was beheaded at the Tower). It is said that as *An Gof* was dragged to Tyburn on his hurdle, he boasted that '. . . he should have a name perpetual, and a fame permanent and immortal'.[24] Indeed, he has.

Although Henry VII lost no time in his despatch of the three ringleaders, he was remarkably sparing of blood in his dealings with the other rebels. He may, indeed, have felt a bond of 'Celtic sympathy', with his Welsh and Breton connections, his 'descent from Arthur', his Cornish colleagues, and, as Bacon suggests, a genuine compassion:

> . . . the King did satisfy himself with the lives of only three offenders for the expiation of this great rebellion . . . Whether it were that the King put to account the men that were slain in the field, or that he was not willing to be severe in a popular cause, or that the harmless behaviour of this people that came from the west of England to the east without mischief almost, or spoil of the country, did somewhat mollify and move him to compassion: or lastly that he made a great difference between people that rebel upon wantonness and them that did rebel upon want.[25]

Vergil agreed that Henry VII took pity on the poor Cornishmen and '. . . had their lives spared out of consideration of their rustic simplicity'. However, he also suggested a deeper and more political reason for Henry's restraint:

> . . . the king would have ordered that the dismembered corpses of Thomas Flammock (sic) and Michael Joseph should be displayed in various places throughout Cornwall, in order that the penalties of treason might be widely known and seen: but when he heard that those who had stayed at home were not cowed by the catastrophe that had befallen their fellows, but were still keen to begin a rebellion if they were roused in any way, Henry changed his mind for fear he might embarrass himself with even greater burdens at a time when he considered it enough to end civil strife . . . .[26]

This leniency was in vain, however, because Cornwall was still in uproar, and because Perkin Warbeck—the pretender whose Scottish support had precipitated the crisis in the first place—had seen the potential of Cornish unrest. Seizing the opportunity, Warbeck made his way from Scotland to Cornwall via Ireland, arriving with a couple of hundred supporters at Whitsand Bay, near Land's End, on 7 September 1497. Leaving his wife in the safety of St Michael's Mount, he determined upon an early attack on Exeter and was proclaimed Richard IV at Bodmin (the chief town of Cornwall but also Flamank's former home). The second Cornish rising of 1497 was underway.

Although the grander families steered clear of Warbeck, he gathered round him the lesser gentry and yeomen who formed the backbone of Cornwall and represented the groundswell of Cornish opinion against Henry VII. Amongst them were John Nankivell of St Mawgan, Walter Tripcony and John Tregennow of St Columb, Nicholas Polkinghorne of Gwinear, Humphry Calwodeley of Helland, Otes Philip of Polwhele, Thomas Gosworthdogga of Crowan, and John Trehanneck of St Teath. However, their support for Warbeck was not an eleventh hour conversion to this pretended remnant of the Yorkist cause (Otes Philip, for one, had suffered before at the hands of the Yorkist Henry Bodrugan). Rather, they used Warbeck as a focus and as a catalyst in their desire to regroup after the disaster of Blackheath. To that extent, the Warbeck rising was really the second act of the 'An Gof' rebellion.

By 17 September, Warbeck was at Exeter with a Cornish army some 6,000 strong. He demanded the city's surrender but the gates were closed against him. After a brief attempt against the North Gate, the Cornish attacked East Gate in strength and broke through, probing as far as Castle Street before meeting stiff resistance from reinforcements hurriedly rushed to the scene. Little by little the Cornish were pushed back, out of the city. Next day they renewed their attacks but this time without success, although as ever the Cornish archers caused distress—not least when Exeter's chief defender, the Earl of Devon, was struck in the arm by an arrow. In a change of plan, Warbeck decided to leave Exeter and press on eastwards to Taunton. In a grisly aside, which shows that the Cornish were still motivated by outrage against the Scottish tax rather than love for Warbeck, it was recorded that as the rebels lay in Somerset:

> . . . a rebel and rover named James . . . took the provost of Penrhyn [sic, i.e. Glasney], and so brought him unto the forsaid town of Taunton, and there tyrannously dismembered him in the market place, and after shewed unto the people that he was one of the chief procurers and occasioners of the rebellion of the Cornish men by reason that he, being admitted a commissioner in those parts, levied of them much more money than came into the King's use, which caused great murmur and grudge among the commons towards the King, and lastly rebellion as after ensued.[27]

By this time, however, Henry VII was already moving against the rebels. He sent Daubeney forward to engage the Cornish but when it was reported that Daubeney's scouts were already at Glastonbury, Warbeck's nerve failed him and he deserted his army. He was soon captured at Beaulieu, on the south coast of England, and was later kept at court as a curio (and for his own safety, the Milanese envoy observing that 'it was necessary to guard him well, in order that the men of Cornwall may not murder him'), until, involved in further indiscretions, he was finally executed. Henry himself reached Taunton on 4 October, receiving the surrender of those Cornish who remained there, and went on to Exeter where a host of Cornish prisoners with halters around their necks were brought before him. He spoke to the crowd, pardoning the rebels for their actions, at which point the prisoners threw their halters in the air and cheered 'God save the King!'

Indeed, as earlier in the year, Henry VII proved remarkably sparing of blood in seeking retribution. The chief ringleaders were executed but for the rest, Henry was satisfied with a rigorous programme of fines which, as well as bringing a heavy financial punishment upon Cornwall, would also help to fill his coffers. According to A. L. Rowse, the extent of the fines levied against Cornwall meant that '. . . the Cornish were not only defeated but humiliated',[28]adding further to the dire economic situation which Cornwall found itself in at the end of the fifteenth century.

John Pendyne of Pendeen, near St Just-in-Penwith, was fined £40 for 'the unnatural rebellion by him and others committed and done against our sovereign lord the King as well with the smith who named himself the Captain of Cornwall as with Perkin Warbeck'.[29] Thomas Tregos of St Anthony and Thomas Budockshide of Budock paid a fine of ten marks for Master Nicholas Wyse, vicar of Constantine; Master Thomas Allen, vicar of Newlyn, paid £20; Nicholas Enys of Luxulyan paid eight marks for Remfry Enys and William Penrose; and Nicholas Enys and William Trewynnard paid

Today Constantine is peace and tranquillity but in 1497 and 1548-49 it was a hot-bed of Cornish rebellion. In later centuries it boasted tin and copper mines, and numerous granite quarries.

£30 for John Tresynny of Penryn.(This Tresynny had been one of *An Gof's* captains at Blackheath and there is an amusing story that, back in Cornwall at Padstow, he had beaten-up the notorious Roger Whalley of Egloshayle—who had also been at Blackheath—before the two of them had gone off to Whitsand Bay to meet Warbeck!). Other fines were exacted on a parish-by-parish basis, so that Breage paid four marks, Illogan three marks, Grade forty shillings, St Stephen-in-Brannel four marks, Lawhitton four marks, Redruth £4, Camborne £4, Wendron forty shillings, St Agnes five marks, and so on.

It is tempting to see Cornwall in the aftermath of 1497 as both broke and broken, overtaken by poverty and cowed-down in the face of the Tudor regime. Rowse considers that 'exhaustion kept the county quiet for half a century',[30] while Julian Cornwall agrees that 'After 1497 Cornwall retreated into quiescence for another 50 years'.[31] However, it is difficult to gauge with certainty the mood of the Cornish in the years after the 'An Gof' and Warbeck risings. They may, indeed, have retreated into introspective isolation, licking their wounds (financial as well as physical) and turning their backs on England until the next great intrusion by the Tudor state in 1549 demanded their attention once again. There is, however, evidence, circumstantial but compelling, to suggest that in fact the Cornish remained resentful and potentially rebellious, a restlessness that required attention and appeasement.[32]

What one may term anti-English sentiment was demonstrated throughout the subsequent period, Norden writing in the reign of Elizabeth that the Cornish '. . . seem . . . yet to retain a kind of concealed envy against the English, whom they yet affect with a desire of revenge for their fathers' sakes, by whom their fathers received the repulse'.[33] Similarly, Richard Carew noted that enquiries from visiting Englishmen would frequently be rebuffed with the terse retort '*meea navidna cowzasawzneck*' (I will not speak English):

> One point of their former roughness some of the western people do yet retain, and therethrough in some measure verify that testimony which Matthew of Westminster giveth of them together with the Welsh, their ancient countrymen, namely, how fostering a fresh memory of their expulsion long ago by the English, they second the same with a bitter repining at their fellowship; and this the worst sort express in combining against and working them all the shrewd turns which with hope of impunity they can devise.[34]

Moreover, it must be observed that in the immediate aftermath of 1497 Henry VII treated Cornwall with a leniency that was not characteristic of the era or of the Tudor regime. This may have reflected personal compassion, as Bacon suggested, but a more likely explanation (as per Virgil) is that Henry VII was well aware that the Cornish were 'not yet cowed by catastrophe' and required careful treatment. The pacification of Cornwall would not be easy. It may be significant, for example, that, despite the initial rigour of the post-1497 fines and attainders (outlawing), by 1500 the process was being reversed. Indeed, as early as 1500 William Barrett of Tregarne (Flamank's brother-in-law) had been pardoned for his part in the rebellions, and in 1506 there was a spate of reversals of attainder. James Tripcony (son and heir of Walter Tripcony, who was apparently executed after 1497) received the property of his father, as did William Brabyn of St Mabyn (son of the late John Brabyn). Other reversals of attainder in that year included those

The granite face of contemporary Helston conveys something of the gritty independence which made the town a focus of rebellion in 1548 and 1549.

relating to Thomas Polgrene of Polgrene, Thomas Gosworthdogga of Crowan, Nicholas Polkinghorne, John Trehannek, and John Tregennow. The property of William Antron of Antron (who had been MP for Helston in 1491-92 and was executed after 1497) was restored to his son Richard in 1512.

Equally significant was Henry VII's Charter of Pardon of 1508, a move clearly designed to win the pacification and renewed accommodation of Cornwall by not only restoring the Stannaries (on the payment of a fine of £1,000; how typical of Henry!) but also through enhancing the constitutional status of the Stannary Parliament. Both the privileges of the tinners and the legislative capacity of the Parliament were extended, providing a curious contrast with the general Tudor concern to centralise government and discourage local usage. Coming so soon after the crisis of 1497, this must be seen as a deliberate strategy to restore the constitutional accommodation of Cornwall. The Charter of Pardon extended the definition of tinner (and thus the jurisdiction of Stannary Law) to include almost anyone connected in one way or another with the tin trade, not merely the extractive process itself.

The extension of the Stannary Parliament's legislative powers was even more significant. The Charter of Pardon of 1508 confirmed the establishment of a Parliament of twenty-four Stannators (or Members of Parliament), the Mayors and Councils of the Stannary Towns (Lostwithiel, Truro, Launceston and Helston) having the right to nominate six each. The Parliament thus constituted was afforded the right to allow or disallow '. . . any statute, act, ordinance, provision, restraint, or proclamation . . . made by the King, his heirs, successors, or the Prince of Wales, Duke of Cornwall, or their Council . . . to the prejudice of any tinner, or any other person having to do with black or white tin'.[35] It was this right of veto that lent the Parliament its ultimate power, and which gave it the Westminster-like characteristics noted by Lewis and the ambience of territorial semi-independence emphasised by John Rowe.[36] The Charter of Pardon of 1508 was, therefore, a powerful reaffirmation of Cornwall's distinctive place within the state. Indeed, this distinctive position was shortly to be reflected in the Coronation procession of Henry VIII in 1509 when there were:

> . . . the nine children of honour, upon great coursers [horses], apparelled on their bodies in blue velvet, powdered with fleur de lys of gold, and chains of goldsmith's work, every one of their horses trapped with a trapper of the king's title, as of England, and France, Gascony, Guienne, Normandy, Anjou, Cornwall, Wales, Ireland, wrought upon velvets with embroidery and goldsmith's worth (sic).[37]

In Cornwall itself, there was certainly evidence that such accommodation was necessary and that the Cornish were not yet sufficiently appeased. For example, the unflattering gargoyle representations of Henry VII and his wife, Elizabeth of York, on the late fifteenth-century church-tower of Uny-Redruth are probably a good (and rather bold) indication of how the Tudor regime was viewed in Cornwall at the time.[38] More substantial was the evidence of the Cornish miracle play *Beunans Meriasek* (the Life of St Meriasek), written c1500 and no doubt first performed during the era under discussion.

Although written in the Cornish language and focused upon the district of Camborne, celebrating a saint with a cult in both Cornwall and Brittany,

Beunans Meriasek has been seen traditionally as very much a standard late medieval *vita*, composed in the wider tradition of European miracle plays, with the aim of asserting the fundamental tenets of late medieval Christendom. The play as it has survived consists of three distinct components or stories, woven together. Although scholars have tended to view the construction as disharmonious, strands of continuity and meaning can be discerned. Professor Brian Murdoch believes that the play dwells upon three grand themes: the relationship between Church and State; the combating of evil and the conversion of unbelievers; and the role of the Saints, clergy and Virgin Mary as intercessors. The duty of the State is to defend the Church and to avenge its representatives. In *Beunans Meriasek*, argues Brian Murdoch, the victory of the virtuous Duke of Cornwall over the pagan King Teudar is the dramatic assertion of this role.

As Professor Murdoch has pointed out, this insistence on the primary duty of the State to defend the Roman Catholic Church, highlighting as it does the obligations of temporal rulers towards the Papacy, combined with other Catholic features of the play (such as the emphasis on Marianism), to ensure that *Beunans Meriasek* swiftly became politically incorrect in the eyes of Reformation England: '. . . it is not hard to see why the play could no longer be performed a mere generation or so after its composition'.[39] Indeed, as we shall see, Cornwall was to emerge as a focus of popular opposition to the Reformation, a resistance expressed in the rebellion of 1549 in which the Cornish clergy played a major role. From that perspective, *Beunans Meriasek* had become a subversive document, a vehicle for Cornish sentiment as well as a statement of global Papal pretensions.

However, *Beunans Meriasek* was potentially a subversive document before that date. In the aftermath of 1497, the play may have reflected the mood of Cornish discontent, its performance giving expression to a continuing unrest.[40] Put simply, the argument is that we may equate the villainous King Teudar of the play with Henry Tudor (as Henry VII was still known popularly in Cornwall and elsewhere). As Dr Whetter has observed:

> When the play was written Henry Tudor was on the English throne and, following the 1497 rebellions and the banishing of popular (sic) figures like Henry Bodrugan, the new king was *persona non grata* with the Cornish people. When Teudar was routed on the stage in 1504, the 184 'manucaptors' representing nearly every parish in Cornwall, who had all to pay heavy fines after the rebellion, must have been very well pleased.[41]

It is not quite that easy, however, for the degree of 'coincidence' in the relationship between 'Teudar' and 'Tudor' is open to debate. Murdoch, for example, considers that although the villainous King Teudar of the play might be based on historical 'fact' (he is the semi-legendary Dark Age figure, the Teudar who persecuted Irish missionaries), '. . . any link with the Tudors seems highly unlikely except on an accidental basis'.[42] Indeed, it has been suggested that the component parts of the play may in fact have been written before 1497, and that the surviving text dated 1504 is actually an edited collation designed specifically for performance. And yet, if this is the case, then the desire to edit and perform *Beunans Meriasek* in the immediate aftermath of 1497 may well indicate a Cornish sophistication which saw the play (in particular the contest between the Duke of Cornwall and King Teudar) as a telling metaphor for the relationship between Cornwall and the

Tudor state. As Dr Jonathan Wooding has observed:

> . . . defeat by the Duke of Cornwall may well have been a statement of the locals' disillusionment with the distant king. The fact that the play itself was in the local language, probably not understood by English onlookers, might serve to reinforce the 'underworld', or slightly subversive quality of it.[43]

To this is added the important observation by Dr Lynette Olson that the central theme of *Beunans Meriasek* is that of *tyranny*. It is this that provides the links and continuity between the three otherwise disparate parts of the play, and which gave the play its powerful resonance in post-1497 Cornwall. It is not just that 'Teudar' might be equated with 'Tudor'—whether coincidentally or by design—or that the Duke of Cornwall is a metaphor for Cornish resistance, or even that the Cornish language provides a *frisson* of subversion, but rather that the play is about the nature of tyranny and can thus be seen as a contemporary commentary on the Tudor regime. Or, at the very least, its performance in Cornwall in the immediate aftermath of 1497 can be seen in that light. Certainly, there is an uncanny imagery in *Buenans Meriasek*, conveyed beautifully in Dr Myrna Combellack's excellent English translation of the play, in which we see the Duke of Cornwall fighting not only for the universal Church but also for Cornwall and against tyranny:

> Of all Cornwall, Duke am I,
> As was also my father.
> A great lord in the country,
> From Land's End to the Tamar.
> I am dwelling in—no lie—
> Castle an Dinas itself,
> In Pydar.
> And up on the high ground,
> I've another castle sound,
> Which is named Tintagel,
> Where my chief dwelling is found.[44]

The references to Castle-an-Dinas with its connotations as a seat of royal power and, even more significantly, to Tintagel are, in dramatical terms, important in establishing the popular legitimacy of the Duke of Cornwall and his right to rule in Cornwall. Here, paradoxically, we observe the deployment of the Arthurian tradition *against* the Tudor 'British project'. And if the play imbues the Duke of Cornwall with righteous legitimacy, then it is careful to invest King Teudar with an illegitimate and pagan tyranny which in the immediate aftermath of 1497 would have spoken volumes in Cornwall:

> I will crush the Duke of Cornwall
> Under my feet, with all his people,
> Just like grains of sand.[45]

Murdoch considers that Teudar is 'seen as an interloper in Cornwall', an outsider whose unwelcome and unwarranted intrusions are to be resisted. Stripped of its religious allusions (Mahound is Mohammed), the following has an important temporal message for the Cornish people:

Dedicated to the Saints Martin and Meriadoc (or Meriasek), Camborne church is a reminder of the parish's link with the important Cornish language Miracle Play, *Beunans Meriasek (the Life of St Meriasek).*

Well now—Teudar is my name,
Reigning Lord in Cornwall.
That Mahound gets holy fame
Is my charge, without fail,
Both far and near.
Whoever worships any
Other God shall have many
Pains: and a cruel death, I fear.[46]

In the final part of the play, an unnamed Tyrant asserts the nature of his power in unequivocal terms that again would have struck a chord in post-1497 Cornwall:

I am a Tyrant without
Equal, prince under the sun.
Though mad and rough men, no doubt,
Will fight me . . . .[47]

The significance of *Beunans Meriasek* as a vehicle for Cornish sentiment has been noted in a different context by David Thomas in his analysis of the Wardens of Camborne church and parish. *Beunans Meriasek* is, of course, 'the Camborne play' and St Meriasek (or Meriadoc) is today the joint patron of Camborne, along with the (Gaulish) St Martin. Until the Cornish Celtic Revival of the late-nineteenth and twentieth-centuries, however, Meriasek's patronage was largely forgotten, the conventional wisdom insisting that St Martin had supplanted him in Camborne long before the Reformation. David Thomas has shown, however, that '. . . popularly speaking, by the reign of Elizabeth I (1558) it was St Martin who had been eclipsed and not St Meriasek. The Gaulish saint is last mentioned, significantly enough, in 1549 . . . St Meriasek . . . lingers on until 1562 . . . .'[48]

David Thomas suggests that knowledge of *Beunans Meriasek* kept this patronage alive and accounted for the persistent references to Meriasek in the Camborne church accounts in the sixteenth century. Moreover, he also argues that the preferred use in the 1540s of *Meriasek* (the Breton and Cornish-language form of the name) rather than the 'Anglicised' *Meriadoc*, might be a clue to a stiffening of Cornish resolve in the process leading up to the Reformation. The vitality and relevance of *Beunans Meriasek* continued to hold the imagination of local Camborne people until the middle of the sixteenth century, while the medium of the Cornish language and the appeal to a Breton saint were important resources in the resistance of unwelcome intrusion and change.

Intriguingly, Dr Whetter has suggested that *Beunans Meriasek* may have been written partly with the intention of bolstering St Meriasek at the expense of St Martin. He notes that Master John Pascoe, who was rector of Camborne for forty-four years, obtained a prebend at Glasney College in 1463 and became Provost there in 1476. He considers that Pascoe was sympathetic to the Glasney literary tradition of Cornish-language writing and, as a Camborne man, probably encouraged the groundwork that led to the production of *Beunans Meriasek*. Pascoe in fact resigned the Provostship of Glasney in the autumn of 1491 (he was by then well into his eighties, an extraordinarily old age for those times), to be replaced by Sir John Oby, the vicar of St Gluvias (also at Penryn), who presumably continued the work initiated by Pascoe.

Bodmin glimpsed through the early morning mist from the Old Coach Road, a sight that must have greeted the massing Cornish rebels in 1497 and again in 1549.

It is startling to discover that this was the same John Oby who was notorious as a tax-collector in the Hundred of Kerrier, the over-zealous (and greedy) official whose activities may have sparked the first resistance in St Keverne in 1497. It was the very same Provost of Penryn who was discovered amongst the Cornish throng in Taunton and publicly dismembered there. Quite what Oby was doing in Taunton has not been established (was he there *incognito* as a spy, or had he been recruited to Warbeck's cause?).

His fate, however, is merely an exemplar of a wider paradox in sixteenth-century Cornwall—the reaction of the Cornish to the suppression of the religious houses. On the one hand, we know that the Cornish took their religion seriously. As we saw in Chapter Five, the fifteenth-century had witnessed a renewed enthusiasm for Cornish churches (at a time when the tin industry was apparently in depression, many churches were rebuilt at great expense with their characteristic Cornish towers). At the same time, there was a similar enthusiasm for re-establishing or even inventing Celtic Saints in church dedications. Glasney College had continued as a focus for literary scholarship in the Cornish language, producing the important *Beunans Meriasek*. Indeed, the suppression of Glasney in the 1540s may well have been a significant catalyst in the process that provoked Cornish opposition to the Reformation and precipitated their Prayer Book Rebellion of 1549.

On the other hand, however, the extreme reaction to John Oby suggests strongly that the ecclesiastical establishment of monks, friars and so on was no more popular in Cornwall than it was elsewhere, with a reputation for indolence, greed, and corruption, and with resentment of the rents and tithes that they levied. When the Dissolution of the smaller monasteries was ordered in 1536, many in Cornwall would have welcomed the disappearance of the religious houses at Tywardreath, Bodmin, Launceston, St Germans and elsewhere. However, there is evidence that the Dissolution in Cornwall was handled with some caution and care, a sensitivity that recognised the potential for unrest. For example, the main agent for the Dissolution was himself a Cornishman, Dr John Tregonwell, the lawyer who had already arranged the divorces of Katharine of Aragon and Ann Boleyn. Settlements were often generous, so that the Prior of St Petroc at Bodmin received an annual pension of over £66, his opposite number at Launceston being awarded the annual sum of £100. Indeed, in 1539 (the same year that the short-lived Council of the West was set up to enforce the changes) there was talk of creating a Cornish diocese, with its seat at Bodmin or St Germans, an act of accommodation that might have done much to reconcile Cornwall to the changes wrought by the Reformation. But it was not to be, and Henry VIII instead used the resources he had earmarked for this project on a war with France.

Not without reason did the government watch Cornwall carefully. Although the Cornish had not risen in support of the 'Pilgrimage of Grace', the great rebellion of the North Country, there were those who were sympathetic to that cause—notably one Carpyssack of St Keverne who in 1537 was arrested and probably hanged for expressing his beliefs. In 1538 came the destruction of Henry Courtenay, Marquis of Exeter, (his 'crime' being his misfortune to have been descended from Edward IV); amongst those arrested with him, and sent to the Tower, was his chief agent in Cornwall, Walter Kendall, accused of raising forces in Cornwall in support of the Marquis. In Courtenay's place, Sir John Russell, one of the King's men (from an old Dorset family), was promoted to take charge of Cornwall and the wider South West. He was given the Stewardship of the Duchy of Cornwall, was made Lord Warden of the Stannaries, and was appointed President of the Council of the West. However, Cornwall seemed to be quiet, and in 1544 the Council was disbanded.

In 1548 came the first major signs that all was not well.[49] Henry VIII had died the previous year, his work being continued by the government of Protestant councillors which guided the boy-king Edward VI. A new Chantries Act necessitated the appointment of commissioners in every county to create inventories of church possessions such as bells, vestments, ornaments and plate. This intrusion caused alarm in Cornwall, where the compulsory keeping of parish registers was already seen as an unwarranted imposition, a potential governmental device for raising further taxation. Commissioners were appointed in Cornwall to undertake the task, but in 1548 the unpopular William Body (who had purchased a lease of the archdeaconry of Cornwall and had already been involved in a disturbance in St Stephen-by-Launceston) arrived to undertake his own investigation. He ordered the incumbents and churchwardens of Penwith deanery to his headquarters in Glasney College, and a hostile demonstration ensued. Although the government restrained Body and asked him to explain himself, it in fact made matters worse when it ordered the removal of all 'popish' images from churches and asked William Body to carry out this work in Cornwall.

Body arrived in Helston on 5 April 1548, with the intention of removing images from the church. However, he was soon confronted by an angry mob, led by Martin Geoffrey, priest of St Keverne, and William and John Kilter, yeomen of Constantine. Others came from nearby parishes such as Grade, Mullion, Ruan Minor, Gwennap, Illogan, Redruth, and Perranzabuloe, but most were St Keverne and Constantine men. Body hid in a house near the church but he was dragged outside and murdered; the mortal blows were struck by William Kilter and Pascoe Trevian. Two days later there was a mob of some 3,000 people in Helston, and there was open talk of rebellion. However, Sir William Godolphin and his fellow justices of the peace made an appeal for assistance, and the payments in kind contributed by St Winnow, Morval, Lanteglos, Boconnoc, Launceston, Stratton, and elsewhere in Cornwall to help quell the disturbance, show that this was in fact a localised insurrection. As the *Black Book of Plymouth* put it, '. . . the Commons were pacified by the gentlemen of the country with small trouble'.[50]

William Kilter of Constantine was a character reminiscent of Michael Joseph *An Gof*, and Carew has bequeathed us an engaging story: 'For activity, one Kilter, committed to Launceston gaol for the Cornish commotion, lying there in the Castle green upon his back, threw a stone of some pounds' weight over the tower's top which leadeth to the park'.[51] Kilter and Trevian were hanged, drawn and quartered, and a number of the others held at Launceston were hanged. In London, Martin Geoffrey the priest was drawn from the Tower to Smithfield where he was hanged, drawn and quartered, his head being displayed on London Bridge. A 'traitor of Cornwall' was also executed on Plymouth Hoe, with quarters later displayed on poles in Plymouth and Tavistock.

In January 1549 the Act of Uniformity was passed. This was the epitome of the 'Tudor revolution in government', a self-confident, centralist instrument which abolished the diversity of religious practices that had existed hitherto and dictated one form of worship that was to be enacted throughout the realm. Moreover, there was to be a *Book of Common Prayer*, with services in English to which all must conform. For Cornwall, the Act of Uniformity was the epitome of Tudor intrusion. Instead of the accommodation to which Cornwall was by now so accustomed, there was to be no 'special case' dispensation for the Cornish, no separate or sensitive treatment. Moreover, not only was Cornwall to be subject to centralist dictat but the English language was to be imposed upon a population that was only partly English-speaking and which, in the west, still contained a great many monoglot Cornish-speakers. The Cornish were outraged. There were disturbances at Penryn and Marazion, and at Bodmin the insurgents rallied around Henry Bray, the mayor, and two local leaders of the Catholic gentry—Humphry Arundell of Helland (whose grandfather Humphry Calwodely had risen in 1497) and John Winslade of Tregarrick. Other leaders of this fast-growing rebellion included Nicholas Boyer (soon to be Bray's successor as mayor of Bodmin), Thomas Holmes of Blisland, Robert Smith of St Germans, William Harris, James and Henry Rosogan, and a number of priests, including Roger Barret, John Thompson, Richard Bennett, and Simon Morton.

Meanwhile, at Sampford Courtenay in the mid-west of Devon, rebellion was also brewing. Situated just north of the Dartmoor mass, the folk of Sampford Courtenay, like others in remote north and west Devon, probably looked as often towards Cornwall as they did to the softer, lowland country of the east and, as Dr Mark Stoyle has noted, the Dartmoor tinners (as Stannary men and subjects of the Duchy of Cornwall) had more in common with their Cornish colleagues than their Devon compatriots.[52] This moulded their loyalties and determined their actions in the Civil War, and the same was probably true a hundred years earlier in the Prayer Book Rebellion of 1549. Certainly, the Cornish and Sampford Courtenay rebels made common cause. Those Cornish gentry who opposed the rebellion sought sanctuary (with varying degrees of success) in the castles of St Michael's Mount and Trematon, while the rebels themselves crossed from Cornwall into Devon and laid siege to Exeter.

The Cornish had by now drawn up a petition to the King, declaring that the new Service was:

> . . . like a Christmas game . . . we will have our old service of Mattins, Mass, Evensong and Procession in Latin as it was before. And so we the Cornish men (whereof certain of us understand no English) utterly refuse this new English.[53]

Archbishop Cranmer retorted that there were more people in Cornwall who understood English rather than Latin, but he was missing the point, for Latin was familiar (if not always understood) all across Cornwall, whereas English was not. Moreover, as Carew noted, the Creed, the Commandments and other elements had been said in Cornish since time immemorial, something that the Act of Uniformity was specifically designed to eradicate. While the demands were made, Lord Russell, representing the King, moved his forces westwards to Honiton. Yet he dared not try to lift the siege of Exeter until his reinforcements of foreign mercenaries had arrived. The Cornish, for their part, had been persuaded by the intervention of the vicar of St Thomas, Father Welsh, himself a Cornishman from Penryn (and said to be an accomplished wrestler and archer), not to destroy Exeter by firing fireballs into its midst. Instead, the Cornish decided to advance against Russell before he was reinforced, and at Fenny Bridges battle was joined. John Hooker, the Devon historian, noted that 'The fight for the time was very sharp and cruel, for the Cornishmen were very lusty and fresh and fully bent to fight out the matter'.[54] However, they were pushed back by Russell, though he dared not pursue them.

Soon after, the mercenaries arrived under Lord Grey. On 3 August he left Honiton in the direction of Clyst St Mary. On 4 August, as he forded the river at Clyst St Mary, the alarm was sounded and, fearing ambush, Grey ordered that all the prisoners be killed. On the following day, in the principal engagement of the Prayer Book Rebellion, Grey found himself in the midst of a fight which he later conceded was more hard-fought than any other war he had known. The rebels were forced to retreat, the Devon men cutting north up the Exe valley where they were overtaken by Sir Gawen Carew who left their leaders hanging on gibbets from Dunster to Bath. Russell proceeded into Exeter, lifting the remnants of the siege and dealing with the rebels. Welsh, the Cornish vicar of St Thomas who had saved Exeter from burning, was hanged from his church-tower, with, as Hooker noted, '. . . having a holy-water bucket, a sprinkle, a sacring bell, a pair of beads and such other like popish trash hanged about him'.[55] The Cornish rebels, meanwhile, had taken up new positions at Sampford Courtenay. Russell advanced to engage them and, after stiff resistance, managed to enter the village on the night of 7 August. The rebels fled in the direction of Launceston, including Humphry Arundell who was captured and, with other rebel leaders, hanged, drawn and quartered at Tyburn.

In contrast to Blackheath in 1497, there were several thousand Cornish casualties in the engagements of 1549, and the aftermath was equally bloody. The clergy implicated in the Prayer Book rebellion were singled out for particular attention. Richard Bennett (vicar of St Veep and St Neot), Simon

Poundstock Church, where in 1549 Simon Morton, the vicar, was a leader of the Prayer Book Rebellion.

Morton (vicar of Poundstock) and William Alsa (vicar of Gulval) were certainly executed, as was the vicar of Pillaton. Amongst those attainted were the vicars of St Cleer, St Keverne, and Uny Lelant. Miraculously, the vicar of Constantine seems to have escaped attention. The demise of Simon Morton was celebrated in London in a Protestant ditty of the day:

> The vicar of Poundstock with his congregation
> Commanded them to stick to their idolatry;
> They had much provision and great preparation,
> Yet God hath given our king the victory.[56]

Lord Russell was given the Earldom of Bedford for his services, but the actual pacification of Cornwall was delegated to Sir Anthony Kingston. In 1497 the pacification had been cautious, sparing blood and soon resorting to renewed accommodation as attainders were reversed and as the Charter of Pardon of 1508 restored and enhanced the Stannaries. In 1549, however, the Tudor state was determined to crush all resistance within its peripheries. Much more than in 1497, Cornwall in the aftermath of 1549 was firmly under the Tudor thumb. Certainly, Kingston set about his task with enthusiasm and diligence. As Richard Carew observed, in Cornwall 'Sir Anthony Kingston, then provost-marshal of the king's army, hath left his name more memorable than commendable . . . .'[57]

Two stories in Grafton's *Chronicle* serve to illustrate the manner in which Kingston did his business.[58] Nicholas Boyer, who had replaced Henry Bray as mayor of Bodmin, 'had been busy among the rebels, but some that loved him said that he was forced thereunto'. Kingston wrote to Boyer, expressing his desire to visit Bodmin and to dine with him. Boyer was delighted, thinking himself off the hook, and 'seemed to be very joyous thereof and made for him very good preparation'. On the day Kingston arrived, he requested that gallows be erected, for there was unfinished business to be attended to. Boyer readily complied, and the party then sat down to a hearty dinner. After the meal, Kingston took Boyer by the hand and asked to be shown the gallows. He asked, 'Think you they be strong enough?' Boyer opined that they were. 'Well then', said Kingston, 'get you even up to them, for they are provided for you'. The mayor cried out, 'I trust you mean no such thing to me'. Grimly, the provost-marshal replied, 'Sir, there is no remedy. You have been a busy rebel, and therefore this is appointed for your reward'.

Sir Anthony Kingston played the same trick, and with equal success, at St Ives where the Portreeve, John Payne, was hanged. Kingston's black humour is also glimpsed in the execution of William Mayow of Clevyan, hanged from the tavern sign-post in St Columb. However, the second of Grafton's stories is both tragic and cynical, a dreadful cameo that tells us something of life in early modern Cornwall and yet, uncomfortably, might just as easily be a tale from contemporary Bosnia or Rwanda. A miller near Bodmin, also implicated in the Prayer Book Rebellion, was tipped-off that Kingston was after him. Thinking quickly, he called his servant and explained that he had to go away: 'If there come any to ask for me, say that thou art the owner of the mill, and that thou hast kept the same this four years, and in no wise name not me'. Sure enough, Kingston soon arrived at the mill and quizzed the young servant. The servant answered as his master had instructed, and Kingston ordered that he be strung-up from a nearby tree as a rebel. The servant pleaded that he was not the miller, to which Kingston responded 'Well then, you are a false knave to be in two tales. Therefore hang him up'. After the execution, a passer-by commented, 'Surely this was but the miller's man?'. Kingston quipped, 'Well then, could he ever have done his master better service than to hang for him?'.

These individual stories, horrific though they are, are merely illustrations of the wider process of subjugation in Cornwall after 1549. Chief amongst the casualties was the Cornish language. The suppression of Glasney College had robbed the language of both scholarship and status. The imposition of the *Book of Common Prayer* meant that English was now heard in every Cornish church. The miracle plays, as vehicles of popular culture in the Cornish language, were either suppressed as subversive or allowed to fossilise as half-understood relics from earlier times. Interestingly, Nicholas Udall (born in Southampton but thought to be of Cornish provenance), one of the 'divines' asked to comment on the demands of the Cornish rebels, had recommended that the Prayer Book be translated into Cornish so that all the people of Cornwall might enjoy the benefits of the new Service. His recommendation fell on deaf ears. Similarly, in 1563 legislation that provided for the Bible and Prayer Book to be translated into Welsh made no mention of Cornish, although three years earlier a conference of the Anglican Church had moved that '. . . it may be lawful for such Welch or Cornish children as can speake no English to learn the Praemises in the Welch tongue or Cornish language'[59]. It may be that Cornish was already considered to be in terminal decline; or perhaps Cornish was now irrevocably tainted as a 'popish' tongue, the Tudor grip on Cornwall now so complete that accommodating measures were no longer necessary. Whatever the case, John Norden, writing in Elizabeth's reign, considered that:

Lanherne, near St Mawgan-in-Pydar, ancient seat of the recusant Catholic Arundells, but now a Carmelite convent.

> . . . of late the Cornish men have much conformed themselves to the use of the English tongue . . . from Truro eastward it is in manner wholly English. In the west part of the country, as in the Hundreds of Penwith and Kerrier, the Cornish language is most in use among the inhabitants, . . . yet there is none of them in manner but is able to converse with a stranger in the English tongue, unless it be some obscure people that seldom confer with the better sort. But it seems that in a few years the Cornish Language will be by little and little abandoned.[60]

Norden was right in his predictions (although not in his detail; as we saw in Chapter Five, Cornish was still being spoken east of Truro at St Ewe in 1595). However, the old ways were not abandoned overnight. Indeed, during the brief reign of Mary Tudor (1553-58), the revival of Catholicism had brought a glimmer of hope for the Cornish language. In 1555 Edmund Bonner, Bishop of London, published a series of homilies which shortly after were translated into Cornish by one John Tregear. Discovered as recently as 1949, these *Tregear Homilies* comprise the last examples of Cornish that we have in the Middle Cornish period, although already they display many of the characteristics of the language in its Late Cornish phase. The link between the Cornish language and Catholicism was also exhibited in the activities of John Kenall, vicar of St Columb Major (where Mass was still being said in 1590), who according to Carew bore 'the principal love and knowledge of this language', and in the work of Richard Pendrea, a Catholic priest in exile who in 1600 preached before King Philip III of Spain in Cornish.

At a wider level, Cornish Catholicism also endured. Indeed, in 1584 the vicar of Kilkhampton protested that he had never heard of the new Prayer Book! The centre of Roman Catholicism in Cornwall, however, was Lanherne, the seat of the Arundells, situated between St Columb Major and Mawgan Porth. Sir John Arundell was despatched to the Tower for his beliefs in 1584; he died there six years later. The Arundells were related by marriage to another prominent Cornish Catholic family, the Tregians of Golden, near Probus, and Francis Tregian—who had succeeded to Golden in 1575—provided sanctuary for a seminary priest, one Cuthbert Mayne, who conducted illegal Catholic services.

In June 1577 Tregian and Mayne were arrested, and sent to Launceston gaol. Mayne was tried by a grand jury of Cornish gentry (one of whom was the then young Richard Carew). He was subsequently hanged, drawn and quartered in the market place in Launceston, with 'quarters' later displayed at Bodmin, Wadebridge, Tregony (near Golden), and Barnstaple (Mayne's home town). His head was impaled on the gate at Launceston Castle, but was eventually taken to Lanherne where it was preserved as a saintly relic. Mayne was the first of several hundred seminary priests and Jesuits executed in the second half of Elizabeth's reign; other unfortunates from Cornwall included John Hamley of St Mabyn and John Cornelius of Bodmin. Other Cornish Catholic families, such as the Penkivells of St Minver, also suffered persecution, while Nicholas Roscarrock—author of the *Lives of the Saints*—was tortured and imprisoned in the Tower. During his incarceration he scratched his name on the cell-wall. There is also a verse, said to be in his hand:

> Be vertuouus and assure thyselfe
> thou canst not then but thrive;
> in only vertw is it sayfe
> that men themselves survive.[61]

However, although the Catholicism that had endured with such courage and tenacity reflected much that was redolent of medieval and early modern Cornwall, a vibrant and assertive Protestantism that emerged in the years after 1549 was also indicative of much that was Cornish. As we have seen above and in Chapter Five, the Cornish were readily co-opted in the 'British project'. The very fact of their participation was evidence of the validity and

Trerice—one of the seats of the Arundell family, now cared for by the National Trust.

The Edgcumbes of Cotehele began the construction of Mount Edgcumbe, overlooking Plymouth Sound, in 1547. The Duke of Medina Sidonia allegedly coveted this splendid house, and announced that it would be his home once the Spanish Armada had succeeded in its invasion. In 1941 Mount Edgcumbe was hit by a German incendiary bomb, but reconstruction commenced in 1958.

success of that project, while the recognition and exploitation of Cornish distinctiveness by the English state was both an act of accommodation (the Cornish fought in their own units) and a means of tapping Cornish military prowess and *esprit de corps*. In 1544, for example, Henry VIII's success at the siege of Boulogne was due largely to the efforts of the younger William Godolphin and a contingent of Cornish miners. In the same way, the Cornish sea-faring tradition was put to good use. When the ill-fated *Mary Rose* foundered off Portsmouth in 1545, its captain was the Cornishman, Roger Grenville of Stowe, father of Richard Grenville of the *Revenge*.

Beautifully restored in recent times, Arwenack (at Falmouth) was home to the turbulent Killigrew family.

From that perspective, the rebellions of 1497 and 1549 were evidence of the temporary failure of such a strategy. And while the aftermath of 1549 was harsh and bloody, with no evidence of a desire to accommodate those who had lately rebelled against the Tudor state, there was accommodation of another sort—ample reward for those who (like their counterparts in the North Country) were prepared to sign-up as the local collaborative elite. Indeed, many of the Cornish gentry had profited from the dissolution of the religious houses, or from the confiscation of rebel property, and some built new seats or extended existing ones: Trerice, Mount Edgcumbe, Port Eliot, Menabilly, Godolphin, and so on. The loyalty of the Cornish gentry was also rewarded with the granting of numerous town charters, a new mechanism of constitutional accommodation which by 1548 had provided Cornwall with no fewer than forty-four Members of Parliament at Westminster (almost the equivalent number to that allocated to Scotland at the Union in 1707; Looe, with its constituent parts, West and East, had the grand total of four MPs). In this way, the Cornish gentry, modest though it was when compared to the grandeur and wealth of the English peerage, came to enjoy a distinctive role of its own in the affairs of state.

This was especially so as relations with Spain deteriorated, when Cornwall was suddenly in the front line and of enormous strategic importance to England. As Halliday put it, 'Cornish nationalism was merged, though never submerged, in a greater English nationalism, which in Elizabeth's reign meant enmity with Spain and abhorrence of its religion and Inquisition'.[62] The Spanish threat had led to the construction in 1540 of the new 'castles' (in reality, modern fortresses) at Pendennis and St Mawes. The two were designed to be complementary, guarding the Carrick Roads, the entrance to Falmouth Haven. Pendennis dominated the high-ground on the western promontory of that name; St Mawes was almost on the water's edge on the eastern side of the estuary. Both castles were extremely well-appointed; an intriguing touch at St Mawes was the cheery inscriptions built into the walls: GAUDEAT EDWARDO NUNC DUCE CORNUBIA FELIX (Let fortunate Cornwall rejoice that Edward is now her Duke) and EDWARDUS FAMA REFERAT FACTISQUE PARENTUM (May Edward resemble his father in fame and deeds).

The 1550s were ostensibly a time of peace but in fact a vigorous unofficial war was being waged against Spanish shipping by the privateers and pirates of Cornwall, notably the Killigrew family of Arwenack. John Killigrew was Captain of Pendennis Castle but he spent much of his time assisting his sons John (later Sir John), Peter and Thomas in the capture and plunder of Spanish vessels. Sir John succeeded his father as Captain of Pendennis in 1567, the year before the revolt in the Spanish Netherlands led to increased privateering in the Channel and a further deterioration in relations with Spain. In December 1568 a rumour that John Hawkins had been killed on the Spanish Main prompted the seizure and spoil of Spanish ships then lying in Fowey and Saltash. In the fifteen-year cold war that followed, the Killigrews became the centre of a major privateering operation, operating on the edge of (and very often beyond) the law. Peter Killigrew made a fortune provisioning the pirates who operated from the Helford River, notably the infamous Captain Hicks of Saltash. Although it suited the government to turn a blind eye to this private-enterprise warfare, timely interventions (such as that which reprimanded and imprisoned Sir John Killigrew in the early 1580s) made it plain that there were clear limits to this independent behaviour.

The Mount's Bay fishing village of Mousehole, scene of the daring Spanish raid in July 1595 when Mousehole, Paul church, Newlyn and Penzance were all set ablaze.

St Mawes Castle, the Tudor fortress assisting Pendennis with the defence of Falmouth Haven.

Sir John died in 1584, to be succeeded as Captain of Pendennis by his son, John Killigrew. The conflict with Spain was now acute, and in 1588 the Spanish Armada made its famous but abortive journey of invasion. In serious escalations of the war, in 1590 Spain occupied Brittany (posing a direct threat to Cornwall), while squadrons of the Royal Navy cruised as far as the Azores to intercept Spanish treasure ships. In 1591, Richard Grenville of Stowe, in his ship the *Revenge*, was trapped by a Spanish fleet of fifty-three vessels. Although hopelessly outnumbered, Grenville fought on for fifteen hours, earning his reputation as doyen of the Cornish sea-dogs.[63]

In 1595 the war was brought even closer to Cornwall, when in the early morning of 23 July four Spanish galleys landed a raiding party of some two hundred men at Mousehole. They set fire to the village and to Paul church, and four locals were killed trying to organise a defence—James Keigwin, John Pearce Peyton, James of Newlyn, and Teck Cornall. Meanwhile, Sir Francis Godolphin had ridden to Penzance to investigate. He quickly gathered an impromptu body of defenders and made for Mousehole, only to be outflanked by the Spanish who had re-embarked in their galleys and sailed for Newlyn. The full force of four hundred Spaniards was landed; they fired Newlyn and Penzance and Sir Francis was powerless to do anything to stop them.

Henry VIII's mighty fortress at Pendennis. Designed to deter the Spanish, Pendennis in fact saw action in the Civil War when it was defended for the Royalists by John 'Jack for the King' Arundell.

Just off the coast at Mousehole is Merlin's Rock and so, it was said, was fulfilled the ancient Cornish prophecy:

> Ewra teyre a war mearne Merlyn
> Ara lesky Pawle Pensanz ha Newlyn
>
> They shall land on the Rock of Merlin
> Who shall burn Paul, Penzance and Newlyn.[64]

The Mousehole raid alarmed the government and re-emphasised the strategic significance of Cornwall. Elizabeth herself understood the political importance of the loyalty and confidence of the Cornish gentry, and under her patronage they had found favour at court—Edmund Tremayne as Clerk of the Privy Council, William Killigrew as groom of the Queen's Chamber, Henry 'Hal' Killigrew as senior diplomatic envoy. She said (so it is alleged) that 'The Cornish gentlemen are all born courtiers, with a becoming confidence', an observation reflected in the old Cornish adage that 'a Trelawny was never known to want courage, a Grenville loyalty, or a Godolphin wit'.[65]

At the end of this period, Carew observed that all Cornish gentlemen were 'Cousins', but in the ensuing seventeenth-century, in the contest between King and Parliament, both this kinship and the implied relationship with the Crown (through the Duchy) were to be severely tested. Moreover, the Civil War in Cornwall was to demonstrate that, despite the cataclysms of 1497 and 1549, and despite Tudor efforts to co-opt the gentry, there remained a profound popular consciousness prepared to assert and defend its Cornishness in the face of external intrusion.

Notes & References (Chapter 6)

1. A.L. Rouse, *Bosworth Field and the War of the Roses*, Panther, London, 1968, p.184.

2. Christopher Haigh, 'Reformation and Inflation 1450-1625', in Christopher Haigh (ed.), *The Cambridge Historical Encyclopedia of Great britain and Ireland*, Cambridge University Press, Cambridge, 1985, pp.142-146.

3. A.L. Rouse, *Tudor Cornwall*, Cape, London, 1941, repub. Dyllansow Truran, Redruth, 1990, p.9.

4. A.L. Rouse, *The Expansion of Elizabethan England*, Cardinal, London, 1973, p.15.

5. Rowse, 1973, p.6.

6. Haigh, 1985, p.144

7. C.S.L.Davies, 'Government and Politics in England 1450-1553', in Haigh (ed.), 1985, p.154.

8. Helen M.Jewell, *The North-South Divide: The Origins of Northern Consciousness in England*, Manchester University Press, Manchester, 1994, p.57.

9. Jewell, 1994, p.61.

10. Rowse, 1941 and 1990, remains an excellent introduction; see especially chapter five, 'Feudal Anarchy and Social Unrest'. See also, William J.Blake, 'The Cornish Rebellion of 1497', *Journal of the Royal Institution of Cornwall*, No.62, Vol.XX, Part 1-1915.

11. Penry Williams, 'Wales: Integration and Conformity', in Haigh (ed.), 1985, p.162.

12. A.L. Rowse, *Court and Country: Studies in Tudor Social History*, Harvester, Brighton, 1987, p.140.

13. Rowse, 1941 and 1990, p.117.

14. Blake, 1915.

15. Robert R.Pennington, *Stannary Law: A History of the Tin Mining Law of Cornwall and Devon*, David and Charles, Newton Abbot, 1973, p.19.

16. Again, Rowse, 1941 and 1990, remains the best account of this confrontation. Blake, 1915, is still very useful and there is interesting material in Julian Cornwall, *Revolt of the Peasantry, 1549*, Routledge, London, 1977, especially chapter two, 'A Land Apart'.

17. Francis Bacon, *Life of Henry VII*, 1641 ed., p.163.

18. Polydore Vergil, *Anglica Historia*, in David C.Douglas (gen.ed.) and C.H.Williams (ed.), *English Historical Documents*, London, 1967, p.118.

19. Vergil, p.134.

20. Bacon, p.148-149.

21. Bacon, p.171.

22. Edward Hall, *Chronicle*, 1548; cited in Rowse, 1941 and 1990, p.126.

23. *The Great Chronicle of London*, cited in Rowse, 1941 and 1990, p.127.

24. Hall, cited in Rowse, 1941 & 1990, p.128.

25. Bacon, p.156.

26. Vergil, pp.135-136.

27. Douglas (gen.ed.) and Williams (ed.), 1967, p.118.

28. Rowse, 1941 and 1990, p.136.

29. Rowse, 1941 and 1990, pp.138-139.

30. Rowse, 1941 and 1990, p.140.

31. Cornwall, 1977, p.47.

32. Philip Payton, '"a . . . concealed envy against the English": A Note on the Aftermath of the 1497 Rebellions in Cornwall', in Philip Payton (ed.), *Cornish Studies: One*, University of Exeter Press, Exeter, 1993.

33. John Norden, *Description of Cornwall*, cited in Rowse, 1973, p.45.

34. Richard Carew, *The Survey of Cornwall*, ed. F.E.Halliday, Melrose, London, 1953, p.139.

35. Pennington, 1973, p.20.

36. G.R.Lewis, *The Stannaries: A Study of the Medieval Tin Miners of Cornwall and Devon*, 1908, repub. Bradford Barton, Truro, 1965, p.127; John Rowe, *Cornwall in the Age of the Industrial Revolution*, Liverpool University Press, Liverpool, 1953, repub. Cornish Hillside, St Austell, 1993, p.13.

37. Edward Hall, *Chronicle*, in Douglas (gen.ed.) and Williams (ed.), 1967, p.148.

38. Frank Mitchell, *Redruth Parish Church: St Euny's*, Dyllansow Truran, Redruth, 1987, p.6.

39. Brian Murdoch, *Cornish Literature*, Brewer, Cambridge, 1993, p.115.

40. Payton, 1993.

41. James Whetter, *The History of Glasney College*, Tabb House, Padstow, 1988, p.105.

42. Murdoch, 1993, p.118.

43. Jonathan Wooding, *St Meriasek and King Tudor in Cornwall*, First Australian Conference of Celtic Studies, July 1992, p.6.

44. Myrna Combellack, *The Camborne Play: A Verse Translation of Beunans Meriasek*, Dyllansow Truran, Redruth, 1988, pp.96-98.

45. Combellack, 1988, p.104.

46. Combellack, 1988, p.45.

47. Combellack, 1988, p.141.

48. David Thomas, 'The Wardens of Camborne Church and Parish, 1534 to 1980; with Guild and Chapel Wardens, 1534 to 1558', *Cornish Studies: 6*, 1978.

49. Rowse, 1941 and 1990, remains the best introduction to the events of 1548-49; also good is Cornwall, 1977, while a useful discussion is John Sturt, *Revolt in the West: The Western Rebellion of 1549*, Devon Books, Exeter, 1987.

50. Cornwall, 1977, p.54.

51. Carew, 1603 (1953), p.135.

52. Mark Stoyle, *Loyalty and Locality: Popular Allegiance in Devon during the English Civil War*, University of Exeter Press, Exeter, 1994, p.151.

53. Cornwall, 1977, p.57.

54. Rowse, 1941 and 1990, p.275.

55. F.E.Halliday, *A History of Cornwall*, Duckworth, London, 1953, p.183; Halliday's chapter on the Tudors is a useful summary of the period.

56. Rowse, 1941 and 1990, p.283.

57. Carew, 1603 (1953), p.196.

58. Rowse, 1941 and 1990, pp.285-286; Cornwall, 1977, pp.201-204.

59. Crysten Fudge, *The Life of Cornish*, Dyllansow Truran, Redruth, p.26.

60. John Norden, *Description of Cornwall*, 1728, p.26.

61. Nicholas Orme (ed.), *Nicholas Roscarrock's Lives of the Saints: Cornwall and Devon*, Devon and Cornwall Record Society, Exeter, 1992, p.9.

62. Halliday, 1953, p.185.

63. A.L. Rouse, *Sir Richard Grenville of the 'Revenge'*, Cape, London, 1937.

64. P.A.S. Pool, *The History of the Town and Borough of Penzance*, Corporation of Penzance, Penzance, 1974, p.28.

65. Thurston Peter, *A Compendium of the History and Geography of Cornwall*, Houlston, London, 1906, p.191.

CHAPTER 7

'There is much danger in a Cornish hugg'

C O R N W A L L

'There is much danger in a Cornish hugg'

As we have seen in Chapter Six, the Tudor era was pivotal in the creation of modern Cornwall. The impact of 'the Tudor revolution in government' was felt as early as the 1490s, the intrusion of the Tudor state undermining the very fabric of what we may call 'Celtic-Catholic' Cornwall and posing a serious threat to the constitutional accommodation that had made Cornwall politically 'a land apart'.

The Cornish reacted against this process, twice in the rebellions of 1497 and again in the rising of 1549. But they were not successful in resisting the encroachment of Tudor power—in particular the Protestant Reformation and the imposition of the English language. The instruments of accommodation faired rather better, however, the Charter of Pardon of 1508 restoring and enhancing both the privileges of the tinners and the authority of the Stannary Parliament. This demonstrated the Tudor regime's recognition of the limitations of its own power in the opening years of the sixteenth-century but it also reflected the significance of the Duchy of Cornwall (the principal mechanism of accommodation) as a governmental device for wooing and rewarding the Cornish gentry. This process of co-opting the gentry was further assisted by the dissolution of religious houses and the granting of numerous borough charters, the latter precipitating a new accommodation based around the acquisition of no fewer than forty-four Cornish MPs. The war with Spain also enhanced the status of the Cornish gentry, encouraging their enthusiastic embrace of Protestantism and allowing them to deploy (often to their own profit) their own maritime assets in the war effort.

At the accession of James I & VI, then, in 1603, Cornwall had experienced a century and more of turbulent, traumatic change. In a sense, the seventeenth-century was to offer 'more of the same'. The Civil War had a major impact in Cornwall, as it did in other parts of these islands, but it had a particular Cornish dimension which only now is being appreciated in its full complexity. The Cornish gentry, tied closely to the Crown through the institution of the Duchy of Cornwall but now (in some quarters at least) with a strong ideological commitment to Protestantism, found itself split in its loyalties. The more Anglicised gentry, concentrated for the most part in South East Cornwall, often with Puritan sympathies, was drawn into the Parliamentary camp, rather like those Cornish gentlemen who had distanced themselves from the Tudor risings.

The rest, more conservative and more 'Cornish', made common cause with the lesser gentry and yeomen farmers (those who had made the rebellions of 1497 and 1549) to resist this further intrusion by what became the 'Cromwellian state'. Indeed, Cornish popular opinion was overwhelmingly on their side, and in the determination to confront this latest intrusion we hear more than an echo of the passions and motives of 1497 and 1549. As Dr Mark Stoyle has suggested, the last stand of Sir Richard Grenville as the war drew to a close was conducted with the intention of making Cornwall a semi-autonomous Royalist statelet, independent of the control of Parliamentarian England:

> This suspicion that the county's inhabitants meant to use their support for the King as a stepping-stone towards their own independence was aroused again in 1645, when the Cornish commander Richard Grenville proposed that the Prince of Wales, then titular commander of the King's forces in West Devon and Cornwall, should seek a separate peace with Parliament, effectively establishing Cornwall as an autonomous state.[1]

However, the Parliamentary victory in Cornwall was complete and, notwithstanding the Restoration in 1660, the erosion of the remaining attributes of Celtic-Catholic Cornwall continued apace. The Duchy and Stannaries never fully recovered from the Cromwellian assault, beginning their long slide into stagnation and eventual metamorphosis, while the upheavals of the Civil War further accelerated the decline of the Cornish language. The Cornish economy, meanwhile, despite those upheavals, revived and diversified in the wake of Cornwall's new-found strategic maritime importance. Most significant, however, was the development of tin mining which, despite this economic diversification, had emerged by the end of the seventeenth-century as the single most important determinant of Cornish prosperity, heralding the central role that mining was to play in the construction of industrial Cornwall.

Mary Coate's *Cornwall in the Great Civil War and Interregnum*, first published in 1933, was the first attempt to assess in detail the characteristics of the Civil War in Cornwall. This important text has stood the test of time but in recent years there has been renewed interest in the subject, resulting in several articles and books by Dr Mark Stoyle and Dr Anne Duffin.[2] This activity, in turn, has resulted in a vigorous historiographical debate, an academic argument as to how best we might understand and write the history of Cornwall in this period. Dr Stoyle has complained that, ever since Mary Coate's intervention, historians have tended to down-play and underestimate the strength of popular Royalist sentiment in Cornwall. Dr Duffin, in contrast, has complained that Coate over-estimated and over-simplified Cornish Royalist allegiance, and offers an alternative perspective which emphasises Parliamentarian and Puritan sympathies, especially in South East Cornwall. This apparent conflict of interpretation is resolved, at least in part, in a recognition that Mark Stoyle is concerned principally with popular opinion, the beliefs of ordinary people, while Anne Duffin has focused on the gentry. As Dr Stoyle has graciously admitted, 'The two approaches complement, rather than contradict each other, therefore'.[3] Dr Duffin, equally graciously, concedes that 'Stoyle's conclusion that religion was the primary influence upon popular allegiance in Cornwall is entirely convincing . . . .'[4]

The economic history of Cornwall in this period has been tackled by Dr James Whetter, most notably in his *Cornwall in the Seventeenth Century* which provides a clear picture of economic expansion. This is complemented by his other writings, including *The History of Falmouth* (Falmouth was very much a product of seventeenth-century development) and *Cornish Weather and Cornish People in the Seventeenth Century*.[5] To these must be added the painstaking investigations by Dr Todd Gray into the maritime and agrarian issues of the day, presented in illuminating detail in his *Early Stuart Mariners and Shipping: The Maritime Surveys of Devon and Cornwall 1619-35* and *Harvest Failure in Cornwall and Devon: The Book of Orders and the Corn Surveys of 1623 and 1630-1*.[6]

However, to catch the flavour and to gain an insight into the life of Cornwall at the beginning of this period we can do no better than to return to Richard Carew and his *Survey of Cornwall* of 1602. Carew has long-since served as a primary source for those investigating early modern Cornwall, and yet he is rarely understood in his full context. At one level he is presented merely as an antiquarian observer, laboriously recording events and anecdotes (as a later Victorian rector might) which, with the passage of the years, are now for us an important window in the daily happenings of those times. At another level, Carew is presented as the typical Cornishman of the era, enthusing about his 'native county' (for example, he writes with pride of Cornish prowess in archery and wrestling) and bequeathing to us an authentic Cornish voice and an authentic Cornish commentary on those times.

Both approaches, however, are missing something. Richard Carew needs to be understood as both 'insider' and 'outsider', a member of the Anglicised Cornish gentry whose sympathies and connections are in one sense Cornish, and yet who writes from the margins of Cornwall. This 'marginality' is both geographical (his home at Antony was at the most south-eastern tip of Cornwall, immediately opposite Plymouth) and cultural. For all his apparent 'Cornishness', Carew is in fact presenting himself as a typical 'Englishman' of the Renaissance. It is in this spirit that his *Survey of Cornwall* was conceived, written and presented. And this is how we must interpret it today.

Nowhere is Carew's Renaissance 'Englishness' more apparent than in his essay 'The Excellency of the English Tongue'. As well as advocating the inherent superiority of English over other languages, he is also at pains to identify personally with the language. He sets out to '. . . prove that our English language, for all, or most, is matchable, if not preferable before any other in use at this day, I hope the assent of any impartial reader will pass on my side'.[7] In the *Survey of Cornwall* he refers to 'the Saxon, our natural language' and reveals his sketchy (to say the least) knowledge of Cornish when, for example, he says that *Pulstean* means 'The Miry Head' (in fact, it means tin pool or pit) and that *Crueg braaz* is Cornish for 'The Great Borough' (it actually means the great barrow or burial mound; Carew has presumably misunderstood an interpreter). He was on safer ground, perhaps, when he reported that which he more readily understood; for example, his repetition of the old Cornish adage:

> By Tre, Pol, and Pen
> You shall know the Cornishmen.

As far as the current status and future prospects of the Cornish language were concerned, he considered that,

> . . . the English speech doth still encroach upon it and hath driven the same into the uttermost skirts of the shire. Most of the inhabitants can speek no word of Cornish, but very few are ignorant of English; and yet some so affect their own as to a stranger they will not speak it, for if meeting them by chance you inquire the way or any such matter, your answer shall be, *Meea navidna cowzasawzneck*, 'I can speak no Saxonage'. The English which they speak is good and pure, as receiving it from the best hands of

> their own gentry and the eastern merchants, but they disgrace it in part with a broad and rude accent, somewhat like the Somersetshire men . . . .[8]

Apart from misunderstanding the Cornish phrase (significantly, it means 'I *will* not speak English'), Carew's observations reduce the Cornish language to a device to deceive visitors. The Cornish gentry, meanwhile, have a clear duty to impart the English language and to encourage improving contact with traders from east of the Tamar. Although the English thus learned is of the highest standard, the rustic tones in which it is spoken is something of an embarrassment. Even more telling, perhaps, is Carew's description of what must have been the dying days of the Cornish-language Miracle Plays (or 'gwary miracle' as Carew calls them, *gwary* being the Cornish for 'play'). Stripped of their religious significance by the Reformation (the more 'subversive' examples no doubt suppressed altogether), the plays had become chaotic parodies for the amusement of simple country folk. Carew explains this, but behind the patronising description of harmless fun is a restrained contempt which reveals Carew's cultural distance from his countrymen:

> The gwary miracle, in English, a miracle play, is a kind of interlude, compiled in Cornish out of some scripture history, with the grossness that accompanied the Romans' *vetus comedia* . . . The country people flock from all sides, many miles off, to hear and see it, for they have therein devils and devices to delight as well the eye as the ear. The players con not their parts without book, but are prompted by one called the ordinary, who followeth at their back with the book in his hand, and telleth them softly what they must pronounce aloud. Which manner once gave occasion to a pleasant conceited gentleman of practising a merry prank; for he undertaking (perhaps of set purpose) an actor's room, was accordingly lessoned (beforehand) by the ordinary, that he must say after him. His turn came: qoth the ordinary, 'Go forth man, and show thyself'. The gentleman steps out upon the stage, and like a bad clerk in a scripture matters, cleaving more to the letter than the sense, pronounced these words aloud. 'Oh (says the fellow sofly in his ear) you mar all the play'. And with this his passion the actor makes the audience in like sort acquainted. Hereon the prompter falls to flat railing and cursing in the bitterest terms he could devise; which the gentleman with a set gesture and countenance still soberly related, until the ordinary, driven at last into mad rage, was fain to give over all; which trouse [jest], though it break off the interlude, yet defrauded not the beholders, but dismissed them with a great deal more sport and laughter than twenty such gwaries could have afforded.[9]

The cultural gulf between gentry and populace illuminated by Carew helps further to resolve the Stoyle/Duffin paradox. Anne Duffin is right to point to the Parliamentarian and Puritan predisposition's of significant parts of the Cornish gentry (although she wrongly takes her cue from John Chynoweth's flawed analysis to suggest that this reflects a wider Anglicisation of Cornish society at this time)[10] while Mark Stoyle is certainly correct in emphasising the strength of Cornish particularism that lay behind popular support for the Royalist cause.

Anne Duffin has estimated that there were some 321 gentry families in Cornwall in the years leading up to the Civil War. Although this does not include the more obscure lesser gentry, for whom few records survive, it does encompass a broad spectrum from minor country gentlemen, through newly-emergent merchant families (such as the Rashleighs of Fowey), to the new peers (Cornwall's first) created in 1625 and 1628 respectively—Richard, 1st Baron Robartes of Truro (son of a wealthy Truro wool and tin dealer) and John, 1st Baron Mohun of Okehampton (born at the Mohun family seat of Boconnoc). Approximately one-third of these gentry constituted the ruling elite in Cornwall, and about a quarter of the greater gentry was concentrated in the Hundred of East (Wivelshire)—the territorial subdivision of South East Cornwall that lay between the Looe and Tamar rivers. Significantly, as we have seen, Richard Carew of Antony hailed from the eastern fringe of this Hundred, while Lord Robartes' Lanhydrock estate was situated in that part of East Cornwall where the boundaries of the Hundreds of Trigg, Pydar, Powder and West (Wivelshire) came together.

This concentration of the more significant (and Anglicised) gentry in South East Cornwall was reflected in Cornish religious divisions.[11] Although seventeenth-century Puritans were quick to point to 'popish' tendencies in Cornwall, it is a mistake to paint too simplistic a picture of Cornish religious allegiances at the time. In some areas the Anglican Church had remained deeply conservative (Mass being celebrated at St Columb Major in 1590, for example) while, despite the persecution and decline of Roman Catholicism, pockets of Catholic recusants did survive. In addition to individual Catholic families in the 1640s, such as the Trevillions of St Clether and the Tremaynes

Lanhydrock, now a National Trust property, was in the seventeenth century the seat of the Puritan and Parliamentarian Robartes family.

of St Kew, the influence of Sir John Arundell of Lanherne ensured a concentration of recusants in the Hundred of Pydar, especially in the parish of St Mawgan-in-Pydar. However, Puritanism was also part of the Cornish religious pattern, Anne Duffin's analysis of seventeenth-century Cornish wills revealing a surprisingly widespread use of Calvinistic language (for example, references to 'predestination' and the 'elect'). From the mid-sixteenth-century until the 1620s, Calvinism (i.e. Puritanism) had been the dominant theology of the Church of England but even in the days of Elizabeth it had been a minority religion in Cornwall. Its one area of strength was in South East Cornwall, mirroring the concentration of Cornish gentry in that locality.

By the late 1620s the anti-Calvinist element had gained the upper-hand in the Anglican Church, signalling a return to High Church theology and ritual. This was reflected in Cornwall where, for example, in the 1620s and 1630s churches such as St Neot, Poughill and Feock erected framed paintings of the King's Arms or placed the Ten Commandments and other key texts upon the walls. More attention was paid to church restoration and to the purchase of plate and vestments. This re-assertion of High Church practice no doubt grated amongst Puritans in Cornwall as it did elsewhere, but for the gentry—again, especially in South East Cornwall—it simply added to an already growing catalogue of complaints and discontents. Cornwall had suffered, probably disproportionately, from the effects of Charles I's war with France and Spain. Local men had been pressed into dubious military adventures that had gone badly wrong, coastal fortifications such as Pendennis and St Mawes had been neglected and ill-provisioned (at a time when 'Turkish' pirates from North Africa were an ever-present menace along the Cornish coast), and the Forced Loan of 1626 had required the inhabitants of Cornwall to pay some £2,000.

Amongst the so-called Cornish 'loan refusers' who declined to contribute were Sir Richard Buller, Andrew Manaton of Trecarrel and Nicholas Trefusis of Landue—all three in the Hundred of East, the latter two within the parish of Lezant. They were also Puritans and adhered to the Cornish faction that had grown up around Sir John Eliot and William Coryton. Eliot, indeed, had emerged on the wider stage as a key opponent of Stuart taxation and one of the chief critics of the influence of the King's favourite, the Duke of Buckingham. Eliot was sent to the Tower, where he died three years later in November 1632. When his son asked that his body might be returned home to Port Eliot, in St Germans, Charles I gave his famous reply: 'Let Sir John be buried in the parish in which he died'.[12] Seemingly cruel and heartless, Charles' response no doubt reflected the fact that the parish of St Germans lay deep in the Hundred of East. To send Sir John's body home might needlessly inflame local passions; burying him in London would be unpopular but invisible and soon forgotten.

In the Long Parliament between 1640 and 1642, a number of Cornish Puritans acted together as a coherent force under the leadership of Sir Alexander Carew and the Bullers (Sir Richard and Francis) in the Commons and Lord Robartes in the House of Lords. Politically, most of the 44 Cornish MPs were moderate 'constitutionalists' but, with the increasing realisation during 1642 that compromise was impossible, leading Cornish families such as the Grenvilles of Stowe, the Vyvyans of Trelowarren, and the Killigrews of Arwennack, began to form a Cornish coalescence that was to declare for the King. Despite the new perspectives that have been drawn recently, Mary Coate's judgement of more than sixty years ago still holds good, emphasising as it does:

Port Eliot, in the parish of St Germans in the Hundred of East, is a product of the late eighteenth and nineteenth centuries. An earlier house stood on higher ground, the residence of Sir John Eliot who died in the Tower of London in 1632.

> . . . the passionate attachment of the Cornish to their own county and their own race . . . again and again this local patriotism, born of racial difference and geographical isolation, knit together in a common unity men of differing political and religious opinions.[13]

The minority of Parliamentarian sympathisers—the more Anglicised gentry, concentrated in South East Cornwall—took refuge nearby in Puritan Plymouth but their marginalisation in Cornwall did not mean that they would not be active or significant in Parliament's cause. On occasions families were split, as in the tragic case of Sir Alexander and John Carew, the grandsons of Richard Carew of Antony. They were both executed but by opposing sides, one by Parliament (Sir Alexander had tried to defect to the Royalists but was betrayed) and the other by the Royalists.[14] Hugh Peters, from Fowey, was counted amongst the Regicides responsible for the execution of Charles I, as were the Cornish representatives on the Commission that signed the King's death-warrant: John Carew, Gregory Clement and William Say. A. L. Rowse has described Peters as a 'Puritan propagandist' and 'a religious malcontent', opining that 'Hugh Peters was about the most vilified man in the whole Civil War period . . . .'[15] Indeed, a popular rumour at the time was that Peters was the masked executioner on the scaffold. His real crime, however, was to preach against the King and to be implicated as one of Cromwell's cronies. When, finally, Peters was himself executed a macabre folk-ditty did the rounds:

> Sing hey-ho, my honey,
> My heart shall never rue,
> Twenty-four traitors now for a penny,
> And into the bargain—Hugh.[16]

Stamford Hill re-enacted.

Sir Bevill Grenville emerged as the focus for those Cornish gentry who chose not to side with Parliament; he also became a powerful focus for popular sentiment in Cornwall. A moderate constitutionalist himself, he brought together the various factions and set himself up as champion of Cornwall, establishing a personal military leadership that placed him in command of the new Royalist Cornish Army that had begun recruiting in earnest in October 1642. Like Michael Joseph *An Gof* and Bishop Trelawny (and David Penhaligon in our own time), Bevill Grenville has become embedded in the iconography of Cornish patriotism. His memory today is especially strong in his native North Cornwall, particularly in the district of Stratton—near his former seat at Stowe, and close to the site of the battle of Stamford Hill—where every year the 'Sealed Knot' organisation re-enacts his famous victory over the Roundhead intruders. In the early nineteenth-century, the Rev Robert Stephen Hawker, vicar of Morwenstow in that same tract of North Cornwall, himself a High Churchman resistant to Puritan views, gave expression in verse to a romantic Cornish Royalism that is with us still:

The Tree Inn at Stratton, where Bevil Grenville and the Royalist Officers are reputed to have stayed before the battle of Stamford Hill.

Arise! and away! for the King and the land;
 Farewell to the couch and the pillow:
With spear in the rest, and with rein in the hand,
 Let us rush on the foe like a billow.

Call the hind from the plough, and the herd from the fold
 Bid the wassailer cease from his revel:
And ride for old Stowe; where the banner's unrolled,
 For the cause of King Charles and Sir Beville.

Trevanion is up, and Godolphin is nigh,
 And Harris of Hayne's o'er the river:
From Lundy to Looe, 'One and all' is the cry
 And the King and Sir Beville for ever!

Ay, by Tre, Pol and Pen, ye may know Cornishmen,
 'Mid the names and the nobles of Devon;
But if truth to the King be a signal, why then
 Ye can find out the Granville in heaven.

Ride! ride! with red spur, there is death in delay,
 'Tis a race for dear life with the devil;
If dark Cromwell prevail, and the King must give way,
 This earth is no place for Sir Beville.

So at Stanford he fought, and at Lansdowne he fell,
 But in vain were the visions he cherished . . .
For the great Cornish heart, that the King loved so well,
 In the grave of the Granville is perished.[17]

Although Hawker's view was of course retrospective, his image of a passionate, personal relationship between Cornwall (exemplified in Bevill Grenville) and the Crown was reflected in the propaganda of the time—by both sides. In 1644, for example, the besieged Parliamentarian garrison in Plymouth, suffering constant harassment from the Cornish, declared that it was '. . . eager to be avenged on the cursed Cornish who are as very heathen as the ignorant Welsh that know no religion nor God, but the King is more than God in that country and Wales'.[18] Later, the Parliamentarian leader Fairfax complained of the depth of Cornish sentiment, writing with clear frustration that 'Prince Charles is called the Duke of Cornwall altogether by the Cornish'.[19] The King's or Cavalier camp was as quick to point to the Royalist sympathies of the Cornish. For example, Sir John Birkenhead, the perceptive editor of the Royalist journal *Mercurius Aulicus*, drew a telling and sophisticated comparison between Cornwall and Wales (in the latter, only the heavily Anglicised 'Little England beyond Wales' of Pembrokeshire had declared for Parliament):

> Pembroke is the only remnant of Wales (if it be true Welch) which rebels against his Majestie, for as Pembroke (still called little England beyond Wales) forsook their allegiance when all other Welch counties stood loyal to his Majestie; so Cornwall (which is little Wales beyond England) proved themselves true Brittaines, when no English county stood intirely for his Majestie.[20]

Mark Stoyle has also made much of the comparisons and similarities between Cornwall and Wales in this period. Both became hotbeds of popular Royalist allegiance, and both were singled out for particular contempt by English Roundhead pamphleteers. Thus both the Welsh and Cornish were guilty of 'paganisme' and, in the estimation of one Parliamentarian critic, '. . . when posterity shall see the Gospell shine cleere there [in Wales and Cornwall], they will know what Turks their ancestors were, and what advantage this rebellion had from thence by their forefather's ignorance'.[21] In Wales and Cornwall, as in Ireland and Scotland, argues Stoyle, ethnicity was a profound determinant of a Royalist allegiance which was in turn an integral part of the Welsh, Cornish, Irish and Scots national identities that had by then emerged.

Dr Stoyle also makes much of the contrasts between Cornwall and Devon in the Civil War. Although Devon was essentially Puritan in sympathies and Parliamentarian in politics, it in fact exhibited a considerable diversity in culture and popular loyalty. South, South East and even remote North Devon were indeed generally supportive of Parliament but mid-Devon was noticeably more Royalist. Royalist sympathy was especially characteristic of the Dartmoor tinners (Duchy of Cornwall and Stannary men) who—as in the rebellion of 1549—had more in common with the Cornish than their Devon compatriots. As Stoyle wisely remarks, '. . . it is too often forgotten that Devon was a marcher (or border) county, the River Tamar forming a racial frontier between Anglo-Saxon England and Celtic Cornwall'.[22]

However, as Stoyle admits, the march in fact straddled the Tamar. The far north-east of Cornwall, the Hundred of Stratton, was—in the words of the Royalist historian Clarendon—'the only part of Cornwall eminently disaffected to the King'. It was geographically remote from the rest of Cornwall, and was characterised by English rather than Celtic placenames. In 1645 the parishes of Stratton, Whitstone, Bridgerule, Marhamchurch, Launcells and Poundstock rose against the Royalists, and in 1646 there was a further rising in Morwenstow and Kilkhampton. Stoyle's explanation is that the Stratton district was in effect an 'English enclave in north-east Cornwall', a 'little England in Cornwall' where popular sympathies were often Parliamentarian rather than Royalist and where the inhabitants '. . . preferred to co-operate with the people of north-west Devon rather than with their fellow Cornishmen'.[23] An intriguing aside here is that Stratton Hundred was, of course, the home of Sir Bevill Grenville, darling of the Cornish Royalist cause, a powerful affirmation of Stoyle's argument that in Cornwall (and elsewhere) popular allegiance in the Civil War was usually a function of culture and religion rather than deference to the preferences of local gentry.

A bench-end in Kilkhampton church, deep in Grenville territory but in a district that rose against the Royalists in 1646.

Taking an overview of the rest of Cornwall, Mark Stoyle insists that 'The vast majority of the common people supported the King, a fact that was demonstrated again and again as the war progressed'.[24] He concedes that West Cornwall was more solidly for the King than was the East but he notes that, in terms of popular allegiance, Bodmin, Liskeard and the countryside around Saltash were clearly Royalist areas. And just as Stratton remained unmoved by Grenville's Royalism, so the tenants of Lord Robartes of Lanhydrock in South East Cornwall were not persuaded to embrace his Parliamentary and Puritan enthusiasms. Again the deference model is discredited, and Dr Stoyle argues that explanations for Cornwall's support for the King must be sought in Cornish popular and religious culture, and in the institution of the Duchy of Cornwall. Despite the activity of the Puritans, their impact was limited geographically and socially, in the manner described above. The populace as a whole was religiously conservative—Roundhead pamphleteers described Cornwall as '. . . a corner of ignorants . . . a place full of superstitious and popishly affected persons . . . a pagan principality'.[25] And, as Stoyle notes, in the far west in the 1640s there was still a substantial Cornish-speaking population, linguistically and culturally resistant to English influences—not only to Puritan religious teachings but to the stream of scurrilous ballads and newsheets that had done much to tarnish the monarchy elsewhere.

Although the Duchy as an institution had suffered neglect in the closing years of Elizabeth's reign, it had been reinvigorated under the early Stuarts, emerging as a political device to reinforce Stuart aims. In Cornwall, the effect was to re-emphasise once again the constitutional peculiarity and political accommodation inherent within the Duchy, while also encouraging the common Cornish to support the Stuart cause. The Parliamentarians, by contrast, were seen from the beginning as external intruders, inheritors of the Tudor mantle who intended to impose foreign ways upon Cornwall. It was no co-incidence when in July 1646 the Parliamentarian troops of the Earl of Essex, having crossed the Tamar, not only desecrated the church of St Bartholomew in Lostwithiel but—in an act of great symbolic importance—gutted the Duchy Palace, the physical manifestation of Cornwall's claim to separate political existence. The Duchy, through the Stannaries, had played a vital part in securing Cornwall for the King, and the Cornish tinners were the backbone of the small Cornish army that time and again checked superior Roundhead forces. The export of Cornish tin was vital in acquiring funds for the purchase of the King's munitions.

Sir Ralph Hopton had arrived in Cornwall in September 1642 to rally the Cornish volunteers and to secure key points, such as Launceston Castle. A Parliamentarian force was rushed to Cornwall but in January 1643 it was routed at the battle of Braddock Down, near Liskeard, its remnants driven across the Tamar at Saltash. In April a second Parliamentarian force crossed into Cornwall, this time in the north, but it too was checked and defeated, driven from Cornwall at the battle of Stamford Hill. The stature of Sir Bevill Grenville was confirmed, and the 'Cornish Foot' had earned itself an enviable reputation.

The remains of the so-called Duchy Palace in Lostwithiel, built by Earl Edmund in 1289 as administrative centre of the Earldom (later Duchy) of Cornwall, a reminder of the considerable degree of independence Cornwall enjoyed in earlier times. Parliamentary forces went out of their way to reduce this important Cornish symbol.

St Bartholomew's church at Lostwithiel, notable for its Breton-style spire but desecrated by the Roundhead troops in 1646.

It was now time for the Cornish to take the offensive, and they did so spectacularly, winning the battles of Lansdowne and Roundway Down and participating in the capture of Bristol at the end of July. However, Sir Bevill Grenville had been struck down and killed leading his men to victory at Lansdowne, while amongst those killed in the bloody fight at Bristol were the other Cornish leaders, Nicholas Slanning and John Trevanion. To these losses was added that of Sidney Godolphin, the Cavalier poet, who earlier in the year had been shot in a skirmish in the Devon village of Chagford, expiring in the porch of the *Three Crowns* inn. Taken together, these losses were a grievous blow to the Cornish army and to the King's long-term prospects in the West:

> The four wheels of Charles's Wain,
> Grenville, Goldolphin, Trevanion, Slanning, slain.[26]

Clarendon, the contemporary Royalist historian, lamented the loss of Grenville, 'the most generally loved man in Cornwall', while of Sidney Godolphin he wrote:

> Though everybody loved his company very well, yet he loved very much to be alone, being in constitution inclined somewhat to melancholy, and to retirement amongst his books; and was so far from being active, that he was contented to be reproached by his friends with laziness . . . Yet the civil war no sooner began . . . than he put himself into the first troops which were raised in the west for the king; and bore the uneasiness and fatigue of winter marches with an exemplar courage and alacrity; until by too brave a pursuit of the enemy, into an obscure village in Devonshire, he was shot with a musket . . . to the excessive grief of his friends, who were all that knew him; and the irreparable damage of the public.[27]

Clarendon may be accused of bias, but let Godolphin speak for himself:

> When then our sorrows we apply
> To our own wants and poverty,
> When we look up in all distress,
> And our own misery confess,
> Sending both thanks and prayers above,
> Then, though we do not know, we love.[28]

However, the gloomy, stunned sense of loss that has come down to us through the ages has obscured the subsequent feats of Cornish arms in the Civil War. Even Mary Coate considered that the capture of Bristol ended the career of the Cornish army as a fighting force, when in reality of course the Old Cornish—as the original army was known—went on to reduce the whole of Dorset to Royalist control and to participate in the siege of Plymouth (1643), the siege of Lyme (1644), the Lostwithiel campaign, the siege of Taunton (1645), and various other actions. Moreover, little attention has been given to the New Cornish Tertia of 1644-46, fresh troops which were raised in the aftermath of the Lostwithiel campaign of 1644 and became what one contemporary observer called 'Sir Richard Grenville's creatures'.[29]

The Lostwithiel campaign (which resulted in the torching of the Duchy

The recently restored Stuart House in Liskeard, where the Duke of Cornwall (later Charles II) was reputed to have stayed during his time in Cornwall.

Palace) was an attempt by the Roundheads to take advantage of a number of reverses experienced by the Royalists. Lord Robartes had advised—wrongly—that an invading Parliamentary force would be welcomed by the populace of South East Cornwall and when in July 1644 Essex crossed the Tamar and penetrated as far as Bodmin and Lanhydrock, he found himself in the midst of hostile country. His forces were defeated at Lostwithiel and Fowey, Essex himself noting that '. . . the country people being violent against us, if any of our scouts or soldiers fall into their hands they are more bloody than the enemy'.[30] Indeed, the slaughter in the 'Cornish mousetrap' (as Cornwall was known) was one of the most nightmarish experiences of the Parliamentarian forces in the entire Civil War. Of the seven thousand who had marched in to Cornwall, only one thousand escaped across the Tamar.

Having driven the Roundheads from Cornwall once more, the Royalists prepared to redeploy their forces to the main theatre of war up-country. This would leave Cornwall only lightly defended, and to prevent a Parliamentarian counter-attack from besieged Plymouth, Sir Richard Grenville (brother of the late Sir Bevill and a defector from the Roundhead cause) was entrusted with continuing the Plymothian blockade. By the end of 1644 Grenville had raised between five and six thousand men, a remarkable achievement which reflected the power of the Grenville name and the decision by Sir Richard to present himself as a specifically Cornish leader. The new 'tertia' (division) thus raised consisted of four regiments (though later reduced to three): those of Grenville himself, John Arundell, Richard Arundell, and Lewis Tremaine.

In January 1645 the New Cornish Tertia was unleashed upon Plymouth but the attack failed, despite the individual success of one of the Arundell regiments. Shortly after, Grenville was ordered to Taunton, leaving the Cornish trained bands (the militia) to maintain the watch on Plymouth. However, he was badly wounded at Taunton, even before an attack could be launched, and was evacuated to Exeter, leaving his troops in the care of Sir John Berkeley who—being a 'foreigner'—did not enjoy the confidence of the officers and men. In May 1645 Berkeley was replaced by Lord George Goring, who managed to antagonise the Cornish even further, leading to wholesale desertions.

The Prince of Wales (Duke of Cornwall), who had been given titular command of all Royalist forces in South West Britain, invited the by now recovered Grenville to resume his old command but, with Goring forced to abandon Taunton in the face of a Parliamentarian advance, there was no immediate way of giving Grenville back his troops. The Prince retired to the safety of his Cornwall, and belatedly Grenville was able to recover and regroup the remnants of his tertia. By the end of October Sir Richard had decided to concentrate his forces at Okehampton to resist the inevitable Parliamentarian advance. However, he was compelled to withdraw to Cornwall, leaving a core of defenders in Okehampton, because the activities of Goring in North Cornwall had provoked an anti-Royalist uprising. Grenville posted troops along the Tamar to keep Goring's marauding and plundering troops out of his territory. Having thus secured Cornwall, Grenville expended considerable effort in trying to persuade the Prince to set-up a neutral, semi-independent statelet within his Duchy. As Mary Coate put it, Grenville's energies were '. . . directed more to the saving of Cornwall than to the preservation of the Royalist cause'.[31]

However, the Prince was determined to fight on and in January 1646 Sir Richard Grenville was imprisoned, first in Launceston and then safely out of

Tresillian Bridge, where the Cornish army formally surrendered to Fairfax's Roundhead forces on 12 March 1646.

the way on St Michael's Mount, his Cornish particularism now seen as a threat to Royalist war aims. Meanwhile, the New Cornish Tertia suffered a stinging defeat at Torrington in North Devon, although many of its soldiers managed to make it back across the Tamar. Thereafter, the Royalist forces continued to retreat back into Cornwall. The Prince managed to escape into exile, as did Grenville who extricated himself from the Mount (as a turncoat, he would almost certainly have been executed by Parliament), and the formal surrender of the Royalist army to Fairfax occurred at Tresillian Bridge on 12 March 1646. St Mawes Castle surrendered without a fight, the Mount held out for another month, and Pendennis resisted until the August when finally John Arundell— 'Jack for the King'—proudly surrendered and marched out of the castle with 'colours flying, trumpets sounding, drums beating'. The Civil War in Cornwall was all but over.

As the above indicates, the conduct of the war in Cornwall and the activities of the Cornish forces—the Old Cornish as well as the New Cornish Tertia—emphasised the particular Cornish dimension of the conflict. One result of this Cornish particularism was the contrasting imagery of the Cornish displayed by both sides, Royalist as well as Parliamentarian, in their respective propaganda. As well as applauding (or denigrating) the Royalist sympathies of the Cornish, such propaganda also drew images of the Cornish *as a people*.[32]

The Royalists, for their part, were careful to emphasise the military prowess of the Cornish. In 1643 the Royalist journal *Mercurius Aulicus* declared that the Roundheads had 'lately received the Cornish hugge', an allusion to the Cornish reputation as wrestlers as well as to their recent victories, and in 1645 the Parliamentarians were warned 'that there is much danger in a Cornish hugg'. Interestingly, the Parliamentarians themselves adopted the phrase, using it ironically in descriptions of operations against the Cornish, as in the gratuitous note of a raiding party from Plymouth which attacked the besiegers 'and gave eight or ten of them the Cornish hug'. From a metaphor for military prowess, 'the Cornish hug' had become a casual off-hand phrase for killing. *Mercurius Aulicus*, however, continued to extol the Cornish as 'brave', 'stout', 'resolute', linking this courage to devotion to the King's cause. Thus the 'gallant Cornish . . . are all resolved to spend their lives for his Sacred Majestie' and 'no Prince in Christendom hath better subjects [than the Cornish] . . . they still value their honour and consciousness above their blood'.

However, behind these fulsome public utterances was a more private concern about the behaviour of the Cornish and the wisdom of arming them. Skirmishing between Cornish regiments and other Royalist units (particularly Prince Maurice's cavalry) was not unknown and in 1644 Cornish soldiers refused to let 'beastly, buggering' Frenchmen of the Queen's Guard enter Cornwall. There was rivalry between Irish and Cornish regiments, the two groups insulting each other as 'Cornish Choughs' and 'Irish Kernes' respectively. Concern that the Cornish might be working to their own agenda was also present, as in 1644 when its was observed that the Royalists at Oxford 'exclaim against Cornwall . . . it is believed that now the King has armed them they will suffer neither his Majesty's nor his Excellency's forces to come among them'. As Mark Stoyle has observed,

> . . . Cornish soldiers tended to serve in exclusively Cornish regiments, under the command of their own officers. The more one examines the evidence, in fact, the more forcefully one is struck by the impression that the Cornish were fighting as a people, rather than simply as supporters of Charles I.[33]

The Parliamentarians, for their part, were in no doubt about the treacherous and devious ways of the Cornish. Depicted as beggarly, poverty-stricken quasi-papists, an unsavoury picture of the Cornish was drawn by Roundhead propagandists. Hopton's army was dismissed as '4,000 almost starved pore Cornish' and, such was this contempt, that at the siege of Lyme in 1644 the Roundhead garrison declared it would 'give no quarter to any Irish or Cornish'. After the disaster of the Lostwithiel campaign, the Roundheads were especially vigorous in their condemnation of the 'cruel Cornish', the 'cursed Cornish', the 'perfidious Cornish', one account condemning the 'heathenish Cornish, who pillaged our foot' and another (in a vivid echo of English accounts of Irish atrocities against Protestants in the rebellion of 1641) describing how men and women were stripped naked and thrown into the river. Those Parliamentarian soldiers who had almost starved in Cornwall, 'mean either to give the Cornish a dieting in requital here, or send them to Break-fast in another world'.

The Cornish as trogdolytic pagans was a favourite Roundhead theme, raising the spectre of the 'Cornish mettal-men' of 'heathen . . . Hellish, Cornwall'. As one pamphleteer put it, 'the men of Cornwall are very heathens, a corner of ignorants and atheists, drained from the mines'. The Cornish were also plunderers, 'Cornish Choughs' to their detractors, the magpie-like kleptomania of the chough a useful allusion in the attempt to stereotype and smear. Moreover, the Cornish were characterised as 'rebels' and 'traitors'. Not only did they 'rebel' (in the ideological language of the Roundheads) against the will and sovereignty of Parliament, but also their

St Michael's Mount was held for the King during the Civil War, and Richard Grenville was imprisoned here briefly. The St Aubyn family acquired the Mount after the Civil War, and live there still. This is the Blue Drawing Room, which contains some fine Rococo Gothic plaster-work, and dates from the time of Sir John St Aubyn of whom Sir Robert Walpole is reputed to have said: 'All . . . men have their price except the little Cornish Baronet'.

historical reputation was as rebels against authority. The Prayer Book Rebellion of 1549 had been known popularly (to Carew and others) as 'the Commotion', and a telling comparison was being made in 1642 when one Parliamentarian referred to 'Cornwall's second commotion'.

And yet, despite all this and the Roundhead cries for revenge in the aftermath of Lostwithiel, the Parliamentarian subduel of Cornwall was not the vicious blood-bath that had been threatened and feared. Instead, as in their cautious treatment of the Welsh, the Parliamentarians listened to explanations (from the likes of Hugh Peters) that the rustic and gullible Cornish had been deceived by the Cavaliers and duped by their religious leaders. However, in 1646 Peters also warned his Roundhead colleagues that there was 'a common muttering among [the Cornish] that their country was never conquered'. As Stoyle observes, the inference was that many Cornish had seen the Civil War as a war between Cornwall and England. In an echo of Henry Tudor's policy after 1497, the Parliamentarians knew that they would have to tread carefully in their pacification of Cornwall. They were sparing of blood and, as in the case of Sir Richard Vyvyan, who was able to hold on to his family seat at Trelowarren, Fairfax's intervention prevented the wholesale ruin (and alienation) of the Cornish gentry. Even so, Royalist leaders such as Sir Francis Godolphin had sought exile overseas, while the fines that were imposed almost destroyed Jonathan Rashleigh of Fowey and forced the Bassets to sell St Michael's Mount to the St Aubyn family (who have held it ever since).

And in other respects the Parliamentarians did 'go for the Cornish jugular'. As in 1549, the priests were seen as dangerous opinion leaders. Amongst those driven from their livings were the vicars of Ludgvan, Lanivet, St Cleer, Warbstow, St Goran, St Keverne, St Buryan; in other words, from all across Cornwall. The rood screens and rood lofts of some Cornish churches were dismantled after the Parliamentary victory, and stained glass windows were smashed—although, mercifully, those at St Neot survived, despite the fact that the vicar there also had lost his living. In a firm attack on the constitutional accommodation of Cornwall (and its Royalist connotations), both the Duchy of Cornwall as an institution and the Stannary Parliament were abolished, while Cornish representation in the Westminster Parliament was reduced from forty-four to twelve. A County Committee was set-up to run Cornwall, mindful that even yet 'Cornwall was cavileerish enough . . . .[34]

Indeed, significant Royalist sympathy did remain active in Cornwall. The Trelawny and Arundell families were implicated in Royalist intrigues, and the Scillies survived under the leadership of Sir John Grenville as a base for Royalist privateers until captured by Admiral Blake in May 1651. Meanwhile, a potentially serious rebellion had broken out in Cornwall in May 1648. At Penzance, Parliamentary troops were able to nip a local rising in the bud but across on the Lizard peninsula the men of Mullion and St Keverne (the by now traditional home of Cornish rebellion) prepared to march on Helston. At the Iron Age earthwork at Gear, near Trelowarren, they were met and defeated by the troops from Penzance in the so-called 'Gear Route'. In 1655 Cornish Royalists refused to join an ill-planned and ill-fated rising in Wiltshire, which had attempted to break into Dorset and Devon with a view to rousing the Cornish, although in the spring of 1657 a number of Cornish Royalist sympathisers was arrested as a precaution.

In September 1658 Cromwell died, and in 1660 in the Restoration of the monarchy, Charles II became king. Sir John Grenville (Bevill's son) became Earl of Bath, Viscount Lansdowne. The Duchy and Stannaries were restored, as were Cornwall's forty-four MPs, and Penzance—the seat of the rising in 1648—was rewarded with its elevation to the status of Stannary town. Although, in practice, the restored institutions of accommodation did not fully recover their semblance of semi-autonomy, moving again towards stagnation and eventual metamorphosis, their restoration was a politically astute means of recognising and rewarding Cornwall's particular role in the Royalist cause. Certainly, despite their rebellious reputation, the Cornish steered well clear of Monmouth's western rising of 1685, once again showing no inclination to make common cause with the Puritan enthusiasts of Devon and Somerset (and thus escaping the later attentions of Judge Jeffries). However, the imprisonment of Bishop Jonathan Trelawny by James II two years later in 1687 caused resentment and discontent in Cornwall, although not to the extent suggested by R.S. Hawker's romantic evocation of the event:

> A good sword and a trust hand!
> A merry heart and true!
> King James's men shall understand
> What Cornish lads can do!
>
> And have they fixed the where and when?
> And shall Trelawny die?
> Here's twenty thousand Cornish men
> Will know the reason why!

Out spake our Captain brave and bold:
A merry wight was he:-
'If London Tower were Michael's hold'
We'd set Trelawny free!

'We'll cross the Tamar, land to land:
The Severn is no stay:
With "one and all", and hand in hand;
And who shall bid us nay?

'And when we come to London Wall,
A pleasant sight to view,
Come forth! come forth! ye cowards all;
Here's men as good as you.

'Trelawny he's in keep and hold:
Trelawny he may die:
But here's twenty thousand Cornish bold
Will know the reason why!'[35]

Jonathan Trelawny was born in March 1650, a member of the well-known landed family from South East Cornwall whose properties and connections are remembered in the rhyme:

Trelawne, Trelask, Trelay,
Ashleighcross, little Bell Hay,
And Trendaway.[36]

In the Civil War the Trelawnys had been Royalist supporters, and after the Restoration this loyalty brought them preferment, Jonathan Trelawny rising in the Church of England and establishing a reputation as a successful Tory Churchman. His celebrated confrontation with the Catholic James II was a result of his refusal, as Bishop of Bristol, to read James' second Declaration of Indulgence which granted toleration to Catholics and Dissenters. Trelawny was one of the so-called 'Seven Bishops' who joined in this refusal, considering the Declaration an affront to the status of the Anglican Church (James II recalled that 'My Lord of Bristol was the most saucy of the Seven'). Trelawny had assisted in the suppression of the Monmouth rebellion in 1685, and in 1687 had acted as the king's watchdog in the meeting of the Stannary Parliament of that year, keeping an eye out for undue assertions of Cornish independence. He was thus outraged when the king accused him of rebellion:

> Rebellion, Sir! I beseech your Majesty do not say so hard a thing of us; for God's sake! Do not believe we are or can be guilty of rebellion! It is impossible for me or my family to be guilty of rebellion! Your Majesty cannot but remember that you sent me to quell Monmouth's rebellion and I am as ready to do what I can to quell another. We will do our duty to your Majesty to our utmost in everything that does not interfere with our duty towards God.[37]

Trelawny and the rest of the Seven Bishops were committed to the Tower and charged with seditious libel. However, they were acquitted by the jury

And shall Trelawny Die? The chair and crook of Bishop Jonathan Trelawny are preserved in Pelynt church.

that examined them, part of the run of occurrences in which James II gradually lost control of events in his realm. In Pelynt, Trelawny's native parish, the bells were rung in triumph, and there were celebrations at neighbouring Looe. However, there was no Cornish rebellion (or threat of rebellion) of the kind suggested by Hawker. Despite the Declaration incident, Trelawny remained loyal to James II during the deteriorating period that led to James' flight and his replacement by William and Mary in the 'Glorious Revolution' of 1688. It was not until 5 November 1688 that Trelawny thought it tactful to write to William of Orange, welcoming his actions to preserve the Law and the Protestant Church. Even then he stopped short of offering William his unequivocal support, and in Parliament he was one of those who resisted the plan to offer the throne to William and Mary. He only gave his assent when he realised that it was necessary to do so, bowing to the inevitable. Today, when Cornish rugby supporters are known as 'Trelawny's Army', and when these supporters at Twickenham in 1989 sported 'Trelawny's Second Invasion' sweatshirts, it is ironic that it is Trelawny's non-rebellion that is routinely celebrated while 1497 and 1549 have generally slipped from public view.

Inevitably, the dramatic events of the seventeenth-century had an important impact upon Cornwall. In economic terms, however, there was less dislocation than might have been expected. The fact that agriculture dominated both land use and employment probably accounted for this (agriculture is often more flexible than other kinds of production, and there is less opportunity for infrastructural destruction), while the opening- up of increased contact with the outside world may have provided new opportunities and promoted the evident growing coastal shipping. As James Whetter observes, what is most striking about the Cornish economy in this period is its stability and resilience in the face of war, disruption and uncertainty. However, behind this stability there was change and development.

The early seventeenth-century was a time of relative prosperity, although the coincidence of bad harvests and plague outbreaks in 1626 and 1627 was certainly deleterious. And Cornwall was by no means wealthy, the tax commissioners in 1623 apologising for the poor return from Cornwall: 'The scarcity of money, decay of coast fishing, loss by tin mines, and low price of cattle and wool, prevent it being larger'.[38] Although the war years were surprisingly un-disruptive, those areas that witnessed actual engagements between the rival armies were of course affected. Thus in the parish of Linkinhorne in South East Cornwall, '. . . the Country was much impoverished in the Late Civil Warre being the Thorowfare for all Armies which had occasion to March East and West'.[39]

The period 1650-1680 saw a general rise in prosperity (Whetter suggests that the Commonwealth, however it might have been viewed in Cornwall, was actually a stimulus to economic development). The Hearth Tax of 1662 revealed that the principal concentration of wealth continued to be in South East Cornwall but it also indicated a new concentration of wealth around Falmouth Haven, hinting at a general shift in economic activity from east to west that was by then underway. In the years after the 'Glorious Revolution' in 1688, despite the apparent return of political normality, the expansion of the Cornish economy was checked by poor harvests and renewed outbreaks of plague. Tinners were by now implicated in the periodic 'food riots' that would bring them notoriety in the eighteenth-century.

Throughout the seventeenth-century, agriculture dominated the Cornish economy in terms of employment. But farms were small, over half consisted of less than fifteen acres, and a full eighty percent was under forty acres. Much farming was of a part-time and subsistence nature, combined with other occupations such as fishing (of an inevitable seasonal nature) and tin mining. There was some regional specialisation within Cornwall; for example, moorland areas were used for cattle-rearing while the lowlands (with their richer grazing) were used for fattening. Agriculture was generally diversified, including animals like cattle, sheep, pigs and horses, together with crops of barley, wheat, oats and, occasionally, flax and hemp. By 1676 there were references to 'Cornish potatoes', and, despite the subsistence level of much of Cornish farming, surplus corn produce was increasingly exported to destinations that included France, Spain and the Canaries, as well as Plymouth, Exeter, London and Bristol.

Fishing was also significant, and during the seventeenth-century, the populations of fishing ports like St Ives and Mevagissey grew markedly. The pilchard fishery was the most important, and during the course of the century it became more concentrated in Cornish waters (fewer pilchard shoals ventured further east along the South Devon coast) while the pilchard season itself expanded. Although generally considered a summer harvest, pilchards were increasingly caught during the winter months, as in January 1671 when a large catch was landed at Mevagissey. The herring fishery was also important, while Looe and Fowey specialised in the catching of ray for export to Brittany. Hake and conger were exported to Spain and Mediterranean countries. There was also a thriving inshore fishery specialising in shellfish, and in Cornish rivers salmon and peal were caught. The Cornish also participated in the development of the Newfoundland cod fishery although, compared to the major involvement of Devon ports such as Dartmouth and Bideford, their impact was limited.

Similarly, compared to the Devon cloth industry, the Cornish trade in wool and cloth was modest. Nevertheless, it did create wealth and employment, especially east of the Fowey-Camel line where, as Dr Whetter observes, the Cornish economy was increasingly geared to the stimulus of contact with Devon. Cloth was exported to Devon, and Devon merchants visited Cornish towns to purchase both wool and finished cloth. The prevalence of the placename Vellandruckya (and its localised English equivalent, Tuckingmill), meaning fulling mill, attest to the widespread existence of cloth-making in Cornwall in this period. Although the export of cloth overseas was banned (so as to support the indigenous industry), Cornish producers did engage in smuggling operations—as in 1661 when it was discovered that a St Malo vessel was regularly carrying illicit cargoes of wool and tin from Fowey to Brittany.

Sea traffic, both coastal and international, increased during the seventeenth-century. The rapid development of Falmouth Haven led to the exploitation of hitherto latent resources—both on land and in the sea—and export markets grew. As Whetter observes, Cornwall '. . . had a near monopoly of both tin and pilchards in Britain, and indeed, in Western Europe . . . tin mining and pilchard fishing were geared almost entirely to overseas markets . . . '.[40] Of these two, tin was to prove the more significant: 'The exceptional feature of the Cornish economy in the seventeenth-century was tin mining'.[41] The expansion of tin was dependent on a number of factors. The near-monopoly position was important (tin was used extensively in seventeenth-century society for the manufacture of pewter) but also significant was the high price of tin after the Civil War and the abandonment of the practice of 'pre-emption' (discussed below). To these were added the increasing interest in tin exhibited by merchants anxious to diversify into new and profitable areas, and the improvements in technology. There were advances in drainage and pumping and the application of water-power, and by the end of the century gunpowder had been introduced for blasting. Indeed, Whetter considers that in mining and other Cornish industries, '. . . developments in this century laid the foundations for technical advances and expansion in output in the eighteenth'.[42]

Godolphin Hall, west of Helston, the ancient home of the Godolphins, the family which played such a major role in the events of seventeenth-century Cornwall.

The early part of the seventeenth-century, however, had witnessed a decline in tin mining in East Cornwall, especially around Callington and Stoke Climsland, although further west in mid-Cornwall there were important tinworks in the neighbourhood of St Austell—notably the Great Hewas or Poldragon mine in St Ewe. Further west, there was considerable activity, especially at Godolphin Bal (or Ball), the vast tinwork near Helston said to have employed some three hundred hands and counted as the source of the Godolphin family's wealth. A survey of 1618 noted some four hundred specialist tinners ('spallers') in West Cornwall: forty at St Just-in-Penwith, forty in Wendron, thirty-six at Breage, and thirty each at Sithney, Gwennap and Redruth. By the second half of the century tin mining had expanded in west and central Cornwall. In Gwennap parish mines such as Ting Tang and Poldice had already acquired the fame that would characterise them in later centuries, and there was a steady rise in the number of mines and blowinghouses in the areas of St Agnes, Penzance, Kenwyn and St Allen. In 1697 the traveller Celia Fiennes noted some twenty mines at St Austell and a further hundred tinworks between there and Tregony. Although the tinners shared in the general economic depression at the end of the century, the volume of tin production had in fact increased two-and-a-half fold during the course of the seventeenth-century.

As James Whetter has written, '. . . by the second half of the century . . . tin mining, in parts of the centre and west, was monopolising resources of labour and capital to a degree not known before'.[43] Before the Civil War, the Duchy of Cornwall had maintained a tight control over the production of tin through the royal prerogative of pre-emption—the right of the crown to purchase all metal produced by tinners and to sell it as it saw fit. In practice, pre-emption was normally farmed out to London pewterers in contracts which allowed these pre-emptors to purchase all the tinners' metal at a fixed rate, normally for a period of seven years. This practice was defended as a means of preventing the exploitation of tinners, giving them security when times were bad, but it also militated against the tinners when the demand for tin was high and the price of tin-based commodities rose. Here the tinners (unlike the pewterers) did not share in the increased revenue and wealth, a factor which helped retard the development of Cornish mining in the first half of the seventeenth-century. However, the victory of Parliament in the Civil War swept away the Duchy and its administrations, and amongst the casualties was pre-emption. The effect was dramatic, leading to tin price rises, an expansion of output, and increased profitability which in turn led to the further expansion of the industry. The impact was so marked that, after the Restoration, attempts to restore pr-emption were doomed to failure. As Whetter has concluded, 'by the end of the century . . . tin mining had become the dynamic element in the economy, the main force for prosperity—or depression, as the case might be'.[44]

Despite the general expansion and resilience of the Cornish economy, tin had nevertheless emerged as the central, crucial feature of Cornish economic activity, a main determinant of prosperity or poverty in Cornwall—as it was to be for the next two centuries or more. Copper mining, too, had reappeared in Cornwall in the latter part of the seventeenth-century. It had first emerged a century before but had languished because the available technology was then insufficient to support the mining of deeper copper lodes. However, the technological advances of the seventeenth-century, together with the abandonment in 1689 and 1693 of the royal monopoly of copper mining, aroused new interest and facilitated the industry's development. By the early nineteenth-century copper had outstripped tin as Cornwall's principal metal, and together these two metals dominated and shaped the Cornish economy in its industrial hey-day.

But if the Cornish economy was resilient in the seventeenth-century, then the Cornish language was less so, and one of the principal effects of the upheavals and new contacts was the further decline in Cornish. Richard Symonds, a Royalist officer who served in Cornwall during the Lostwithiel campaign in 1644, noted that 'This language is spoken altogether at Goonhilly and about Pendennis, and at Land's End they speak no English. All beyond Truro they speak the Cornish language'.[45] However, Symonds' knowledge was probably second-hand (his duties were unlikely to have taken him west of Truro), and the likelihood was that Cornish was by then under even more pressure than when commented upon by Carew. Indeed, many of the younger Cornish-speakers serving in the Royalist army would have been up-rooted from their Cornish-language communities (although some of the Cornish regiments will have been Cornish-speaking, at least in part). Additionally, it may also be the case that the economic resilience emphasised by Whetter was in fact responsible for still further pressure upon the language. The development of coastal shipping and the growing contact with Devon merchants in the cloth trade, together with other increased external contacts, would all have been vehicles for the spread of English in this period.

In 1662, after the Restoration, the naturalist John Ray visited the far-west of Cornwall, making the acquaintance of one 'Dickan Gwyn' (Dick Angwin of Bojewyan) and noting that:

> Mr Dickan Gwyn lives not far off, in St Just Parish, who is the only man we could hear of that can now write the Cornish language. We met none here but what could speak English; few of the children could speak Cornish, so that the language is like, in a short time, to be quite lost.[46]

In fact, Ken George has estimated that the number of Cornish-speakers fell from approximately 22,000 in 1600 to some 14,000 in 1650, and from there to a small core of about 5,000 in 1700. By 1750 there were 'very few', and the language had disappeared as a spoken vernacular by 1800.[47] Dick Angwin was one of a small group of Cornish scholars who, in the closing decades of the seventeenth-century and the opening decades of eighteenth, recognised that they were witnessing the rapid demise of their language and decided to do something about it. They corresponded in Cornish, collected words and verses and proverbs, gave accounts of the state of the language, and even (in one case) did work on the medieval literary manuscripts. John Keigwin of Mousehole, grandson of the Keigwin killed in the Spanish raid of 1595, took it upon himself to translate into Cornish Charles I's famous *Letter of Thanks* to the Cornish people for their help in the Civil War, the English version of which still hangs in many Cornish churches.

At nearby Newlyn was Nicholas Boson. As a child his mother had prevented him from learning Cornish by forbidding the servants and neighbours to speak to him in anything but English, a strategy we may accept as typical of the time. However, Boson later picked-up the language and became a devotee. His *Nebbaz Gerriau dro tho Carnoack* (A Few Words about Cornish), written in the late seventeenth-century, tells the familiar story of decline:

> Gun Tavas Carnoack eu mar pu hez, uz na ellen skant quatiez tho ewellaz crefhe arta, rag car greeg an Sausen e thanen en pow idden ma an kensa, an delna ema stella teggo warno tha hep garra tho tha telhar veeth buz dro tho an Aulz ha an more, el eu a va clappiez lebben oggastigh eu durt pedn an wollaz tho an karrack looez, ha tuah Poreeah ha Redruth, ha arta durt an Lizard tuah Helles ha Falmouth: ha an powna, an idna deu Codna teer ez en fester a dro tha iggens moldeer, ha buz quarter, en po hanter an lester na; en telhar idden ma ha gul ma mouy Sousenack clappiez dre eza Curnooack, rag radden el bose keevez na el skant clappia, na guthvaz Curnooack, buz skant Denveeth buz ore guthvaz ha clappia Sousenack; rag hedna he volden kallick eue tho gweel

dotha gurtaz ha dose a dro arta, rag ugge an Teez goth tho merwal akar, ny a wele an Teez younk tho e clappia le ha le, ha lacka ha lacka, ha an dena eue a vedden heha durt Termen tho Termen.[48]

Boson also provided an English translation, so that the above becomes:

> Our Cornish tongue hath been so long in the Wane, that We can hardly hope to see it increase again, for as the English confined it into this narrow Countrey first, so it presseth on still leaving it no Place but about the Cliff & Sea, it being almost only spoken from the Lands-End to the Mount & towards St Ives and Redruth, and again from the Lizard to Helston, and towards Falmouth: and these parts in the narrowest two necks of Land, containing about twenty Miles in Length, and not quarter or half that Breadth, within which little Extent also there is more of English spoken than Cornish, for here may be found some that can hardly speak or understand Cornish, but scarce any but both understand and speak English; therefore it seems difficult to stay & recover it again, for the old Men dying away, We find the young Men to speak it less and less, and worse & worse, and so it is like to decay from Time to Time.

Among Nicholas Boson's other Cornish language works are *The Duchess of Cornwall's Progress* and the *John of Chyanhor*, the latter a Cornish version of the international tale known generally as 'The Servant's Good Counsels'. His kinsmen (the precise relationships are not known) were Thomas Boson and John Boson, who both wrote in Cornish. Amongst several pieces by John Boson is his letter dated 17 February 1712 to William Gwavas, containing a lament and epitaph for James Jenkins, another of this group of scholars:

> Lebbn duath Tavaz coth ny en Kernow
> Rag kar ny Jenkins gelles durt an Pow
> Vor hanow taz ny en Eue tha Canow.[49]

Or, in English:

> Cornwall now Mourne thy Tongue just lost and gone
> Jenkins, our Cornish Bard is fled among
> The Saints to sing his Everlasting Song.

Another interesting survival is the Cornish language inscription prepared by Thomas Boson for William Gwavas' silver hurling ball (even today, the silver ball used in the Shrove Tuesday hurling contest between 'town' and 'country' at St Columb has an inscribed motto). Gwavas provided the English translation:

> An pelle Arrance ma ve resse,
> gen mere Hurleyey, Creve, ha brosse,
> Do Wella Gwavas, an Deane gentle,
> an Kensa journa a messe Heddra an Centle,
> en plew Paule, in Cernow Teage
> an Blooth Creste an Arleuth whege
> Meele Sithcans ha hanter Deege.[50]

This Silver bale was given
With many Hurlers Stronge & greet
To William Gwavas gent.
the first day of September was the tyme
in the parish of paule in Cornwall faire
in the year of our Sweete Lord Christe
a thousand seven hundred & the half of ten (vis) fiue

Nicholas Boson's account of the state of the Cornish language is complemented in an analysis of its decline by William Scawen. Scawen lived at Molenick in the parish of St Germans, many miles east of the Cornish-speaking area. However, he had served in the Royalist army during the Civil War, where no doubt he had encountered the language, and after his appointment as Lord Warden of the Stannaries at the Restoration he would again have met Cornish speakers. He was persuaded to take an active interest in the language, when in 1678 he and others attending Launceston Assizes were upbraided by the Lord Chief Justice, Sir Francis North, for allowing its decay. Thereafter, he devoted himself to Cornish until his death in 1689. He drew attention to one of the last monoglots (named elsewhere as Chesten Marchant of Gwithian, who had died c1676) whose English was so slight that she had to make habitual use of an interpreter. He also listed a number of reasons for the decline of Cornish. Amongst these were the loss of intimate contact with Brittany, the demise of the Miracle Plays, a general apathy towards the language, the dismissive attitude of the gentry (shades of Carew), the proximity to Devon (which he would have felt keenly at St Germans), contact with outsiders (especially traders in tin and fish, and ministers of religion), the lack of a Cornish Prayer Book, and the failure of people to correspond in Cornish or to preserve Cornish manuscripts.

William Gwavas (1676-1741) and Thomas Tonkin (1678-1742) were two other members of this group of Cornish enthusiasts. Gwavas, although born in Suffolk, was from the family long established at Gwavas in the parish of Sithney, near Helston. He lived most of his life in Penzance, and was in close contact with Keigwin, the Bosons, Oliver Pendar of Newlyn, James Jenkins of Alverton (honoured in the Boson epitaph), John Odger at the Lizard, and 'several ancient persons in Paul, St Just, St Keverne etc. both men and women that could speak the modern Cornish'.[51] Gwavas also wrote in Cornish to an unnamed correspondent in America, an intimation that there were Cornish speakers amongst early emigrants to that continent. William Tonkin spent his later years at Gorran (having lost the family property at Trevaunance, St Agnes, in a law suit!) and devoted himself to a wide range of antiquarian activities, from natural history to topography. Amongst his Cornish language activities, he composed a song eulogising William of Orange and collected from one Edward Chirgwin, c1698, a Cornish version of the well-known folk-song 'Where are you going, my pretty maid?':

Pelea era why moaz, moz, fettow, teag,
 Gen agaz bedgeth gwin, ha agaz blew mellyn?
Mi a moaz tha'n venton, farra, wheag,
 Rag delkiow fevi gwra muzi teag.
Pea ve moaz gen a why, moz, feyyow, teag
 Gen agaz bedgeth gwin, ha agaz blew mellyn?
Greuh mena why, farra wheag,
 Rak Delkiow fevi gwra muzi teag.[52]

Whither are you going pretty fair maid, said he,
With your white face and your yellow hair?
I am going to the well, sweet sir, she said,
For strawberry leaves make maidens fair.
Shall I go with thee pretty fair maid, he said,
With your white face and your yellow hair?
Do if you will sweet sir, she said,
For strawberry leaves make maidens fair.

The activities of the Cornish enthusiasts had caught the attention of Edward Lhuyd, the Oxford scholar who embarked on an exhaustive comparative study of the Celtic languages (and in so doing became a founder of modern Celtic Studies), and this in itself must be seen as one of the triumphs of those concerned Cornishmen who strove to protect and promote their language.[53] Lhuyd painstakingly recorded all he could of the Cornish tongue (he came to Cornwall armed with a letter of introduction from none other than Bishop Jonathan Trelawny, who had earlier encouraged the work of John Keigwin) and he discovered that it was yet spoken in a string of some twenty-five parishes from Land's End to the Lizard. Although Lhuyd saw little future for the Cornish language other than as an antiquarian curio for gentlemen (he compared it unfavourably with Welsh and Breton which were still widely spoken by all classes in their respective countries), he was nonetheless sensitive enough to appreciate and record a rhyme given to him in 1700 by the parish clerk of St Just-in-Penwith:

An lavar koth yw lavar gwir,
Na boz nevra doz vaz an tavaz re hir;
Bez den heb davaz a gollaz i dir.

The old saying is a true saying,
A tongue too long never did good:
But the man with no tongue lost his land.[54]

In a sense, this stands as a telling epitaph for the experience of Cornwall and the Cornish people in the seventeenth-century, not least with respect to their fortunes in the Civil War. As in 1497 and 1549, the Cornish had fought for their privileges as they understood them, against an increasingly intrusive English state that was less and less inclined to make allowances for Cornish difference. And yet this difference had been a formidable force, harnessed with considerable success by the Royalist side and feared, abused, appeased and finally subdued by the Parliamentarians. Keigwin, the Bosons, Scawen and the rest lamented the loss of what they saw as the last of old Cornwall, and in many respects they did truly witness the end of an era.

However, in yet another of the delightful paradoxes that characterises Cornish history, the new Cornwall that emerged from this century of trauma and conflict was equally as Cornish as that which had gone before. The incipient industrialisation noted by James Whetter, with the powerful determining characteristics of Cornish mining, wrought a new Cornwall radically different from its earlier incarnation but one that wholly different and built a modern, assertive Cornish identity based on the notion of industrial prowess.

Notes & References (Chapter 7)

1. Mark Stoyle, '"Pagans or Paragons?": Images of the Cornish during the English Civil War', *The English Historical Review*, Vol.CXI, No.441, April 1996.

2. Mary Coate, *Cornwall in the Great Civil War and Interregnum, 1642-1660*, 1933, repub. Bradford Barton, Truro, 1963; Mark Stoyle, *Loyalty and Locality: Popular Allegiance in Devon during the English Civil War*, University of Exeter Press, Exeter, 1994; Mark Stoyle, April 1996; Mark Stoyle, '"Sir Richard Grenville's Creatures": The New Cornish Tertia, 1644-46', in Philip Payton (ed.), *Cornish Studies: Four*, University of Exeter Press, Exeter, 1996; Anne Duffin, *Faction and Faith: Politics and Religion of the Cornish Gentry Before the Civil War*, University of Exeter Press, Exeter, 1996.

3. Stoyle, April 1996.

4. Duffin, 1996, p.211.

5. James Whetter, *Cornwall in the Seventeenth Century: An Economic History of Kernow*, Lodenek Press, Padstow, 1974; James Whetter, *The History of Falmouth*, Dyllansow Truran, Redruth, 1981; James Whetter, *Cornish Weather and Cornish People in the Seventeenth Century*, Lyfrow Trelyspen, St Austell, 1991.

6. Todd Gray, *Early Stuart Mariners and Shipping: The Maritime Surveys of Devon and Cornwall, 1619-35*, Devon and Cornwall Record Society, Exeter, 1990; Todd Gray, *Harvest Failure in Cornwall and Devon: The Book of Orders and the Corn Surveys of 1623 and 1630-1*, Institute of Cornish Studies, Redruth, 1992.

7. 'The Excellency of the English Tongue', in Richard Carew, *Survey of Cornwall*, 1602, ed. F.E. Halliday, Melrose, London, 1953, p.303.

8. Carew, 1602 (1953), p.127.

9. Carew, 1602 (1953), pp.144-145.

10. John Chynoweth, 'The Gentry of Tudor Cornwall', unpub. PhD, University of Exeter, 1994.

11.See Duffin, 1996, especially chapter 2.

12. A.L. Rowse, *A Cornish Anthology*, Macmillan, London, 1968, p.117.

13. Coate, 1933 & 1963, p.351.

14. F.E. Halliday, *A Cornish Chronicle: The Carews of Antony from Armada to Civil War*, David and Charles, Newton Abbot, 1967.

15. A.L. Rowse, *Four Caroline Portraits*, Duckworth, London, 1993, p.97.

16. A.L. Rowse, *The Regicides and the Puritan Revolution*, Duckworth, London, 1994, p.159.

17. Anon, *A First Cornish Anthology*, Tor Mark Press, Truro, 1969, p.16.

18. Coate, 1933 and 1963, p.162.

19. Coate, 1933 and 1963, p.199.

20. Stoyle, 1994, p.241.

21. Stoyle, 1994, p.239.

22. Stoyle, 1994, p.149.

23. Stoyle, 1994, p.151.

24. Stoyle, 1994, p.233.

25. Stoyle, 1994, p.237.

26. F. E. Halliday, *A History of Cornwall*, Duckworth, 1959, p. 226.

27. Rowse, 1968, p.58.

28. Helen Gardner (ed.), *The New English Book of English Verse*, Oxford University Press, Oxford, 1972, p.307.

29. Stoyle, 1996; for the career of Sir Richard grenville, see also, *Sir Richard Grenville of the Civil War*, Phillimore, London, 1969.

30. Coate, 1933 and 1963, p.147.

31. Coate, 1933 and 1963, p.147.

32. The following examples of Royalist and Parliamentarian propaganda are drawn from Stoyle, April 1996.

33. Stoyle, April 1996.

34. Coate, 1933 & 1963, p.290.

35. Rowse, 1968, p.5.

36. M.G. Smith, *Fighting Joshua: A Study of the Career of Sir Jonathan Trelawny, bart, 1650-1721, Bishop of Bristol, Exeter and Winchester*, Dyllansow Truran, Redruth, 1985, p.5.

37. Smith, 1985, p.48.

38. Whetter, 1974, p.13.

39. Whetter, 1974, p.13.

40. Whetter, 1974, p.176.

41. Whetter, 1974, p.173.

42. Whetter, 1974, p.173.

43. Whetter, 1974, p.172.

44. Whetter, 1974, p.173.

45. P.A.S. Pool, *The Death of Cornish, 1600-1800*, Penzance, 1975, p.8.

46. Pool, 1975, p.16.

47. Kenneth George, 'How many People spoke Cornish Traditionally?', *Cornish Studies*, 14, 1986.

48. Oliver J. Padel, *The Cornish Writings of the Boson Family*, Institute of Cornish Studies, 1975, p.24-25.

49. Padel, 1975, p.48.

50. Padel, 1975, p.38.

51. Pool, 1975, p.17.

52. William Pryce, *Archaeologia Cornu-Britannica*, Redruth, 1790, p.224; see also Kenneth H. Jackson, *A Celtic Miscellany*, Penguin, London, 1971, pp.221-222.

53. See Derek R. Williams, *Prying into Every Hole and Corner: Edward Lhuyd in Cornwall in 1700*, Dyllansow Truran, Redruth, 1993.

54. Pryce, 1790, p.229.

CHAPTER 8

The Large Continent of Cornwall

C O R N W A L L

'The Large Continent of Cornwall'

From the dislocation and uncertainty of the Civil War and Glorious Revolution, there emerged in the late seventeenth and eighteenth centuries a new Great Britain (re-invented in the Act of Union in 1707) which was soon to exercise global diplomatic, commercial, military and maritime power, in the process undergoing the world's first 'Industrial Revolution' and forging an incomparable Empire.[1]

This was the 'British project' re-invented with a vengeance, and, as this chapter sets out to demonstrate, it was a process in which Cornwall and the Cornish had often a significant (and always a distinctive) role to play. In an echo of the early Tudor period, when Richard Edgcumbe emerged as key negotiator in defining England's diplomatic relationships with her Celtic neighbours, so at the very beginning of this era it again fell to a Cornishman (symbolically and not altogether co-incidentally) to adopt an instrumental role in constructing this new Britain. This Cornishman was Sidney Godolphin, nephew of the 'Cavalier Poet' of the same name killed by Roundheads in that 'obscure village in Devonshire', a member of the family which found its fortunes restored in the preferment given to Royalist sympathisers (Cornish among them) after 1660.

Made wealthy from the tin of Godolphin Ball, the family mine near the family home of Godolphin in West Cornwall, Sidney Godolphin was plunged early into the life of Court and international diplomacy. He was politically very astute. Charles II, always a shrewd judge of men (and women), remarked that 'he was never in the way, and never out of the way', while another contemporary observer decided that '. . . being naturally dark and reserved, he became adept at Court politics . . . his talent for unravelling intricate matters and exposing them to easy view was incomparable [and] . . . joined with a felicity of wit . . .'[2]. Godolphin used this political skill to tack his way through the difficult diplomatic waters of the late seventeenth century. He was one of Charles II's 'Triumvirate' which ran the affairs of State but even then he had an eye to the future, maintaining a careful correspondence with William of Orange. Nonetheless, like Bishop Trelawny, he remained loyal to James II almost to the last moment (advocating a Regency after James' flight), switching allegiance to the Prince of Orange only when it was necessary to do so.

Godolphin stayed in office under William and Mary for as long as the Whigs remained in favour, but he was at the height of his power and influence as Lord High Treasurer in the reign of Queen Anne. From 1702 to 1710 he ensured that sufficient resources were allocated to underwrite the Duke of Marlborough's ruthless and stunning military exploits on the Continent, all the while remaining the cosy 'Mr Montgomery' of Anne's domestic fantasies. Considered a 'safe pair of hands', it was Godolphin who guided the delicate negotiations that led to the Act of Union between England and Scotland in 1707. Of course, the Crowns of England and Scotland had already been joined in 1603, creating a proto-'Great Britain', but it was the Act of Union that forged the new State. Godolphin, as part architect of the Union, had played a pivotal role in the creation of the new Britain.

However, the forging of a 'British identity' to match this new State was a lengthy and complex affair. As Daniel Defoe noted, it had been a Union of policy and not of affection.[3] When a 'Britishness' did eventually emerge, it was an identity conditional on the link between commerce, industry and Empire, more to do with Britain's activities overseas than dependent on the construction of a unified identity at home. As Professor P.J.Marshall has written, the '. . . Empire did more than reflect the Britishness of the British in Britain, it helped to focus and develop it'.[4] The extent to which individuals and groups adopted this Britishness depended very much on their particular stake in the emerging Empire. Thus (for example), while Lowland Scots embraced the new Britishness with Protestant entrepreneurial enthusiasm, the Catholic Irish (colonised at home and 'doubly colonized'[5] abroad) were on the whole less than keen.

Moreover, as Linda Colley has emphasised, the construction of a British identity did not mean the integration and homogenisation of disparate cultures within these islands. Rather, Britishness was superimposed over an array of internal differences within Britain (and, to some extent, Ireland) as a result of the Imperial experience. Sometimes, paradoxically, the embrace of Britishness by a particular group was matched by the symbiotic enhancement of particularist regional sentiment. Again we may take the Lowland Scots as an example. At home but increasingly abroad in the Empire, the Lowlanders deployed separate ethnic identity as an economic device —to be Scots was to be uniquely qualified for the demands of commercial activity or the rigours of colonial expansion. In short, to be a Scot was to be a kind of 'super Briton'.[6]

As we shall see in Chapter 10, with its emphasis on emigration, the Scots experience was mirrored in the Cornish. Again responding to the imperatives of commerce, industry and Empire, the Cornish used their distinctive identity as an economic device. At home but more especially abroad, the Cornish were not only 'Cousin Jacks' (inate inheritors of mining expertise) but also 'Ancient Britons' —again, a race of super-Britons, able to trace their impeccable British credentials back to the time of Boadicea and beyond.[7] But more than this, the Cornish were involved in the practical assertion of Britishness, assisting in the global projection of British maritime power. In a fascinating echo of the earlier feats of Cornish arms, from Sluys and Agincourt to Calais and Grenville and the Elizabethan sea-dogs, the eighteenth and nineteenth centuries witnessed a major contribution by the Cornish to the growth in British sea-power. And yet, in a paradox typical of Cornwall but also of the new Britishness, this contribution also served to point-up the distinctive characteristics of the Cornish identity.

It is relatively easy to point to a list of distinguished Royal Navy officers of the period who hailed from Cornwall, or, indeed, to remind ourselves of the strategic importance of Cornwall at the Southwestern tip of Britain. Falmouth, in particular, a child of the seventeenth century, grew-up in the eighteenth as an important operating base for the Royal Navy and for the Packet service, also developing Naval refit and training facilities. The Falmouth Packet service was set up as early as 1688-89 and was in existence until 1850, the port acting as the Post Office's point of departure for its more far-flung mail services overseas. At various times destinations included Spain, Portugal, the Mediterranean, the West Indies, Canada, the United States, Mexico, and Central and South America. As well as being an impor-

Crossing the Tamar to England, with Devonport in the background. The Torpoint Ferry emphasises the Tamar as the divide between Cornwall and Devon but also affirms the historic link between Torpoint and the neighbouring Naval Dockyard.

tant contribution to the economic life of Falmouth, the Packet service also brought a dash of colour and excitement. Often only lightly-armed but carrying diplomatic despatches and sometimes bullion as well as mail, the Falmouth Packets (at the height of the service, there were some forty all told) had often to run the gauntlet of enemy and privateering attacks in various parts of the world.[8]

The co-ordination of the Packet service with Royal Naval operations had become so intimate by 1823, that in that year its control was passed to the Admiralty. Ostensibly a move for the better, Admiralty control in fact led to the introduction of the so-called 'coffin brigs', vessels so poorly designed for the tasks that they were asked to perform, that they often foundered. Of the first twelve entering service, the *Hearty, Redpole, Thais, Ariel, Calypso* and *Myrtle* were lost at sea with all hands after only a few months in service, with the *Briseis* lost soon after. New ships were introduced from 1842 but already the Admiralty was looking to 'privatise' the Packet operation, reaching a series of agreements with commercial shipping lines for the carrying of mails, a process that was completed in 1850—the last year of the Falmouth Packets. Although the decline and eventual demise of the Packet service was a blow to the local economy, Falmouth as a port was already diversified, in effect a regional outpost of the maritime dimension of the new Britishness.

The 1841 Census Returns emphasised Falmouth's close connection with the sea and maritime activities. As well as mariners and seamen, there were provisioners, sailmakers, ropemakers, tallow chandlers, shipbuilders and shipwrights. In 1806 there was even a Cornish Naval Bank in Falmouth which, like other Cornish financial institutions, survived as a viable organisation long enough to be absorbed later in the century by the large London banking interests. Although Falmouth as a maritime centre with global connections was (in Cornish terms) beyond compare, at the other end of Cornwall, Torpoint had also developed as an important Naval town. Situated immediately opposite Devonport dockyard, Torpoint became both residence for Naval personnel based at Devonport and a centre for the myriad economic activities associated with the maritime life of the Tamar estuary. In the Census Returns of 1851 we find the expected mariners, watermen, Naval officers, ropemakers, riggers, sailmakers, caulkers, dockyard labourers, bargemen, boatswains, and so on.[9]

At a sentimental level, the link between Cornwall and British maritime power in this period is exemplified in Trafalgar, the great battle fought on 21 October 1805 in which the combined French and Spanish fleets were destroyed by Admiral Lord Nelson. Not only was it Lieutenant Pascoe, from near Torpoint, who recommended to Nelson the famous flag signal 'England expects . . .' (prompting the Admiral's kindly response, 'That will do nicely, Mr Pascoe') but it was Cornwall where both the great victory and the Admiral's death were first announced. According to popular tradition, the schooner *HMS Pickle*, despatched from Trafalgar for Falmouth (where she arrived on 3 November with the bitter-sweet news), encountered a Penzance fishing boat off the Lizard. The message was passed on, and relayed by the dutiful fishermen to the Mayor (Thomas Giddy) who announced the dramatic news during a ball in the Penzance Assembly Rooms (today the dining room of the Union Hotel). Suitably moved, he led the guests up the hill out of Penzance for a memorial service in the mother church at Madron.[10] Apocryphal or not, the story has passed into Cornish lore, remembered each year in a solemn service in Madron church. As A. L. Rowse has it:

> With one impulse the gathering poured
> Out in the street above the Bay,
> Up the hill to Madron church
> There to give thanks, and grieve and pray.
>
> For all the fallen along with him.
> And every year, as if time should stay,
> The faithful gather there in church
> Still to remember Trafalgar Day.[11]

Of all the Cornish Navy men of this era, perhaps the best known (at least internationally) is Admiral William Bligh, born in St Tudy in 1754, who has achieved fame (or is it infamy?) as a result of both 'the Mutiny on the *Bounty*' and the later 'grog mutiny' in New South Wales. As to the former, Bligh's own account of the mutiny in *HMS Bounty* at Tahiti in 1789, and his subsequent forty-two day journey to Timor in an open boat, can be read in a facsimile version of his own log.[12] The latter mutiny, often seen as a result of Bligh's thoroughgoing attitude to discipline in what was then a convict colony, was in fact a *coup d'etat* by the New South Wales Corps which resented the restraints on its activities imposed by a succession of Naval Governors of the colony, of which Bligh was the last. The officers of this 'Rum Corps' had cornered much of the economic activity of New South Wales (by 1799 they owned thirty-two percent of cattle in Australia, 40 percent of goats, fifty-nine percent of horses and seventy-seven percent of sheep) and, according to Robert Hughes, they were 'Grasping, haughty, jealous of their privileges and prerogatives, [they] . . . were on top and meant

Flushing, across the water from Falmouth, home of Cornish mariners in the past as it is today.

to stay there'.[13] Bligh was deposed by these men on 26 January 1808, the twentieth anniversary of European settlement, and a military junta ruled for two years. None of those responsible was hanged or even severely punished, but on his return to Britain in 1811 Bligh was promoted Rear Admiral and, in 1814, Vice-Admiral of the Blue.

Other Cornish maritime careers were almost equally as eventful, and again point to Cornish participation in the new Britishness founded on Empire and expansion. The little-known Charles Penrose, for example, was born in Penryn in 1759, joining the Royal Navy as a Midshipman in 1775. He served in the West Indies in 1790-96, a time of conflict with France, and in 1810 was appointed Commodore in command of Gibraltar. Amongst other exploits, he sailed to Algiers to force the Bey to release his Christian slaves, an action followed-up in 1816 with a further expedition against the Bey of Algiers under Viscount Exmouth, a member of the celebrated Pellew family (*his* brother, Isaac Pellew, born in 1761 at Flushing, near Falmouth, was Captain on the Newfoundland Station in 1789).

James Silk Buckingham is better-known than Penrose but deserves to be even more so, as sailor, explorer and maritime reformer. Born in Flushing in 1786, Buckingham's varied and colourful career took him from early service in the Packets and, briefly, the Royal Navy, to his later activities as a liberal reformer. He spent time in the Middle East and India (founding the liberal

Calcutta Journal newspaper in which he exposed the excesses of the East India Company) and was later MP for Sheffield. In 1836 he chaired a Parliamentary Select Committee on Shipwrecks which, in the estimation of maritime historian David M.Williams, produced a set of proposals for which '. . . Buckingham might justly be said to be as deserving as Plimsoll of the accolade of "the Sailor's friend" and to be recognised for his much wider vision of the relationship between the state and the merchant service'.[14]

Affected, no doubt, by the fate of the 'coffin brigs', Buckingham was determined to achieve better standards at sea. Amongst his proposals was the codification of maritime law; the better classification of ships; the examination of officers; the establishment of registry offices, savings banks, asylums and nautical schools for seamen; the institution of courts of inquiry into shipwrecks; the formation of tribunals to arbitrate in disputes between owners, officers and men,; and various other measures from the promotion of 'maritime improvement' to the better survey of vessels. Many of these were later enshrined in legislation. As well as being a major contribution to the safety of British shipping and the welfare of British sailors at a time of expanding commercial and Imperial maritime traffic, Buckingham's activities also offer a hint of the improving, philanthropist culture that had by then developed in Cornwall. In another context, for example, Buckingham was also an avid composer of temperance propaganda.

Qintessentially Cornish in another respect was Admiral Edward Boscawen, Lord Falmouth, born at Tregothnan in 1711. Known with respect and even affection as 'Old Dreadnought' or 'Wry-necked Dick' (the latter nickname a response to an unpleasant neck wound that he had received in action), Boscawen has won recognition in the annals of Naval history on two counts. First, he was an extremely successful commander, and among a string of exploits was his famous action off Lagos in 1759 which resulted in the dispersal of a French fleet, with various ships captured or destroyed, the prizes including the famous 'fighting' *Temeraire.* Secondly, he was one of the first to recognise the importance of cleanliness, fitness and high morale in a maritime fighting force. He introduced a modicum of hygiene into his ships and attempted to provide something like a balanced diet for his men. Again, like Buckingham after him, he can be seen as materially improving the conditions of sea-faring men at a time of British expansion overseas.

However, from a Cornish perspective, there is a further point of interest, put by the distinguished Naval historian, Nicholas Rodger:

> What is clear is that many sea officers from Cornwall, and most notably Edward Boscawen, were very conscious of their identity, and very ready to identify and favour their fellow Cornishmen; moreover it appears that they used this connection to overcome some of the manning problems endemic to their service.[15]

Boscawen's sense of Cornish identity is easily demonstrated, although its strength does require some comment. Notwithstanding the Cornish particularism of the Grenvilles and other Royalist leaders in the Civil War, the evidence of Richard Carew (or earlier figures such as Carnsew or even Trevisa) suggested the inexorable spread of Anglicisation amongst the gentry and literate classes in Cornwall. However, the invention of the new Britishness allowed, even encouraged the cultivation of Cornishness - even the 'residual' Cornishness of the gentry. Whilst 'Cornish' and 'English' might be in tension, if not mutually exclusive, 'Cornish' and 'British' could be complementary, even mutually supportive, especially against the background of maritime and Imperial expansion. Thus on 6 November 1756, Elizabeth Montagu wrote to her old friend Mrs Frances 'Fanny' Boscawen, the Admiral's wife, commenting on the political situation and expressing the hope that Edward Boscawen might again be included in the Admiralty Board:

> . . . in these days of discontent, all are pleased with *him,* and I assure you it will discredit any new administration if he is excluded his share in it. No! that cannot, shall not be; it would put the very ocean in a storm, and the large continent of Cornwall into a rebellion.[16]

The significance of this is two-fold. First of all, Mrs Montagu was aware of the Admiral's developed sense of Cornish identity. Although in 1756 the new assertive Cornishness born of industrial prowess was in its infancy (if not still embryonic), there was in the English mind, in addition to the accommodation of Cornishness fostered by the reinvention of Britishness, memory of a Cornish identity —such as that observed a hundred years before in the Civil War —which commanded respect, perhaps even fear, and yet (for such a small territory) seemed to English observers somehow inordinately puffed-up and self-important. Hence the half-mocking, half-reverential allusion to the 'large continent of Cornwall' and the danger of 'rebellion'. Mrs Montagu was not alone in this opinion. In 1745 it was said with feeling of the 6,000 Cornish militiamen raised in response to the Jacobite scare, 'They all express great readiness to defend their country, but they mean their county'.[17] In similar vein, Dr Johnson employed Cornwall as a *reductio ad absurdam* to demonstrate the impossibility of independence for the thirteen American colonies. Just as American claims were outrageous and wrong-headed, so too would be the claims of a an equally preposterous and jumped-up '*Cornish* Congress at Truro', Cornish and American impudence being equally absurd in their naïve posturing: . . . let it be supposed for a moment that Cornwall, seized with the Philadelphian frenzy may resolve to separate itself and judge of its own rights in its own parliament. A congress then might meet at Truro and address the other counties in a style not unlike the language of the American patriots:

> We the delegates of the several towns and parishes of Cornwall hold it necessary to declare the resolutions which we think ourselves entitled to form by the inalienable rights of reasonable beings . . . Know then that you are no longer to consider Cornwall as an *English* county . . . but as a state distinct and independent, governed by its own institutions . . . We are the acknowledged descendants of the earliest inhabitants of *Britain,* of men who before the time of history took possession of the island . . . Of this descent our language is a sufficient proof . . . Such are true Cornishmen. But who are you? Who but the unauthorised and lawless children of intruders, invaders, oppressors? . . . Independence is the gift of nature. No man is born the master of another. Every *Cornishman* is a free man.[18]

Dr Johnson intended this as some kind of sophisticated joke but the heady juxtaposition of Cornwall, England, Britain, America, along with the allusions to revolutionary notions of 'inalienable rights' and 'freedom' and 'gifts of nature', suggested a more subtle appreciation of Cornish sensibilities. Like Mrs Montagu, Dr Johnson was almost incredulously aware of the strength of Cornish particularism.

The second point to note in Elizabeth Montagu's letter is the suggestion of the personal importance of this sense of identity to Admiral Boscawen. And, as Nicholas Rodger has described, this had practical importance for the way in which the Royal Navy did its business. The Navy suffered periodic manning crises in the eighteenth century, due the fact that it was essentially demobilised in peacetime. The cycle of conflicts with France meant that the Navy was forever growing and shrinking, the Admiralty sometimes adopting drastic measures (such as the press gang) to respond rapidly to manpower shortages. Boscawen, however, made much of his Cornishness and Cornish connections to recruit the men he needed—so much so that his wife gently accused him of constructing 'a little Navy of your own making'.[19] Although it would be wrong to assume that the men crewing his ships were overwhelmingly Cornish, Boscawen did go out of his way to select Cornish sailors for key jobs. Thus in 1756, for example, he replaced an unsatisfactory officer in his flagship with one Lieutenant Jacob Lobb from Penzance. 'You approve, I believe', the Admiral wrote to Fanny Boscawen, 'of my taking and encouraging good men from that part of the world'.[20] He also put in a good word for Cornish officers with other commanders, on one occasion writing to Lord Anson in support of a young man to explain that '. . . he is very well recommended by Cornish friends'.[21]

Boscawen also recruited Cornishmen for the lower-deck, as in 1755 and 1756 when he engaged a large body of men from the Penzance area. His patronage was much sought after, and his death in 1761 (when aged only 49) was described as '. . . an event that greatly affects this country, there being a vast number of Cornishmen whose bread, and hopes of preferment depended entirely on him'.[22] However, Boscawen was not the only Cornish officer to give preferment to his own kind. When the *Juno* was hurriedly commissioned in 1770 in response to the Falklands Islands crisis, sixty men were swiftly recruited in West Cornwall by an officer with Cornish connections. Similarly, Edward Pellew (later Viscount Exmouth), born in Dover but of a strongly Cornish family and considered Cornish by all who knew him, commanded a semi-independent frigate squadron, based in Falmouth, in the early French Revolutionary wars. When he commissioned the *Nymphe* in 1793, the ship had 104 Cornishmen in her company, and his *Arethusa* and *Indefatigable* were also to a considerable degree, 'Cornish ships'. Perhaps even more than Boscawen, Pellew had constructed his own private Cornish Navy.

The experience of men like Boscawen and Pellew emphasised the paradox at the heart of the new Britishness. On the one hand, the strategic importance of Cornwall was confirmed, towns such as Falmouth and Torpoint growing in response to the spread of British maritime power—military and commercial—with Cornishmen playing significant roles in the projection of this power overseas. On the other hand, however, Cornish particularism was often at the heart of such Cornish behaviour, accounting for the independence of attitude and action in men such as Boscawen and Pellew, and reinforcing Cornwall's 'difference' in the eyes of external observers. At a wider level this paradox was even more pronounced, and, despite the apparent complementarity of 'Cornish' and 'British', in practical terms this led to considerable tension and sometimes conflict. The activities of the Royal Navy and the Packet service represented a high degree of intervention in Cornwall by the state, drawing Cornwall closely into the policy delibera-

In times past the craggy cliffs and rocks of the Lizard peninsula emphasised its sense of wild remoteness.

tions of the 'centre', but in other respects Cornwall remained firmly apart in the 'periphery'—especially with regard to popular behaviour and beliefs.

The independence of action that had long before created that mood of 'feudal anarchy' in medieval Cornwall, and had made such difficulties for the Tudor state and for the Parliamentary cause, survived into the eighteenth (and even nineteenth) centuries. To external observers, Cornwall was 'West Barbary', an unsavoury and potentially dangerous land characterised by wrecking and riot and smuggling. According to one visitor in 1775, the Cornish were '. . . very strange kind of beings, half savages at best . . . They are as rough as bears, selfish as swine, obstinate as mules, and hard as the native iron'.[23] Another agreed that Cornwall was '. . . upon the whole a dismal country . . . inland dwellings are a vast distance from neighbours . . . the prospect chiefly over barren lands'.[24]

As in earlier times the tinners were singled out for particular disdain, and not without reason—as Eric Hobsbawm and George Rude have commented, '. . . Cornwall was one of the chief centres of food rioting in the country . . . the tinners were regarded as almost beyond the pale of civilization'.[25] In 1709, 1727-29, 1748, 1757, 1766, 1796-99, 1810-13, 1831 and 1847, the Cornish rioted against food shortages and high prices, behaviour that was deemed an everyday part of Cornish life until at least May 1847 when hungry and angry miners forced 'fair prices' for corn at Callington market and tinners and clayworkers looted shops in St Austell, action that was threatened again in the hard times of the 1860s and was exhibited in part in the Camborne Riots later in the century. Even in the 1850s, according to A. K. Hamilton Jenkin,[26] miners in the more remote, western parts of Cornwall —notably the districts of Breage and Sithney—could scarcely venture from their parishes for fear of being assaulted. The ancient rivalry between the twin mining towns of Camborne and Redruth was routinely played out, with scant regard for such rules as there were, in the traditional hurling matches held on neutral ground in Illogan parish.

Inter-parish competition was also evident in the practice of 'wrecking' where different communities would vie with each for the spoils of ships that had come to grief on Cornwall's notoriously dangerous and rocky coast. Robert Hunt furnished a grim picture of such an affray, perhaps apocryphal but nonetheless telling in its description of an event which (as Hunt put it) took place 'about a hundred years since':

> A wreck took place near the Lizard, and the Breage-men being nearest, were soon upon the spot to appropriate whatever flotsam and jetsam might come their way. Returning laden with their spoils, they were encountered at the Great Tree [at Cury] by the Wendron-men bound on a similar errand, and a fight, as a matter of course, ensued, which was prolonged to the following day. The contest is said to have been a terrible one, each party being armed with staves . . . These fights between parishes were so common in those days that any death occurring in the fray was quietly passed over as a thing of course, and soon forgotten.[27]

To those external observers versed in the excesses of the tinners and other Cornish 'half savages', such behaviour was explained in terms of innate savagery, of deeply ingrained traits that made the Cornish different. It was a fear that led to stories of Cornish folk deliberately luring ships to destruction by the showing of 'false' lights on cliff tops, and which accounted for the mariners 'prayer:

> God keep us from rocks and shelving sands,
> And save us from Breage and Germoe men's hands.[28]

However, for the Cornish the lawless and independent behaviour inherent in riot, wrecking and smuggling was entirely rational. Cornwall was still felt by many to be beyond the reach of English law, and in such circumstances riot as a means to achieve 'fair prices' or the equitable distribution of corn was entirely reasonable. Similarly, smuggling was defended as a response to an external intrusion which was unjustified; customs and duties were imposed from London, smuggling was good business which exploited Cornwall's natural advantages —geographical remoteness from London, a complex coastline, and local contacts with Brittany and the Channel Islands. Indeed, the sea was in all respects a 'harvest-field', as Hamilton Jenkin so aptly described it,[29] a vast resource which offered a multiplicity of opportunities. These were not only the obvious occupations of fishing and maritime trade, or indeed the privateering and piracy of earlier times, but extended to both smuggling and wrecking. Just as smuggling took advantage of Cornwall's location, so too did wrecking: Cornish waters were notoriously dangerous, they were also very busy. While there is no evidence to suggest that ships were in fact lured to their doom, many in Cornwall would have tacitly accepted (even approved of) the spirit of the well-known Cornish saying:

> The *Eliza* of Liverpool came on shore
> To feed the hungry and clothe the poor.[30]

The tranquillity of Porthleven is deceptive-the harbour faces the full fury of the winter storms and the adjacent coastline has witnessed many a shipwreck.

Such an attitude, however, hardly squared with the increasing intervention of central government in the maritime affairs of Cornwall. The contrast itself is interesting, highlighting the complexity of the situation in which Cornwall found itself, a nice paradox juxtaposing the savagery of remote West Barbary with the modernity of global maritime communication. On the ground (and in the sea) it was played out in a contest between wreckers and government officials, the former insistent upon the exercise of 'ancient privileges' and the latter equally insistent upon the rule of law. John Vivian's booklet, *Tales of the Cornish Wreckers*, deserves to be better known than it is, because it makes the point well.[31] In November 1738, for example, a German ship, the *Vigilantia,* was wrecked near Perranuthnoe, on Mount's Bay. Charles Vyvyan of Penzance Custom House hurried to the scene with a squad of soldiers but on arrival found that the wreck had been plundered. When the *Lady Lucy* was wrecked at Gunwalloe on 14 December 1739, the same Charles Vyvyan made his way around the coast from Penzance, only to find that the ship's valuable and attractive cargo of wine, brandy, coffee berries and indigo had already disappeared. A search locally discovered some of the spoils in the possession of the local vicar, the Rev. Thomas Whitford of Cury.

During the stormy winter of 1739-40, several ships were wrecked on the Scillies, and the Scillonians cellared about 3,000 of the 9,000 gallons of brandy brought ashore, on the grounds that it was their traditional salvage right. When the *Jonge Alcida* ran aground near Porthleven in December 1748, the long-suffering Charles Vyvyan could do little to save the cargo because of 'the violence and barbarity of the country people'. The Custom officers had more luck at Downderry in March 1751, however, when they discharged their weapons —first with powder only, and then with ball—to warn off the wreckers intent upon plundering the stranded *Endeavour*. But in the next year at neighbouring Looe, the Custom men were powerless in the face of a huge mob of country folk which dismembered a brigantine that had been bound from London to Penzance. In 1754 a 'parcel of Cornish Barbarians' (as the *Sherborne Mercury* described them) plundered a ship wrecked near Mawgan Porth. The local magistrate managed to save £10,000 worth of raw silk but was assaulted by the mob when he ordered his officers to fire upon the wreckers.

As time went on, the officers did become more successful in their control of wrecks, while the behaviour of local people moderated. However, almost a hundred years later, when the *Good Samaritan* was wrecked on Bedruthan Steps on 22 October 1846 (at the height of the 'Hungry Forties', the year in which the potato famine again hit Cornwall), a new version of the old rhyme appeared on this stretch of the North Cornish coast:

> The *Good Samaritan* came ashore
> To feed the hungry and clothe the poor,
> Barrels of beef and bales of linen,
> No poor man shall want a shillin'.[32]

Smuggling, too, remained a way of life for much of this period, especially notorious stretches of coast including Mount's Bay in the west and Cawsand Bay in the southeast. Unlike the 'commercial organisations' of Dunkirk and elsewhere that had dominated smuggling activities in the eastern Channel, smuggling in Cornwall was usually the result of individual enterprise, such as

The treacherous north coast as Bedruthan Steps, where in 1846 —the height of the 'Hungry Forties'—*The Good Samaritan came ashore/ To feed the hungry and clothe the poor.*

Today a mecca for holiday-makers, two hundred years ago Polperro was the haunt of Cornish smugglers.

that of 'Captain' Harry Carter (1749-1809, the so-called 'King of Prussia [Cove]') who wrote his own *Autobiography of a Cornish Smuggler*.[33] Again, there is a recurring theme, the defence of what was seen as a legitimate form of livelihood against the increasing intrusion of governmental control and direction. In 1871 Jonathan Couch's *History of Polperro* was published, and in it he described the long contest between the local smugglers and the Preventive service, a struggle which in his day had been conducted within living memory. He recounted, for example, the pursuit of the smuggling smack *Vigilant* by a Revenue cutter in December 1802 in which attempts to cut the *Vigilant*'s rigging by the firing of shot, resulted in the deaths of two of the smuggling party. Similarly, Couch drew attention to the fate of one Robert Mark, shot by Preventive men in 1810. His epitaph in Talland churchyard was equivocal, to say the least:

> In prime of life most suddenly,
> Sad tidings to relate,
> (Here view my utter destiny
> And pity my sad fate,)
> I, by a shot which rapid flew
> Was instantly struck dead.
> Lord! pardon the offender who
> My precious blood did shed.
> Grant him to rest and forgive me
> All I have dome amiss;
> And that I may rewarded be
> With everlasting bliss.[34]

The contest between smugglers and Preventive men has been sketched more recently by the authors John Vivian in 1969 and Cyril Noall in 1971.[35] Again, in marked contrast to the perhaps more romantic portrayals of smuggling, what emerges from these accounts is the sheer violence and brutality of the 'trade', together with evidence of the frequent recourse to firearms and other weapons. Near Constantine Churchtown in November

The imposing mass of Penally Point guards the entrance to Boscastle harbour, one of the few havens on the dangerous coast between Padstow and the Devon border.

1828, for example, there was a violent confrontation between a large party of smugglers (armed with pistols, bludgeons and knives) and two Custom officers, in which one of the latter was beaten extensively and left for dead. At nearby Gweek in September 1840, a band of smugglers, angry that their contraband had been confiscated, forced their way into the Helford Custom House and recovered the loot. And human violence was not the only danger that the officers faced. On the coast of North Cornwall, beyond the River Camel, the Preventive men operating from Boscastle and Bude had an especially lonely and inhospitable stretch of cliffs to patrol. In January 1822 the Boscastle Preventive men were returning from a foray from Bude, when the wind and sea got up and the boat (perhaps carrying too much sail) was upturned off St Gennys. Locals observing the tragedy from the cliff tops were powerless to help, and all five men were drowned. Again, there is another apt north coast rhyme:

> From Hartland Point to Padstow light
> Is a watery grave by day or by night.

Jonathan Couch considered that the decline of smuggling in his time had been inevitable, the contest between smuggler and government at root an unequal one:

> These determined measures for the extinction of the 'free trade' [smuggling] struck consternation in the minds of all engaged in it; but, though active opposition was not politic, the people de-

> termined one and all, to offer as much passive resistance as was safe [but] . . . In no long time the contraband trade became too dangerous to be profitable, antipathies wore out, the preventive men made themselves more agreeable to the people . . . .[36]

In other respects, too, the march of modernity changed the nature of eighteenth and nineteenth-century Cornwall. Like the Parish Clerk of St Just-in-Penwith, from whom Edward Lhuyd had collected the rhyme about the fate of land and language in 1700, the Cornish language scholars of the late seventeenth and early eighteenth centuries had mourned what they saw as the last of old Cornwall. Certainly, the decline of the language had continued apace, a process that might have gone entirely unnoticed if it had not been by chance that the minor English antiquary, Daines Barrington (1727-1800), had become intrigued by his brother's experiences in Cornwall.[37] In 1746 Captain Samuel Barrington, one of the many Royal Navy officers whose duties brought them to Cornwall, engaged a Mount's Bay mariner said to be able to communicate in Cornish with Breton sailors.

Captain Barrington's antiquarian brother was mildly fascinated, and proceeded in 1768 (over twenty years later!) to make a tour of West Cornwall in search of Cornish speakers. At last at Mousehole he was introduced to an old fishwife called Dolly Pentreath who, according to Daines Barrington, spoke in a language that sounded very much like Welsh. Dolly insisted that she talked no English until she was twenty, that she had sold fish in Penzance in the Cornish language until the age of twelve, and that she was now the last speaker of the old tongue. Others in Mousehole might understand what she said but there was none with whom she could hold a conversation.

Dolly Pentreath died in December 1777 but, despite her subsequent reputation as 'the last Cornish speaker', she was certainly survived by others with a knowledge of the tongue. Barrington had noted other Cornish speakers who had died before Dolly (two nurses, Jane Cock and Jane Woolcock, both from Newlyn) but he also indicated three others who survived her. There was an unnamed inhabitant of Truro (probably a mining engineer called Tompson), John Nancarrow of Marazion (no more than forty years of age in 1777), and William Bodinar, a Mousehole fisherman. In July 1776 Bodinar wrote a testimonial in both Cornish and English. The English reads:

> My age is 65. I am a poor fisherman. I learnt Cornish when I was a boy. I have been to sea with my father and 5 other men in the boat, and have not heard one word of English spoke in the boat for a week together. I never saw a Cornish book. I learnt Cornish going to sea with old men. There is not more than 4 or 5 in our town can talk Cornish now, old people 80 years old. Cornish is all forgot with young people.[38]

After Bodinar (who died in 1789), the trail becomes difficult. When John Whitaker visited Cornwall in 1799 he was told variously of an old man at St Levan and old woman at Newlyn, both of whom spoke Cornish, but he failed to find either of them. In 1808 the Rev Richard Warner scoured West Penwith without success in his search for Cornish. But there were echoes. In 1859 Mathias Wallis of St Buryan certified that his grandmother, Ann Wallis, who had died in her 90th year some fifteen years beforehand, had spoken Cornish, as had one Jane Barnicoate who had been dead only two years. John Davey of Boswednack in the parish of Zennor, who died in 1891, was said to have had a traditional knowledge of the language and be able to 'converse' (but with whom?) in it in a few simple subjects. Thereafter, various snippets of the language apparently survived—not only as attested dialect words in the Cornish version of English but also at Newlyn in fishermen's counting rituals, perhaps even into the 1920s or 30s.

The inexorable process of cultural change occurred in other areas as well, although for those who viewed or experienced it, the evidence was sometimes conflicting. Although the reality was that Cornishness was both surviving and changing in response to new conditions, for some the question was more stark: was Cornwall stubbornly maintaining its sense of difference in the face of change, or was it rapidly becoming more or less like anywhere else? At one level, the Cornish retained many of their customs and superstitions —belief in the mystical and healing qualities of holy wells, the practice of Cornish wrestling and hurling, the celebration of Midsummer's Day and St Piran's Day, the Padstow 'Obby 'Oss and Helston Furry, the observance of Celtic saints and their feasts. The notion of Cornish 'nationality' also survived, demonstrated quite unselfconsciously in Hamilton Jenkin's telling account of an incident in a nineteenth-century dame school. A pupil, asked to describe Cornwall, declared that '. . . he's kidged to a furren country from the top hand'.[39] According to Hamilton Jenkin, the answer was '. . . heard by the whole school with much approval, including old Peggy [the school-dame] herself'. The 'furren country' to which Cornwall was 'kidged'(joined) was, of course, England, the 'top hand' being the Tamar border in the east.

Boswednack, Zennor, where John Davey (1812-1891) was said to have been one of the last to possess a traditional knowledge of the Cornish language.

As ever, the miners were seen as the chief repository of Cornish distinctiveness, their particular customs and superstitions a clue to the meaning of what it was to be Cornish.

Given the inherently dangerous conditions in which they laboured, it is not surprising that many of these superstitions focused on death and portends of death.[40] Occasionally voices from nowhere would suddenly alert a miner to the fact that he was stepping into danger, as in the case of John Lean who was working underground in Wheal Jewell (in Gwennap parish) and was warned miraculously, 'You are in the winze!'. Sure enough, Lean discovered that he was indeed standing on the very edge of a winze (an underground communication shaft)—another step would have plunged him to almost certain death. On other occasions, 'death hands' would appear, ghostly hands clutching lighted candles in the depths of a shaft—to have the misfortune to see one was to receive intimation of one's own impending doom. At Wheal Vor, in the parish of Breage, the appearance of a black dog in an engine house was a similar portend, as was the appearance of a white hare (a superstition shared by Cornish fishermen, who would refuse to put to sea if they had by chance encountered such a hare).

Central to the lore of Cornish mining were the 'knackers' or 'knockers', the 'tommyknockers' of North American mining legend introduced in the States by emigrant Cousin Jacks. In Cornwall, the knockers were ugly sprites, variously defined as Christian souls trapped in pergatory or Jews' spirits enduring perpetual punishment. They were also seen as underground Buccas and, just as croft country at surface would be left uncultivated as an offering to Bucca, so in the mines a prudent miner would leave a portion of his 'croust' or 'crib' (lunch) as an offering. Properly treated, Buccas could be friendly and helpful, leading a miner towards especially rich parcels of ground or guiding him away from danger. But once wronged or neglected,

The Crowns engine houses at Botallack, near St Just. It is not difficult to understand why superstition played such an important role in the lives of Cornwall's mining and sea-faring folk

the Buccas could be vindictive enemies. There is the well-known story of Tom Trevorrow who fell foul of the Buccas in just this way. Stopping to eat his fuggan (Cornish heavycake), he heard the eerie singing:

> Tom Trevorrow! Tom Trevorrow!
> Leave some of thy fuggan for bucca,
> Or bad luck to thee to-morrow!

Foolishly, Tom ignored the warning and continued to eat every last scrap. He then heard the menacing tones of the Buccas:

> Tommy Trevorrow! Tommy Trevorrow!
> We'll send thee bad luck tommorrow;
> Thou old curmudgeon to eat all thy fuggan,
> And not leave a didjan for bucca.

It was said that, thereafter, Trevorrow was dogged with ill-fortune, so much so that he had to leave mining to find work on the land.

Although, in popular fancy, the miners were the epitome of the Cornish frailty for superstition, in fact the lives of fishermen were no less governed by taboos.[41] White hares were a sign of ill-luck, but so too were 'bullhorns' (snails), while the mention of any kind of wild animal when at sea was strictly forbidden. Clergymen and churches were also taboo. A parson spotted near a boat that was preparing to put to sea was a bad sign, and even worse was to mention a 'church-related' topic when away from land. This posed problems when using churches as navigational aids (for example, St Keverne was important for a boat off the Manacles reef and making for Falmouth, and likewise off Plymouth the tower of Maker and spire of Rame were useful daymarks), and it is said that fishermen were inclined to refer enigmatically to 'cleeta'—a dialect word inherited from the Cornish language, meaning 'belltower'.

The medieval spire of St Germanus' church at Rame, in what author Tony Carne has called *Cornwall's Forgotten Corner*, is a useful daymark for mariners.

This and other taboos and tales remained in currency in the last century, to be recorded by the likes of Hunt and Bottrell, and to be retold later by A. K. Hamilton Jenkin. Certainly, observers east of the Tamar were much impressed by these 'quaint survivals', and were still careful to depict Cornwall as the land of difference. Wilkie Collins visited Cornwall in the middle of the nineteenth century and emphasised that this was:

> . . . a county where, it must be remembered, a stranger is doubly a stranger, in relation to provincial sympathies; where the national feeling is almost entirely merged in the local feeling; where a man speaks of himself as Cornish in much the same way that a Welshman speaks of himself as Welsh.[42]

George Henwood, writing in the *Mining Journal*, thought that the Cornish were '. . . particularly proud of their parentage, to a degree almost rivalling that of the Welsh, and refer to King Arthur and Trelawney as demigods and patterns of virtue and patriotism'.[43] Even at the end of the nineteenth century, W. H. Hudson, the naturalist, felt moved to describe what he called 'the remote and most un-English county of Cornwall', opining that there were few '. . . Englishmen in Cornwall who did not experience that antipathy or sense of separation in mind from the people they live with, and are not looked at as foreigners'.[44]

However, for the Cornish themselves, the picture was more complex. In a situation that anticipated most strikingly the paradox that engages many of us in late twentieth-century Cornwall, while external observers in the nineteenth century were impressed by continuity, for internal commentators it was change that was principally of note. For some, this change was not always for the better and represented loss, the doggerel poet Henry Quick of Zennor (1792-1857) lamenting the impact of modernity upon his native Cornwall:

> The Cornish drolls are dead, each one;
> The fairies from their haunts have gone:
> There's scarce a witch in all the land,
> The world has grown so learn'd and grand.[45]

And yet, one of the recurring features of Cornish history is for observers to mistake cultural change for cultural extinction. For while the eighteenth and nineteenth centuries did witness striking changes, with the demise of the Cornish language to boot, the new Cornwall that emerged from the onslaught of modernity continued to be profoundly 'different'. Indeed, that 'residual' Cornishness felt so strongly by the likes of Admiral Boscawen (and observed so acutely by Mrs Montagu and Dr Johnson) was not only accommodated within the new Britishness but was re-invigorated by socio-economic change to produce a new, dynamic identity founded on industrial prowess.

Notes & References (Chapter 8).

1. See, Linda Colley, *Britons: Forging the Nation 1707-1837*, Pimlico, London, 1994.

2. A.L.Rowse, *The Early Churchills: An English Family*, Macmillan, London, 1956, p.160.

3. Rowse, 1956, p.159.

4. P.J.Marshall, 'Imperial Britain', in P.J.Marshall (ed.), *The Cambridge History of the British Empire*, Cambridge University Press, Cambridge, 1996, p.319.

5. Robert Hughes, *The Fatal Shore: A History of the Transportation of Convicts to Australia 1787-1868*, Pan, London, 1988, p.181.

6. Colley, 1994, especially p.6. and Chapter 3.

7. Ronald M.James, 'Defining the Group: Nineteenth-Century Cornish on the North American Mining Frontier', in Philip Payton (ed.), *Cornish Studies: Two*, University of Exeter Press, Exeter, 1994; Philip Payton, 'Paralysis and Revival: The Reconstruction of Celtic-Catholic Cornwall, 1890-1939', in Ella Westland (ed.), *Cornwall: The Cultural Construction of Place*, Patten Press, Penzance, 1996.

8. James Whetter, *The History of Falmouth*, Dyllansow Truran, Redruth, 1981; David Mudd, *The Falmouth Packets*, Bossiney Books, St Teath, 1978; John Beck, *Captain John Bull of the Falmouth Packet Service*, South West Maritime Historical Society, Exeter, 1996.

9. Gladys and F.L.Harris, *The Making of a Cornish Town: Torpoint and Neighbourhood through Two Hundred Years*, Institute of Cornish Studies and University of Exeter Extra Mural Department, Redruth/Exeter, 1976.

10. P.A.S. Pool, *The History of the Town and Borough of Penzance*, Corporation of Penzance, Penzance, 1974, p.111.

11. A.L.Rowse, *Transatlantic: Later Poems*, Tabb House, Padstow, 1989, p.35.

12. William Bligh, *The Mutiny on Board HMS Bounty*, Pageminster, Guildford, 1981.

13. Hughes, 1988, p.111.

14. David M. Williams, 'James Silk Buckingham: Sailor, Explorer and Maritime Reformer', in Stephen Fisher (ed.), *Studies in British Privateering, Trading Enterprise and Seamen's Welfare, 1775-1900*, University of Exeter Press, Exeter, 1987, p.117.

15. Nicholas Rodger, '"A Little Navy of Your Own Making": Admiral Boscawen and the Cornish Connection in the Royal Navy', in Michael Duffy (ed.), *Parameters of British Naval Power, 1650-1850*, University of Exeter Press, Exeter, 1992, p.82.

16. Cited in Rodger, 1992, p.82.

17. Cited in Colley, 1994, p.81.

18. Cited in A.L.Rowse, *The Little Land of Cornwall*, Alan Sutton, Gloucester, 1986, repub. Dyllansow Truran, Redruth, n.d. (c.1992), pp.299-300.

19. Rodger, 1992, p.85.

20. Rodger, 1992, p.86.

21. Rodger, 1992, p.86.

22. Rodger, 1992, p.87.

23. *Old Cornwall*, Vol.1., 1925.

24. *Old Cornwall*, Vol.7., 1972.

25. E.J.Hobsbawm and George Rude, *Captain Swing*, Penguin, London, 1973, pp.98 and 106.

26. A.K. Hamilton Jenkin, *The Cornish Miner*, 1927, repub. David and Charles, Newton Abbot, 1972, p.284.

27. Robert Hunt, *Popular Romances of the West of England*, 1865, p. 198.

28. Philip Payton, *The Cornish Miner in Australia*, Dyllansow Truran, Redruth, 1984, p.74.

29. A.K. Hamilton Jenkin, *Cornwall and it People*, 1932-34, repub. David and Charles, Newton Abbot, 1983, p.2.

30. John Vivian, *Tales of the Cornish Wreckers*, Tor Mark Press, Truro, n.d., p.3.

31. Vivian, n.d.

32. Hamilton Jenkin, 1932-34 and 1983, p.66.

33. Harry Carter, *The Autobiography of a Cornish Smuggler*, 1894, repub. Bradford Barton, Truro, 1971.

34. Jonathan Couch, *History of Polperro*, 1871, repub. Frank Graham, Newcastle-upon-Tyne, 1965, p.32.

35. John Vivian, *Tales of the Cornish Smugglers*, Tor Mark Press, Truro, 1969; Cyril Noall, *Smuggling in Cornwall*, Bradford Barton, Truro, 1971.

36. Couch, 1871 and 1965, pp.42-43.

37. P.A.S. Pool, *The Death of Cornish*, Pool, Penzance, 1975, p.25.

38. Pool, 1975, p.27.

39. Hamilton Jenkin, 1927 and 1972, p.274.

40. Hamilton Jenkin, 1927 and 1972, pp.293-296.

41. Hamilton Jenkin, 1932-43 and 1983, pp.258-259.

42. Wilkie Collins, *Rambles Beyond Railways*, Richard Bentley, 1851, p.124.

43. Cited in Roger Burt (ed.), *Cornwall's Mines and Miners*, Bradford Barton, Truro, 1972, p.220

44. W.H. Hudson, *The Land's End: A Naturalist's Impression of West Cornwall*, 1908, repub. Wildwood, London, 1981, p.34.

45. P.A.S. Pool (ed.), *The Life and Progress of Henry Quick of Zennor*, Dyllansow Truran, Redruth, 1994, p.43.

CHAPTER 9

So Many Brilliant Ornaments

CORNWALL

'So Many Brilliant Ornaments . . .'

The Cornish economy was one of the very first in the world to industrialise, the early and successful application of steam power facilitating the development of deep mining and achieving for Cornwall an envied place in the forefront of technological innovation. Sadly, this is not always recognised today and Cornwall remains historiographically invisible in most accounts of industrialisation in Britain (thus, for example, George Stephenson, and not Richard Trevithick, is routinely trumpeted as 'inventor' of the railway locomotive).

At best, Cornwall has been acknowledged as some kind of side-show, the complex experience of Cornish industrialisation marginalised and dismissed in gross over-simplification, such as that in Maxine Berg's otherwise impressive *The Age of Manufactures*: '. . . in the middle of the nineteenth century mining suddenly declined and the region was rapidly transformed into a holiday resort'.[1] The main reason for this invisibility has been the lack until recently of a satisfactory Cornish historiography, the means of understanding and critically articulating the ways in which Cornwall's history might be read (and written). It has also been a function of Cornwall's isolation from the 'focus' of industrialisation elsewhere in Britain, far removed as it was from areas such as the Midlands and North. Early de-industrialisation exacerbated this invisibility, while, paradoxically, Dr John Rowe's vitally important *Cornwall in the Age of the Industrial Revolution* (first published as long ago as 1953) probably appeared too early to have had the impact that it deserved in the later studies that emerged of comparative regional industrialisation. The same, perhaps, was true of the impressive string of Cornish mining books produced by the prolific D. Bradford Barton in the 1960s.[2]

However, there is evidence that at last things are beginning to change. Not only is there a new Cornish historiography, vigorously debating the manner in which Cornwall's history has been interpreted and portrayed, but on the wider stage scholars have begun to take an increased interest in comparative regional industrialisation. Crucially, it is now recognised that the process of industrialisation promoted regional differentiation rather than homogeneity. In contrast to an earlier generation of writers which stressed what it saw as increased cultural and social uniformity in Britain as a result of the industrial experience, a new wave of historical geographers, economic historians and political scientists has shown that industrialisation both perpetuated and reinforced regional differentiation.

Commentators such as Jack Langton, Pat Hudson and Derek Urwin have argued that the Industrial Revolution gave new meaning to regional identities, the often highly specialised and distinctive forms of industrial activity that emerged becoming defining cultural icons.[3] As Dai Smith put it, '. . . there was an explosion into industrial pre-eminence of regions *as* regions'.[4] South Wales was coal, Clydeside shipbuilding, and so on. In Cornwall, glasses were raised to the toast, 'fish, tin and copper'. Even the greater mobility associated with industrialisation served to promote diversity rather than homogeneity, contact with others precipitating an often bewildered recognition of how different people could be. Thus in the emerging coal-fields of County Durham in the Northeast of England,

> . . . there was a combination of Lancashire, Cumberland, Yorkshire, Staffordshire, Cornish, Irish, Scottish, Welsh, Northumbrian and Durham accents. All these and more tongues were to be heard in a marked way; and not only that, but the families in each group gravitated together and formed a common bond.[5]

The strong but often simply defined images of regional distinctiveness gained common currency and acquired widespread meaning. 'Dame Wales', for example, was seen as being responsible for almost literally 'feeding' the world with coal, the new Wales no longer a dark periphery but a modern society capable of playing its own distinguished role in the further advance of Imperial Britain. In the North of England, the 'difference' that had characterised the medieval period and had posed such problems for the assertion of Tudor rule, was re-invented in the Imperial-industrial era. An urban civic pride was everywhere apparent, on the one hand presenting the North as possessing unifying cultural traits (in contradistinction to the South) but also pointing to an intricate relationship of 'northern' subcultures from the Midlands to Tyneside.

Intriguingly, Professor Hugh Kearney has identified Cornwall as both integral and exceptional to this 'northern' pattern—integral in that Cornwall exhibited economic and social behaviour akin to that of the northern subcultures but exceptional in that Cornwall was neither in nor of the North.[6] The experience of Cornwall, Kearney implies, had much more in common with the North than the South of which it was ostensibly a part, and yet was in the final analysis unique and incomparable. Indeed, the economic historian Sidney Pollard has described Cornwall as one of the early and highly distinctive regions of industrialising Britain:

> . . . it was tin and copper mining and smelting which formed the basis of one of the most advanced engineering centres in the world to the 1840s, and of a complex industrial society exhibiting early developments of banking and risk- sharing to deal with the particular needs of local industry as well as a remarkable attempt to cartelize copper in the 1780s.[7]

As we saw in Chapter Seven, Cornwall at the end of the seventeenth century was already acquiring the characteristics that would facilitate its early place in Britain's Industrial Revolution. Although it was tin that was (and still is) popularly associated in the public mind with Cornish mining, it was in fact the expansion of copper that gave the initial impetus to technological advance. As early as the 1680s, there was a number of important copper producers in the neighbourhood of Redruth, and by 1720 some 6,000 tons of copper ore were being raised annually in Cornwall. Names such as Great Wheal Busy, Roskear, Dolcoath and Cook's Kitchen were already prominent amongst the major Cornish mines. As they became ever deeper, so new technologies were sought to deal with the problem of water. The old 'rag and chain' pumps were no longer enough, and one device was to improve the network of drainage tunnels, or 'adits'. In 1748 the Great County Adit was commenced as a project to keep Poldice (and eventually a great many other mines in Gwennap and environs) free from water inundation but deep

The clock tower of Great Consolidated Mines, or 'Consols' as it was known in Gwennap parish—once 'the richest square mile on earth'. In 1857 Consols was taken over by the neighbouring United Mines to form the extensive Clifford Amalgamated which survived until 1869-70. Today, this area — United Downs—is an eerie wasteland.

mining was also to require the early application of steam-driven pumps.

The discovery of extensive copper deposits in Anglesey in North Wales in 1768 caused much alarm in Cornwall and threatened the Cornish monopoly, but the Welsh reserves were worked out with surprising rapidity, so that by the 1790s Cornish copper was again experiencing expansion. In 1809 a tramway was opened to link the major mines of Scorrier and St Day to Portreath on the north coast (facilitating both the export of ore and the import of coal), and in 1824 a similar tramway was constructed from the Gwennap mines to the port of Devoran on the River Fal. By then the parish of Gwennap alone was responsible for more than a third of global production of copper ore, while mining in Cornwall was technologically the most advanced in the world. The mine names of Gwennap were like a Cornish litany on the lips of mine-owners, adventurers (shareholders), captains (managers), and tributers and tutworkers (the miners): Wheal Fortune, Wheal Virgin, Poldory, Ale and Cakes, Wheal Cupboard, Wheal Maid, Wheal Unity, Wheal Gorland, Wheal Jewell, Wheal Damsell, Ting Tang, Wheal Squire . . . . In 1757 it was said that in its first fortnight of operation, Wheal Virgin had produced copper ore to the value of £5,700, a vast amount in those times.

From 1810 onwards the Cornish copper industry began to look beyond its Gwennap and Camborne-Redruth heartland—eastwards to the district around St Austell Bay (mines such as Crinnis, Fowey Consols, and Lanescot) and westwards to St Just-in-Penwith, at the very end of Cornwall, where Levant mine was soon established as a major producer. The subject of a detailed and painstaing 'biography' by Cyril Noall (he also wrote similar pen-pictures of the neighbouring mines of Botallack and Geevor), Levant is perhaps best remembered for the terrible accident there in 1919 when thirty-one miners lost their lives.[8] Today, however, Levant is the focus of a remarkable preservation project, where the National Trust and Trevithick Society have pooled their expertise to restore to use (with full steam) the Cornish engine that had lain there neglected since the mine's closure in 1930.

In 1836 there was a further series of spectacular copper discoveries, this time in East Cornwall, at Caradon Hill on the southern edge of Bodmin Moor. Although long since a quarrying and tin-working district, the discovery of copper transformed St Cleer and Linkinhorne, changing them almost literally overnight from remote, sparsely populated parishes whose economy was based predominantly on small farming and moorland grazing, to the latest centre of Cornish industrialisation. Mines such as South Caradon, Caradon Consols and Gonamena were soon to acquire an international reputation. At first the change was traumatic. For a while St Cleer was called 'Hell up by Liskeard', a commentary on the unsavoury social conditions that had been established there, John Allen writing in his history of Liskeard in 1856 :

> A great demand was created for labourers, the population of the district suddenly and largely increased, small cottages and single rooms became frightfully crowded—fever and immorality were the natural consequences. All kinds of provision met a steady sale, the markets were thronged, the roads were worn into dangerous ruts, the dialect of the people grew more provincial and Cornish than before, and the singing tone of the West was imported with full effect.[9]

An aerial view of the mining landscape around Botallack, on the cliffs to the north of St Just-in-Penwith.

The spectacular situation of Levant, the 'mine beneath the sea', in the St Just mining district, with Pendeen Watch lighthouse in the background.

In a remarkably short time the district was recast, becoming almost uncannily reminiscent of the western mining areas rather than the pastoral east of which it had been so lately a part. Villages such as Tremar Coombe, Darite, Common Moor, and Pensilva (formerly Bodmanland), together with St Cleer Churchtown itself, developed solid rows of miners' cottages and the more substantial captain's dwellings, architecturally reminiscent of the country around Redruth and St Day. Many miners (and often their families too) did indeed move up from the west of Cornwall, noticeably from the district of Breage where Great Wheal Vor was run down with disastrous effect in 1846-47.[10]

The discovery of silver-lead in the neighbouring parish of Menheniot (soon to lead to the rise of mines such as Wheal Trelawny) and further south at Herodsfoot, confirmed the eastwards shift in the focus of Cornish mining. This shift was again emphasised by further discoveries of copper in the Tamar valley around Callington and Gunnislake, leading to the rise of mines such as Holmbush, Gunnislake Clitters, Prince of Wales, and Hingston Down Consols. In 1844 there was yet another significant discovery of copper, this time on the Devon bank of the Tamar. Mines such as Wheal Anna Maria, Wheal Josiah and Wheal Fanny coalesced into the mighty Devon Great Consols, that westward fringe of Devon becoming to all intents and purposes a trans-Tamar extension of Cornwall—mines with Cornish names, worked by Cornish methods and by Cornish hands, their output measured and categorised as Cornish ore. Again, technological advance facilitated the rapid development of these new finds. The Liskeard and Caradon railway was opened in 1844, assisting the export of ore and the import of coal at the port of Looe. Similarly, there was an enormous growth in Tamar river traffic, associated with new quays such as that at Morwellham.

The jagged remains of copper mining on the bleak slopes of Caradon Hill, near St Cleer.

Mitchell's 30 inch *whim (winding)* engine at East Pool mine, near Carn Brea, preserved by the National Trust and managed now by the Trevithick Trust.

The dynamic impact of copper overshadowed the more prosaic performance of tin, although in the latter third of the last century tin production (ironically) outlasted that of copper. And while the expansion of copper may have precipitated the technological advances of this period, it was the experience of tin over decades and centuries that had largely moulded the fabric and culture of Cornish mining. The names of the late eighteenth and early nineteenth-century tin bounds in St Agnes parish have an almost timeless euphony: Goonlaze Goath, Great Carnmeal, Little Wheal an Culliack, Great Wheal an Cracke, Codnacoose, Middle Park Broaze, Great Bounds Henver, Wheal Mena. So to in the district of Wendron: Hetch an Rose, Hagarowal, Balreath, Stennack, Baldees, Goonreath, Park Tottle.[11] However, the controlling influence of merchants and smelters (alongside the role of the East India Company as a major purchaser of Cornish tin in the latter part of the eighteenth century) had established and circumscribed the operations of the tin market, while what Barton has called 'the fetters of coinage' (the dues payable to the Duchy of Cornwall) retarded the expansion of the Cornish tin industry in the years before 1838.[12]

Nonetheless, by 1800 the demand for tin-plate in the British domestic market was beginning to expand rapidly, offering the Cornish industry a new and readily accessible market place. By 1815 the tin-plate works of South Wales had become established as the principal destination for Cornish produce, a position they would maintain for decades to come. As early as 1810 a veritable tin boom was underway in Cornwall, leading to the working of Great Wheal Vor and a number of other mines in the neighbourhood of Helston and Marazion, as well as in other districts such as St Just-in-Penwith where mines such as Wheal Spearne, Carnyorth Moor, Bosorne, and Wheal Bellan were in production by 1815. Overseas competition (that from the Malay Straits being felt as early as 1813) would dog the performance of Cornish tin throughout the century but the abolition of 'coinage' in 1838 was a welcome boost to the industry, helping it to ride the depression of the 1840s more easily than it might otherwise have done. Between 1850 and 1864 there was vigorous activity, as demand from the Welsh tin-plate works surged ahead and as many of the old copper mines turned to tin. Dolcoath had turned from copper to tin as early as 1838, her copper deposits increasingly worked out, but with tin lodes fortuitously discovered at depth, and the example was followed by other Camborne-Redruth mines. A further tin boom in 1870-72 accelerated this process, leading to the rise of South Frances and other tin mines along the Great Flat Lode south of Carn Brea, and to the development of Wheal Owles and North Levant on the cliffs to the north of St Just.

Writing for the *Mining Journal* in the mid-1850s, George Henwood pondered the might of Cornish mining as he quite literally saw it from atop Carn Brea,

> There we sat, on the summit of this hill, in the centre of some of the richest mines ever worked in this or any other country. There, at our feet, lay the Carn Brea Mines (so called from the mountain) with the numerous family of East, North & Carn Breas. There away west, Tincroft, Dolcoath, Cook's Kitchen, and Stray Park, all of which have been wrought for generations without sign of exhaustion. On a parallel with these, to the north, lie the Seatons (sic), the Roskears, the Croftys, the Pools, the Tolguses . . . we turn round to the east, and our vision is greeted by the sight of the Treleighs, the Pedn-an-drea, the Cupids, the Gramblers, the ancient Sparnon, the famous Bullers and Bassets, the Old and New Penstruthal, the glorious old Tresavean, the pride and boast of Gwennap, notwithstanding her famous Great Consols or United Mines—all these may be seen by the mere twist of a heel. Another move displays the Frances, the Rosewarnes, and at a distance of a few miles radius may be discerned the whole of the western mines. Oh! a glorious sight it is from the top of Carn Brea Hill![13]

The technological innovation that underpinned this impressive pageant of industrialisation also prompted the emergence of Cornwall as a principal centre of engineering expertise, particularly with regard to the mechanical application of steam power. The development of the Cornish beam engine—for pumping, winding, ore-crushing, and the operation of man-engines—exemplified this process, with Cornish engines built not only for use in Cornwall but for export across the globe. As Barton has put it, '. . . by 1850 Cornishmen had more experience of deep mining, and with it deep pumping, than the rest of the world put together'.[14] Even as early as 1716 there was one steam-powered Newcomen engine at work in Cornwall, possibly at Great Wheal Vor or nearby Godolphin Ball. Others followed, and in the 1770s the more economical Watt engines arrived on the Cornish scene. By then Cornish engineers, with more experience than anyone else, had their own ideas for the further development of steam and pushed and tested Watt's patents to the limit.

James Watt's patents lapsed in 1800, and at once the floodgates were opened, precipitating in Cornwall an era of enthusiastic, almost feverish experimentation. Cornish engineers competed with one another to perfect the beam engine and to achieve ever-greater feats of efficiency, their efforts recorded in careful detail in Lean's *Engine Reporter*, a journal founded in 1810 to record the 'duty' achieved by the principal engines at work in Cornwall. 'Duty' was defined as the number of pounds of water raised one foot high by the consumption of one bushel of coal. Thus in 1814, for example, at Wheal Druid in Illogan Highway, a 28 inch engine in the care of J. Pearce (engineer) achieved an average duty of 15,330,619. In the same year a 42 inch engine at Wheal Damsel, in Gwennap parish, achieved 15,827,733, and the average figure for the 48 inch engine at Tincroft, near Camborne, was 20,217,011.[15] Individual engines acquired individual reputations, and were often much sought after second-hand if they became surplus to requirement as a result of a mine's expansion or (alternatively) closure. In 1834, for example, a 50 inch engine was removed from Wheal Anna in Perranzabuloe parish to Wheal Fortune copper mine in Illogan Highway (not to be confused with other Wheal Fortunes in Gwennap, Breage, Ludgvan, and St Mellion), the re-erection of the engine in its new Illogan home being supervised by J. Sims, one of the several celebrated engineers from that family.[16]

The reputations of engineers were at least as important as the engines they designed or nurtured. Arthur Woolf was one such engineer, a legend in his own lifetime amongst the Cornish mining fraternity. Even more important (but insufficiently recognised in his own time) was Richard Trevithick (known variously as 'Cap'n Dick' or the 'Cornish Giant'), born in the parish of Illogan in 1771, who in 1812 successfully introduced his high-pressure engine at Wheal Prosper in Gwithian—in effect the prototype for the generation of 'Cornish engines' that was to follow. Trevithick was also responsible for the invention of the self-propelled steam locomotive, the prototype for which was trialed in Camborne on Christmas Eve 1801, an event commemorated in the much-sung Cornish song 'Goin' up Camborne 'ill':

> Goin' up Camborne 'ill, Comin' down,
> Goin' up Camborne 'ill, Comin' down,
> The 'osses stood still, the wheels turned aroun',
> Goin' up Camborne 'ill, Comin' down.
>
> White stockins, white stockins she wore,
> White stockins, white stockins she wore,
> White stockins she wore, the same as before,
> Goin' up Camborne 'ill, Comin 'down.[17]

The next step was the invention of the railway locomotive, achieved by Trevithick at Penydaren in South Wales in 1804. In 1808 he exhibited another railway engine, 'Catch-me-who-can', on a circular track in central London, while in 1805 one of his design of locomotives was introduced at the Wylam colliery in the Northeast of England—the prototype from which was developed the 'Newcastle school' of locomotives of George and Robert Stephenson. In 1814 Trevithick was asked to design a series of pumping and winding engines and other equipment for the reworking of silver mines in

Peru, a challenge to which he rose with relish. He himself travelled to South America in 1817, and there he remained for a decade—ensnared in all kinds of adventures from civil wars to hazardous river crossings and encounters with alligators—before returning home. Never one to plan in advance, Trevithick moved from one project to another, and died impoverished and relatively obscure in Dartford, south-east London, in 1833 at the age of sixty-seven. Trevithick saw that he had not enjoyed the public recognition (outside of Cornwall) or financial success that he deserved, and a few months before his death wrote to his old friend, the Cornish technocrat Davies Gilbert:

> I have been branded with folly and madness for attempting what the world calls impossibilities, and even from the great engineer, the late Mr James Watt, who said to an eminent scientific character still living, that I deserved hanging for bringing into use the high-pressure engine. This so far has been my reward from the public; but should this be all, I shall be satisfied by the great secret pleasure and laudable pride that I feel in my own breast from having been the instrument of bringing forward and maturing new principles and new arrangements of boundless value to my country. However much I may be straitened in pecuniary circumstances, the great honour of being a useful subject can never be taken from me, which to me far exceeds riches.[18]

Amongst other Cornish engineers of the period was William Sims (another of that family), who in 1816 introduced numerous improvements to his engines at Wheal Chance, in Gwennap. At Wheal Hope, in Gwinear parish, Samuel Grose acquired an enviable reputation as one of the greatest practical engineers of his day, a reputation enhanced by the outstanding duty achieved by his 80 inch engine at Wheal Towan in the early 1830s. The period 1825 to 1850 witnessed a continuing improvement in duty performance in the competition between the various engines and engineers, with the highest duty ever recorded by Lean (an extraordinary 107,000,000) being achieved by the far-famed 85 inch Ale and Cakes engine (Taylor's) at United Mines in Gwennap in 1842. Other well-known engineers, who established Cornish, British and in some cases even international reputations, included the Cornish-adopted Hornblowers (originally from the Midlands), John Hocking, Michael Loam (who invented the man-engine, allowing miners to ride from the depths instead of climbing ladders), William West, and the incredible Michell dynasty whose activities spanned almost the entire period of Cornish steam engineering—from the late eighteenth to early twentieth centuries.

The rise of the Cornish beam engine was facilitated in part by the establishment of numerous engineering foundries in Cornwall, including those at Wadebridge, St Austell, Charlestown, St Blazey, Redruth, Tuckingmill, St Just-in-Penwith and elsewhere. Amongst the leaders were Harvey's of Hayle and the Perran Foundry at Perranarworthal, near Truro. Established soon after 1780, Harvey's was already a major concern by the turn of the nineteenth century, playing a central role in the growth of Hayle as an industrial port. A notable achievement was the manufacture of massive pumping engines in the 1840s to assist the Dutch government in its draining of Haarlem Meer. Perran's hey-day was from the 1820s until the 1860s, its engines in demand from across the world—from Burra Burra and Moonta in South Australia, to Real del Monte in Mexico, and Kimberley in South Africa. Also of international significance was Holman Brothers of

Camborne, an engineering firm which, by the end of the nineteenth century, was exporting pneumatic rock drills and other mining appliances to destinations as diverse as the silver-lead-zinc workings of Broken Hill in Australia and the gold mines of South Africa's Rand. Thus in 1894, when representatives of the *Mining World* visited Holmans, they found some 250 workmen engaged in a range of activities from the manufacture of pulverisers, amalgamators, and stamps to pumping and winding engines for steam or compressed air. In the fitting shop:

> . . . we found some thirty men employed on overtime making Cornish drills for delivery in various parts of the world. Every detail is made in duplicate, so that customers may depend upon obtaining, without delay, duplicates of any part of the machine they order . . . .[19]

In December 1884 an order from Spain had been fulfilled for twenty-four drill bits and spare valve tappets and pins for each, while in June of the following year two rock drills plus parts and spares had been supplied to New Zealand. In the same month a steam winch and two drills were sent to Australia. Further items were sent to Spain during 1886. Later, in May 1903, a compound pumping engine and associated pitwork was supplied to the Broomassie Mines in West Africa (at a cost of £1,205), while in August 1908 a major order from the La Blanca Mine, Pechuca, Mexico was fulfilled for a compound hoisting engine, two Lancashire boilers, and a steel headframe, together with a variety of other appliances, the total cost being some £5,489. Later still, between 1906 and 1909, pneumatic stamps, Acme tables, pulversisers and buddles, wagons and elevators, and woodwork for buildings, were supplied at a cost of £6,636 to the Aramayo-Francke Mines in Bolivia.

Although (despite early attempts at Polrudden and a more sustained effort by the Cornish Copper Company at Hayle) there was little development of copper smelting in Cornwall, the growth of engineering foundries was reflected in the spread of tin smelting. Modern smelters, using the reverberatory furnace and employing coal as fuel, gradually replaced the ancient charcoal-fired 'blowing houses' that had hitherto been characteristic of Cornwall. Amongst the tin smelters that existed in a score or more of Cornish towns and villages, perhaps the best known (and most important) were Chyandour and Trereiffe at Penzance; Carvedras, Calenick and Trethellan in Truro; Treloweth at St Erth, and Angarrack near Hayle. Lead smelting was also carried out in Cornwall, notably at Point on Restronguet Creek and at Par, the former owned by the noted Michell family of Truro and the latter by J.T. Treffry—the so-called 'King of Mid-Cornwall'.

Improvements in transport and communications assisted the industrialisation of Cornwall. The mineral tramways of Portreath, Gwennap and Devoran, and of Caradon and Looe, were matched by the appearance of other railways serving mines and clayworks—notably the complex of mineral lines in mid-Cornwall (of which the Treffry viaduct is a splendid memorial), the Pentewan railway, the clay lines to Wenford and Ruthern Bridge, and the East Cornwall Mineral Railways at Calstock. The significance of these systems was not their ability to feed into the main line (the Royal Albert Bridge, linking Cornwall's railways to the rest of Britain, was not opened until 1859) but rather the connection that they made between mines and quarries on the one hand, and ports and harbours on the other. New ports were established as part of this process—Portreath, Par, Pentewan, Hayle,

Newquay, Charlestown, Trevaunance, Bude and others—while long-established harbours such as Fowey, Looe and Saltash were re-equipped to allow the export of minerals or the import of coal, timber and other materials for the mineral industry.[20] Although the topography of Cornwall did not lend itself to the construction of canals, there were some attempts at canal building, notably the Bude Canal in the North Cornwall-North Devon border country.

Situated in the dramatic Luxulyan Valley, the Treffry Viaduct is a masterpiece of Cornish civil engineering, and is today in the care of the Cornwall Heritage Trust.

Alongside the practical engineers who developed the beam engines and managed the mines and other engineering establishments, was the new breed of Cornish industrialist which emerged during the technological advance of the eighteenth and nineteenth centuries. These industrialists—capitalists, innovators, inventors, reformers—brought a particular single-mindedness and determination which prompted the re-definition of Cornish society as modern and progressive, and which helped mould a re-defining Cornish identity based on industrial prowess. The great families had their role to play in this process; some well-established, and others which had only lately gained wealth and status. Among the former were the Bassets of Tehidy, an ancient family which acquired new riches from Dolcoath and other mines in the Camborne-Redruth district. One of their number, Francis Basset, the Lord de Dunstanville, is commemorated on the great monument that crowns Carn Brea, erected in 1836. It is said, probably correctly, that Basset's funeral was the biggest Cornwall has ever known.[21] He died in London in February 1835, and the procession of his coffin from the Capital to and within Cornwall had all the air of a State occasion. He did indeed lie 'in state'—in Launceston, in Bodmin and in Truro, with local worthies encouraged to pay their last respects. At Truro the shops were closed in melancholy deference to his greatness, and the bell of St Mary's was tolled in his honour. The funeral itself, marked by the closure for the day of all the local mines, drew a procession of some 20,000 people from Tehidy Park to Illogan church.

The sylvan setting of Treffry Viaduct is apparent in this view.

Also influential and well-regarded, though perhaps not on such a grand a scale, was the Fox family of Falmouth, Quakers who had made their money as merchants and then invested wisely in copper ventures such as North

In 1808 John Trevanion engaged John Nash, the architect, to build a 'castle' at Caerhays. In 1853, the building—still unfinished—was acquired by the Williams family of Scourier, who proceeded to establish a magnificent garden.

Downs and United Mines. Robert Fox, born in Falmouth in 1789, interested himself in scientific phenomena such as magnetism and the internal temperature of the earth, and in recognition of his contribution to science was elected Fellow of the Royal Society in 1848. His brother, Charles Fox, was a founder of the Royal Cornwall Polytechnic Society in 1833 (an important vehicle for the propagation of the literary and scientific flowering in Cornwall in that period) and was later President of the Royal Cornwall Geological Society. Robert's daughter, Caroline Fox, was no less successful in the construction of an intellectual career, her diaries recording her contacts with John Stuart Mill, Carlyle and other learned gentlemen of the day. Members of the Lemon family, though perhaps less scholarly than their Fox counterparts, were equally influential. They owed their rank to the efforts of William Lemon of Germoe, an ordinary village boy who rose to become manager of a Penzance smelting works and who, with great foresight, made the financially advantageous step of introducing Newcomen and his engines to Cornish mining. As befitted his new power and prestige, Lemon moved to Truro (his name is commemorated there in Lemon Street and Lemon Quay), dominating that town's civic life until his death in 1760, passing on a healthy inheritance to his successors.

The Williams family of Scorrier were equally successful, living almost literally in the midst of the vast mining landscape that their energies and investments had helped to create. In 1853 they acquired from the impecunious Trevanions the part-completed Caerhays castle at Porthluney Cove, in the softer, gentler country around Gorran Haven. The Williamses not only completed and restored the castle (it had been begun in 1808, with John Nash as architect) but—in a manner that was echoed elsewhere in nineteenth-century Cornwall as it was discovered that exotic plants from

America, Asia and Australia could thrive in the mild Cornish climate—they also created a magnificent garden. Trengwainton, Glendurgan, Trebah, Trelissick, Trewithen, Heligan and other gardens up and down Cornwall were similarly part of this new Cornish fashion, creating a gardening culture that was recognisably Cornish (few other areas of Britain could hope to emulate its style and diversity) and which should be seen as an integral part of the Cornish scientific and artistic accomplishment of the period.[22]

Joseph Thomas Treffry of Place, Fowey (here carved by Neville Northey Burnard) the creator of the Treffry viaduct, changed his name from Austen to Treffry when he became High Sheriff in 1838.

The Treffry family of Place, at Fowey, had earned a niche in Cornish history almost without equal, and it was perhaps for this reason that Joseph Thomas Austen assumed the Treffry surname (from his mother's line) when he became High Sheriff in 1838. He had also inherited Place through his mother, extensively rebuilding and restoring it between 1813 and 1845, creating the familiar outline that we recognise today. However, it is not so much for his work at Place that J.T. Treffry is remembered as the 'King of Mid-Cornwall' but rather for his development of mines, quarries, ports and railways (including the Treffry Viaduct) around Fowey and St Austell. John Keast, Fowey's historian (author of *The Story of Fowey*), has carefully detailed the life and achievements of J.T. Treffry in a fond biography called simply *The King of Mid-Cornwall*, describing at length Treffry's many projects and achievements. As well as developing Newquay harbour and founding the port of Par, Treffry built a canal from Par to his nearby mines (Fowey Consols and Lanescot), connecting them in turn by mineral railway to the Luxulyan granite quarries and the china clay district around Roche.[23] Somehow, he also found time to farm some 1,000 acres near Place. As the *West Briton* newspaper concluded in its obituary of 1 February 1850, 'Joseph Thomas Treffry . . . was not an ordinary man'.[24]

Also less (or more) than ordinary was Sir Humphry Davy, the 'mercurial chemist' as Anne Treneer described him in her biography, the larger-than-life Cornishman who has long since been the butt of the affectionate rhyme:

Sir Humphry Davy
Abominated gravy
He lived in the odium
Of having discovered sodium.[25]

Sir Humphry Davy, with his miner's lamp, surveys the scene from his vantage point at the top of Market Jew Street in Penzance.

Born at Varfell, Ludgvan, near Penzance, in 1778, Davy quickly made his mark in scientific circles (his *Researches Chemical and Philosophical chiefly concerning Nitrous Oxide and its Respiration* was published as early as 1799) and was by 1803 a Fellow of the Royal Society (of which he was later President). He was knighted in 1812. In 1815 he invented the miner's 'safety lamp' (of use to coal miners rather than the hard-rock men of his native Cornwall), and it is a measure of the man that he refused to take out a patent on this invention, lest it compromise or restrict its general application. He assisted in the establishment of the Zoological Society in 1825 (which exhibited its collection in Regent's Park), and as a poet expressed his appreciation of natural history:

The mighty birds still upward rose
In slow but constant and most steady flight,
The young ones following; and they would pause,
As if to teach them how to bear the light,
And keep the solar glory full in sight.
So went they on till, from excess of pain,

Bickford's dynamite factory at Tuckingmill, near Camborne, where the safety fuse was invented and manufactured. In the background are the mill and headframe of New Cook's Kitchen Shaft at South Crofty, Cornwall's last tin mine.

> I could no longer bear the scorching rays;
> And when I looked again they were not seen,
> Lost in brightness of the solar blaze.[26]

The list of Cornish scientific worthies could be extended almost *ad infinitum*. John Couch Adams, born in the remote moorland parish of Laneast in 1819, discovered the planet Neptune and went on to become Professor of Astronomy at Cambridge and President of the Royal Astronomical Society. William Bickford, born at Tuckingmill, near Camborne, invented the miner's safety fuse in 1830 and erected a factory at Tuckingmill dedicated to the manufacture of these fuses. Jonathan Couch, born in Polperro in 1789 and author of the *History of Polperro*, was also an important marine scientist and produced several definitive treatises, including his *History of British Fishes* (1860-65). Goldsworthy Gurney, born near Padstow in 1793, was responsible for a number of significant experimentations and inventions, not least Bude Castle itself which was built to demonstrate that it was possible to construct buildings on concrete rafts. Henry Trengrouse, born in Helston in 1772, invented the rocket-and-line apparatus for saving lives in shipwrecks and also introduced the cork life jacket.

The archetypal Cornishman of the age, however, was Davies Gilbert, who as technocrat, inventor, reformer, antiquarian, patron of both arts and sciences and encourager of the likes of Trevithick and Davy, exemplified the energy and self-confidence of Cornish society. Even in his own time his reputation was exceptional, known to all in the business of improvement and reform as the 'Cornish Philosopher'. He is the subject of a full length biography by Dr A. C. Todd, but suffice it here to note that his career as Member of Parliament, Fellow and President of the Royal Society, and chairman of numerous Parliamentary committees led him to advocate and embrace many 'improving' causes—technical education, the application of steam power, agricultural reform, road construction, Poor Law reform. As a Parliamentarian he was a useful political voice for the practical and theoretical scientists with whom he associated, and we see in his activities an echo of the work and concerns of that other Cornish MP, his contemporary James Silk Buckingham, the maritime reformer. Gilbert retired to his Sussex home in later life, where he died in 1839. Memorials on the church walls of both Eastbourne and St Erth record the maxim by which he had lived, drawn from the third hymn of Synesius:

> Nor love thy life, not hate: But what Thou liv'st
> Live well. How long or short, permit to Heaven.[27]

The heady mix of Trevithick and Davy, Lemon and Fox, Basset and Williams, Treffry and Gilbert, Bickford and Gurney, made for an astonishing concentration of intellectual activity and inventiveness in Cornwall. Cornish society became remarkably self-confident and assertive, and Cornishness was expressed increasingly in terms of technological and scientific advance—in particular in its practical manifestations in mining and steam engineering. Thus in 1839 Thomas Lean (of *Engine Reporter* fame) could insist that:

> Great as are the advantages which this nation [Britain] in general enjoys from the invention of the steam engine, and the successive improvements which it has received; there is, perhaps, no place in particular, where those advantages have been greater, or more

> evident, than in Cornwall. The very existence of its deepest, most extensive, and most productive mines, is owing, not merely to the invention of the steam engine, but to the state of great perfection to which that machine has been brought in that county . . . the improvements which the engine has, for many years, received, are due to native engineers; whose skill and watchful care, maintain it in its present state, or add continually still further improvements . . . .[28]

Twenty years later the message was even more confident and expansive, George Henwood in 1859 explaining with evident pride:

> The Cornish are remarkable for their sanguine temperament, their indomitable perseverance, their ardent hope in adventure, and their desire for discovery and novelty . . . to this very cause has science to boast of so many brilliant ornaments who claim Cornwall as their birthplace.[29]

This spirit was reflected in the foundation and rapid rise to pre-eminence of Cornwall's learned bodies, the Royal Cornwall Geological Society (1814), the Royal Institution of Cornwall (1818), and the Royal Cornwall Polytechnic Society (1833), each of which became an important vehicle for the new Cornishness based on industrial modernity. At a more popular level, the same improving spirit motivated the many mutual-improvement and educational bodies that had grown-up by the 1850s: the St Austell Useful Knowledge Society, the St Austell Literary Society, the Launceston Philosophical Society, the Liskeard Institution, and so on. As Dr Roger Burt has noted, such institutions displayed a 'distinctive Cornish hue', not least in their passion for mining:

> The most noticeable 'Cornish' sector of the educational system were the non-vocational institutions: 'Non- vocational' in the sense that they had no specific commitment to providing instruction in basic literacy or for any particular profession, but highly 'Cornish' in that their programmes reflected the district's consuming interest in mining affairs and related subjects.[30]

Mining as a central plank of the Cornish identity was firmly established by the middle of the nineteenth century, asserted by the Cornish themselves and acknowledged by external observers. For the latter, the habits of the miners had always been the distinguishing features of Cornishness but increasingly the image of 'West Barbary' was left behind, to be replaced by a new stereotype which emphasised a diligent and industrious modernity. Bernard Deacon, who with great skill has mapped this shifting imagery, has drawn attention to the diary of Thomas Preston of Norfolk, who in 1821 wrote:

> . . . the mines of Cornwall occupy the attention of the principal inhabitants. As you advance to the west, so you hear them more and more talked about till you arrive at Truro; there their whole ideas are immersed in the value of the shares of such and such a mine; if you go to Redruth, then it is the weight of a piece of ore or the quality of what was raised or dug up yesterday.[31]

Although there was in this (and other) descriptions, an inference that the further west one travelled in Cornwall, the greater was the predominance of mining and thus more pronounced the sense of Cornishness, mining had in fact become a geographically and culturally unifying factor by the 1850s. By then, the industry directly employed one third of the working population of Cornwall, with still more working in support activities and ancillary trades. As discussed above, the focus of copper mining had shifted from West to East Cornwall from the late 1830s, John Allen noting that an influx of western miners to Liskeard had made that district visibly and audibly more 'Cornish'. Even the most far-flung parts of Cornwall could boast their Cornish mines—Wheal Morwenna at Morwenstow, Wheal Tamar at Saltash, Wheal Carew at Torpoint—the very Cornishness of their names leaving no doubt as to their significance as cultural icons as well as economic enterprises. But the economic aspect of this new territorial unity was also significant. Just as mining had drawn West and East Cornwall together, so the decline of the Devon cloth industry had undone the former economic links between Devon and East Cornwall. These, in turn, were replaced by the eastwards expansion of Cornish mining which spilled across the Tamar to make Tavistock to all intents and purposes a Cornish town, Devon Great Consols by now the focus of a 'Greater Cornwall' which spread out towards the Dartmoor hills.

At its most developed, the pride in Cornish achievement verged on arrogance or even chauvinism. As Bernard Deacon has noted, in 1857 Herman Merivale wrote 'The thorough Cornishman's respect for his own shrewdness and that of his clan is unbounded, or only equalled by his profound contempt for "foreigners" from the east . . .'.[32] There was in such an attitude, perhaps, a coalescence of the new pride in industrial prowess with an older mistrust of intrusion from across the Tamar. And yet, in other respects, this modernity was no respector of traditional beliefs. Henry Quick may have regretted the passing of the old ways, but informed opinion in Cornwall was insistent that the march of progress was all to the good. Thus Davies Gilbert welcomed the demise of the Cornish language. Although his antiquarian interests extended to the remnants of the old tongue, prompting him to publish an edition of the passion poem *Pascon agan Arluth* (the 'Passion of

The open-air cathedral of Cornish Methodism. John Wesley's preaching place at Gwennap Pit.

Our Lord') in 1826, he emphasised that 'No one more sincerely rejoices than does the editor of this ancient mystery that the Cornish dialect of the Celtic or Gaelic languages has ceased altogether from being used by the inhabitants of Cornwall'.[33] Cornish, of course, would have been an obstacle to progress, an impediment in an English-speaking industrial environment, an irrelevant relic from less enlightened days. Even Matthew Arnold, Cornish on his mother's side (she was a Penrose from Constantine), favoured the decline of the Celtic languages on such grounds, despite his professed enthusiasm for Celtic literature and cultures.[34]

Thus while the trumpeting of industrial prowess could be fiercely Cornish, it also welcomed—even encouraged—the disappearance of those attributes that had hitherto marked Cornwall as different. This complex paradox was also evident in the impact of Methodism in Cornwall. Although Methodism was central to the improving culture of modernity, disapproving as it did of ancient customs from wrestling to wrecking, its very success was dependent upon its ability to adapt to Cornish conditions. Moreover, in earning its place in the forefront of the new Cornishness, Methodism became an integral part of the increasingly assertive Cornish identity. As Dr D. H. Luker has put it, there was '. . . an increasingly articulated regional sensitivity on the part of the Cornish which fuelled an exaggerated identification of Methodism as 'theirs" .[35]

The changes wrought by John Wesley and his Methodist followers in Cornwall are easily charted, although the transformation was no doubt neither as immediate nor as complete as contemporary Wesleyan propagandists and later sentimental interpretations have suggested. Nonetheless, the impact of Methodism must be counted an important influence in the decline of wrecking and smuggling. Although Cornish smugglers had sought to reconcile their traditional pursuit with the demands of their new religion by describing the import of contraband as 'Free Trade' (something liberal-minded Methodists might be expected to support), John Wesley was in no doubt that smuggling was an 'abomination'. At St Ives in July 1753, for example, he rebuked members of the local Methodist society for indulging in smuggling and warned that they must cease the practice or 'see my face no more'.[36] He was also hard on wreckers, denouncing 'that scandal of Cornwall, the plundering of wrecked vessels', and similarly took a dim view of riot as a means of popular expression: 'I took a view of the ruins of the house which the mob had pulled down a little while before, for the joy that Admiral Matthews had beaten the Spaniards. Such is the Cornish method of thanksgiving'.[37]

As well as disapproving of such behaviour, the Methodists also took a positive role in the establishment of mutual improvement and educational institutions, their commitment to self-help permeating so many aspects of late eighteenth and nineteenth-century Cornish life. In 1817 one observer could write with feeling that '. . . those local habits which might once have been deemed unconquerable, have almost completely disappeared'.[38] Wesley's personal impact was phenomenal. In 1781, at the age of seventy-eight years, he could attract a crowd of twenty-thousand adoring followers when he preached at Gwennap Pit, that extraordinary spot in the heart of Cornwall's mining country destined to become the cathedral of Cornish Methodism. Seventy years later, in 1851, sixty per cent of the Cornish population was Methodist. Many others belonged to other Nonconformist sects, while only twenty-seven per cent were Anglicans. As Dr Bruce Colman has observed:

> Though the [Southwest] peninsula was thus rather more non-conformist than the average for England and Wales, Devon was hardly exceptional while Cornwall's condition was far enough from the norms of southern England to place it firmly in the 'Celtic fringe' of religious practice.[39]

Indeed, those areas of Devon where Methodism was strong were not the old Dissenting districts of East Devon (so important in the Civil War) but those parts of the west and north where contact with Cornwall was close. The Cornish mining influence in the neighbourhood of Tavistock was an important influence, and further north there was another 'Greater Cornwall' in the North Devon border country where the Bible Christian denomination (founded by William O'Bryan—or Bryant—from Gunwen, Luxulyan) took root. It was not unknown for contemporary observers to mistakenly imagine that Shebbear, the Bible Christian training college, was actually in Cornwall.[40]

Paradoxically, although Methodism often disapproved of Cornish individualistic behaviour, its very success depended in part on the individualistic and independent strains in Cornish society. It would be unwise to suppose that the Cornish lived in a state of perpetual anarchy, unable to form any kind of association or co-operative venture, with individuals unable to recognise or defer to points of view alternative to their own. Thus in 1824 Hitchens and Drew could note of the Cornish that a '. . . spirit of independence not only pervades their general actions, but it enters into their various views, and incorporates itself with their conflicting opinions', while in the same breath explaining an 'equally conspicuous feature':

> . . . accustomed to associate in bodies, they mutually encourage each other to perseverance, even on occasions when all rational hopes of success have taken their leave. Hence 'One and All' accompanied by three huzzas will infallibly reanimate their spirits, in the midst of a doubtful exploit.[41]

However, as Dr A. C. Todd has noted, the individualistic and independent aspects of Cornish behaviour were an important function of a society in which there were 'No great families in the English sense . . . differences between social groups were never as clearly marked as elsewhere'. Tenant farmers sported a long tradition of independence as a result of the weakness of the manorial system in Cornwall, while, it has been argued, the scattered Celtic settlement pattern left farmers on their remote properties physically isolated from external influences. To this was added the impact of the 'tribute' and 'tutwork' system of employment in the Cornish, in which part of the entrepreneurial function was performed by the miner himself. Individual sections of a mine (pitches) were contracted out to individual miners (tributers), or—more commonly—small groups of miners (pares) as a result of open-bidding on 'survey day'. Prior to this bidding, each pitch was inspected by a mine agent (captain) to ascertain the value of the ore that it contained. Each pitch would then be offered at a 'captain's price'. For a rich section of ground the captain's price would be relatively low, perhaps a few shillings in the pound (so that a tributer or pare would no be excessively remunerated for the ore that they raised) but for lower-grade pitches the captain's price would be high—encouraging miners to work indifferent ground. Occasionally pitches were let at captain's prices but more often there was vigorous downward bidding, as tributers anxious to work particular pieces of ground competed against one another. The lowest bidder would win the contract, and then would be expected to furnish all the materials he (or they) would need to work the ground—pick and gad, tallow candles, powder, timber and so on.

Tributing was thus something of a gamble. An apparently rich section of ground might unexpectedly fail, although a rich pocket of high-grade ore (a sturt) in otherwise poor ground might give a lucky tributer or pare a handsome reward during that particular 'take' or contract period. Tutwork was similar to tributing in that it too paid by results and offered a form of self-employment, but here the contract was concerned with the amount of ground mined rather than the value of ore won—tutwork was thus often reserved for the driving of levels or sinking of shafts. Although the bidding process set miner against miner, tribute and tutwork was generally well-liked, not least because it gave the individual miner an opportunity to benefit directly from his own enterprise, energy and expertise.

Lead, kindly Light, amid the encircling gloom . . . Keep thou my feet; I do not see / The distant scene—one step enough for me: J. H. Newman's well-known hymn was a firm favourite in Cornwall's mining communities. The imposing facade of Camborne Centenary chapel conveys the strength and self-confidence of Methodist culture in nineteenth-century Cornwall.

If the organisation of the mining industry both reflected and perpetuated the individualistic and independent strains in Cornish society, then so too did fishing. In the absence of large commercial groups, the Cornish fishing industry was generally in the hands of small men who owned their own vessels or, more often, the small co-operative companies (seines) that had emerged: by the beginning of the nineteenth century, almost every Cornish cove and harbour had its seine—such as the 'Dolphin' of Mevagissey or the 'Trusty' of St Mawes. Like the ributing pares, the seines might encourage co-operation between groups of workers (often family-related) who were prepared to pool their resources and expertise, but the wider effect was to emphasise individual enterprise and action.

It was against this background of individualism and independence that Methodism took root and flourished in Cornwall. In the absence of nucleated villages, many people lived isolated from the remote churchtowns—physically insulated from the influence of church and vicar—and with relatively few figures of squire-like authority to encourage their religious conformity.

The established Church of England was perpetually weak in Cornwall (perhaps never having fully recovered from the trauma of 1549), the remoteness of the episcopal centre in distant Exeter making adequate supervision of often lacklustre incumbents an impossibility. Henry Pelling has noted the 'failure of ecclesiastical adaptation that gave a special stimulus to the growth of Nonconformity', and John Pearce has argued that 'The Wesleys and their itinerants restored heart religion to Cornwall . . . The Cornish were moved as they had not been moved for centuries'.[42]

In the rapidly expanding mining districts, with the social problems, overcrowding and poverty associated with a burgeoning and mobile population, the Methodists found fertile ground in which to plant their ideas. Their emphasis upon self-help and improvement provided constructive and practical support, while the pre-occupation with the 'next world' helped to alleviate some of the despair in this. Although some mighty piles were erected later as memorials to the triumph of Methodism in Cornwall (for example, Centenary Chapel in Camborne), the Methodists in their embryonic phase needed neither paid clergy nor purpose-built premises to begin their work. Local preachers provided the evangelical edge to the Methodists' efforts, and individuals' homes could serve as meeting places until chapels were built. The commitment to self-help meant that Methodists were good at raising money and acquiring land to build their chapels, individual society members often donating materials, labour and sometimes land towards the cause. As F. W. Bourne observed of Cornish chapels:

> The great majority of these have been built by the self- denying efforts of the poor rather than by the encouragement and generosity of the wealthier classes. The power and effectiveness of the Voluntary principle may be here [Cornwall] witnessed on a large scale. The people generally put their shoulder to the wheel, and preferred to help themselves rather than be dependent on the charity of others—they trusted almost wholly to God's blessing on their own exertions.[43]

The Methodists were also mobile, able to follow the shifting population from one new area of concentration to another (vide the profusion of chapels in the St Cleer district), forever responding to new opportunities. Periodic revivals served to renew evangelical drive if complacency seemed dangerously close at hand, and the fact that local preachers were decidedly 'of the people' meant that they could communicate and gain trust in a way that was often not possible for Anglican parsons. Notable amongst these preachers were Peter Jaco, a Newlyn fisherman, called by Charles Wesley a 'fisher of men, ordained by Christ alone'; Samuel Drew, born at Tregreghan Mills (near St Austell) in 1756 and later a literary figure of note; Richard Hampton (the famous 'Foolish Dick') from Porthtowan; Thomas Rosevear from near Camelford; and Samuel Dunn from Mevagissey. The list, in fact, is endless.[44]

The most celebrated 'Methodee', however, was Billy Bray, the subject of F.W. Bourne's moving and delightful biography, *The King's Son*. Known for his wit, vitality, even eccentricity, Billy Bray was a miner, born at Twelveheads, near Truro in 1794. In addition to his personal characteristics, it was his reputation as a practising Methodist that brought him recognition in his own time and has ensured his place today in Cornish folk-memory. His energy and enthusiasm was behind the building of several chapels, while his determination to put what he preached into practice was demonstrated most dramatically in the story told by Bourne, where Bray returned home one day with a little boy and little girl, one under each arm. Explaining to his perplexed (and, one imagines, long-suffering) wife that, as the children's mother had died and the father had deserted them, they were now to live with them rather than being sent to the workhouse: 'The Lord can as well feed them here as He can in the union . . . Here, my dears, this is your home now'. As Bourne put it, Billy Bray '. . . lived out in his life the teaching and promises that he believed in his heart'.[45]

Professor John Rule has suggested that one of the attractions of Methodism in Cornwall was the relative simplicity of its theology (especially in the unsophisticated Bible Christian sect) which appealed to the superstitious frailties of the Cornish people.[46] Certainly, there is evidence that superstition was often swapped for Methodism, not least in the mines where (as we saw in Chapter Eight) superstitious belief focused often on death and portends of death. The industry took its steady toll on the unwary and unlucky, mining accidents in the last century occurring on an almost regular basis. Cyril Noall's catalogue of *Cornish Mine Disasters* makes shocking reading, not least for the gratuitous and incidental way that fate seemed to deal out death when it was least expected and least deserved.

To take one example, on 11 July 1866 an inexperienced youngster, fifteen year-old Josephus Trevithick, was working in the 160 fathom level in Tincroft mine, Illogan, when he was asked by two comrades to bring up a brace of heavy spanners from the bottom of the level. Mistaking his whereabouts, he went further up the shaft than was necessary. His brother-in-law, William Carpenter, exclaimed, 'Josephus, why do you bring up the spanners here for; they are wanted down on the sollar'. As Noall puts it, 'Without answering, Trevithick turned to go down, slipped his left hand and his right foot and fell a distance of seven fathoms. He was still alive, but unconscious, when found, and died shortly afterwards'. The horror of sudden and unexpected violence is also conveyed in an account of an accident at Binner Downs mine, near Leedstown, in 1828 when a seventy-two year-old miner called Speer was killed by the breaking of a chain on a steam whim (winder). As the kibble (bucket) approached the top of the shaft, its chain parted. The kibble was sent hurtling to the bottom but the section of the chain still attached to the whim recoiled, wrapping itself several times around Speer's arm. His arm and shoulder were almost wrenched off, exposing his heart and lungs. He died instantly and, it is said, left a bedridden wife without anyone to care for her—their three sons having already been killed in mining accidents.[47]

Even for those for whom familiarity with the mining environment ameliorated their worst anxieties, underground remained a fearsome place. As John Harris, the nineteenth-century miner-poet, asked so penetratingly:

> Hast ever seen a mine? Hast ever been
> Down it in its fabled grottoes, walled with gems,
> And canopied with torrid mineral belts,
> That blaze within the fiery orifice?
> Hast ever, by the glimmer of the lamp,
> Or the fast-waning taper, gone down, down,
> Towards the earth's dread centre, where wise men
> Have told us that the earthquake is conceived,
> And great Vesuvius hath his lava-house,
> Which burns and burns forever, shooting forth
> As from a fountain of eternal fire?
> Hast ever heard, within this prison house,
> The startling hoof of Fear? the eternal flow
> Of some dread meaning whispering to thy soul?[48]

In such circumstances, the ready appeal of Methodism is not hard to understand. Offering practical help and moral support in this world, and anticipating the glories of that to come, Methodism encouraged a faith (or fatalism, depending upon one's point of view) which equipped the individual to face the danger of the mine. In the words of one Cornish hymn:

> Far down in the earth's dark bosom
> The miner mines the ore:
> Death lurks in the dark behind him
> And hides in the rock before
> Yet never alone is the Christian
> Who lives by faith and prayer;
> For God is a friend unfailing,
> And God is everywhere.[49]

There was in such belief a strange mixture of joy and melancholy, hope and dread, a reflection perhaps of the general Victorian predilection for pathos and sentimentality but with an edge that was decidedly Methodist and

Cornish. The point is even more strongly made in the Cornish 'burying tune':

> 'Sing from the chamber to the grave',
> I hear the dying miner say;
> 'A sound of melody I crave
> Upon my burial day'.
>
> 'Sing sweetly whilst you travel on
> And keep the funeral slow;
> The angels sing where I am gone
> And you should sing below.
>
> 'Then bear me gently to my grave,
> And as you pass along,
> Remember, 'twas my wish to have
> A pleasant funeral song'.[50]

Of course, such sentiment was by no means restricted to life (and death) in the mines, but was reflected more widely in Cornish life as a whole. As a stroll around any Cornish churchyard will reveal, infant mortality was high in the nineteenth century, and although the loss of children to disease and accident was commonplace, that did not make it any easier to bear. Again, the Methodists had an important role to play in making this life bearable and in focusing upon the redemption yet to come. And again, the personal experience of John Harris is for us a poignant illumination of those times. His daughter Lucretia died on 23 December 1855; the following are stanzas selected from a lengthy poem written in her memory:

> And art thou gone so soon?
> And is thy loving gentle spirit fled?
> Ah! is my fair, my passing beautiful,
> My loved Lucretia numbered with the dead?
> Ah! art thou gone so soon?
>
> I miss thee, daughter, now,
> In the dear nooks of earth we oft have trod
> And a strange longing fills my yearning soul
> To sleep with thee, and be, like thee, with God!
> I miss thee, daughter, now.
>
> I miss thee at thy books,
> Lisping sweet Bible-accents in my ear,
> Showing me pictures by the evening lamp,
> Beautiful emblems thou dist love so dear:
> I miss thee at thy books.
>
> Farwell my beautiful!
> Thy sinless spirit is with Christ above:
> Thou hast escaped the evils of the world:
> We have a daughter in the meads of love.
> Farewell, my beautiful!

Hush, murmuring spirit, hush!
It is the Lord, He only hath given:
And he hath taken—blessed be His name!—
The gem, which fell from paradise, to heaven:
I bow and kiss His rod.[51]

We are indebted to D. M. Thomas, Professor Charles Thomas and, more recently, Paul Newman for making the works of John Harris more widely known and appreciated, and for making them more accessible. But Harris was just one (albeit significant) part of a wider Cornish literature spawned by Methodism in the nineteenth century. Journals such as the *Bible Christian Magazine* and the *Cornish Banner* were vehicles for this literature but most of it appeared elsewhere, for example in novels such as those by the prolific Hocking brothers (Silas and Joseph, born in St Stephen-in-Brannel in 1850 and 1855 respectively) which seemed endlessly to dwell on Methodist themes. Amongst the poets was James Dryden Hosken, the 'Helston postman', born in 1861, who in his searching poem 'When the Son of Man cometh, shall He find Faith on the Earth?' asked questions that seemed to have particular relevance for the industrial Cornwall that we have discussed above:

What has this splendid world of might,
This orb of intellectual light,
To do with poverty and loss,
And old-world stories of the Cross?[52]

But if Hosken had sounded a cautionary note about the world that they had built, for others progress could only mean things getting ever better, the very evidence of Cornish life bearing witness to the transformation from 'West Barbary' to a new world of 'improvement'. Within that century of progress the stereotypical picture of the Cornish miner had changed from pagan savage to that portrayed by J. Henry Harris in his *Cornish Saints and Sinners*, the unusual travel book written in similar *genre* to Jerome K. Jerome's *Three Men in a Boat*:

We saw some bal-maidens; [female mine workers] from the train, and heard them singing. . . One girl starts singing, and the rest join in; and very sweet singing it is when heard in the open. The surface men catch on, and there's just sweet harmony, whilst the stamps are dancing, and the great bob is going up and down, pumping out water. Nothing stops them when the orchestra is in full swing. The men generally sing, too, when coming and going, and they like a hymn with a good, rousing march tune. After the night and early morning shifts, the hills and valleys are tuneful . . . .[53]

However, behind this benign, light-hearted, even idyllic portrayal of Cornwall-tamed was a darker reality that was realised but slowly; that Cornwall's experience of industrialisation, seemingly unassailable, was in fact flawed and already moving inexorably towards crisis and an untimely end. Cornish copper stumbled in the 1860s, tin faltered in the 1870s, and even in the 1850s the Cornish beam engine was at the zenith of its development, a prelude to its subsequent fall from grace. The Great Emigration, noticeable even by the 1840s, was interpreted as the ultimate triumph of Cornish genius, with Cousin Jacks and Jennies scattered across the globe, but it was in fact evidence of the calamity that was about to overtake Cornwall.

Notes and References (Chapter 9).

1. Maxine Berg, *The Age of Manufactures 1700-1820*, Fontana, London, 1985, p.125.

2. John Rowe, *Cornwall in the Age of the Industrial Revolution*, Liverpool University Press, Liverpool, 1953, repub. Cornish Hillside, St Austell, 1993; D.Bradford Barton, *A History of Copper Mining in Cornwall and Devon*, Bradford Barton, Truro, 1961, revised ed. 1968; D.Bradford Barton, *The Redruth and Chasewater Railway 1824-1915*, Bradford Barton, Truro, 1961, 3rd ed. 1978; D.Bradford Barton, *The Cornish Beam Engine*, Bradford Barton, Truro, 1965, repub. Cornwall Books, Exeter, 1989; D.Bradford Barton, *A History of Tin Mining and Smelting in Cornwall*, Bradford Barton, Truro, 1967, repub. Cornwall Books, Exeter, 1989; D.Bradford Barton, *Essays in Cornish Mining History*, 2 Vols., Bradford Barton, Truro, 1968 and 1970.

3. John Langton, 'The Industrial Revolution and the Regional Geography of England', *Transactions of the Institute of british Geographers*, NS 9, 1984; Pat Hudson (ed.), *Regions and Industries: A Perspective on the Industrial Revolution in Britain*, Cambridge University Press, Cambridge, 1989; Pat Hudson, *The Industrial Revolution*, London, 1992; Derek W. Urwin, 'Territorial Structures and Political Developments in the United Kingdom', in Stein Rokkan and Derek W.Urwin, *The Politics of Territorial Identity: Studies in European Regionalism*, Sage, London, 1982; Derek W.Urwin, 'The Price of a Kingdom: Territory, Identity and the Centre-Periphery Dimension in Western Europe', in Yves Meny and Vincent Wright (eds.), *Centre-Periphery Relations in Western Europe*, George Allen and Unwin, London, 1985.

4. Dai Smith, *Wales! Wales?*, George Allen and Unwin, London, 1984, p.17.

5. Jack Lawson, 'A Man's Life', quoted in W.H.B. Court, *British Economic History 1870-1914: Commentary and Documents*, Cambridge University Press, Cambridge, 1965, p.97.

6. Hugh Kearney, *The British Isles: A History of Four Nations*, Cambridge University Press, Cambridge, 1989, p.149.

7. Sidney Pollard, *Peaceful Conquest: The Industrialisation of Europe 1760-1970*, Oxford University Press, Oxford, 1981, p.14.

8. Cyril Noall, *Levant*, Bradford Barton, Truro, 1969.

9. John Allen, *History of the Borough of Liskeard*, Liskeard, 1856, p.398.

10. Bernard Deacon, *Migration and the Mining Industry in East Cornwall in the Mid-Nineteenth Century*, Department of Economic History, University of Exeter, Exeter, 1985, pp.6-7.

11. Maurice H.Bizley, *Friendly Retreat: The Story of a Parish*, 1955, repub. St Agnes Museum Trust, St Agnes, 1994, pp.74-80; A.K.Hamilton Jenkin, *Wendron Tin*, Wendron Forge, Helston, 1978, p.21.

12. Barton, 1967 and 1989, p.17.

13. Roger Burt (ed.),, *Cornwall's Mines and Miners*, Bradford Barton, Truro, 1972, pp.171-172.

14. Barton, 1965 and 1989, p.252.

15. Thomas Lean, *On the Steam Engines in Cornwall*, 1839, repub. Bradford Barton, Truro, 1969, pp.13-30.

16. T.A.Morrison, *Cornwall's Central Mines: The Northern District 1810-1895*, Alison Hodge, Penzance, 1980, p.120.

17. A.L.Rowse, *A Cornish Anthology*, Macmillan, London, 1982, p.128.; for an excellent biographical sketch of Trevithick see James Hodge, *Richard Trevithick 1771-1833*, Shire Publications, Princes Risborough, 1973, repub. 1995; for a biography of Woolf see, T.R. Harris, *Arthur Woolf 1766-1837: Cornish Engineer*, Bradford Barton, Truro, 1966.

18. Quoted in Hodge, 1972 and 1995, p.44.

19.Brian Hollowood, *Cornish Engineers*, Holmans, Camborne, 1951, p.37; for discussions of Cornish foundries and smelters see also Edmund Vale, *The Harveys of Hayle*, Bradford Barton, Truro, 1966; A.C.Todd and Peter Laws, *Industrial Archaeology of Cornwall*, David and Charles, Newton Abbot, 1972; W.H.Pascoe *The History of the Cornish Copper Company*, Dyllansow Truran, Redruth, 1981.

20. Alan Kittridge, *Cornwall's Maritime Heritage*, Twelveheads, Truro, 1989.

21. Michael Tangye, *Tehidy and the Bassets*, Dyllansow Truran, Redruth, pp.62-63.

22. See Helen McCabe, *Houses and Gardens of Cornwall*, Tabb House, Padstow, 1988.

23. John Keast, *The King of Mid-Cornwall: The Life of Joseph Thomas Treffry 1782-1850*, Dyllansow Truran, Redruth, 1982; see also John Keast, *The Story of Fowey*, 1950, repub. Dyllansow Truran, Redruth, 1983.

24. *West Briton*, 1 February 1850.

25. Rowse, 1968, p.79; see also Anne Treneer, *Humphry Davy: The Mercurial Chemist*, London, 1963.

26. Rowse, 1968, p.237.

27. A.C.Todd, *Beyond the Blaze: A Biography of Davies Gilbert*, Bradford Barton, Truro, 1967, p.286.

28. Lean, 1839 and 1969, p.1.

29. Burt (ed.), 1972, p.232.

30. Roger Burt, *The British Lead Mining Industry*, Dyllansow Truran, Redruth, 1984, p.123.

31. *Old Cornwall*, Vol.7, 1972.

32. Herman Merivale, 'Cornwall', *The Quarterly Review*, 102, 1857.

33. Davies Gilbert, *Mount Calvary*, 1826, p.v.

34. A.L.Rowse, *Matthew Arnold: Poet and Prophet*, Thames and Hudson, London, 1976, pp.12-16; Victor Edward Durkacz, *The Decline of the Celtic Languages*, John Donald, Edinburgh, 1983, pp.202-204.

35. D.H.Luker, 'Cornish Methodism, Revivalism and Popular Belief c1780-1870', unpub. PhD, University of Oxford, 1987, pp.xv, 322, 290.

36. Cyril Noall, *Smuggling in Cornwall*, Bradford Barton, Truro, 1971, p.12.

37. F.E.Halliday, *A History of Cornwall*, Duckworth, London, 1959, pp.267, 271.

38. Heard's *Gazeteer of the County of Cornwall*, Truro, 1817, cited in Bernard Deacon and Philip Payton, 'Re-inventing Cornwall: Culture Change on the European Periphery', in Philip Payton (ed.), *Cornish Studies: One*, University of Exeter Press, Exeter, 1993.

39. Bruce Colman, 'The Nineteenth Century: Nonconformity', in Nicholas Orme (ed.), *Unity and Variety: A History of the Church in Devon and Cornwall*, University of Exeter Press, Exeter, 1991, p.140.

40. *People's Weekly* (Moonta, South Australia), 12 July 1902.

41. Fortescue Hitchins and Samuel Drew, *The History of Cornwall: Volume 1*, Helston, 1824, p.710.

42. Henry Pelling, *Social Geography of British Elections 1885-1910*, Macmillan, London, 1962, p.160; John Pearce, *The Wesleys in Cornwall*, Bradford Barton, Truro, 1964, pp.24-25. See also, A. C. Todd, *The Cornish Miner in America*, Bradford Barton, Truro, 1967, repub. Clark, Spokane (Washington), 1995.

43. F.W.Bourne, *The King's Son*, repub. as *I Can't Help Praising the Lord: The Life of Billy Bray*, Bridge Publishing, Monmouth, 1987, p.28.

44. Thomas Shaw, 'Representative Methodists 1742-1930', in Sarah Foot (ed.), *Methodist Celebration: A Cornish Contribution*, Dyllansow Truran, Redruth, 1988.

45. Bourne, 1987, pp.49, 86.

46. John Rule, 'The Labouring Miner in Cornwall c1740-1870', unpub. PhD, University of Warwick, 1971, p.258.

47. Cyril Noall, *Cornish Mine Disasters*, ed. Philip Payton , Dyllansow Truran, Redruth, 1989, pp.25, 28.

48. Quoted in Paul Newman, *The Meads of Love: The Life and Poetry of John Harris 1820-84*, Dyllansow Truran, Redruth, 1994, p.142.

49. Philip Payton, *The Cornish MIner in Australia*, Dyllansow Truran, Redruth, 1984, p.166.

50. A.K.Hamilton Jenkin, *The Cornish Miner*, 1927, repub. David and Charles, Newton Abbot, 1972, p.283.

51. Quoted in Newman, 1994, pp.162-164.

52. Quoted in Charles Thomas, 'The Reflection of Methodism in Cornwall's Literature', in Foot, 1988, p.50.

53. J.Henry Harris, *Cornish Saints and Sinners*, John Lane, London, 1906, pp.221-222.

CHAPTER 10

'If you haven't been to Moonta'

CORNWALL

'If you haven't been to Moonta'

Hindsight is a remarkable facility. From our position at the close of the millennium, we can look back across the sweep of Cornish history, and in focusing on the nineteenth-century can view with some astonishment the profound change that was wrought in Cornwall in less than one hundred years. From that self-confident vibrant society at the forefront of industrial achievement at the turn of the nineteenth-century, Cornwall was reduced to the depopulation and dereliction lamented by the *West Briton* newspaper in November 1894:

> There was a time when Gwennap was alive with the clang of stamps, and thousands of tons of copper ore went down the Carnon Valley to Devoran for shipment; when the Perran and St Agnes districts were busy hives of activity, and East Wheal Rose was a name to conjure by. Where are they now? . . . gone to the limbo of forgotten things.[1]

And, as one visitor to Cornwall put it in 1893, 'the Cornish miners have mostly emigrated'. To find the Cornishman engaged in his traditional pursuit one would have to travel to the farthest ends of the earth, even to distant Australia where '. . . in some Wooloomooloo, or other place of name infinitely repetitive, you shall who seek, find him'.[2]

The contrast is for us a familiar one, but for informed Cornish men or women at the opening of the last century, such a fall from grace was too remote a possibility to be even contemplated. From their perspective, the century ahead was full of promise, laden with opportunities for the further advancement of Cornwall, its society and economy. For these reformers and innovators (such as those identified in Chapter Eight), their overriding aim was the construction of a modern society in which the motive power was a self-confident and assertive Cornish identity. However, with the benefit of hindsight, we can see that even by 1815 things were beginning to go sour. The Napoleonic Wars, of course, had brought uncertainty and even the danger of invasion. But the peace that followed was not the happy release that many desired. Instead, in response to fears of reform or even revolution, there was a period of political repression. *Habeas Corpus* was suspended in 1817, and in 1819 the so-called Six Acts introduced a series of draconian measures, ranging from the banning of seditious assemblies to restrictions on the press.

In Britain as a whole, this repression only redoubled the efforts of those pressing for reform. The newly-emergent 'middle classes', in particular, demanded an enhanced role in the political process, exerting pressure on the more liberally-inclined Whig party to achieve electoral reform. This was realised finally in the Great Reform Act of 1832, the first cautious step towards popular democracy in Britain in which the franchise was extended and a whole array of electoral anomalies and abuses were addressed.

In Cornwall, the reformers had their own version of this agenda. As elsewhere, this meant questioning the value and purpose of existing institutions, pressing for their metamorphosis or abolition, as well as a quest for more modern and relevant bodies. This involved querying the worth of ancient institutions such as the Duchy of Cornwall, while also calling for new institutions which might more adequately reflect the modernity of Cornwall's status and identity. The early emergence of those Cornish learned bodies—the Royal Geological Society of Cornwall, the Royal Cornwall Polytechnic Society and the Royal Institution of Cornwall—was part of this process (in other circumstances they might even have coalesced into something like the 'civic universities' that emerged later in the industrial North of England), a clear signal to observers of a developed and reformist civic pride founded upon the territory of Cornwall.

Such considerations were also important in debates concerning ecclesiastical and local government reform. There was, for example, an increasing clamour for the creation of a Cornish diocese, for what was then the Archdeaconry of Cornwall, to break away from Exeter and become a See in its own right. Although seemingly at odds with the overwhelmingly Methodist flavour of nineteenth-century Cornwall, the desire for a Cornish diocese represented not only an Anglican concern to respond to the failings of the Church of England but a wider determination that modern Cornwall should acquire its own institutions. Writing in the *Cornwall Register* of 1847, the Rev John Wallis (vicar of Bodmin) considered that the creation of a Bishopric of Cornwall would be 'an act of tardy justice. For 800 years we have been deprived of our ancient See'.[3] In fact, it would take another thirty years of politics and planning to achieve the creation of the Cornish diocese in 1877, with its new cathedral in Truro (not Bodmin, as Wallis had hoped, or St Germans or St Columb as others had advised), an event which—as A. L. Rowse has put it—unleashed an 'astonishing stream of Cornish patriotism'.[4]

The desire to achieve a Cornish diocese was mirrored in concern for local government reform. Again, John Wallis voiced a wider anxiety when he asked 'Where will county administration soon be?' His fear was that growing centralisation posed a threat to local freedom of action and to the territorial integrity of Cornwall: 'Already the new Auditor's district runs up nearly to Okehampton, and omits a part of Cornwall—the Union of Stratton', while 'The recent arrangement for the new County Courts has made a deeper inroad on Cornwall, by attaching the Unions of Stratton, Camelford, Launceston, and St Germans, to Plymouth'. He considered that 'The remedy, however, is in our own hands. Let Cornishmen combine, and attend to the history and statistics of Cornwall as their own peculiar duty'. His view was that 'Cornwall should be treated as an Island. *One and All* is our motto'. The achievement of Cornu-centric policies and perspectives, however, would be no easy task, for 'There is an array of interest in London, adverse to the independence and prosperity of the provinces, which needs to be watched, and constantly, with a vigilant eye'.[5] In fact, when the confused overlapping and unaccountability of mid-nineteenth-century local administration was finally addressed, the resultant Local Government Act of 1888 based its new county authorities on traditional boundaries. The border and territorial extent of Cornwall were thus confirmed, and, to the satisfaction of those like John Wallis, a measure of accountable local self-government was conferred.

Against the background of this reformist drive for institutional status, the more ancient and already faltering symbols of constitutional accommodation became less relevant as icons of Cornishness, and were open to scrutiny. If

The ruined engine house of East Wheal Lovell is a familiar sight on the Helston—Penryn road, a silent memorial to Cornwall's mining heyday and typical of the two hundred or so engine houses that still mark the old Cornish mining districts.

The foundation of a Cornish diocese and the construction of Truro Cathedral, with its Breton ambience, epitomised the triumph of nineteenth-century Cornwall, but also anticipated the Celtic Revival and Anglo-Catholic movement.

Truro Cathedral—the medieval ambience of a modern building.

their activities were seen as detrimental to the best interests of the new Cornwall, then there was no hesitation in offering criticism. The Duchy, for example, was in the early nineteenth century the butt of much criticism, not least because of the retarding effect of 'coinage' (dues payable to the Duchy) on the tin industry. As the radical *West Briton* (increasingly the voice of reform) put it, 'Surely the tin mines are not to be sacrificed in order to supply a revenue for the Heir Apparent?'[6] In response to such attacks, 'coinage' was abolished in October 1838, although compensation for this loss was still payable, as were the rents and royalties from mines and quarries on Duchy land, to say nothing of the income from properties owned by the Duchy itself. As Roger Burt and Graham Haslam have both noted, the Duchy of Cornwall in the early nineteenth-century was at a low point, seen as keen to extract its revenues but extremely reluctant to plough anything back.[7] Partly in response to this feeling, Albert, the Prince Consort, was appointed Lord Warden of the Stannaries in 1842, with a wide-ranging brief to reform the organs of the Duchy of Cornwall. He achieved this with his characteristic diligence and enthusiasm, and effectively completed the Duchy's long transition from instrument of constitutional accommodation to economic enterprise. This was enshrined in the Duchy of Cornwall Management Act of 1863, and when the Local Government Act became law in 1888 there was no mention of a special constitutional status afforded to the Duchy (although the High Sheriff continued to be appointed by the Duchy, and not the Crown itself).

As an integral part of the Duchy of Cornwall, the Stannary system also experienced criticism and demands for change. Although still popular in the early nineteenth-century, and seen as a mechanism by which the characteristics and interests of Cornish mining could be protected from external intrusion, the growing need to attract outside capital meant that the Stannary system was increasingly vulnerable to criticism that it was merely part of the retarding infrastructure of a discredited Duchy. Although some reformers might have been attracted to the idea of a Cornish Parliament, the Stannary Parliament had last met in 1752 and, with its archaic constitution, was hardly a model of modern democracy. In the reforming spirit that led to the Great Reform Act of 1832, suggestions that the Parliament should meet again were hardly treated seriously. The Stannary Courts, however, were a different matter, and remained busy for as long as Cornish mining was important enough to warrant their separate existence. They continued to conduct their business according to Stannary Law, until their last case was heard in 1896.

Just as the reforming rationale of 1832 meant that the Stannary Parliament was unlikely ever to meet again, so that same reforming zeal dealt a death-blow to another feature of Cornwall's accommodation—the curious situation in which Cornwall sent no fewer than forty-four MPs to the Westminster Parliament. Although observers such as Davies Gilbert and John Wallis regretted the reduction in visibility, status and influence that a fall in representation might mean (in fact, the number of Cornish MPs was cut to twelve), there was general agreement that many of those forty-four MPs had rarely put Cornish interests at the top of their agendas. Although Angus Calder has pointed to a 'Cornish mafia which played a large role in the politics of Walpole's England',[8] many MPs owed their loyalty to the Duke of Cornwall (the Prince of Wales controlled many of the Cornish seats), and were thus drawn into the bitter political in-fighting between George III and his Heir, Prince George Augustus. In addition to this Ducal influence, Cornwall was also notorious for its 'rotten' and 'pocket' boroughs, where the franchise was severely restricted or votes were bought and sold. In 1747, for example, Thomas Pitt had complained of the expense in his securing Grampound. In 1829 the representation of Mitchell was decided by only seven voters. Penryn was controlled by Lord Falmouth, Fowey was in the hands of the Rashleigh family, and Callington was in the gift of Lady Orford.[9]

The decline of the old mechanisms of accommodation, and their replacement by new institutional expressions of Cornishness, was matched elsewhere in the Cornish politics that had emerged in the aftermath of reform. As in Britain as a whole, the political contest was between two parties, the Liberals (which grew out of the old Whigs) and the Conservatives (the Tories), but politics in Cornwall developed its own distinctive hue. The widespread extension of the franchise in 1885 is often identified as the real turning-point in modern British politics, where the style of party-political contestation that we recognise today, together with its underlying political culture, was finally established. Professor Edwin Jaggard, however, has argued that for Cornwall, 1885 represented continuity rather than change, the enduring features of Cornish political behaviour having been established between 1832 and 1885. Two features moulded this continuity: the emergence and then enduring strength of a Liberal-Nonconformist nexus, and the failure by local Tories to grasp the electoral realities of post-1832 politics.

Of the latter, as Edwin Jaggard observes, even as late as the 1850s the Conservatives still '. . . revealed a preference for the interventions of wealthy and supposedly powerful parties like the Tremaynes, Bassets, Carews, Vyvyans, Edgcumbes and Bullers whose heyday was more than half a century in the past'.[10] Many of the notable families, as improvers and reformers, had in any case found a home in the Liberal camp. As T. A. Jenkins has noted, '. . . the Trelawnys were typical examples of the Cornish tradition of lesser aristocratic families with radical leanings . . .', while William Molesworth of Pencarrow was similarly a 'Radical Aristocrat'.[11] Moreover, the Liberals proved adept at organising voter registrations and other local activity, ingraining themselves into the fabric of Cornish society.

The organisational ineptitude of the Tories was against the background of prevailing socio-economic conditions not conducive to Tory vitality; as Henry Pelling put it, '. . . the strength of Nonconformity, the weakness of large landowners, the generally small scale farming, and the paucity of nucleated villages . . .'.[12] Although John Wesley and his early followers were politically conservative, advocating a passive and philosophical acceptance of one's lot in this life, Cornish Methodism as it developed was swiftly wedded to the political cause of the Liberals. This was especially true of those Methodist sects that, for various reasons, had parted company with the Wesleyans to form their own independent denominations. The Primitive Methodists, with their origins in the Midlands, had some appeal in Cornwall (notably in the mining areas) and were from the beginning a working-class movement associated with political and social radicalism. More indigenously Cornish were the Bible Christians, equally strong in the countryside (especially in the North Cornwall-North Devon borderland where first they were established in 1815) and in the mining districts. As Thomas Shaw noted, while 'Politically, Cornish Methodists have tended to be Liberals', the Bible Christians especially '. . . were radicals of the old Liberal school'.[13]

Methodism, as we saw in Chapter Nine, was much concerned with the individual and his or her betterment, leading to the emergence of all manner of temperance, educational, literary and 'improving' societies, and even prompting the development of a rudimentary welfare system (the 'club and doctor' funds) in larger mines. It also prompted the growth of a liberal philanthropy, manifested (for example) in the generosity of those who had done well up-country or abroad, and were inclined to make contributions to deserving institutions back home. J. Passmore Edwards, born at Blackwater, near Redruth—whose generosity allowed the foundations of hospitals, institutes and public libraries throughout the length and breadth of Cornwall—is the best remembered, his name still displayed prominently on the facades of public buildings in towns such as Truro and Liskeard.[14] In general, Cornish Methodism exhibited a strongly egalitarian strand, reflecting the potential for socio-economic mobility and the relative lack of class consciousness in nineteenth-century Cornwall. Its theology, stressing concern for the needy and the equality of men before God, matched the political ideology of Cornish Liberalism. And just as Methodism had emerged as a significant element of the new Cornishness, so Liberalism too was seen to be distinctly 'Cornish'.

By the 1830s (the 'Reforming Thirties', as they were known) radicalism was becoming a force to be reckoned with in Cornwall (it is often not realised that one of the leaders of the Chartist cause, who campaigned throughout Britain on a range of reformist issues, was William Lovett, a Cornishman born in Newlyn in 1800).[15] However, not all Cornish radicals were convinced of the possibility of reform at home, and, increasingly, many turned to the cause of emigration as a means of constructing a better life abroad, based on the principles of religious freedom, social and economic mobility, and civil liberty. Emigration was in that sense a Cornish institution, an integral part of popular culture but also an expression of the reformist aims of Cornish society.

The dark days of repression after the end of the Napoleonic Wars in 1815 had found many in Cornwall questioning the institutions of Church and State. Tithes payable to the Church of England by a predominantly Methodist population at a time of high rents, were a cause of much discontent, reflected in 'The Cornish Emigrant's Song' written in this period by the Rev R. S. Hawker:

> Oh! the eastern winds are blowing;
> The breezes seem to say.
> 'We are going, we are going,
> To North Americay.
>
> 'There the merry bees are humming
> Around the poor man's hive;
> Parson Kingdom is not coming
> To take away the tithe.
>
> 'There the yellow corn is growing
> Free as the king's highway;
> So, we're going, we're going,
> To North Americay.[16]

South Australia, founded in 1836, soon became an important destination for emigrant Cornish folk and quickly earned a reputation as a 'Paradise of Dissent', a society in which Nonconformist values were respected and where Nonconformist aspirations might be met. Its early advocate was John Stephens (who later edited the radical *South Australian Register* in Adelaide), the son of a Cornish miner-turned-Methodist-minister. In 1839 Stephens wrote his *The Land of Promise*, in which he explained Wakefield's utilitarian principle of 'systematic colonisation' that underpinned the foundation of South Australia, emphasising in the process that the new colony was a haven of religious liberty in which Wesleyan, Baptist and Independent denominations were already well-established: 'Persons who have had experience of all the other colonies . . . agree in awarding the palm of decided excellence to this new settlement'.[17]

The United States of America had built a similar reputation, a land of the free in which (it was argued) those brought up in the tradition of self-help and improvement could hardly fail to flourish. The fact that it was merely across the water, 'the next parish after Land's End' in Cornish parlance, made the States especially attractive as a destination—for example, for Samuel James, a yeoman farmer on the Lizard peninsula. In assessing the attractions of America, James listed the reasons why he wished to leave Cornwall. Foremost amongst these was the need 'To escape the heavy charges of supporting certain useless institutions'. To this was added the desire 'To escape from

Not Callington, Cornwall, but Callington, Australia. Now a quiet village outside Adelaide, Callington was once a thriving community of Cornish miners and their families.

supporting a State religion . . . [and] To live under free and useful institutions'.[18] James finally left Cornwall in April 1842, sailing from Falmouth for New York in the *Orient*, along with 188 other like-minded Cornish emigrants from the neighbourhoods of Helston, Camborne and Redruth.

To these political and religious motives for emigration, was added the agricultural depression that had dogged Cornwall since the end of the Napoleonic Wars. Indeed, things went from bad to worse, the 1840s earning the reputation in Cornwall (as elsewhere) as the 'Hungry Forties'. The failure of the potato crop, in particular, caused widespread hardship and distress, especially during 1845-47. William Allen, an emigration agent at Penzance in the heart of the potato-growing district of Penwith, warned that '. . . there is great excitement in this county and neighbourhood. Many persons in the Penzance district are preparing to emigrate to South Australia, and among them a fair proportion of first rate miners'. As one colonial newspaper went on to explain, 'Mr Allen says business was dull in Cornwall, and as the crop in his neighbourhood participated in the general failure, much distress was felt and anticipated'.[19] Sadly, little has been done in Cornwall today to mark the impact of the potato blight of 1845-46, in contrast to Ireland and Scotland where activities have ranged from scholarly treatises to television programmes and school and college projects. Again, Cornwall has remained historiographically invisible, the National Curriculum affording Cornish schoolchildren few opportunities to learn about their own land, and with the local media seemingly unable to respond to all the possibilities that present themselves.

Be that as it may, Cornwall suffered greatly during the Hungry Forties and, as in Ireland and Scotland, emigration was an important safety valve.[20] In Cornwall it was a means of preventing mass starvation, although it did lead to significant pockets of depopulation—the population of Stratton Hundred in north-east Cornwall fell by some ten percent during the 1840s, while one contemporary observer, J.R. Leifchild, estimated that in 1849 nearly five percent of the Penzance Poor Law Union district had emigrated to Australia and New Zealand. As he put it, 'Emigration has tended to keep down the Cornish population'.[21]

As in earlier times, miners took to the streets to express their distress and outrage. Despite the repeal of the Corn Laws, bad harvests had doubled the price of grain, aggravating the already serious situation caused by the potato failure. After the hard winter of 1846-47, bands of starving miners marched on towns such as Penzance, Helston, Redruth, St Austell, Wadebridge, Callington and Launceston to prevent the export of corn and to force 'fair prices'. At Wadebridge in May 1847, '. . . a large body of men from the Delabole quarries . . . mixed with others (streamers, china clay men, and tinners from Roche, Luxulyan, St Austell &c) . . .' lay siege to the town: '. . . between three and four hundred men . . . each armed with a bludgeon . . . they presented a most formidable appearance and created great consternation'.[22] Likewise in Helston, 'Coinage Hall Street was thronged with miners from the bottom to the Market House on the top of the street, all armed with shovel handles and pick handles'. Such demonstrations sometimes had the desired effect, as in the Helston riot where '. . . a great quantity of bread [was] distributed among the hungry poor',[23] but for many, a surer solution to their problems was emigration.

Moreover, by the 1840s, though the Cornish were reluctant to admit it, wider structural problems in the Cornish economy were beginning to make themselves felt. Although the Cornish economy had been one of the first to industrialise, and although Cornwall had been at the leading edge of industrial advance, the Cornish experience of industrialisation was in fact imperfect, overspecialised and incomplete. An unwillingness and inability to diversify was to leave Cornwall with few options for the future and little room to manoeuvre as it felt the impact of an internationalising global economy, while the Cornish educational system and subsequent skills base found themselves highly but dangerously (over) specialised. And, as Dr Roger Burt has written:

> The greatest *deficiency* in Cornwall's mineral wealth was without doubt its lack of *coal.* This proved to be a near fatal flaw in terms of the county's general industrialisation and long-term economic welfare. The smelting and manufacture of its metallic minerals was generally forced out of the region to areas where fuel was plentiful and cheap. The secondary industries which developed within the county related only to primary mining and quarrying activity.[24]

From its earliest days, the Cornish copper industry had been locked into an unequal relationship with the South Welsh and (to a lesser extent) Bristol smelting interests. The Swansea 'ticketing' system, introduced in 1725, where potential purchasers of copper ore were required to submit 'tickets' (bids) for the lots in which they were interested, tended to keep the price down, to the detriment of the Cornish industry. Put simply, the relatively few purchasers were well known to one another, and so was the likely nature of their several bids. This resulted in a general disparity between the low prices paid for copper ore and the high price asked for manufactured copper groups. Cornish attempts to raise the price of copper ore and dismantle the ticketing system, through the establishment of a marketing cartel in 1785, came to nought—partly through the untimely intervention of the Anglesey scare. By the time equilibrium was restored, the South Welsh interests had consolidated their position, so much so that in the early 1800s some Cornish capitalists decided that 'if you can't beat 'em, join 'em' and set-up their own smelting works in Wales.

The Cornish 'cost-book' system probably also militated against the best long-term interests of Cornish industry, its structure encouraging a short-termism which opted for immediate profit maximisation at the expense of long-term capital investment. Under the cost-book system, meetings of shareholders (adventurers) were held regularly, usually at two-month intervals, where the progress of a mine would be reviewed. If the mine was in difficulties or still at a developmental stage, then 'calls' would be levied on the shareholders at a level determined by the meeting. If, however, the mine was profitable, then dividends would be declared and paid out. The cost-book was thus a single fund which received all income (including calls) and expended all cash for whatever reason, including capital expenditure. In other words, capital expenditure was accounted an operating cost.[25] In the hey-day of Cornish mining, the cost-book system proved equal to the task financing even the largest Cornish mines, but even then adventurers were often more interested in short-term profit maximisation rather than long-term planning— 'picking the eyes' out of a mine by plundering its best reserves, irrespective of market conditions, or sinking crooked (and ultimately inefficient) shafts to follow lodes so that ore might be won while sinking.

Additionally, the cost-book system was viewed with suspicion by outside investors. At first, this was seen as advantageous, a means of keeping the 'wise men from the east' at bay, but eventually the rising power of the City of London became irresistible. Cornish mines needed greater investment, and the prospect of vast profits tempted the speculators of the metropolis. Their demands that the cost-book system be replaced by more conventional limited liability companies caused resentment, while those City capitalists who did take an interest in Cornish mining were often drawn unwittingly into the net of sharp share-dealing that emerged in Cornwall in the mid-nineteenth-century. As Leifchild noted wryly:

> The keen Cornish miners have a kind of proverb amongst them, which they keep pretty closely to their own companies, and which is to this effect:— That the county is divided into two classes, Cornish men and 'Lun'oners', and that it is the privilege of the former to live—not by the mines, but by the latter; in other words, by the speculation of strangers. There is much truth in this.[26]

In fact, the result of such suspicions was to bring Cornish mining into further disrepute, widening the rift between Cornish and 'foreign' adventurers, and encouraging City capitalists to look overseas for their investments—in the mines of the future, rather than those of the past in Cornwall. The Cornish themselves were persuaded to prop-up ailing mines in the vain hope of better days ahead. John Rowe states the case plainly, arguing that the Cornish expended their efforts and finances far too long in shoring-up their mining industry, with the result that '. . . the industrialisation of textile manufactures in northern England left it too late in the day to promote spinning, knitting, and lace-making in Cornwall'.[27] Cornwall had been left behind by other regions, many with the additional advantage of local coal deposits. Roger Burt has suggested that the overall sale of ore from Cornish mines never did repay the total investment in the industry, a significant factor in explaining the Cornish economy's failure to diversify.[28] Indeed, Leifchild's view in 1855 was that:

> It is well known to the experienced, that in Cornwall . . . mines, in the aggregate, form a losing concern. I repeat that the quantity of copper annually extracted from Cornwall, is not worth the money annually spent in Cornwall in copper-mining. Therefore, while a few people gain very large profits, many people lose money by mining. Mining is a lottery . . . .[29]

The descent into crisis has been described in the several narrative histories of Cornish mining, examining in detail the collapse of copper and decline of tin in response to changing economic conditions. Although the 1850s had witnessed the peak of Cornish copper production, the figures were in a sense 'artificially' boosted by the younger mines of East Cornwall, the older West Cornwall districts already in terminal decline. Many of the western mines were by now extremely deep (and therefore very costly to work) and, although some had fortuitously struck tin at depth, more than a few were virtually worked-out. To make matters worse, rich and easily accessible copper ores had been discovered overseas—in the United States, in Chile and Cuba, and in South Australia. Even distant South Australia, where there were significant copper discoveries in the 1840s, 1850s and 1860s, could compete successfully with the Cornish industry. As the Royal Geological

Society of Cornwall noted, South Australia was a wool-exporting colony. Thus:

> . . . the wool-ships on account of the lightness of the cargo are obliged to take in a large quantity of ballast, and they are therefore glad to take lead and copper ore at a merely nominal rate of freight;—at the time in question about eight to ten shillings per ton. That circumstance was considered as bringing their mines, as it were, actually into Europe, or at all events as placing them upon equal footing with European mines . . . .[30]

After 1856 there was a marked decline in the output of Cornish copper, culminating in the great crash of 1866 in which the industry was one of the victims of the financial crisis precipitated in Britain by the collapse of the Overend-Gurney Bank.[31] As Edmund Newell has explained:

> The problem was not a cyclical fluctuation or short-term market shock but was deep-seated in the changing nature of the market: the world supply of the metal was increasing despite falling prices—to depress still further the price of ore in the unprotected British market.[32]

The problems facing the Cornish industry were reflected in the falling prices realised at the Swansea ticketings for what the Cornish termed 'ore copper'—i.e. as much ore as will make a ton of fine copper. In January 1860 the price had stood at £102.18s. A year later it had fallen to £86.2s, while in 1862 it fell to £84.5s and in 1863 to £79.10s. In 1864 there was an encouraging if temporary rally, the price climbing to £94.19s, but in 1865 and 1866 there was a fall to £80.14s and £80.18s respectively. By January 1867 the price had slumped to a disastrous £71.16s, at which no Cornish mine could hope to make a profit. The *West Briton* warned that '. . . the price of 1860 will not be realised again, the production of Chili (sic) and Australia . . . being now so very large that the decreasing yield of the Cornish mines makes very little difference to prices'.[33] This was reflected in the wholesale closure of the Gwennap mines and, after 1866, in other areas too—Crenver and Wheal Abraham near Crowan, Perran Great St George at Perranporth, and Fowey Consols. Even those Camborne-Redruth mines that had turned from copper to tin (among them Dolcoath, South Crofty, Tincroft, and Cook's Kitchen) felt the pinch, tin prices having fallen from £71.11s per ton in 1860 to only £45 in 1866, several tin mines also being abandoned in that fateful year. In January 1867 the *West Briton* gave a gloomy assessment of the previous year:

> The year now ended is one of the most disastrous for the mining interests of Cornwall during the present century . . . the failure of banks and public companies, leading to panic, distrust, an absence of speculation . . . high rates of discount which locked up money . . . all the miseries and privations have fallen upon us which await crushed speculators, a partially-employed working class, and a general languor and depression in trade.[34]

The unusually severe winter of 1866-67 caused much distress in Cornwall. At St Ives problems stemming from the abandonment of local mines were exacerbated by '. . . great distress among the fishermen's families, the late pilchard season having proved a failure'. At Callington, 'In consequence of the stoppage of mines . . . there is great distress among the poor and labouring classes'. In the Helston district, the closure of mines '. . . has thrown hundreds of men and children out of employment, producing a state of things which is only possible to conceive on actual inspection'.[35] A Cornwall Distress Fund was set up to co-ordinate relief efforts and to raise money. In January 1868 the Fund was able to vote £50 to help 197 families in Sithney, Breage, Germoe, Godolphin and Carnmenellis. Likewise, £100 was voted for St Just-in-Penwith, £50 for Lelant, £50 for East Penwith (Camborne-Redruth), £60 for Tywardreath, and £30 for Callington. Again, emigration was seen as one solution to the problem of destitution, with the Fund being used to help miners' wives and their families to join husbands who were already overseas.

Each and every one of the Gwennap copper mines was silent by 1871. Although a few copper producers struggled on elsewhere, the Cornish copper industry was virtually dead. Tin outlived copper, although it too suffered in 1866, dominated as it was by the triple concerns of the costs of production, the market price of tin, and the effects of overseas competition. However, the disruption in 1869 of tin supplies from the Straits as a result of civil disturbances in the Malay States, provided a welcome breathing-space. The early 1870s witnessed a veritable tin boom in Cornwall, even to the extent of revealing an acute shortage of skilled labour as a result of the emigration that had occurred. However, the *West Briton* noted that the general mood was one of caution, so that:

> In the Redruth district, although tin is high, and times should be better, there appears to be a feeling of general depression among the labouring classes—a longing to be off somewhere, anywhere, in fact, to escape the grinding process now being brought to bear upon mine labour.[36]

The Cornish were right to be cautious, for 1873 brought falling tin prices. In April 1874 'There is quite a panic in the West Cornish mines',[37] with the abandonment of major concerns such as Balleswidden, Wheal Owles, North Roskear, and Wheal Seton, together with the partial closure of Botallack. In January 1875 it was reported with deep regret that 'In the history of mining in Cornwall it has known no such disastrous year as that of 1874'.[38] In fact, forty-seven tin mines had been closed in Cornwall in that year. But 1875 was to prove marginally worse, resulting in the abandonment of a further forty-eight Cornish tin mines, and 1876 another thirty-seven were closed. Thanks to continuing technological innovation (not least by Holman's of Camborne), the tin industry survived the catastrophe of the 1870s (albeit in greatly reduced form) but the 1880s—a time of international economic downturn—were no better. Straits tin was back in full production, and both Tasmanian and Bolivian tin were significant competitors. By 1896 the Cornish industry was facing extinction with only nine mines still in production, a precarious situation in which Cornwall limped into the twentieth-century.

The decline of copper and tin mining in Cornwall was accompanied by the fall from grace of the Cornish beam engine. It had reached the pinnacle of its development by 1850, and was thereafter in decline. The widespread closure of Cornish mines from the 1860s onwards boosted the trade in

The dramatic remains of Cornish mining, at Wheal Owles near St Just-in-Penwith. In the foreground is the Cargodna or West Wheal Owles engine home; in the background is Wheal Edward.

second-hand engines, thus retarding the construction of new ones and precluding further design improvement. Overseas markets dried-up as foundries were opened abroad to meet local demands, and the emergence of new technologies meant that the Cornish engine became increasingly old-fashioned. In Cornwall standards of maintenance fell as unprofitable mines desperately tried to cut costs in time-expired machinery, and the competitive spirit reflected only recently in Lean's *Engine Reporter* was swiftly a thing of the past. Indeed, in 1895 only seven engines were recorded in the *Engine Reporter*. By 1903 the number had fallen to just four, and in 1909 that once august and internationally renowned journal ceased publication altogether.

The demise of the beam engine, with its knock-on effects for the engineering and manufacturing industries in Cornwall, was part of a wider fall in demand from the mining industry for goods and services of all kinds. Paradoxically, where demand was maintained, it was for increasingly specialist and technologically-advanced equipment for deployment in the unequal fight to save the Cornish mining industry. Thus, Chris Schmitz has observed, as the industry became less competitive and less viable, so it demanded increasingly complex technology.[39] Deeper mining required more efficient pumping, while more complex or leaner ores (such as would have been discarded as valueless in earlier times) required more advanced milling and concentrating equipment at the surface. Thus the diminishing Cornish industrial base was locked into ever-more specialised production, with little opportunity for diversification. Although the introduction of compressed air drills in the 1880s and the use of compressed air winches seemed to intimate reassuring technological advance, the reality was that Cornish mining was then of only marginal importance. As John Rowe has put it:

> A long historic past, during which many myths and traditions had developed, delayed recognition of the fact that, early in the twentieth-century, Cornish mining had so drastically declined that in realistic terms it was only of minor significance.[40]

The fortunes of the mining industry in nineteenth century Cornwall were reflected to some degree in those of the other Cornish staples, agriculture and fishing. As we have seen already, the post-Napoleonic depression in agriculture was followed by the 'Hungry Forties' in which the Cornish potato crop was all but obliterated. Thereafter, Cornish farming also suffered in the agricultural depression of the 1870s and in the international downturn of the 1880s. In some respects, however, Cornish agriculture was well-suited to the peculiar characteristics of the land. The prevalence of the 'outfield' system (in common with other areas of highland Britain) in land adjacent to moors and wastral allowed the cultivation of bonus crops in good years without having to reduce the area devoted to livestock, while the predominance of ley-rotation farming (with its temporary grassland) made good use of the mild, wet climate. However, Cornish agriculture in the first half of the nineteenth century was geared inevitably to meeting the demand for food from the rapidly expanding mining population. Not only did this lead to the reliance upon potatoes, especially in West Penwith, but also it encouraged an emphasis upon arable farming—as Worgon put it in his 1808 survey of Cornish farming: '. . . there is nothing like corn sacks for making money, they are very fond of the plough . . .'.[41]

But Cornwall, with its acidic soil and heavy rainfall, was not entirely suitable for the production of wheat and other crops. Although the soil could readily be prepared with sand from local beaches, or even with rotting pilchards, other factors were beyond the farmer's control. The rapid decline in the mining population after mid-century saw a consequent fall in local demand for arable produce, while Cornish farmers were by no means equipped to compete in wider markets. Cornwall was no match for the excellent wheat country of the Midlands and East Anglia or, indeed, after the repeal of the Corn Laws, for the imported corn of Australia and North America. As John Rowe has observed, Cornish farming was in deep depression by the 1850s as a direct result of its over-dependence on corn.[42] Moreover, many Cornish farms were marginal concerns, their surpluses small, which precluded investment in modern machinery. Similarly, the hill-farming character of Cornwall often did not lend itself to the introduction of such equipment. The Cornish contented themselves with a range of relatively modest innovations (for example, the 'Cornish plough'). As Andrew Jewell has noted, 'Adoption of those technical inventions which promoted English lowland farming from the early eighteenth century fully penetrated only a few districts inside the Devon border'.[43]

At length, Cornish farming did adapt to new conditions, the depression years of the 1870s and 1880s resulting in much land being switched to mixed farming and permanent pasture. There was a move to dairy farming and, aided by the connection to the British railway network in 1859, to horticulture in West Cornwall and the Tamar Valley. By 1880 there were twice as many cattle on cultivated land in Cornwall than was the average in England and Wales, and there were eight sheep for every seven elsewhere and three pigs for every two. Although this shift in emphasis may have helped Cornish agriculture ride the difficult years of the 1870s and 1880s more easily than it might otherwise have done, Cornwall remained out of step with developments elsewhere—Cornwall was turning to cattle at a time when English lowland farming was redoubling its emphasis on arable crops. The apparently favourable figures of 1880 reflected Cornish difference rather than superiority; in fact, Cornish farms remained remarkably small and under-capitalised.[44]

In the fishing industry, Cornwall had established a near-monopoly of pilchards in the seventeenth-century, and this encouraged a Cornish reliance on pilchard seining which lasted well into the nineteenth-century. The demand for pilchards remained fairly constant in the last century, coming—as it had done traditionally—from the Roman Catholic countries of Europe. The irony of this situation was not lost on the largely Methodist Cornish:

> Here's a health to the Pope
> And may he repent,
> And lengthen six months
> The term of his Lent.
> It's always declared
> Betwixt the two poles
> There's nothing like pilchards
> For saving of souls.[45]

However, despite this continuity, complemented in the last century by demand from communities in the West Indies and (for pilchard oil) from the Royal Navy, the reliance on pilchard seining proved deleterious to Cornish interests because the pilchards themselves progressively quit Cornish waters. The reason for this change in the pilchards' habits has not yet been satisfactorily explained. A general change in the nature of the Gulf Stream (which brought the pilchards to Cornwall in the first place) is the favoured explanation, although more recent research has suggested a more complicated story in which temperature change was but one factor alongside other considerations such as the species and size of zooplankton food, and the direction of water movements.[46] Today, the huer's hut at Newquay bears silent witness to the former importance for fishing communities of the pilchards' arrival. The huer or watchman would scan the sea for the tell-tale 'stain', and, spotting the shoal, would shout a triumphant 'Hevva!' to alert his colleagues in the harbour below. Another traditional fishing toast is eloquent testimony to the vital importance of the pilchards' arrival:

> Long life to the Pope
> Death to our best friends.
> And may the streets run in blood.[47]

Alas, the 'friends' proved inconstant, and in the 1830s they made no appearance for several successive seasons. Occasionally, there were still bumper years (as in 1871 when a record 46,000 hogsheads was exported) but the general pattern was one of gradual decline, with the pilchards increasingly deserting the inshore waters. By 1872 they had disappeared from the entire stretch of coast between Cawsand and Mevagissey, leaving the rump of the seining industry in the western districts around St Ives and Newlyn. Looking for explanations, the Cornish were inclined to pour at least some of the blame upon 'foreign' drifters from the southern and eastern coasts of England, who were increasingly fishing in Cornish waters and who, it was claimed, were dispersing the pilchard shoals before they had had a chance to come onshore. The foreign drifters certainly had a technological advantage over their Cornish seining competitors, a superiority accentuated at the end of the century by the introduction of East Coast steam trawlers with their greater flexibility, range and endurance. The railway connection in 1859 had facilitated the penetration of London markets by fresh Cornish fish, and many Cornish seiners turned their attention from the failing

On the cliff road above Newquay is the Huer's Hut, where the huer or watchman once scanned the sea to spot the pilchard shoals, crying 'Hevva!' when the fish were in sight.

pilchards to the abundant mackerel. Unfortunately, the East Coast men had the same idea. The Cornish boats were outclassed, the *West Briton* lamenting in 1891 that '. . . this is probably the first year in which not a single seine has been put in the water'.[48]

In fact, seining struggled on but a fierce animosity had developed between the Cornish and the East Coast 'Yorkies' (as they were known), an animosity expressed in Cornish Methodist hostility to 'Yorkie' Sabbath-breaking. As the *West Briton* explained in May 1877:

> The Cornish fishermen suspend work on Sundays, but the east country fishermen, who come to St Ives in the season have no such scruples. Last year there was a disturbance, and this year the St Ives men have again prevented the others from landing at the St Ives pier fish caught on Saturday night or Sunday.[49]

The issue smouldered on for another two decades but came to a head in an extraordinary paroxysm of violence at Newlyn in May 1896, when the Cornish destroyed the entire catch, some 100,000 mackerel landed by the Lowestoft boats. This incident, described in detail by John Corin in his *Fishermen's Conflict*, led to serious rioting and to the deployment by the government of three hundred and fifty soldiers, and to no fewer than three Naval gunboats in Mount's Bay.[50] Law and order was restored, and the situation smoothed over, but the reality was that for Cornish fishing—like mining—things had altered irrevocably.

The economic marginalisation that progressively overtook Cornwall as the nineteenth-century wore on precipitated a widespread exodus, building swiftly upon the experiences of the 'Reforming Thirties' and 'Hungry Forties'. The result was the 'Great Emigration', a sustained movement of people (miners and others) which was to characterise the Cornish experience until the years before the outbreak of the Great War in 1914. A. C.Todd considers that 'It seems reasonable to suppose that Cornwall lost at least a third of its population . . .'[51] in the last century, while Dudley Baines offers some frightening statistics. Between 1861 and 1900, he says, Cornwall lost no less than 10.5 percent of its male population overseas and 7.0 percent to other counties (far and away the greatest percentage loss of any county), with a corresponding loss of 5.3 percent of the female population overseas and 7.1 percent to other counties. This amounted to some 118,500 people. Baines concludes that although 'This is not as high as from the famous regions of Italy . . . it must be remembered that mass emigration from Italy lasted not much more than twenty years. Cornwall was probably an emigration region comparable to any in Europe'.[52] More unnerving still are statistics which indicate that, between 1861 and 1900, 44.8 percent of the Cornish male population aged fifteen to twenty-four left for overseas, with a further 29.7 percent leaving for other counties. Over the same period and in the same age group, 26.2 percent of Cornish females went overseas while 35.5 percent went to other parts of Britain.

Of course, this picture was complicated considerably by the oft-repeated process of emigration, counter-emigration, and renewed emigration, where individuals (or even families) might spend their lives gravitating between Cornwall and a variety of overseas destinations. The pattern was made more complex still by the international mobility that emerged, with many Cornish folk (especially the miners) roaming within and between the continents of the world, especially their mining districts. The most obvious impact within

Tamblyn's Row. The name suggests Redruth or Liskeard but this is Mineral Point, Wisconsin, U.S.A., a mining town established by Cornish emigrants—Cousin Jacks and Jennies—in the mid nineteenth-century.

Cornwall itself was the very visible depopulation that occurred—the populace of Breage and Germoe fell by 27 percent between 1841 and 1851, that of Tywardreath by 29 percent between 1861 and 1871, and that of St Just-in-Penwith by 27 percent between 1871 and 1881. Perranzabuloe lost 22 percent of its population between 1871 and 1881, and St Cleer lost 25 percent during the same decade and a further 22 percent between 1891 and 1901.[53]

Complementing the push factors—those circumstances that encouraged individuals to leave Cornwall—were the corresponding 'pull' factors, the considerations that drew Cornish emigrants to a multiplicity of destinations across the globe. Fortuitously, even before the 1840s, when emigration first emerged as a significant feature of Cornish life, a range of potential destinations for Cornish emigrants had already appeared. Miners had been engaged to work in Mexico as early as the 1820s, and in the 1830s the lead deposits of Wisconsin were being opened-up with the help of Cornish miners. By 1850 there were perhaps as many as nine thousand Cornish folk at Mineral Point in that State. In the 1840s the Real del Monte silver mines in Mexico

Cornish engine house at Real del Monte, Mexico

Morphett's engine house, Burra Burra mine, South Australia. Constructed in 1858, this building was restored in 1986 as part of the Burra Mine Museum. Although the 80 inch engine, built at Perran Foundry in 1857, has disappeared long-since, remains of pit-work and the balance - box survive.

attracted a flurry of Cornish emigrants, as did the iron mines on the shores of Lake Huron in Canada. In 1843 and 1844 the 'Copper Rush' in the Keweenaw district of upper Michigan drew Cornish miners and their families from both Wisconsin and Cornwall itself, the 'Lakes' region destined to remain a major focus of Cornish concentration in America for generations to come.

Five years later, gold was discovered in California, triggering an enthusiastic response from Cornwall where hundreds of miners (and others) clamoured to become 'Forty-niners'. At first, individuals had easy pickings but soon quartz gold was discovered at depth—and this required the particular expertise of the Cornish miners. Consequently, as A. L. Rowse has noted, 'It is probable that there are more Cornish people in California than in any other state in the Union'.[54] Grass Valley and Nevada City became predominantly Cornish towns, and the 'Cousin Jacks'—as the Cornish were known—found their way across America: from North Carolina in the 1850s and Utah in the 1860s, to New Mexico in the 1870s and Arizona in the 1880s. Colorado, where a significant element of the population of Gilpin County and the appropriately-named Leadville was Cornish in the 1880s, was another important focus, as were the copper mines of Butte, Montana, in the same decade. In each of these districts the Cornish were recognisable as a distinct ethnic group, the contemporary American journalist, Wells Drury, noting their '. . . religious fervour . . . independence, thrift, geniality, excitability, contempt for familiar dangers . . . with what zest they can sing their fellowship song "One and All", and their old patriotic ballad, "And Shall Trelawny Die" . . .'.[55]

Fortunately, the Cornish settlement of the United States has been well-documented. In addition to the magnificent contribution of what is effectively a Cornish-American trilogy—the *Cornish in America* by Dr A. L. Rowse , Dr A. C.Todd's *The Cornish Miner in America*, and Dr John Rowe's *The Hard-rock Men*—there has been a profusion of other work, from local histories such as that by Jimmy Jewell to the more scholarly essays of Ronald M.James.[56] At home in Cornwall, the indefatigable efforts of Moira Tangye have established a 'Cornish-American Connection', a collaborative effort by the Murdoch House Educational Trust and the Institute of Cornish Studies (University of Exeter) in which a vast data-base now records details of those who emigrated from Cornwall to America in the last century.

Morphett's winding house, Burra Burra min, contained a 20 inch whim engine built at the Perran Foundry in 1860.

Australia has been equally significant in the story of the Cornish diaspora. South Australia, in particular, has drawn the attention of those engaged in the study of the emigrant Cornish. Special tribute is due to the work of the late Ian Auhl, who in the 1970s almost single-handedly drew attention to the international significance of the Burra township and its distinctive Cornish landscape, leading to the latter's eventual preservation by an enlightened and informed State government as a State Heritage centre. Ian Auhl was also responsible for an impressive string of books and articles, culminating in his definitive *The Story of the Monster Mine: The Burra Burra Mine and its Townships 1845-1877*. A later period in South Australia's Cornish mining history is sketched in Oswald Pryor' delightful *Australia's Little Cornwall*, first published as long ago as 1960, while the Cornish heritage of Yorke Peninsula's 'Copper Triangle' has caught the attention of more recent writers such as Roslyn Paterson. Greg Drew and Jack Connel have produced their important *Cornish Beam Engines in South Australian Mines*, which charts the parallel emigration of Cornish engines to the colony and the impact there of Cornish technology and mining methods.[57]

Cornish kibbles (buckets) and pit-work in the Australian sun at Burra Burra mine.

South Australia occupies a special place in the vast panorama of the Cornish diaspora. Although there had been some limited transportation to the Penal Colonies from Cornwall, the first major movement of Cornish people to the Antipodes did not occur until the foundation of South Australia in 1836. The very first mineral discoveries in Australia were made at Glen Osmond, just outside the colonial capital of Adelaide, in February 1841 by two Cornish miners (remembered today only by their surnames, Hutchins and Thomas), and by April of that year Australia's first metaliferous mine—Wheal Gawler—was in production. However, it was the discovery of copper—at Kapunda and at Burra Burra in the mid-1840s—that really put South Australia on the international mining map. Cornish miners flocked to both localities. At the former, the first mining engine in Australia (obtained second-hand from Cornwall) was put to work. The latter was so fabulously rich that its chance discovery seemed to one observer to be surely the result of a miraculous intervention by the spirits of Madron well:

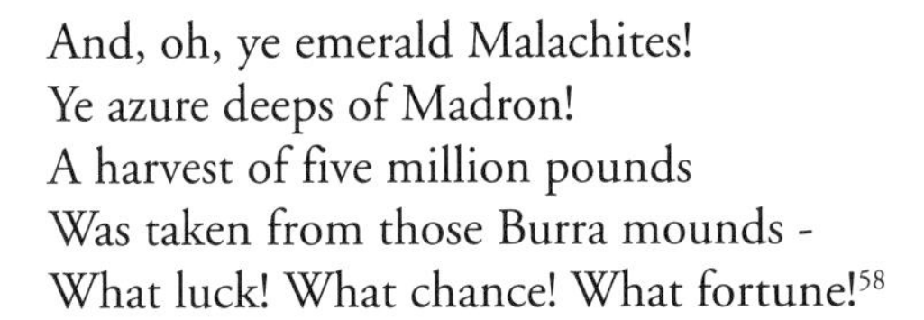

And, oh, ye emerald Malachites!
Ye azure deeps of Madron!
A harvest of five million pounds
Was taken from those Burra mounds -
What luck! What chance! What fortune![58]

Be that as it may, the links between Cornwall and the Burra mine were certainly intimate. The technology, for example, was almost entirely Cornish. Thus in 1852 John Congdon, formerly of the Caradon mines, erected a mighty 80 inch Cornish pump engine which had been especially constructed for the Burra at the Perran Foundry. All manner of other materials was also brought out from Cornwall. Crucibles, essential pieces of kit in the assaying of ore samples, were purchased from the Calenick smelting works near Truro, while stamps and whim engines were ordered from Perran Foundry. The workforce was also largely Cornish. A visitor to the Burra in April 1848 reported that had he met 'A Captain Tre-something and a Captain Pen-something',[59] for the mine's General Superintendent, Captain Henry Roach (originally from the Tresavean mine, Redruth), was careful to appoint Cousin Jacks as his assistants—Matthew Bryant as second captain, Richard Goldsworthy (from Bodmin) as third, William Mitchell as fourth, Samuel Penglaze as grass (surface) captain, Samuel Osborne as chief ore-dresser, and Philip Santo (from Saltash) as clerk of the works. John Congdon was chief engineer, a Mr Boswarva was in charge of clerical work, and two Cornish masons—Ambrose Harris and Thomas Paynter—were engaged to oversee the construction of engine houses. The mines themselves were worked according to the time-honoured traditions of tribute and tutwork.

Three of the Burra townships bore Cornish names—Redruth, Lostwithiel and Copperhouse—and the miners frequented the 'Cornish Arms', the 'Ancient Briton' and the 'Redruth Arms'. At Redruth they lived in streets whose names read like a gazetteer from home: St Dye (reflecting the Cornish pronunciation of 'Day'), Mevagissey, Tregony, Morvah, Sancreed, Crowan, Helston, Ludgvan, Illogan, Truro, Lelant, St Just. The various Methodist denominations were active at the Burra, not least the indefatigable Bible Christians who did much to transform the district from a rough and raw mining camp to a reasonably sober and more-or-less law-abiding community. Cornish wrestling was a popular pastime, the Duke of Cornwall's birthday was observed as a general holiday, and Mid-Summer's Day (though

Constructed in 1864 by John Beaglehole from Helston, Hughes engine house at Moonta Mines, South Australia, once contained a 60 inch Pumping engine built by Harvey's of Hayle in 1862.

falling in winter in Australia) continued to be 'a red-letter day in Cousin Jack's calendar',[60] marked by bonfires and the explosion of powder-charges. In the early days, it seems, the miners also marked St Piran's Day, honouring their patron saint.

Scattered across the expanse of South Australia was a multiplicity of mining sites where the Cornish had lent a hand—sometimes places with unmistakable Cornish names, as in Wheal Blinman, Wheal Prosper, and Wheal Friendship, though often with Aboriginal names that already seemed uncompromisingly Australian, such as Yudnamutana and Mattawarangala. But, after the Burra, the other major concentration of Cornish folk was on the northern Yorke Peninsula, the Copper Triangle of 'Australia's Little Cornwall', comprising the townships of Moonta, Wallaroo and Kadina, where copper had been discovered in 1859-61. As at Kapunda and Burra Burra, Cornish technologies were applied, including the import of engines from Hayle Foundry and William West of St Blazey, and the purchase from Cornwall of all kinds of supplies from pump leather and whim ropes to rivets and Cornish shovels. Theodolites were purchased from W. Wilton of St Day. Under the watchful eye of Captain Henry Richard Hancock (actually born across the border at Horrabridge, making him a 'Devon Dumpling' in the eyes of his Cornish workforce), the twin concerns of Moonta Mines and Wallaroo Mines developed into the colony's principal industrial producers.

In 1873 Anthony Trollope, the novelist, wrote that '. . . so many of the miners were Cornishmen as to give Moonta and Wallaroo the air of Cornish towns', while in 1876 another visitor described the area as 'an Australian Cornwall'. In 1889 a further report explained that the locals '. . . lived isolated from the rest of the colony, remaining more Cornish than Cornwall', while a newcomer to Yorke Peninsula at the turn of the century recorded: 'My first impressions of Moonta Mines was—what had I let myself in for? It was soon made clear that I was a foreigner with habits and opinions to be viewed with suspicion'.[61]

As at the Burra, all kinds of cultural icons appeared to proclaim the district's Cornishness. Cornish wrestling matches were especially popular, with contestants travelling literally hundreds of miles to participate: a memorable occasion was in 1868 when the legendary John H. 'Dancing' Bray of Moonta defeated the Ballarat champion with a superbly executed 'flying mare' throw. 'Then followed a shout such as might have been heard when Sebastopol was captured. It was said that 20 captains who were there declared they had not seen anything equal to it in Cornwall'.[62] The christening of a new engine was an excuse for a lavish public dinner, such as at the starting of the New Cornwall 80 inch engine in 1866 when Captain East invited all the local captains to the festivities, for 'It was a good old Cornish custom to meet together on occasions like the present, and show a friendly feeling, although engaged on different mines'.[63] The Methodists, of course, were also active on Yorke Peninsula, the Rev W.H. Hosken, a Bible Christian preacher from the neighbouring colony of Victoria, writing in 1875 that he was '. . . persuaded that I have never met a finer field of endeavour anywhere in our Connection'.[64] For those born and bred in Moonta and environs, Moonta was 'the hub of the universe'. In wider Cornish lore, there was a well-known saying: 'if you haven't been to Moonta, you haven't travelled'.[65]

Cornish cottage at Moonta Mines, preserved today by the National Trust of South Australia.

And yet, northern Yorke Peninsula was in many ways a forbidding place; isolated, arid and prone to water-shortage, and with the scourge of 'black measles' (typhoid) that decimated the infant population when it struck in the 1870s. Something of a love-hate relationship is evident in the words of

Thomas Burtt whose poem, 'The Solemn Moonta Mines', was written on his returning home after many years, the 'dirge-like sound and muffled reverberations' of the mines at night prompting an equivocal appreciation of that awesome place:

> Hark! methinks I hear the echo!
> Of those solemn Moonta Mines;
> Sadly sounding distant far-off,
> Over flow'rets, trees and vines.
>
> Listen to the ceaseless throbbing,
> Of those engines measured slow;
> Telling many a weary spirit
> How it shares a world of woe.[66]

To concentrate on South Australia, however, should not be to ignore the Cornish impact elsewhere in that continent. During the 1850s, the Victorian Gold Rush established sizeable Cornish communities in Ballarat and (especially) Bendigo. As in California, the development of deep quartz mining led—in the 1870s—to increased capitalisation in the Victorian mining industry, an era in which the Cornish hard-rock miners came into their own. Ann Colman has charted the Cornish impact in Victoria in her impressive Masters thesis 'Colonial Cornish: Cornish Immigrants in Victoria, 1865-1880', and Ruth Hopkins has made that impact more accessible to the general reader in her exhaustive studies *Where Now Cousin Jack?* and *Cousin Jack, Man for the Times: A History of Cornish People in Victoria*. Again, an array of local and family historians (especially Lillian Dell and Joy Menhennet, with their *Cornish Pioneers of Ballarat)* has added to the illumination of the Victorian Cornish. For neighbouring New South Wales, the standard volume is 'One and All: The Cornish in Nineteenth-century New South Wales', a Masters thesis by Patricia Lay. This important work traces the Cornish in both mining and non-mining areas, as well as the great conurbation of Sydney itself, showing how the Cornish tended to 'stick together' in each of these environments, behaving as a distinct ethnic group.[67]

Broken Hill, part of New South Wales but culturally and economically in South Australia, was an important destination for the Cornish in the 1880s as the Barrier silver-lead-zinc mines were opened-up. The Cornish were similarly important in the development of the Westralian goldfields at Coolgardie and Kalgoorlie in the 1890s. In Queensland they mined copper at Peak Downs and gold at Mount Morgan. In the 1870s they made a significant contribution to the rapid development of Tasmanian mining—Mount Bischoff's 'Mountain of Tin—which, ironically, posed such a serious threat to the tin industry at home in Cornwall. Even in the far-flung Northern Territory the Cornish made their mark, 'fossicking' (prospecting) in the outback expanses and putting such hopelessly remote places as Arltunga briefly on the map.

Towards the end of the nineteenth-century, South Africa emerged as an important destination for the Cornish, their influence sketched briefly by Graham Dickason and in greater detail in the as yet unpublished work of Richard Dawe.[68] As early as the 1850s, the Cornish had gone to work the Namaqual and copper mines in the northern Cape, but their major impact came later—on the gold and diamond fields. They participated in the Eastern Transvaal goldrush in the 1870s, and they were on the Witwatersrand in the mid-1880s. The Kimberley diamond fields were also discovered in the mid-1880s, and by 1889 there was a thriving Cornish Association active in the district. Johannesburg had its own 'Cousin Jacks' Corner', where the Cornish would meet to exchange news from home or to find out about latest employment prospects, and the Ferreira Deep mine was said to be manned almost entirely by former Dolcoath miners. In 1895 alone, over two thousand people left Cornwall for South Africa. In 1896 Fanny Moody-Manners, the 'Cornish Nightingale' of operatic fame, toured South Africa, culminating in what she later saw as the greatest night of her life: a concert for the Cornish in Johannesburg. As she recorded in her diary:

> When we arrived at the Park station a perfect mob of people appeared to be waiting for us. They gave a hearty cheer when they saw me, and they also presented me with an illuminated address of welcome. Amongst the people there were many I had known in my Redruth days, or who had at least known some member of my family. Indeed, it seemed as if every Rand man who had hailed from the rocky moorland, every Jack from Camborne or Redruth, every fisherman from Mount's Bay, and every reefman who claims the Duchy as his native heath, had made it his business to be on the platform that morning.[69]

That night she delivered her concert, and in return she was given a diamond tiara with the fifteen bezants of the Cornish arms picked out in diamonds, and with the motto 'One and All' in silver and jewels. As an encore she sang her favourite Cornish songs, including an arrangement of 'And Shall Trelawny Die?' which had been especially written for the tour. As one Johannesburg newspaper recorded, 'And as she sang, these big men of Cornwall wept. They did not applaud, they hid their faces from each other and went quietly away when she had finished'.[70]

Such expressions of Cornish consciousness and solidarity marked a briefly significant international Cornish identity that had emerged by the closing decades of the last century. Of course, in addition to those principal destinations of North America, Australia and South Africa noted above, many other corners of the globe could also boast their Cousin Jacks and Jennies. New Zealand was an important destination, and so too were Chile (or Chili, as the Cornish spelt it, immortalised in Chili Road in Illogan Highway) and Brazil, Cuba and India. The Cornish also turned-up in Brittany, France, Spain, Portugal, Angola, Turkey, Norway and elsewhere, giving real meaning to the old Cornish adage, 'Wherever in the world a hole is sunk in the ground, you will be sure to find a Cousin Jack at the bottom of it, searching for metal'. Closer to home, the Cornish were to be found in the coal mines of South Wales and the North of England, and in metal mines in the Lake District and the Pennines. They mined for copper in Ireland, and for both coal and iron in Scotland.

Few individuals or institutions in Cornwall were not touched by the Great Emigration and, as we have seen, the Cornish identity expanded to insist that 'if you haven't been to Moonta, you haven't travelled'—or, indeed, that those born overseas in Cornish communities were equally as 'Cornish' as those born in Cornwall itself: 'If a cat has kittens in the oven this doesn't make them into pasties'.[71] At the time, the Great Emigration was seen as the culmination of the Cornish experience, the highpoint of a Cornish achievement that—having established Cornwall in the forefront of technological advance—now took its energy and expertise to the four points of the com-

It is difficult to imagine today that in the mid nineteenth century, Padstow was a major focus of Cornwall's 'Emigration Trade', thousands of emigrants sailing for Quebec, the emigrant ships bringing Canadian timber on their return.

pass. The reality, of course, was tragically different, for emigration was a symptom of Cornwall's flawed industrial base, and the mechanism by which Cornwall was shorn of the most skilled and brightest and youngest elements of its population.

The full story of this complex process has yet to be told in its entirety. But we do have the broad outline, and several specific features can be identified. Within Cornwall itself there developed an 'emigration culture' and a corresponding 'emigration trade', where emigration as a way of life became an integral part of local society and economy. The Methodist commitment to self-help encouraged emigration as a means of getting on, while a sophisticated and shrewd appreciation of those free or assisted passage schemes that were in operation at any one time, led to sometimes widespread bending of the rules by officials to ensure that intending emigrants qualified. The names of the more effective emigration agents have come down to us, including that of Isaac Latimer, a reporter on the staff of the *West Briton*, who in the late 1830s and 1840s acted as agent for South Australia, New South Wales, Van Diemen's Land (Tasmania), and New Zealand. Equally important was W.B.Wilcocks who, although based at the Barbican in Plymouth, controlled a number of sub-agents working across Cornwall, and who in the 1840s and 1850s recruited hundreds of Cornish miners, not least for the South Australian Mining Association (which ran the Burra Burra mine). The work of the agents underpinned the mechanisms of the emigration trade but also involved, often to a remarkable degree, a diverse collection of shipping agents, local provisioners, newspapers, advertisers, printers, publicans, coaching operators, clergymen, solicitors, and a host of other public and business interests.

The extent of this emigration trade in Cornwall is exemplified in the experience of Padstow. With its strategic geographic situation half way along the north coast, Padstow was ideally placed to act as port of departure for many emigrants from mid and North Cornwall, especially between 1829 and 1857. Margaret James-Korany has shown that between 1831 and 1860, some 6,200 emigrants sailed from Padstow for Canada.[72] Indeed, in 1841 Padstow was the third most important departure point for Canada, surpassed only by London and Liverpool. A distinctly Padstonian variant of the emigration trade developed during those years, with emigrant ships sailing for Quebec, and returning two or three months later laden with Canadian timber. Ships such as the *Clio*, *Springflower* and *Economist* were familiar sights in Padstow harbour during that period, contributing significantly to the prosperity of town and harbour.

The international identity that emerged from the Great Emigration had an almost missionary quality. As well as taking Cornish skills to an unfolding world, the emigrants were quite literally part of what they saw as a Christianising, civilising mission. The Bible Christian Missionary Society, for its part, was in no doubt about its role in the Great Migration. Within ten years of the foundation of South Australia, for example, the Bible Christian Connection had more than a thousand members in the colony, with some thirty-seven chapels built, valued at £10,000. Many held the view expressed by John Pearce, that if '. . . the Great Emigration is the crown of Cornish accomplishment, then John Wesley is seen to be its brightest jewel'.[73]

However, more worldly motives were also at work. As Horst Rossler has demonstrated in his fine study of the emigration of Constantine stonemasons in the period 1870-1900, the construction of an international identity was central to the success of the Cornish as emigrants. First of all, there was a network of contacts between the Cornish communities across the world. This allowed up-to-date and accurate information about employment prospect to be circulated and fed back to Cornwall. It also meant that emigrants would be certain of somewhere to stay on arrival abroad. Secondly, the deliberate cultivation of identity gave a community cohesion and solidarity (sometimes in a hostile environment, where there might be competition from other ethnic groups), while also encouraging the assertion of ethnic identity as an economic strategy. In the case of the Constantine stonemasons, their Cornishness and its association with craft tradition, afforded them entry to the otherwise restrictive granite-cutters' union in America. As Rossler has concluded, 'Thus craft tradition, union membership, and ethnic background combined to earn Constantine and other Cornish granite stonemasons a privileged position in an atmosphere in which immigrant labour was often viewed with hostility'.[74]

The Cornish miners, too, in America and elsewhere, made much of the myth of 'Cousin Jack', asserting an innate superiority as hard-rock miners as a result of their Cornish birth or descent. As Ronald M. James has shown, on the North American mining frontier, 'The Cornish expressed ethnicity as an economic strategy . . . they found it expedient to project themselves as ethnically distinct . . .'. Thus,

> Clearly, the Cornish could profit by encouraging others to regard them as the best in their field. A superb reputation, albeit reinforced by exemplary work in the New World ore fields, would be nothing without the members of this elite group being easily recognised. This is probably the most important reason why the Cornish sought to maintain their ethnicity.[75]

The same imperatives can be observed in South Australia, where mining entrepreneurs remained convinced that Cornwall was the foremost repository of mining skills and actively recruited Cornish miners in preference to all others throughout the last century. In contradistinction to the Irish, who deployed 'Celticity' to identify themselves as both non-British and anti-British, the Cornish in South Australia embraced Celtic identity as 'Ancient Britons'—the original Britons of Boadiccea and Caractacus, more British than the English. As Cousin Jacks and Ancient Britons, the Cornish were thus uniquely equipped for their role as pioneers in the vanguard of Empire.[76]

The platforms of Redruth railway station are often deserted today but a hundred years ago they were thronged with Cornish miners journeying to Southampton to join ships bound for South Africa.

However, there was another side to all this, for the creation of an international identity, based on the networking described by Rossler, facilitated the emergence of a 'dependency culture' in Cornwall itself. Here emigration was seen as inherently advantageous for those who remained behind, not only because Cornwall had been relieved of 'surplus' population but because of the construction of what was effectively an informal welfare system. In 1863 the *West Briton* admitted that the scale of emigration is '. . . becoming a matter of grave consideration . . . those who go abroad are the very bone and sinew of the country'. But it also declared that,

> It is, however, highly gratifying to learn that wherever the Cornish miner goes, he is generally well received, and rarely fails not only to benefit himself, but those of his friends remaining at home, by the welcome remittances which arrive by almost every mail.[77]

In 1868 the *Royal Cornwall Gazette* estimated that the recent departure of eight thousand people for destinations overseas had left some '. . . 20,000 persons dependent upon their energies elsewhere'. In January 1879 the *West Briton* identified what it saw as a change in the nature of emigration, with fewer leaving Cornwall as permanent colonists but with more individuals departing as itinerant workers in the world's mining fields. 'Thousands of people in Cornwall are supported [by these emigrants]', claimed the newspaper, for the Cornish miner '. . . leaves the women, the children, and the old people behind—not on the parish, be it said to his honour'.[78] By the end of the century the situation had become even more stark, the arrival of the 'African Mail' from South Africa a major calendar event in Camborne-Redruth and the other depressed mining districts. In January 1902 the *Cornubian* newspaper claimed that 'We are living off South Africa', and in December 1906 the *Cornish Post* explained that 'When the button is pressed in Africa, the bell rings in Cornwall . . . a change in thought and action in South Africa affects the little western county which has contributed so much of the labour and enterprise to . . . the land of gold and diamonds.'[79]

It was estimated in 1905 that there were some seven thousand Cornish miners on the Rand, earning something like £300 per annum each. As Richard Dawe has observed, if the cost of living accounted for perhaps half their wages, then as much as £1,000,000 per year could have been coming home to Cornwall. Thus the prospect of Cornwall in the early 1900s, dependent so pathetically on the diligence of her exiles in distant South Africa, was as far removed as it could be from that of the vibrant, assertive, innovative society that had existed less than a century before. The Cornish mining industry had all but disappeared, along with the financial system that had supported it. The Cornish themselves had become pawns in the hands of what was now (as Gill Burke has argued) an international mining labour market, part of the international mining economy in which market forces sped both Cornish miners and British capital to new destinations abroad.[80] The dawn of the twentieth century was not, for Cornwall, an auspicious one.

Notes & Reference (Chapter 10)

1. *West Briton*, 8 November 1894.

2. Charles G.Harper, *From Paddington to Penzance: The Record of a Summer Tramp from London to Land's End*, Chatto and Windus, London, 1893, p.222.

3. John Wallis, *The Cornwall Register*, Bodmin, 1847, p.15.

4. A.L.Rowse, *The Little Land of Cornwall*, Alan Sutton, Gloucester, 1986, p.278.

5. Wallis, 1847, pp.123 and 125.

6. *West Briton*, 7 September 1832.

7. Roger Burt and Michael Atkinson, 'Mining', and Graham Haslam, 'Modernisation', in Crispin Gill (ed.), *The Duchy of Cornwall*, David and Charles, Newton Abbot, 1987.

8. Angus Calder, *Revolutionary Empire: The Rise of the English-speaking Empires from the Fifteenth Century to the 1780s*, Jonathan Cape, London, 1981, p.476.

9. Ian Soulsby, *A History of Cornwall*, Phillimore, Chichester, 1986, p.104.

10. E.K.G. Jaggard, 'The Age of Derby Outside Parliament: New Orthodoxy for Old?', *Journal of the Royal Institution of Cornwall*, Vol.10, No.1, 1986-87; see also, Edwin Jaggard, *Liberals and Conservatives in West Cornwall, 1832-1868'*, in Philip Payton (ed.), *Cornish Studies: One*, University of Exeter Press, Exeter, 1993.

11. T.A. Jenkins (ed.), *The Parliamentary Diaries of Sir John Trelawny, 1858-1865*, Camden Fourth Series, Vol.40, Royal Historical Society, London, 1990, p.3; Alison Aldburgham, *A Radical Aristocrat: Sir William Molesworth of Pencarrow*, Tabb House, Padstow, 1990.

12. Henry Pelling, *Social Geography of British Elections, 1885-1910*, Macmillan, London, 1962, p.162.

13. Thomas Shaw, *A History of Cornish Methodism*, Bradford Barton, Truro, 1967, p.100; Thomas Shaw, *The Bible Christians*, Epworth Press, London, 1965, p.101.

14. R.S. Best, *The Life and Good Works of John Passmore Edwards*, Dyllansow Truran, Redruth, 1981.

15. Joel Wiener, *William Lovett*, Manchester University Press, Manchester, 1989.

16. A.L. Rowse (ed.), *A Cornish Anthology*, Macmillan, London, 1968 p.6.

17. John Stephens, *The Land of Promise*, Smith Elder and Co., London, 1839, p.85.

18. A.C. Todd with David James, *Ever Westward the Land*, University of Exeter Press, Exeter, 1986, p.9.

19. *South Australian Register*, 20 March 1847.

20. Philip Payton, 'Reforming Thirties and Hungry Forties: The Genesis of Cornwall's Emigration Trade', in Philip Payton (ed.), *Cornish Studies: Four*, University of Exeter Press, Exeter, 1996.

21. J.R. Leifchild, *Cornwall's Mines and Miners*, Longmans, London, 1855, repub. Frank Graham, Newcastle-upon-Tyne, 1968, p.270.

22. *West Briton*, 21 May 1847.

23. A.K. Hamilton Jenkin, *The Cornish Miner*, 1927, repub. David and Charles, Newton Abbot, 1972, p.251.

24. Roger Burt, Peter Waite, and Ray Burnley (eds.), *Cornish Mines: Metalliferous and Associated Minerals, 1845-1913*, University of Exeter Press, Exeter, 1987, p.xxxiii.

25. T.A. Morrison, *Cornwall's Central Mines: The Northern District, 1810-1895*, Alison Hodge, Penzance, 1980, pp.40-41.

26. Leifchild, 1855, p.258.

27. John Rowe, *Cornwall in the Age of the Industrial Revolution*, Liverpool University Press, Liverpool, 1953, repub. Cornish Hillside, St Austell, 1993, p.90.

28. Burt and Atkinson, 1987, p.206.

29. Leifchild, 1855 and 1968, p.258.

30. Seymour Tremenheere, 'Notice respecting the Lead and Copper Ores of Glen Osmond Mines, three miles from Adelaide, South Australia', *Transactions of The Royal Geological Society of Cornwall*, Vol.VI, 1841-46.

31. Philip Payton, 'Cornish Emigration in Response to Changes in the International Copper Market in the 1860s', in Philip Payton (ed.), *Cornish Studies: Three*, University of Exeter Press, Exeter, 1995.

32. Edmund Newell, '"Copperopolis": The Rise and Fall of the Copper Industry in the Swansea District, 1826-1921', *Business History*, Vol.32, No.33, July 1990.

33. *West Briton*, 25 January 1867.

34. *West Briton*, 4 January 1867.

35. *West Briton*, 25 January 1867, 18 June 1867.

36. *West Briton*, 16 May 1871.

37. *West Briton*, 13 April 1874.

38. *West Briton*, 7 January 1875.

39. Christopher Schmitz, 'Capital Formation and Technological Change in South-West England Metal Mining in the Nineteenth Century', in Walter Minchinton (ed.), *Capital Formation in South West England*, University of Exeter, Exeter, 1978.

40. John Rowe, 'The Declining Years of Cornish Tin Mining', in Jeffrey Porter (ed.), *Education and Labour in the South West*, University of Exeter, Exeter, 1975, p.59.

41. G.B. Worgan, *General View of the Agriculture of the County of Cornwall*, London, 1811, p.53, cited in Mark Overton, 'The Crop Returns for Cornwall', in Michael Havinden (ed.), *Husbandry and Marketing in the South West 1500-1800*, University of Exeter, 1973, p.56; see also, Harold S.A. Fox, 'Outfield Cultivation in Devon and Cornwall: A Reinterpretation', in Havinden (ed.), 1973.

42. Rowe, 1953 and 1993, p.249.

43. Andrew Jewell, 'Some Cultivation Techniques in the South-West of England', in Walter Minchinton (ed.), *Agricultural Improvements: Ancient and Modern*, University of Exeter, Exeter, 1981, p.106.

44. For an insight into Cornish farming in this period, see John Rowe, *Changing Times and Fortunes: A Cornish farmer's Life 1828-1904*, Cornish Hillside, 1996.

45. Keith Harris, *Hevva! Cornish Fishing in the Days of Sail*, Dyllansow Truran, Redruth, 1983, p.1.

46. Alan Southward, Gerald Boalch and Linda Maddock (eds.), 'Climatic Change and the Herring and Pilchard Fisheries of Devon and Cornwall', in David J. Starkey (ed.), *Devon's Coastline and Coastal Waters: Aspects of Man's Relationship with* the Sea, University of Exeter Press, Exeter, 1988; for a general history of Cornish seining, see Cyril Noall, *Cornish Seines and Seiners: A History of the Pilchard Fishing Industry*, Bradford Barton, Truro, 1972.

47. Harris, 1983, p.64.

48. *West Briton*, 8 January 1891.

49. *West Briton*, 14 May 1877.

50. John Corin, *Fishermen's Conflict*, David and Charles, Newton Abbot, 1988.

51. A.C. Todd, *The Cornish Miner in America*, Bradford Barton, Truro, 1967, repub. Clark, Spokane (Washington), 1995, p.19.

52. Dudley Baines, *Migration in a Mature Economy: Emigration and Internal Migration in England and Wales, 1861-1900*, Cambridge University Press, Cambridge, 1985, pp.157-159; the complexity of Cornish emigration is evident in family histories such as Keith Skues, *Cornish Heritage*, Werner Shaw, London, 1983; and Henry Blackwell, *From a Dark Stream: The Story of Cornwall's Amazing People and their Impact on the World*, Dyllansow Truran, Redruth, 1987.

53. John C.C. Probert, *The Sociology of Cornish Methodism*, Cornish Methodist Historical Association, Truro, 1971, p.61.

54. A.L. Rowse, *The Cornish in America*, Macmillan, London, 1969, repub. Dyllansow Truran, Redruth, 1991, p.241.

55. Rowse, 1969 and 1991, pp.295-296.

56. Todd, 1967 and 1995; Rowse, 1969 and 1991; John Rowe, *The Hard-rock Men: Cornish Immigrants and the North American Mining Frontier*, Liverpool University Press, 1974; Jim Jewell, *Cornish in America: Linden, Wisconsin*, Cornish Miner Press, Linden, 1990; Ronald M. James, 'Knockers, Knackers and Ghosts: Immigrant Folklore in the Western Mines', *Western Folklore*, 51:2, 1992; Ronald M. James, 'Defining the Group: Nineteenth-Century Cornish on the North American Mining Frontier', in Philip Payton (ed.), *Cornish Studies: Two*, University of Exeter Press, Exeter, 1994; see also, John Rowe, *Cornish Methodists and Emigrants*, Cornish Methodist Historical Association, Truro, 1967; John Rowe, 'The Cornish', in Stephen Thernstrom (ed.), *Harvard Encyclopedia of American Ethnic Groups*, Cambridge (Mass.), 1980; John Rowe, 'Cornish Emigrants in America', *Folklife*, 3, 1965.

57. Ian Auhl and Dennis Marfleet, *Australia's Earliest Mining Era: South Australia 1841-1851*, Rigby, Adelaide, 1975; Ian Auhl, *Burra and District: A Pictorial Memoir*, Lynton, Blackwood, 1975; Ian Auhl, *The Story of the Monster Mine: The Burra Burra Mine and its Townships 1845-1877*, Investigator, Adelaide, 1986; Oswald Pryor, *Australia's Little Cornwall*, Rigby, Adelaide, 1962; Roslyn Paterson, *Thankyou Walter Watson Hughes: Essays on Northern Yorke Peninsula*, Gould, Adelaide, 1993; Diane C. Hancock and Roslyn M. Paterson (eds.), *Cousin Jacks and Jennys: The Cornish in South Australia*, Cornish Association of South Australia, Adelaide, 1995; G.J. Drew and J.E. Connell, *Cornish Beam Engines in South Australia*, Separtment of Mines and Energy, Adelaide, 1993; see also D.B.Barton, 'Cornishmen and Australian Copper', in *Essays in Cornish Mining History*, Vol.1, Bradford Barton, Truro, 1968; Jim Faull, *The Cornish in Australia*, AE Press, Melbourne, 1983; Philip Payton, 'The Cornish in South Australia: Their Influence and Experience from Immigration to Assimilation, 1836-1936', unpub. PhD, University of Adelaide, 1978; Philip Payton, *Pictorial History of Australia's Little Cornwall*, Rigby, Adelaide, 1978; Philip Payton, *The Cornish Miner in Australia*, Dyllansow Truran, Redruth, 1984; Philip Payton, *Cornish Carols from Australia*, Dyllansow Truran, Redruth, 1984a; Philip Payton, *The Cornish Farmer in Australia*, Dyllansow Truran, Redruth, 1987; Philip Payton, 'The Cornish', in James Jupp (ed.), *The Australian People*, Angus Robertson, Sydney, 1988.

58. Cousin Sylvia, *Homing*, Hassell Press, n.d..

59. Payton, 1984, p.35.

60. South Australian Register, 27 June 1863.

61. Anthony Trollope, *Australia*, 1873, repub. University of Queensland Press, St Lucia, 1967, p.684; *Yorke's Peninsula Advertiser*, 4 August 1876; W.G. Spence, *Australia's Awakening*, Workers' Trustees, Sydney, 1909, p.27; South Australian Archives, D3627(L), Stanley Whitford, 'An Autobiography', addendum by Sir Lennon Raws.

62. 'Autobiography of Thomas Cowling', pp93-94 (in possession of Mr John Cowling, Adelaide).

63. *Wallaroo Times*, 31 March 1866.

64. *Bible Christian Magazine*, combined volume, 1876, p.37.

65. Pryor, 1962, p.148.

66. Thomas Burtt, *Moonta Musings in Rhythmic Rhyme*, Yorke's Peninsula Advertiser, Moonta, 1885, p.2.

67. Ann Colman, 'Colonial Cornish: Cornish Immigrants in Victoria, 1865-1880', unpub. MA, University of Melbourne, 1985; Ruth Hopkins, *Where Now Cousin Jack?*, Bendigo Bicentennial Committee, Bendigo, 1988; Ruth Hopkins, *Cousin Jack, Man for the Times: A History of the Cornish People in Victoria*, Hopkins, Bendigo, 1994; Lillian Dell and Joy Menhennet, *Cornish Pioneers of Ballarat*, Ballarat Branch of the Cornish Association of Victoria, Ballarat, 1992; Patricia Lay, 'One and All: The Cornish in Nineteenth-century New South Wales', unpub. MA, Australian National University, 1992.

68. Graham B. Dickason, *Cornish Immigrants to South Africa*, Balkema, Cape Town, 1978; Richard D. Dawe, 'The Effect Chinese Labour Had on the Cornish Miner in South Africa', unpub. paper, Middlesex Polytechnic, 1984; Richard D. Dawe, 'The Role and Influence of the Cornish Miner in South Africa, 1886-1925', unpub. MA, Middlesex Polytechnic, 1986; Richard D. Dawe, 'The Cornish in South Africa', unpub. MS, n.d.; see also, A.L. Rowse, *The Controversial Colensos*, Dyllansow Truran, Redruth, 1989.

69. David Mudd, *Cornishmen and True*, Frank Graham, Newcastle-upon-Tyne, 1971, p.33.

70. Mudd, 1971, p.34.

71. Charles Thomas, *The Importance of Being Cornish in Cornwall*, Institute of Cornish Studies, Redruth, 1973, p.12.

72. Margaret James-Korany, 'The "Blue Books" as Sources for Cornish Emigration History', in Philip Payton (ed.), 1993.

73. John Pearce, *The Wesleys in Cornwall*, Bradford Barton, Truro, 1964, p.27.

74. Horst Rossler, 'Constantine Stonemasons in Search of Work Abroad, 1870-1900', in Philip Payton (ed.), 1994.

75. Ronald M. James, 1994.

76. Philip Payton, 'From Cousin Jack to Map Kernow: Re-defining Cornish Ethnicity', *Australian Studies*, forthcoming.

77. *West Briton*, 23 October 1863.

78. *Royal Cornwall Gazette*, 21 January 1868; West Briton, 23 January 1879.

79. *Cornubian*, 31 January 1902; *Cornish Post*, 20 December 1906.

80. Gillian Burke, 'The Cornish Diaspora in the Nineteenth Century', in Shula Marks and Peter Richardson (eds.), *International Labour Migrations: Historical Perspectives*, Temple Smith, London, 1984.

CHAPTER 11

Re-inventing Kernow

CORNWALL

Re-inventing Kernow

The period that stretches from the closing decades of the last century until after the Second World War is one of the oddest in Cornwall's history. It has been characterised as 'The Great Paralysis', a full half-century and more of lethargy and inertia, perhaps even trauma, in which (in marked contrast to all the vigour and movement of the previous two hundred years) very little actually happened.[1] And yet, even as the Cornish economy crumbled in the aftermath of abrupt de-industrialisation, with Cornish society locked into an introverted 'making do', there was in the background a project aimed at nothing less than the 're-invention' of Cornwall. Even more remarkable, this project was an alliance (perhaps even an 'unholy' one) of two quite separate groups, one Cornish and the other 'outsider', whose objectives were entirely different and yet whose interests and strategies were at a crucial point, congruent. This chapter sets out to unravel this conundrum, to try to make sense of the puzzling paradox of 'paralysis' and 're-invention'.

Of course, the paralysis of Cornish society and economy in this period was against the background of intense trauma on the international scene, first in the Great War and then in the Great Depression of the inter-war years, momentous events which caused global dislocation and uncertainty. And yet, despite this shared international experience, Cornwall's socio-economic condition remained highly distinctive and—to those who cared to look in the right direction—highly visible. A survey by the University College of the South West (the embryonic University of Exeter), published in 1947 but drawing largely on the census for 1931, saw that the Cornish economy was '. . . highly differentiated from that of the country as a whole'. Proportionately higher numbers were engaged in service industries and agriculture but, in a remarkable contrast to only a few decades before, there were '. . . fewer in manufacture and mining'.[2] Similarly, the population density of Cornwall in 1931 was an average of 234 persons per square mile, compared to 685 for England and Wales, a legacy of the Great Emigration. The population of Cornwall was actually falling, as it had been since 1861 (with the brief exception of the decade 1901-11), in contrast to even Devon where the population had managed respectable growth.

In unemployment, too, Cornwall was consistently worse off than Devon. In the decade 1929-38, Devon's average unemployment figure (12.3 percent) was less severe than for England (14.8 per cent), while that for Cornwall was 17.7 percent. During the period 1930-33, Cornwall had risen to an alarming 21.6 percent, with Devon on 14.4 percent and England at 18.8 percent. In 1947 it was reckoned that '. . . recovery after the ending of the depression was both more complete and faster in Devon than in Cornwall . . . the persistence of high unemployment in Cornwall suggests a post-world war depression problem more chronic than in either England or Devon'.[3] The extremes of poverty and unemployment were also much greater in Cornwall than in Devon. In the decade 1929-38, for example, Newquay's average percentage unemployment was as low as 7.4 percent, reflecting the growth of the service sector there, while St Austell and Liskeard (both reliant on a china clay industry that was in the doldrums) recorded 15.8 percent and 17.4 percent respectively. In the old mining and engineering localities, where there was neither china clay nor growth in the service sector to offset the

From fishing and industrial port to tourist magnet—the transformation of Newquay is evident in this panoramic view.

impact of de-industrialisation, the figures were far worse—32.9 percent in Redruth, 22 percent in Camborne, 28.4 percent in Hayle.

Although this evidence pointed the finger of blame at an over-reliance on mining, that inability in the past to diversify, sections of Cornish opinion continued to hope, even lobby for a revival of Cornish tin. There was a hint of recovery between 1906 and 1908, the number of miners employed in the industry rising steeply to some 8,500, but the up-turn was short-lived. Soon the press was bemoaning the high level of unemployment at Gunnislake and in the Tamar Valley as a result of the collapse of mining, while the closure of Wheal Jane spelt gloom for the Truro district. At Camborne, Dolcoath struggled on as the flagship of Cornish mining, bravely attempting to embrace new technologies in the fight to remain viable. As Kenneth Brown and Bob Acton have noted, 'Electric pumps came into use in 1912, but nine years later the mine came to an end, creating a depression in the district from which it has never fully recovered, even today'.[4] In the aftermath of the mine's closure, a reconstructed Dolcoath Company sunk a new shaft (over 300 fathoms deep) at Roskear, to the north of the old workings. This company had collapsed by 1928, however, the Roskear shaft eventually passing into the ownership of nearby South Crofty tin mine.

Although tin, as a strategic metal, was in demand throughout the Great War, the government's policy was to exploit Cornish mines rather than develop them. The aim was to secure supplies for war requirements, not to plan future economic regeneration. The price of tin had been pegged at an artificially low level, mainly as part of a deal with America to secure strategic supplies of copper, and the emphasis was on 'picking the eyes' outof the mines to achieve maximum output. In 1919, with the end of hostilities, mine owners and labour unions alike lobbied the government for continued support (the 'land fit for heroes' presumably extended to those Cornish miners who had ensured adequate supplies for the war effort) but no assistance was forthcoming. As John Rowe has noted, in early 1919 it appeared that the entire remnant of the Cornish mining industry was on the point of collapse, the dreadful Levant man-engine disaster in the October (in which thirty-one miners lost their lives) casting a shadow of despair across the mining districts of Cornwall.[5]

The abandonment of Wheal Grenville, near Camborne, in early 1920 heralded what was to be the worst crisis in Cornish mining, and for a time during 1921 Giew (part of the attempted St Ives Consolidated re-workings) was the only mine in operation in all Cornwall. As Dr Rowe puts it, 'Harrowing tales have been told of the distress prevalent in Cornish mining districts during 1921 and 1922'.[6] In an echo of the 1860s, relief funds were organised (Camborne police station was transformed into an emergency clothing centre), while emigrant communities in North America, South Africa and Australia sent money home to Cornwall. A brief rally in tin prices warranted some expansion in 1926, but the depression years of the 1930s precluded any major development (at its nadir, the industry employed but 426 souls). With the outbreak of the Second World War in 1939, the most recent attempts at reworking—in Breage, Wendron and St Agnes—were swiftly abandoned, leaving only three mines at work: Geevor, near St Just-in-Penwith, and South Crofty and East Pool & Agar in Camborne-Redruth.

But if tin mining was all but obliterated, Cornwall's other major extractive industry, china clay, survived—albeit in straitened circumstances. Although not underground, hard-rock mining like tin, china clay had developed alongside the tinworks of moorland Cornwall—principally on the Hensbarrow uplands beyond St Austell—absorbing much of the terminology, technology and indeed manpower from deep mining.[7] And yet 'clay' was different to 'tin', producing a culture and community of its own: Treviscoe and Foxhole were never quite the same things as St Day and Carharrack. Although overshadowed by copper and tin in the nineteenth century, Cornish clay was already an established industry by the 1820s, serving the needs of potters outside Cornwall. Progress was fitful, however, a function of poor organisation and periodic crises of overproduction. Nevertheless, in the early years of this century, china clay was seen by many as the natural successor to copper and tin, a means of filling the vacuum left by the decline of mining proper. Indeed, there was healthy expansion between 1900 and 1916 (when annual output never failed to exceed half a million tons) but the outbreak of the Great War had disastrous effects, closing off vital export markets. By 1917 production was halved, and after the war things were slow to improve. In 1921 and 1922 there was fearful hardship in the little villages of the china clay country. The American slump of 1929 and the consequent Great Depression dashed hopes of restoring exports to pre-war levels, and by 1932 output had slumped by 40 percent since 1929, the price of china clay by more than 30 percent. Total disaster was averted by amalgamation, a number of producers coming together to form the English Clays Lovering Pochin & Company, which was able to develop a strategic marketing policy and to benefit from economies of scale.

Elsewhere in the 'traditional' Cornish economy, it was difficult to discern rays of hope in that long era of paralysis.[8] Notwithstanding 'Yorkie' competition, the fishing industry had rallied to the point where there were as many as thirteen first-class steam trawlers registered in the ports of Cornwall and Devon in the years immediately after the Great War. However, by 1938 the number had dropped to just two, one of which had not been used since 1925. Of the motor fleets, the one hundred and fifty first-class vessels of 1919 had reduced to ninety-one by 1938, the number of sail craft having declined even more alarmingly. The total number of first-class vessels of varying types registered in Cornwall and Devon had fallen drastically from three hundred and six in 1919 to just ninety-nine in 1938.

Cornish farming, too, exhibited the general languor of this paralysis.

Improvements in grasslands, which would have raised the standards of stock and of milk production, had not occurred, and there was a range of infrastructural deficiencies—from poor buildings to inadequate water supplies. On many Cornish farms, the small number of cattle made milk production an uneconomic proposition. Indeed, in 1939, of the 12,881 holdings in Cornwall, no fewer than 2,116 were sized between one and five acres. Only two farms were in the range five hundred to seven hundred acres, and none was larger than that. In such conditions, a high standard of husbandry (usually with a highly-focused specialisation) was a prerequisite for viability—in Cornwall it was exhibited but rarely.

In explaining the characteristics of this Cornish paralysis, the Exeter survey hinted at a wider appreciation of the situation in which Cornish society found itself, suggesting that in Cornwall '. . . deficient industrial enterprise and industrial inertia must not be overlooked'.[9] This, in turn, reflected the fatalistic edge that had come to define popular culture in Cornwall, a 'making do' in which a hitherto assertive and self-confident identity turned in on itself, becoming instead introspective, even 'fossilised'. The icons of popular Cornishness that had come to typify Cornwall in the closing decades of the last century—male voice choirs, brass bands, rugby football (defined as 'Cornish' because of their intimate expression of community life)—were no longer vibrant assertions of an industrial culture, but inward-looking, defensive, a private and often (for the outsider) impenetrable domain of the Cornish working class. Cornish carols, for example, which only a decade or so before had appeared in editions in places as far-flung as Moonta and Johannesburg, were by the Great War hardly known or heard across the Tamar, though still readily on the lips of congregations in Camborne Wesley or at Paynter's Lane End chapel in Illogan. Although in the industrial North of England, Nonconformists might sing 'While Shepherds Watched' to the tune *Lingum*, as the Cornish did, for the rest there was little knowledge of the florid airs, frequent word repetitions and strong flowing basses that characterised the Cornish carol. When, by chance, they were heard by outsiders, they seemed strangely primitive and naive.

Thomas Merritt, the epitome of the late-nineteenth-century Cornish carol-composing tradition, had died in 1908 at the relatively youthful age of forty-six. As organist, first at Chili Road chapel (now demolished) and then at Fore Street Methodist Church, both in Illogan Highway, he had devoted his life to music, ill-health having forced his early retirement from the mines. Of all Cornish carols, his are the most memorable:

Hark the glad sound! the saviour comes,
  The Saviour promised long,
Let every heart prepare a throne,
  And every voice a song.

He comes, the prisoners to release,
  In Satan's bondage held;
The gates of brass before Him burst,
  The iron fetters yield.

He comes, the broken heart to bind,
The bleeding soul to cure,
  And with the treasures of his grace
To enrich the humble poor.[10]

Let hallelujahs swiftly rise, / And join the triumphs of the skies. The house in Broad Lane, Illogan, where Thomas Merritt—the composer of Cornish carols—was born in 1863.

Jack Clemo's clay country is evoked strongly in this portrayal of a Cornish quarry.

For some outsiders the almost secretive, possessive 'inner-life' of Cornwall in this period, with its inherent suspiciousness, its thrift, was unattractive. During the First World War an exasperated D. H. Lawrence complained that the Cornish were '. . . inertly selfish, like insects gone cold, living only for money, mean and afraid'.[11] In the clay country, a part of Cornwall to experience acute poverty in the inter-war years, this introverted 'making do' was everywhere apparent, reflected in the writings of Jack Clemo, whose psychological disposition and encroaching disabilities (blindness and deafness) made for a particular kind of 'inner life'. Like A. L. Rowse's *A Cornish Childhood*, Clemo's gritty autobiography, *Confession of a Rebel*, affords numerous insights into clay country life in that period.[12] But it also exhibits a particular bleakness, an intimation of the fatalism and resignation that had overtaken many of the clay folk. This same quality is also conveyed in Jack Clemo's short-story 'The Clay Dump', in which the white pyramidal spoil heap behind Lucy Gribble's cottage in Pengarth plays the malevolent role of fate:

> This clay-dump dominated the village and . . . Lucy . . . became fascinated, aroused to a certain identification of the gravelly dune with the heaping up of afflictions in her life. All her hope of enjoyment had been like the flowers that pushed out so pitifully through the turf fringing the dump's base—soon to be burst and flattened and buried by the descending vomit of sand and stone.[13]

Clemo also wrote in Cornish dialect, principally pithy (and often humorous) short stories which appeared in the 1930s in volumes such as *Saundry's Almanack*, published in Penzance, Truro's *Netherton's Almanack*, and the *One and All Almanack* at Camborne. Deadpan statements arrest the reader ('Sammy Chegwidden had traipsed around Pengooth village four times that evening afore he catched sight o' Maria Blake; and he wad'n much better off when he did see her')[14], often conveying that same weary fatalism. More interesting still, however, is the use of dialect as a mechanism to express introspection. The choice of dialect as a medium suggests an exclusive self-sufficiency, signally the Cornish as *cognisente* and almost deliberately excluding the outsider, a means of social commentary in which language clearly defines ownership.

This is story-telling about the Cornish (working class), by the Cornish, for the Cornish. Significantly, when the 'Cornish Celtic Revival' emerged in the late nineteenth and (more strongly) in the twentieth centuries, it eschewed the Cornish dialect of English as a marker of Cornishness and instead (as we shall see) chose the more overtly 'Celtic' symbolism of the Cornish language itself. Dialect was redolent of an Anglophone, industrial age; the Cornish language harked back to an earlier Celticity. Even today these distinctions are observed, dialect marginalised in Cornish culture as the medium for funny stories or risqué jokes, the serious stuff of nation-building left to the Cornish language enthusiasts. Perhaps only the late Dr Ken Phillipps saw a wider and more important role for dialect: '. . . dialect could acquire a certain prestige . . . valued as a blend of shibboleth and talisman, to prove one's identity . . .'.[15]

Be that as it may, in the 1930s, when Jack Clemo was writing his stories, dialect was used to defend rather than to assert identity, to put a protective fence around a community under pressure rather than to proclaim its identity to others. Elsewhere in indigenous Cornish literature, from the 1890s right through to the Second World War and beyond, the same introspection could be observed. Henry Harris' story, 'Cousin Jacky', published in 1901, conveys a pervasive sense of loss, fatalism, even hopelessness, the returning migrant recognising the stark truth that there is nothing for him in Cornwall—the only option is to go abroad again. Similarly, the stories in H. D. Lowry's *Wreckers and Methodists*, which appeared in 1893, articulate a profound sense of loss and regret.[16] Later, in 1937, in Richard Preston's enigmatically-entitled *End of Cornwall*, set in the imaginary fishing cove of Tregwidden in 1933-34, hopelessness is expressed not in resignation but in frustration and anger. One character '. . . even dreamed of a Cornwall cut off from the rest of England; but he soon grasped that that aim was hopeless, meaningless under modern conditions'.[17] Another had gained:

> . . . a vague but stirring impression of the Cornish past . . . his emotional conviction was clear that the Cornish had always been courageous . . . rebelling when goaded into desperation, filled with a strong rebel spirit . . . If only this spirit of independence could be given real purpose.[18]

The same character, Amos Rescorla, visits Gwennap Pit and vents his anger and frustration at the Cornwall gone before:

> Hey there, Wesley and all you ghosts, listen to me. You thought you were doing great work, talking about blood and singing your guts out. But you're dead, Wesley, and your world is dead with you. I'm the new world . . . I've got a better text than any of yours. I'll give you a text, Wesley. The workers have nothing to lose but their chains. Workers of the world, unite! Workers of Cornwall, you're part of it. I'm a worker, that's my name and my country.[19]

However, this testament, eloquent though it is, tells us rather more about the author than about the Cornwall of the period. He has caught the mood of hopelessness and resignation, but in railing against it has dissociated himself from the prevailing fatalism. In reality, the general response to hopelessness was one of quiet stoicism, of patience and forbearance in the face of adversity. Thus in the midst of the terrible crisis of 1921, the mayor of Penzance could note that '. . . there were at Penzance children practically starving and men and women suffering in secret hunger and privation without murmuring'.[20] To individual stoicism was added altruism and community solidarity, the *West Briton* observing with pride that, although 1921 was '. . . the most disastrous year in history . . . one of the striking features in the mining district has been the manner in which poor people have quite literally shared their crusts with one another'.[21] This was, *par excellence*, the culture of making-do. Sven Berlin, an outsider living in Cornwall, tried to grope his way towards an understanding of this condition:

> . . . the Cornish are an emotional, literal people with no art of their own through which to free themselves; these compensations [religion and drink] have therefore become necessary to balance the psychological conflict set up by the severity, insecurity and peninsula nature of their lives . . . this has bred an hard, mercenary, suspicious, clannish, but independent and vivid race of people, who are, however, kind and helpful to one another and show fine qualities among themselves. In spite of their hidebound morality they have a profound love of the fields and the sea.[22]

The Exeter survey was less generous, and displayed an undisguised contempt for much that defined Cornwall in this period:

> . . . in the bleak, lonely areas . . . where the village nucleus may consist merely of an isolated church, with perhaps a few cottages; where the parish is less of a community than a widespread powdering over the landscape of scattered farms; where towns are few and small in size, distances between them great and communications poor—it is here that rural decadence, materially, mentally and spiritually is seen at its lowest depths.[23]

Paradoxically, this paralysis, for all its apparent languor and decay, had served to strengthen rather than erode popular identity in Cornwall. Economically, socially and culturally, Cornwall had become more differentiated from England, emphasising a particularism and distinctiveness which perceptive outsiders were compelled to acknowledge—even if they did not understand or approve of it. This heightened differentiation was also reflected in Cornish politics, where party-political contestation had become 'fossilised' as Liberal versus Conservative at a time when elsewhere in Britain the 'age of alignment' (as Christopher Cook has termed it) had ushered in the new struggle between Conservative and Labour.[24]

Although Professor Jaggard has emphasised the continuities in Cornish politics between 1832 and 1885, there is no doubt that the significant extension of the franchise in 1885 gave a strongly popular edge to the election of that year.[25] This was no more so than in the newly-created 'Mining Division' constituency (based on Camborne-Redruth), where a surge of radical opinion served to elect an Independent Liberal (C.A.V. Conybeare) instead of the presumed favourite, the official Liberal candidate Arthur Pendarves Vivian (who had represented West Cornwall unopposed since 1868). L. L. Price, writing in 1895, described the election as 'an intense and bitter . . . contest between Whig and Radical',[26] and indeed it was. Pendarves stressed his reputation and experience as a good constituency man who supported local interests. Conybeare, however, branded a 'Red-

Hot Radical Agitator' by his opponents, had a long political shopping-list; better conditions for miners, anti-landlordism, abolition of game laws, abolition of the House of Lords, disestablishment of the Church of England, graduated income tax, the local option (for pubs to be closed on Sundays), votes for women, triennial elections, and Home Rule All Round (including Cornwall). This was a portfolio of policies designed to appeal to the traditional Liberal-Methodist nexus in Cornwall but it was also put together with the newly-enfranchised voters in mind, particularly the miners.

Conybeare won the election, and local opinion at the time (echoed recently in Bernard Deacon's assessment) was that the miners were crucial in securing his victory.[27] As one commentator explained, '. . . the creed of the overwhelming majority . . . is neatly, precisely Democratic . . . It is as Cornish as the Cornish pilchard and Cornish humour . . .'.[28] More than fifteen years before Keir Hardy's famous victory as an Independent Labour candidate in Merthyr, when he took on Wales' Liberal establishment and won, Conybeare's success meant that—as Bernard Deacon has so aptly put it—'Redruth and district was at the leading edge of British politics'.[29] However, this status was short-lived, for already the stage had been set for the swift divergence of Cornish politics from the mainstream British experience. To understand this, it is necessary to glance back to the 1860s and 1870s, to what Bernard Deacon has called the 'lost history' of the Cornish working class.[30] Although A.K. Hamilton Jenkin and others have characterised the Cornish miner as resistant to collective action, an 'innate' individualism combining with the competitive effects of the tribute and tutwork system of employment to frustrate attempts at co-operative behaviour, there was in fact a history of combination.

Indeed, if we note that riot was the precursor of strike in Britain as a whole, then we can begin to appreciate that the Cornish miners were in fact renowned (and feared) for collective action throughout the eighteenth and early nineteenth centuries. Miners were still rioting in the 'Hungry Forties', as we saw in Chapter Ten, but even in the 1830s riot had moved almost imperceptibly to strike. In February 1841 there was a brief strike at Fowey Consols and Lanescot to try to force a rise in tribute rates (the leaders were incarcerated in Bodmin Gaol, as though they were rioters), and in 1842 there was a similarly brief strike at Consolidated Mines in Gwennap over working hours and conditions of employment. More concerted action had appeared by the 1850s, particularly in the St Just-in-Penwith district in 1853, 1856, 1857 and 1859. Interestingly, a strike at Bosweddan mine in 1853 was over the alleged victimisation of men who had participated in a food riot some six years before.

The first really determined attempts at organised trade unionism occurred in the East Cornwall and Tamar Valley mines in 1866. There was dissatisfaction with tribute and tutwork contracts, a feeling that the miners had not been able to benefit from copper price rises (albeit temporary) of late 1865, while a visit of striking Newcastle coal-miners had kindled an interest in unionism. The first move was a strike at Wheal Trelawney lead mine (near Menheniot) in January 1866, when the miners demanded better remuneration. Other mines followed, and soon there were reports of miners' meetings being held throughout the district, at Liskeard, Gunnislake, Callington and Tavistock. A Miners' Mutual Benefit Association was set-up in February 1866 to organise the men and their demands, an action which led to lock-outs at Drakewalls and other Gunnislake mines. At Devon Great Consols, near Tavistock, soldiers and special constables were brought in to prevent any invasion of angry miners from across the Tamar. In the Caradon area, the Association took the initiative, declaring strikes at East Caradon and Marke Valley mines. The Caradon strikes continued into the March but already the lock-outs had forced some Association members back to work under the employers' conditions. Thereafter, the strikes collapsed. The year 1866 was in any case a disaster for Cornish copper mining, causing mine closure after mine closure, resulting in high unemployment and emigration—hardly the environment in which an embryonic trade union structure might grow and flourish.

In the early 1870s, however, there was a brief upturn in the tin industry, provoking a correspondingly brief upsurge of renewed collective action amongst the Cornish miners. Grievances focused on two main issues, the low level of remuneration (it was said that 'captain's prices' were kept artificially low at time of tin price rises) and the infrequent payment of wages. The latter was concerned with the practice of working 'one month in hand' (a system which forced miners to draw 'subsist'—an advance on wages—to make ends meet) and the strict adherence to the 'five week month' as a payment period. At the end of 1871 there were miners' protest meetings at St Blazey and in the Caradon and St Just districts. In the Camborne-Redruth area, Tincroft and Carn Brea mines both abandoned the five week month, provoking a strike at nearby Wheal Basset when it proved tardy in following suit. By March 1872 the five week month had been abolished at most Cornish mines, a measure of the speed of the employers' reactions at a time when tin prices were high and skilled labour was in short supply. However, although the miners tried to secure their newly-established position through the creation of a union organisation in Camborne in March 1874, their position by then was already weakened. The tin price had fallen, mines were closing, and those that remained open tried—sometimes successfully, sometimes not—to reintroduce the five week month in the face of opposition.

Although there was sporadic industrial action into the 1880s and 1890s, the Camborne union came to nothing. But there was activity in the china clay industry in 1912 (its violence and trauma immortalised in the excellent 1970s BBC television drama *Stocker's Copper*), when workers struck unsuccessfully for union recognition, wage rises, and an eight hour day. Effective trade unionism was only established under wartime conditions, and there were brief strikes at several mines in 1918, 1919 and 1920, together with the more significant Transport and General Workers Union strike at South Crofty in January 1939 (when miners clashed with police in Pool). By then, of course, mining was of marginal importance to the Cornish economy as a whole, geographically restricted to a few specific areas and employing relatively few people. As Gillian Burke has rightly concluded, 'The diminution of the Cornish industry during these years was most certainly one important factor in the delayed advent of Trade Union organisation on any scale in Cornwall . . .'.[31] But the corollary was also true, that before the diminution of the Cornish industry, Cornish miners were as eager as their Welsh (or English) colleagues to explore the possibilities of combination.

As Bernard Deacon has explained:

> The historical divergence between Cornish metal miners and Welsh coal miners only became marked after the 1866-72 period. While coal mining continued to expand, copper and tin mining entered on a severe protracted slump characterised by large scale unemployment and emigration. Such conditions were hardly conducive to the formation of a permanent trade union.[32]

Indeed, as Bernard Deacon has also pointed out, if one follows the fortunes of emigrant Cornish miners overseas, then one often finds Cousin Jacks at the forefront of trade union and Labour activity.[33] On the mining frontier of America, the Cornish were—according to Richard E. Lingenfelter—'. . . the leaders of the mining labour movement of the West'.[34] Tom Matthews, from Newlyn, who had mined in Michigan and at Butte, and had been President of the Miners' Union of Montana in 1872 (and that State's only Labour member of its House of Representatives), was also a central figure in the establishment of South Africa's Miners' Association in 1902. In South Australia, where employment and other conditions bore close comparison with Cornwall, the Cornish had already precipitated a significant strike at the Burra Burra mine in 1848.[35] Later, at Wallaroo and Moonta, the Cornish miners led important strikes in 1864 and 1874 (the latter coincident with unrest at home), the 1874 upheaval leading to the establishment of a permanent trade union structure on Yorke Peninsula. Wallaroo and Moonta were also a birthplace of the United Labour Party, which was to give South Australia its first Labour Premier in 1912, 'Honest' John Verran from Gwennap. In the 1880s, the South Australian Cornish took their unionism to the new silver-lead-zinc mines of Broken Hill, destined to become a major focus of trade union organisation in Australia.

Back in Cornwall, it is clear that the unrest in the mines in the 1870s had had a radicalising effect in Camborne-Redruth, and that Conybeare had benefited from this. He also received moral support from emigrant Cornish miners, telegrams of encouragement arriving from America during his election campaign. However, he had caught not the highpoint but rather the tail-end of radical activity. The Liberal Unionists (in Cornwall as elsewhere) had broken away from the Liberals in opposition to that party's support for Irish Home Rule, and had entered into an electoral pact with the Conservatives. The 1886 general election was a disaster for the Liberal Party throughout Britain, with scores of seats falling to the Liberal Unionists. In Cornwall, Liberal Unionists took three seats. Two others remained in Liberal hands, and the sixth was held by Conybeare. Although, at first glance, this was a shift to the political right, the success of the Liberal Unionists reflected the fact that—in Cornwall at least—they were not surrogate Tories but quite genuinely Liberals with a Unionist (and Cornish) face.

Certainly, the Liberal Unionists remained a significant force in Cornwall until the 1906 'Liberal Landscape' general election, and indeed re-emerged briefly in 1910 in some strength. Their popularity reflected Cornish unease over the prospect of Irish Home Rule (partly on religious grounds, and partly because Cornish fishermen feared that they might be excluded from Irish waters), an essentially nonconformist anxiety. Such was this feeling that Conybeare was defeated in the Mining Division in 1895, although it must also be said that many of those miners who had supported him a decade earlier had now lost the vote as a result of their dependency on poor relief, or had emigrated to South Africa or America. However, Arthur Strauss, Conybeare's Liberal Unionist successor, served only briefly—until *his* defeat in 1900 by the Radical Liberal W.S. Caine. This further change in political climate was due to the South African War. In addition to genuinely 'pro-Boer' sentiment, there were many in Cornwall who opposed the war because of the disruption it posed to South African mining and thus Cornish welfare. In fact, it was said of Caine, that '. . . out of 700 Cornish miners home from South Africa, 650 voted for him'.[36] Liberal Unionist support in Cornwall was further eroded as a result of Cornish hostility to the Conservative's education policy (which was thought to undermine the nonconformist 'voluntary' principle), and because of Cornish opposition to plans to use Chinese 'coolies' to restore the Transvaal mines to pre-war levels of production. Cornwall objected to this 'Chinese slavery' (the *Cornubian* newspaper thundered, 'Will you vote for Chinese Slavery? If it be not a kind of slavery, what is it?'),[37] and so the 1906 election returned Liberals in every Cornish seat.

The 1906 election reaffirmed Cornwall as heartland Liberal territory, as did that of 1910. In Britain as whole, however, the years between 1910 and the Second World War were marked by a process in which the Liberals were progressively replaced by Labour as the principal radical alternatives to the Conservatives. The fatal point of Liberal downfall, argues Christopher Cook, was reached in 1924, and by 1929 the Liberal Party had slipped too far behind to be an effective force in British politics. At the same time, religious nonconformity had ceased generally to be a factor in radical politics. As Stephen Koss remarked, '. . . Radical Nonconformity, once a force to be reckoned with in national life, was not dormant but dead',[38] replaced by the secular socialism of Labour. In Cornwall, however, the reverse was true. Against the background of a continuing and deep paralysis in Cornish society and economy, which Labour found difficult to penetrate, the nonconformist vote remained (as Dr Garry Tregidga has described it) 'the key factor in the electoral base of Cornish Liberalism'[39] in the 1920s and 1930s. Indeed, in 1929 one commentator ventured to suggest that Cornwall was '. . . the last refuge of Liberalism'.[40]

Although the years immediately after the Great War had been characterised by the bewildering faction-fighting of 'Asquith Liberals', 'Lloyd George Liberals' and so on, the 1929 General Election (which witnessed a modest Liberal revival in Scotland, Wales and parts of rural England) saw a Liberal victory in Cornwall which was spectacular and complete. In the remaining elections of the inter-war period—1931 and 1935—Liberal representation in Cornwall was reduced swiftly to two and then one (with the newly-formed National Liberals additionally taking St Ives), mirroring their even more disastrous performance elsewhere in Britain. They had, however, secured the consolidation of Cornish politics as principally a Liberal versus Conservative contest. They had also perpetuated the concerns of traditional Cornish Liberal nonconformity such as the local option, Prayer Book Reform, and disestablishment of the Church of England. In the Parliamentary career of Isaac Foot, this traditional Cornish liberalism had a powerful voice. He represented Bodmin for much of the period, monopolising the radical vote (Labour did not save its deposit until 1945), instinctively drawing a connection between Cornishness, Liberalism and Methodism. It is said that at Looe the local fishermen painted their boats in Liberal colours in his honour.[41] In his victorious 1922 by-election, a campaigning song was written— 'And Shall Our Isaac Win?'—sung (inevitably) to the tune of '*Trelawny*'. Meanwhile,

> The scenes on Saturday afternoon at the declaration of the poll beggared description . . . the enthusiasm of Nonconformist farmers, of earnest young preachers, of dark- eyed women and fiery Celtic youth had something religious about it. No such fervour could be seen elsewhere outside Wales.[42]

Here is more than a hint of that inward-looking 'inner life', the boundaries of exclusivity and community drawn sharply. In such circumstances, penetration by Labour was made all the more difficult, even when the Labour cause was taken-up by insiders, such as A.L.Rowse. As Garry Tregidga has noted, Labour politicians in Cornwall generally failed to exploit the potential of a nonconformist connection, and those areas where they had some success (such as local government in the clay country in the inter-war period) was when they were prepared or able to act as a surrogate Liberal Party. A.L.Rowse, conversely, went out of his way to expose what he saw as the futility of Cornwall's isolation from the main arena of political debate, which was the Labour-Conservative contest. He complained later of '. . . backward Cornwall, smothered as it was in Nonconformist Liberal humbug', explaining that 'The prime task for Labour was to bring home the futility of going on being Liberal'.[43] In fact, Rowse nearly pulled it off, in 1935 coming second (with 32.1 percent of the vote) as the Labour candidate in the Falmouth and Penryn constituency, paving the way for Labour's historic victory there after the war.

If the Tories appeared passive onlookers in all this, they had in fact quietly improved their position in inter-war Cornwall. As well as benefiting from the wider problems encountered in Britain as a whole by the Liberals, they had also participated in the general 'rehabilitation' of the Conservatives under Stanley Baldwin. Locally, and perhaps crucially, they had benefited from the tone of Liberal anti-Labour invective, which had had the effect of playing into Tory hands. But if Tory participation seemed modest and unassuming, then the political impact of the newly-emergent Cornish-Celtic Revivalists was positively inert. Not only did they eschew the political nationalism of their Celtic revivalist colleagues in Brittany and Ireland, but generally they failed to recognise or exploit the potential offered by the now very distinctive qualities of Cornish politics. In this, as in other areas, the Revivalists had failed to engage with the Cornish paralysis.

For explanations we must turn, then, to the Cornish-Celtic Revival itself, to place the Revivalist reconstruction of Cornwall within a wider 're-invention' that was already underway. Robert Hunt had hinted at the romantic possibilities of myth and legend against the background of dramatic land and seascapes, a heady mix to which other writers soon added the Cornish

St Juliot church, restored by Thomas Hardy in 1872. In evoking his courtship with Emma Lavinia Gifford, Hardy played a major role in the romantic 're-invention' of Cornwall:

Why go to Saint- Juliot? What's Juliot to me?
Some strange necromancy
But charmed me to fancy
That much of my life claims the spot as its key.

folk themselves. For the novelist and poet Thomas Hardy, this was an intensely personal process, his visit to St Juliot in March 1870 launching him into an intense love affair with Emma Lavinia Gifford, sister-in-law of the local rector.[44] Although Emma was apparently not Cornish in the sense of birth or descent, the couple's courtship was conducted against the strikingly majestic coast and country of that part of North Cornwall. Emma Gifford and Thomas Hardy were married and, although (or perhaps because) the marriage was not a happy one, after Emma's death in 1912 Hardy returned in an act of guilt and remembrance to their earliest haunts. His expiatory poems of 1912 and 1913 are some of the finest that he ever wrote:

> O the opal and the sapphire of that wandering western sea,
> And the woman riding high above with bright hair flapping free-
> The woman whom I loved so, and who loyally loved me.
>
> ---
>
> What if still in chasmal beauty looms that wild weird western shore,
> The woman now is—elsewhere—whom the ambling pony bore,
> And nor knows nor cares for Beeny, and will laugh there nevermore.[45]

Robert Louis Stevenson is rarely associated with Cornwall, and yet his place in its romantic construction is assured. To begin with, there was Stevenson's unequivocal depiction of the Cornish as a people apart. In his *Across the Plains*, written in America in 1879, Stevenson described a journey on the Union Pacific Railroad:

> There were no emigrants direct from Europe—save one German family and a knot of Cornish miners who kept grimly to themselves, one reading the New Testament all day long through steel spectacles, the rest discussing privately the secrets of their old-world, mysterious race. Lady Hester Stanhope believed she could make something great of the Cornish; for my part, I can make nothing of them at all. A division of races, older and more original than Babel, keeps this close, esoteric family apart from neighbouring Englishmen. Not even a Red Indian seems more foreign in my eyes. This is one of the lessons of travel—that some of the strangest races dwell next door to you at home.[46]

A.L.Rowse has commented that 'Stevenson was young, and may be forgiven his ignorance'.[47] However, behind Stevenson's prosaic, even curt disclaimer is the hint of something altogether more mysterious and intriguing. This, perhaps, underpins or at least informs his *Treasure Island*, published a few years later in 1883. Although the setting of the early chapters is never made explicit (except for references to going up to Bristol), there is much in the book that suggests Cornwall. Trelawney, the squire's name, is quintessentially Cornish, as this that of his aged retainer—old Tom Redruth. The hero of the tale is Jim Hawkins, and his surname is also common enough in Cornwall. There is today an *Admiral Benbow* inn in Penzance, a sixteenth-century building with a 'smugglers" tunnel that runs down to the harbour, so popular fancy has decided that Cornwall is indeed the story's setting, whether or not that was Stevenson's intention.[48] Put another way, *Treasure Island* is an early example of a *genre* which slips easily into romantic constructions of Cornwall.

Tregerthen, near Zennor, the cottage rented by D. H. and Frieda Lawrence during their dramatic sojourn in Cornwall.

It seems a giant leap from R.L.Stevenson to D.H.Lawrence. But the two writers had, surprisingly, things in common (including a taste for travel and the exotic), not least their complicated estimations of the Cornish. Lawrence thought them 'afraid' and 'selfish', and he also believed that they possessed a pre-Christian outlook on life which placed them beyond the bounds of conventional ethics and morals. As individuals they were inherently intriguing, even attractive. In an essay intended (but never used) as a prologue to *Women in Love* (1916), he defined a 'strange Cornish type of man' with '. . . dark, fine, rather stiff hair and full, heavy, softly-strong limbs'.[49] In *Kangaroo* (1923), the novel that forever ties Lawrence to Cornwall, his *alter ego,* Richard Lovat Somers, contemplates the landscape of West Penwith:

> . . . the twighlight, awesome world of the previous Celts. The spirit of the ancient, pre-Christian world, which lingers still in the truly Celtic places . . . The old Celtic countries never had our Latin Teutonic consciousness, never will have. They have never been Christian, in the blue-eyed, or even the truly Roman, Latin sense of the word. But they have been overlaid by our consciousness and our civilisation, smouldering underneath in a slow, eternal fire . . . .[50]

Kangaroo is remembered chiefly, in its Cornish context, for the 'nightmare' that he and Frieda experienced in Cornwall during the Great War—the suspicions of the locals (Frieda was, of course, German), Lawrence's illness, the squabbling with their friends, their rows and fights, the humiliation of the conscription examination, and then the final official expulsion from Cornwall. However, there is another way of reading the Lawrences' stay at Zennor, and that it is to set it within the context of the 're-invention' of Cornwall. Suddenly, Lawrence's role becomes important, if not central. Although *Kangaroo* is hardly a romantic novel in the accepted sense, the depiction of Celtic Cornwall is highly romantic. Moreover, Lawrence's sojourn in Cornwall established a set of ground rules which are with us still. First of all, in coming to Cornwall in the first place, Lawrence was seeking a geographical and cultural 'Other', a spot immune from the normal metropolitan pressures where he could establish his Ranamin—his planned Utopian community. In that sense, Lawrence was the original New Age traveller, planting within Cornwall a lifestyle with which we remain familiar today. Secondly, he emphasised Celticity as the root of Cornishness, a Celticity that was pagan and submerged but which was enduring and, for those who sought it, accessible. He also established Cornwall and Cornishness, in a very profound way, as subjects sufficiently sophisticated and significant for sustained treatment in serious literature. And in all this there was room for nostalgia, for the incomer to make a sentimental claim on Cornwall:

> He loved the place so much . . . shall I see the foxgloves come out? If only I can stay till the foxgloves come. And he had seen the foxgloves come. Then it was the heather—would he see the heather? And then the primroses in the hollow down to the sea: the tufts and tufts of primroses, where the fox stood and looked at him.[51]

Again, it seems like an incredible jump from D.H.Lawrence to Daphne du Maurier, but we may also spot some similarities between these two writers.

Daphne du Maurier, in contrast to Lawrence, is identified overwhelmingly with Cornwall, in a string of novels such as *The Loving Spirit* (1931), *Jamaica Inn* (1936), *Rebecca* (1938), *Frenchman's Creek* (1941), and *The King's General* (1946). *Rebecca*, especially, achieved international fame, already re-written for the stage by 1940 (with Celia Johnson cast beautifully in the first production as the second Mrs de Winter), and then the subject of a successful Alfred Hitchcock film. It is easy to characterise Daphne du Maurier as the first of the big-house-with-windswept-woman-on-a-cliff-top *genre* of romantic novel writers, her works the forerunner of the multiplicity of 'Cornish fiction' books that were to appear after the Second World War. However, du Maurier's story-telling is for the most part more sophisticated and complicated than run-of-the-mill romance. It has often a disturbing and unsettled quality, reminiscent of Lawrence's equivocal view of Cornwall and the Cornish (what child has not been terrified by Hitchcock's Mrs Danvers, or indeed his film version of *The Birds*?). As Dr Ella Westland has remarked, 'The loveliest places in "du Maurier country" are not the safest refuges'.[52] We can add, too, that Daphne du Maurier was seeking a kind of personal Ranamin, which she found in her increasingly secluded life at Menabilly, and latterly (and more unhappily) at Kilmarth. If not exactly an upper middle-class New Age traveller, she was certainly a seeker of 'Other'. But in finding personal retreat, she helped popularise a particular view of Cornwall in a way that few others have managed.[53]

If Stevenson, Hardy, Lawrence and du Maurier had set the structure of a particular literary 're-invention' of Cornwall and the Cornish in the years between the end of the nineteenth century and the Second World War, then so too had a parallel movement in the world of fine art. From the 1880s, painters had begun to settle in Newlyn, drawn by both its picturesqueness (people as well as place) and the particular quality of the Penwith sunlight which gave clarity to shape and form and made colours strong.[54] An early arrival was Stanhope Forbes who, crucially, saw in Cornwall a striking physical and spiritual kinship with Brittany. He, like many other young artists of the time, had trained partly in Brittany—in his case, in Concarneau. Indeed, he painted Newlyn as though it were Brittany, expressing—perhaps even creating—in his art a powerful visual similarity between the two. Lawrence's evocation of the Celticity inherent in Cornish landscape and people was philosophical, expressed in words, but Forbes was able to give it physical representation. Cornwall looked like Brittany, and the Cornish and Bretons were also physically alike, and both were Celtic countries and Celtic peoples. Stanhope Forbes continued his work at Newlyn until 1940, spanning almost the entire period under discussion here, and his contribution to the 're-invention' of Cornwall cannot be over-estimated.

Forbes, however, was but one among many artists attracted by the particular qualities of West Penwith. As a Cornish adage of the time put it, 'Cornwall is like a Christmas stocking—all the nuts go to the toe'. In Newlyn itself, significant names included Frank Bramley, Thomas Cooper Gotch, Norman Gartin, and Dod Shaw and Ernest Proctor. Sail lofts were converted to artist's studios, and even as early as the 1880s purpose-built studios had been constructed—such as the celebrated Trewarveneth Studio. At nearby Lamorna Cove, another artists' 'colony' (and they were 'colonies', almost all the artists incomers) grew-up. Here the driving force was John 'Lamorna' Birch, who had lodged at Boleigh in 1890 before moving to Lamorna in 1902. Notable amongst the Lamorna set were Harold and Laura Knight, who had arrived first at Newlyn in 1910. Across the Penwith peninsula at St

St Ives, a fishing port in West Penwith, comprehensively 're-invented' in this century by the Great Western Railway and St Ives Society of Artists.

Ives, similar colonies had also emerged. In 1883-84, Whistler and Sickert had spent several weeks there, and before long one after another of the sail-lofts along Porthmeor beach was being converted in artists' studios. From the beginning, and in marked contrast to the more staid 'realism' of the Newlyn school, St Ives was the home of landscape and abstract artists. Amongst others, it attracted the astonishing 'primitive' painter, Alfred Wallis, who was active between 1925 and 1942.[55] In 1926 the St Ives Society of Artists was formed, 'formal' expression of a distinct school that was by then emerging. Later, the arrival of sculptors, such as Barabara Hepworth and Naum Gabo, gave (quite literally) another dimension to the St Ives school.

A further dimension to the artistic expression of West Penwith was the opening of the Minack Theatre at Porthcurno in 1932, fashioned out of a natural amphitheatre halfway down the steep granite cliff, the brainchild of Rowena Cade. Although given over to Shakespeare, Greek tragedies and modern British plays, rather than being the focus of things specifically 'Cornish', Minack was—like the St Ives school—somehow outlandish and exotic, thoroughly un-English in conception and form. To that extent, it too contributed to the 're-invention' of Cornwall as romantic 'Other', with more than a hint of Celticity lent by the painstaking carving of Cornish crosses and Celtic motifs into its concrete structures.[56]

The early and collective impact of this emerging 're-invention' is demonstrated by the interest it provoked in the developing tourism industry, particularly the Great Western Railway.[57] Cornwall as a surrogate Mediterranean resort was a theme dating back to the early nineteenth-century (when the Napoleonic Wars had closed the real Mediterranean off to the small band of British health tourists), and the intimation of the exotic and the foreign was a successful marketing ploy which advocates of the new Cornish tourism hoped to develop in the closing years of that century. The conversion to standard gauge in 1892 and the opening of the 'Westbury cut-off' in 1906, made Great Western Railway journeys to Cornwall quicker and more convenient, making the 'remoteness' of Cornwall more accessible for potential tourists across Britain. Suitably equipped, the Great Western set about

Period drama at the Minack Theatre.

High speed trains are today's successors of the old Great Western Railway. Penzance is end of the line but gateway to West Penwith.

marketing its own construction of Cornwall, in posters and promotional literature drawing heavily on the visual images already produced by Stanhope Forbes and the Newlyn school.

In fact, the Great Western had set up an advertising department as early as 1886, an unrivalled propaganda machine that was to stay in place until nationalisation in 1948 (the Great Western alone of railway companies survived the Grouping of 1923) and whose vast outpourings have been meticulously chronicled by R. Burdett Wilson.[58] In 1904 the Great Western published *The Cornish Riviera*, written by the prolific topographical author A.M. Broadley, in which Cornwall was portrayed as balmy, foreign, exotic. The first edition ran to a quarter of a million copies; there were a further four editions. In the following year, 1905, the Great Western introduced the Paddington (London) to Penzance *Cornish Riviera Limited*, a train which shot to international fame as a result of the careful publicity with which it was promoted. Great Western propaganda reached its apogee in the inter-war era, with a huge array of jig-saws, trains-spotting books, postcards, and essay competitions for girls and boys. Locomotives were given carefully chosen, evocative names such as *Cornubia, Trelawney, Tre Pol and Pen, Trevithick, Chough, One and All, Cornishman.*

Central to this effort was the production of an impressive series of Great Western posters. Two classic early posters were those released in 1906. The first placed a map of Cornwall alongside that of Italy, separated by two young women in 'national costume'. The map of Cornwall was distorted somewhat to produce a mirror image of Italy (there was no mention of scale), helping to reinforce the paradoxical message 'See Your Own Country First'. As the poster explained ambiguously, 'There is a great similarity between Cornwall and Italy in shape, climate and natural beauties'. The second poster emphasised the physical and cultural similarities of Cornwall and Brittany, depicting Cornwall's St Michael's Mount alongside the very similar Mont St Michel in Brittany. The message was: 'Another striking similarity. Beautiful Britain. Beautiful Brittany'. A second period of vigorous poster production occurred in the late 1920s and 1930s. 'The Cornish Riviera', produced c1925 by Louis Burleigh Bruhl, depicted Cornwall as 'the warmest place in Britain and also as a land of legend, superstition and romance, the home of the wild and imaginative'.[59] Ten years later came

Tregenna Castle Hotel, St Ives— a vehicle for the Great Western Railway's creation of 'The Cornish Riviera'.

Ronald Lampitt's highly distinctive (and eventually very famous) 'mosaic' portrayal of Newlyn, part of a co-ordinated poster campaign to popularise Newlyn, Penzance, Newquay, Looe, Perranporth and St Ives as tourist resorts.

Even more than posters, Great Western guide books served as vehicles for Cornwall as the land of 'difference'. As *Through the Window* (1924) explained:

> . . . Cornwall is so distinct from the rest of England as to seem almost another country. This holds true even if one judges only by such superficial characteristics as the names of railway stations and things seen from the carriage windows. Its truth is emphasised as one probes into history, legend, and folk-lore, into the dead Cornish language and stories of the Cornish saints. Here, indeed, is a part of Britain with a culture and character peculiarly its own.[60]

Brunel's magnificent railway bridge spans the Tamar at Saltash. Although the link with England was completed in 1859, the railway did not exploit the potential for mass tourism until much later.

This theme was echoed in S.P.B. Mais' celebrated *The Cornish Riviera*, first published by the Great Western in 1924 and reprinted on several occasions during the 1920s and 1930s. Mais insisted that Cornwall was '. . . a Duchy which is in every respect un-English . . . the Cornish people are not English people'. Thus, 'You may go there [Cornwall] with the idea you are in for a normal English holiday, and find yourself in an atmosphere of war-locks and pixies, miracle-working saints and woe-working witches'.[61] The Southern Railway, too, whose mainline into Cornwall crossed the Tamar at Launceston and penetrated as far west as Padstow, embraced similar language and images: the visitor is '. . . thrown back five thousand years in the British region where successive centuries have failed to efface all trace of legend and romance. There is rich music in the very place names'.[62]

Together, the Great Western and the Southern created the basis for mass tourism in Cornwall in the years between 1918 and 1939. Notwithstanding the impact of the Great Depression upon the ordinary working man and his family, the holiday habit percolated down the class structure as the century wore on, and the prospect of an exotic, mysterious, Celtic Cornwall, more or less on their doorstep, enticed many thousands of eager visitors. But of course, neither the image-creators nor the intended consumers was Cornish, a telling insight into this whole process of 're-invention'. With the Cornish themselves cocooned in their paralysis, it had been left to outsiders—with motivations of their own—to come up with new constructions of Cornwall. For Dr Philip Dodd, writing in *Englishness: Politics and Culture 1880-1920*, this 're-invention' of Cornwall's identity was inherently colonial:

> The fate of Cornwall at the hands of the colonists may be taken as a metaphor for the general relationship between the Celts and the English. The Celts are licensed their unique contribution to and place in the national culture: the cost is that they know their peripheral place as the subject of the metropolitan centre.[63]

Dr Malcolm Chapman goes further, arguing that the very notions of 'Celt' and 'Celtic' are romantic constructions by (principally English) outsiders, terms designed to give expression to a particular reading of an 'Other'—the indigenous peoples of Cornwall, Wales and so on. As we saw in Chapter Three, 'Celt' and 'Celtic' are notoriously imprecise and difficult as concepts, not least in the rarefied realms of academic scholarship where archaeologists, linguists, anthropologists and others devote much time to disputing each other's definitions, assumptions and perspectives. But, as both Philip Dodd and Malcolm Chapman suggest, in modern times 'Celt' and 'Celtic' have been powerful terms (and tools) in the hands of an England defining its relationship with its island neighbours. Dr Chapman considers that '. . . romanticism created the fringe Celtic minorities as figures of wish-fulfilment, of opposition to the prevailing philosophy and actuality of industrialising England'.[64] Dr John Lowerson has added that where economic change has been experienced in Celtic Britain, '. . . it has been largely prompted by the varying requirements of the English. The role played in modern society by tourism, the consumption of place and desired experience, is but the latest example of this'.[65] Thus in Cornwall the combination of literary, artistic and marketing images of Cornwall had the effect of underwriting a new tourism aimed principally at external consumption.

However, this is not the whole story, for what this approach fails to recognise is the role played in this process by the Cornish themselves. Although John Lowerson considered that 'There is a strong element of local collusion, even of pushing the changes along',[66] the unequal power relationship between Cornwall and England demanding a degree of collaboration, there was in fact a more proactive intervention by a certain Cornish elite with its own particular agenda. Put simply, a small but significant element of the Cornish middle class, aware of the enormity of the situation in which they found themselves in the aftermath of industrial collapse, also proposed to 're-invent' Cornwall—by looking back over the debris of the industrial period to a time when Cornwall was more 'purely Celtic' and thus more 'purely Cornish'. This, essentially, was the project of the Cornish Celtic Revivalists, to break out of the cultural paralysis in which Cornwall had found itself by rebuilding the Cornish identity anew.

The antecedents of this Cornish Revival can be traced back as far Robert Stephen Hawker, vicar of Morwenstow from 1824 until 1874, who, as an Anglo-Catholic, found himself out of sympathy with the nonconformist, utilitarian, industrialist culture of nineteenth-century Cornwall. He was an early critic of industrialisation ('What angel could arrive with duties to perform for that large Blaspheming Smithery, once a great Nation, now a Forge for Railways?')[67] and his poetry had more than a hint of the romantic:

> Hearts of old Cornwall, fare ye well!
> Fast fade such scenes from field and dell;
> How wilt thou lack, my own dear land,
> Those trusty arms, that faithful band![68]

In Matthew Arnold, too, partly-Cornish as he was, we see a glimmer of the themes that would come to characterise the Cornish Revival. In addition to his *The Study of Celtic Literature*, with his attempts to penetrate the Celtic psyche, he inherited from his mother (born at Carwythenack—pronounced Crannick—in Constantine) a Cornish sensibility, expressed in a telling letter he wrote to her from Paris in 1859:

> I could not but think of you in Brittany, with Cranics and Trevennecs all about me, and the peasantry with their expressive, rather mournful faces, long noses, and dark eyes, reminding me perpetually of dear Tom [his brother] and Uncle Trevenen, and utterly unlike the French.[69]

The rural Celtic idyll, with its hint of medievalism, (still, incidentally, expressed in the 1990s by the Cornish Nationalist Party, among others), was one theme which informed the Revival. We see it in the work of 'Q', Sir Arthur Quiller Couch, Cornishman and leading literary figure at the turn of the century:

> Helford River, Helford River,
> Blessed may ye be!
> We sailed up Helford River
> By Durgan from the sea.
>
> O to hear the hawser chain
> Rattle by the ferry there!
> Dear, and shall we come again
> By Bosahan,
> By wood and water fair?
>
> All the wood to ransack,
> All the wave explore—
> Moon on Calamansack,
> Ripple on the shore.
>
> —Laid asleep and dreaming
> On our cabin beds;
> Helford River streaming
> By two happy heads.[70]

There is an identical mood in C.C. Vyvyan (Cornish by marriage, and a fan of Matthew Arnold), with a vague tinge of pantheism, again a feature of some Revivalist writing, as of course is the implied fascination with Cornish-language placenames:

> All day and every day, all night and every night, the [Helford] river receives water, his own life-blood, flowing down to him from beside the homes and hamlets of Traboe, Trewince, Tregevas, Lean, Caervallack, Carabone, Gilly, Meanlay, Chygarkye, Treverry, Zula, Nancemerrin, Mellangoose, Treloquithack, Boswidjack, Carwythenack, Treworvack and Treviades; and twice in every twenty-four hours he goes forth to lose himself in the greater continuity of the sea, taking part in a miracle which is the be-all and end-all and renewal of his own life.[71]

Such literary expression was a far cry from other 'indigenous' writing of the era, such as that of Jack Clemo (reflective as it was of the 'paralysis'), but it would be wrong to assume that the Cornish Revival amounted to no more than a whimsical native sighing over the most secret, silent, darkest places of old Cornwall. The project to rebuild what amounted to 'Celtic-Catholic Cornwall', the Cornwall that pre-dated the Protestant-industrial era, was more sharply driven and had distinct objectives. First and foremost amongst these was a determination to achieve general recognition for Cornwall as a 'Celtic nation'. To this end the Cowethas Kelto-Kernuak (the Cornish Celtic Society) was formed in 1901, a cultural group which attracted distinguished supporters such as Sir Arthur Quiller Couch. Its leading lights were

St Columb Major, birthplace of Henry Jenner, the father of the Cornish Revival who—of English and Scottish parentage—'chose from the first to be Cornish'. The church is dedicated to St Columba.

L.C.Duncombe Jewell and Henry Jenner. Duncombe Jewell's intervention was short-lived but powerful, his somewhat eccentric enthusiasm catching the attention of the literati in Cornwall before his mysterious disappearance from the scene. A romantic anti-industrialist, Duncombe Jewell's vision was quintessentially Revivalist and 'Celtic Twilight' in tone:

> I enjoy, with all its drawbacks the Celtic heritage: the love of poetry and colour, the pilgrimage of dreams, the pageant of nature, the devotion to a fixed star of a principle, the desire to pursue ideas to their logical conclusion, no man withstanding.[72]

Henry Jenner, by contrast, was more practical and more scholarly, the backbone of the Revival over many years. He did, however, cultivate a romantic Jacobitism, and also became a Tridentine Catholic. Born in 1848 in St Columb Major in the heart of Cornwall, Jenner was in fact of English and Scottish parentage. As Robert Morton Nance was to note, it was open to Jenner '. . . to choose any of three nationalities. He chose from the first to be Cornish'.[73] An impressive demonstration of this commitment was the publication in 1904 of his *A Handbook of the Cornish Language*, a guide to the history and structure of the language but also an introductory means to learning it.[74] Although at this stage opposed to language revival as a goal (which he considered to be impracticable), he was anxious for individuals to make themselves familiar with Cornish. Moreover, he considered the Cornish language the foremost badge of Cornish nationality, a conviction that was to inform the activities of Revivalists to the Second World War and beyond. In 1904, the same year that the book was published, he addressed the Celtic Congress on the subject of 'Cornwall: A Celtic Nation', a convincing speech which clinched Cornwall's application to join the Congress and be accepted by its peers as a Celtic country.

Although the Great War cut short the early work of the Revivalists and spelt the end of the Cowethas Kelto-Kernewek, victory in 1918 paved the wave for a further wave of Revivalist activity. As Nance put it, 'With peace it became possible for the idea of Cornish nationality to rise again, and starting inconspicuously the Old Cornwall movement and the Cornish Revival as a whole began'.[75] The Old Cornwall movement was a genuine attempt to bring the Revival closer to ordinary people, to give it a grass-roots dimension, its first Society being formed at St Ives in 1920. By 1924 there were enough Societies across Cornwall for a Federation to be formed, and in 1925 the Federation's journal *Old Cornwall* was launched. *Old Cornwall* is for us an important window into the motives and activities of the Revivalists in this period. There is everywhere a concern to establish and elucidate Cornwall's Celticity. The Cornish language, in particular, was seen as central to this identity. In 1926 W.D. Watson wrote that there was '. . . a great renewal of Celtic thought and feeling . . . we Cornish have but relics of our language, and are small in numbers, yet we have our part to play in the movement'.[76] Five years later readers were told that 'The Cornish language is more and more taking its place as the chief token of Celtic nationality in Cornwall',[77] and in 1932 it was claimed that 'The most Cornish thing in Cornwall is the Kernewek'.[78]

Although Jenner had appeared hesitant about reviving Cornish as a spoken language, the inter-war generation of Revivalists had no such reservations. Paradoxically, Jenner's achievements had inspired the new Revivalists, notably Robert Morton Nance and A.S.D. Smith, who set about reviving Cornish with a will. As well as advocating the use of Cornish as a written and spoken language in as many contexts as possible, they also attempted the full-scale reconstruction of the language. Led by Nance but involving the input of Smith and other Revivalists, this reconstruction produced 'Unified' Cornish. Abandoning Jenner's early view that revived Cornish should be based on Late (or Modern) Cornish, the language as it was last spoken, Nance concentrated on the Middle Cornish texts of the medieval Miracle Plays. As well as providing a wealth of linguistic raw material from which reconstruction might be attempted, the plays were also agreeably pre-Reformation and medieval in ambience, an attractive feature for the Revivalists in their quest to reconstruct Catholic-Celtic Cornwall. However, there were gaps and inconsistencies in the material that the plays provided, so Nance employed techniques of internal analogy and borrowed from Welsh and Breton, synthesising and standardising as he progressed. The resultant Unified Cornish met almost unanimous acclaim amongst the Revivalists, A.S.D. Smith declaring that it was '. . . a compact medieval language . . . and little likely to undergo any further change'.[79] English-Cornish and Cornish-English dictionaries soon appeared, as did guides to learning the language—*Cornish For All* (1929), *Lessons in Spoken Cornish* (1931), and *Cornish Simplified* (1939).

Alongside the language, the Revivalists attempted to acquire or revive as many symbols of nationality as possible. A black kilt was introduced (on the basis that the kilt was an accepted Celtic form of dress, and therefore appropriate to Cornwall), while the black and white banner of St Piran was revived as the Cornish national flag. Described in 1826 by Davies Gilbert as anciently the standard of St Piran and the banner of Cornwall, the Rev W.S. Lach-Szyrma (vicar of Newlyn, and recorder of traditional knowledge of Cornish numbers and counting among local fishing families) had encouraged its flying in the last century. In 1888 the flag was even incorporated into the 'Trevithick Window' in Westminster Abbey. Later, in 1936, *Old Cornwall* opined that, 'If we took to this old cross-banner of Cornwall . . . we should probably have Cornwall more in evidence on occasions when the flags of all nations decorate Cornish streets'.[80] Links with Brittany, suggested by Matthew Arnold and Stanhope Forbes, were also seen as important. The Breton language, so close to Cornish, was still widely spoken, and Brittany had remained faithful to the Catholic faith. Placenames and saint's dedications across Brittany echoed those of Cornwall —Saint-Brieuc, Lannion, Loctudy, Saint Guenole, Landevennec —and were the subject of Canon Gilbert Doble who rediscovered the multiplicity of Cornish-Breton religious connections. In many respects, Brittany was for the Revivalists the perfect model in their quest to build a pre-industrial culture in Cornwall.

Cornish wrestling was similarly taken under the Revivalist wing. Although greatly popular in the mining districts in the nineteenth-century, not least as a result of the exploits of the Cornish champion, James Polkinghorne (born in St Keverne, but renowned as publican of the *Red Lion* in St Columb), the Methodists had taken a dim view of wrestling, considering it an unwholesome sport which was dangerous and might lead to moral degradation. By the turn of the century, therefore, wrestling was in decline (in any case, many of its practitioners were by then overseas). The clay country, however, had remained a reservoir of Cornish wrestling skills and knowledge, and after 1918 there was something of revival, with mid-Cornwall families such as the Chapmans of St Wenn and the Gregorys of St Columb playing a major role in popularising the sport. In one sense this was consistent with

Gwary wkek yu gwary tek—Good play is fair play: these words, in Cornish, are uttered at the handshake that precedes every Cornish wrestling match. In1928 William Tregonning Hooper initiated tournaments between the Cornish Wrestling Association and its counterpart in Brittany.

the consolidation of popular culture described above, the private practice of a private Cornish sport in an atmosphere of making-do, but—in a manner that anticipated in a striking way the alliance of popular and Revivalist culture that was to emerge in the 1980s and 1990s—the inter-war Revivalists assisted in the process. In contrast to the nineteenth-century definition of Cornish wrestling as 'classical', it was now 'Celtic', with a Cornish Wrestling Association dedicated to building links with Brittany (where a similar form of wrestling also survived). W. Tregonning Hooper, a member of one of the traditional 'wrastling' families, took the lead in organising inter-Celtic contests with their Breton counterparts.

In the drive to acquire symbols and institutions, one of the long-term objectives of the Revivalists was the foundation of a Cornish Gorsedd, based on (and affiliated to) the Gorseddau of Wales and Brittany. The Welsh Gorsedd had been 'revived' in the late eighteenth-century, and was already a significant Welsh national institution. Its Breton equivalent dated from the early years of this century, and was altogether more modest. In 1928 the Cornish Revivalists at last realised their aim, establishing with Welsh support and approval a Gorsedd (or College of Bards) into which individuals would be admitted as Bards on account of some distinguished contribution towards the 'national Celtic spirit' of Cornwall. In 1928 and each year subsequently, the Bards thus initiated met in open Gorsedd (usually at a stone circle or some other sufficiently atmospheric ancient monument) to conduct its ceremonial business. Dressed in blue robes vaguely reminiscent of Victorian estimations of Druidic dress, the Bards participated in a ceremony which was a subtle blend of Christianity, pantheism and neo-Arthurianism. Swearing loyalty to Cornwall on the Sword of Arthur (Excalibur), the Bards expressed the symbolic belief that King Arthur was not dead. He had taken the form of a Cornish chough and, at the appropriate moment, would come again.

Sir Arthur Quiller Couch had, like other Cornish notables, been persuaded to put his name to Cowethas Kelto-Kernewek, and he was also one of the early Bards of the Gorsedd. However, he was at times a reluctant Revivalist, his string of novels—such as *The Astonishing History of Troy Town* (1888), *The Splendid Spur* (1889), *The Delectable Duchy* (1893), and *The Ship of Stars* (1899)—expressing themes that were clearly Cornish but only incidentally Revivalist. Moreover, his response to the Revivalist suggestion that one aim might be to stage the medieval Cornish-language Miracle Plays, was that '. . . the audience would have to be play-acting even more strenuously than the actors'.[81] Nonetheless, Quiller Couch was instrumental in the establishment of the Revival in the sense that it was he who facilitated its wider socio-economic context. Responding to the crisis in Cornish mining, in 1898 he had encouraged debate in his *Cornish Magazine* on the future of Cornwall. Reluctantly, he agreed with contributors who thought that the future lay in tourism. As he put it:

The assembled Bards sing *Bo Goth Agan Tasow, Old Land of our Fathers,* the Gorsedd anthem. Together with the Grand Bard of Cornwall and other Gorsedd dignitaries on the dais, are representatives of the sister Gorseddau of Wales and Brittany.

> The suggestion is that Cornwall should turn her natural beauty to account, and by making it more widely known, at once benefit thousands and honestly enrich herself . . . Well then, since we must cater for the stranger, let us do it well and honestly. Let us respect him and our native land as well.[82]

In effect, Quiller Couch's role was to recognise the inexorable movement towards a post-industrial economy, and then to wed this to the post- (or pre-) industrial culture of the Revivalists. Although he was to criticise the Great Western's 'Cornish Riviera' as an 'inexactitude', his own 'Delectable Duchy' came very close as a winning slogan in the new iconography of post-industrial Cornwall. From this perspective, the imagery of the tourist industry seems less the inauthentic imposition of an outsiders' agenda, and more an integral part of a wider process of cultural change aimed at re-defining the Cornish identity in the aftermath of industrial collapse. Put another way, there was in fact a high degree of collusion, sometimes overt, between the Cornish-Celtic Revivalists and the image-makers of the Great Western Railway, in which a significant section of Cornish society participated in the creation of touristic images of Cornwall. In deliberately escaping the cultural paralysis of the early twentieth century, the Revivalists had found themselves

From modest beginnings in 1928, the annual Cornish Gorsedd (Gorseth Kernow) has become a major event in Cornwall's cultural calendar. Here the Girls of Cornwall perform their Flower Dance within the Bardic Circle , perhaps the most picturesque part of the Gorsedd ceremony.

in active alliance with the new image-builders. S.P.B. Mais himself acknowledged this process, writing in the preface to the third edition of *The Cornish Riviera*, for example, that '. . . owing to the kindness of the Cornish Association, the Rev. G.H. Doble, Vicar of Wendron, Mr Trelawny Roberts, and other correspondents I have been able to rectify a few inaccuracies. Such help is invaluable, and will, I hope, be continued'.[83]

However, it was not all plain sailing for the Revival. Not only did it experience the greatest of difficulties in penetrating the paralysis of popular culture (in 1937 one newspaper correspondent lamented 'That if we are truthful we have to admit that the revival of the Gorsedd has scarcely touched the lives of common people in Cornwall'),[84] but elements of the literati remained to be convinced. A.K. Hamilton Jenkin was, like Quiller Couch, another reluctant Revivalist. Although he too was an early Bard, his own writings on the 'bygone' social history of Cornish mining seeming to fit the Revivalist mould, he was at root a mining enthusiast. He knew that the recent history of Cornwall had been determined by the fortunes of mining, accounting as it did for the poverty and unemployment of the inter-war era. He thus protested: 'Though in latter years becoming known as 'England's Riviera', the characteristics of Cornwall are in truth the reverse of tropical luxuriance'.[85] He also objected to the Anglo-Catholic tone of the Revival. The building of Truro Cathedral (with its deliberate Breton ambience) had given a powerful focus for the rising Anglo-Catholic movement in Cornwall. By 1933 the principal Cornish-Celtic saints had been accommodated within liturgical observance in the Anglican Church in Cornwall, and the Rev Bernard Walke (the vicar of St Hilary) spoke for many Cornish Anglo-Catholics when he wrote:

> There was nothing here to kindle the faith that gave to Cornwall so many saints or to light again the fire that burnt so fiercely in the day of John Wesley. Only the worship of the Mass, where time and space have ceased to be the supreme realities, and where bread and wine have become the Body, Soul and Divinity of our Lord and Saviour, to be adored and to be offered by man as the all-pervading sacrifice for the sins of the world, only the Mass could ever hope to win back man to the reality of God's love.[86]

Hamilton Jenkin's concern was that there was '. . . a definite change in the doctrine of the Church itself, and one which has unhappily caused a widening rift between it and the chapels'. He quoted one correspondent who had objected that 'When incense is burnt in Truro Cathedral and Confessions are heard there . . . when the validity of the sacraments is made to depend on episcopal ordination and apostolic succession, then, by implication . . . the Methodists . . . are unchurched'.[87] Such concerns came to a head in 1932 when a group of nonconformist fundamentalists (from outside Cornwall, but encouraged from within) attacked St Hilary church, smashing its candles and pictures and carrying off its 'popish' statues. Shortly after, when Bishop W.H. Frere—who had acquired a reputation as an 'Anglo-Catholic socialist'[88]—left Truro, the Low Church J.W.Hunkin (a former Methodist, and Cornishman) was sent down as Bishop to temper the Anglo-Catholic influence in the diocese.

The suspicions aroused by these Anglo-Catholic undertones reflected a broader inconsistency (if not incompatibility) between the Revivalist agenda and the sensibilities of wider Cornish society. The ideological provenance of the Cornish Revival lay firmly within the wider Celtic Revival, itself the off-spring of a European nationalist ideology which stressed the rights of national minorities to self-government. As the success of the Liberal Unionists demonstrated, there was in Cornwall a suspicion of Irish nationalism, a nonconformist fear of Roman Catholicism which housed a wider Protestant-industrial suspicion of Irish notions of Celticity. As noted in Chapter Ten, on the international stage, where the Irish and Cornish diasporas met face to face, competing interpretations of Celticity were often voiced. For the Irish, to be 'Celtic' was to be both non-British and anti-British. For the Cornish, to be 'Celtic' was to be an Ancient Briton, more the British than the English themselves. In appealing to the establishment in Cornwall, therefore, the Revivalists had to studiously avoid the language of political nationalism, and in making claims to Pan-Celtic sentiment had to emphasise that the motivation was purely cultural. Thus at the Celtic Conference held at Birkenhead in September 1917, Henry Jenner carefully dissociated himself from Welsh and Irish calls for Home Rule, and in 1924 he assured an audience in Truro that the Revivalists had no intention of emulating the Irish slogan Sinn Fein (Ourselves Alone): '. . . their version of them was "One and All", a better motto'.[89]

Thurston Peter, in his 1906 history of Cornwall, had struck the note of conventional opinion, when he wrote:

> . . . at the Pan-Celtic congress of 1904 Cornwall was accepted as a separate nation. If the study of the language can be revived so as to enable us more fully to appreciate the few (sic) remains of its literature it will be very desirable, but we have no desire to see Cornwall aping the larger countries of Ireland, Wales and Brittany in their efforts after what they mistakenly suppose will lead to home rule.[90]

Whether through political astuteness or a natural conservatism, Henry Jenner managed to avoid the nationalist label, and in so doing was able to appeal to Cornwall's learned bodies, especially the Royal Institution of Cornwall but also the Royal Cornwall Polytechnic Society, co-opting them in the Revivalist 're-invention' of Cornwall. In 1933, however, a new Revivalist organisation was launched, Tyr ha Tavas (Land and Language), composed mainly of young people whose 'primary aim is to serve Cornwall and Cornish people'. The group '. . . stands for the unity of persons of Cornish birth or descent who value their Cornish heritage, and who desire to maintain the outlook, individualism, culture, and idealism characteristic of their race'.[91] This sounded alarmingly political, even nationalist, and indeed Tyr ha Tavas did try to pressure local MPs into giving greater consideration to Cornish issues. However, at root Tyr ha Tavas was not a political organisation. Certainly, it had little idea of how it might penetrate the socio-economic paralysis of inter-war Cornwall, and concentrated instead on romantic Revivalist themes. It produced a magazine *Kernow*, which sold more copies outside of Cornwall than within.

Like the broader Revivalist movement, Tyr ha Tavas was ultimately unable to relate to the broad mass of Cornish people and their 'fossilising' Methodist working class culture. The triumph of the Cornish-Celtic Revival was not the moving or mobilising of the Cornish people (which it had singularly failed to achieve) but rather the credible 're-invention' of the Cornish identity in the face of industrial collapse and social paralysis. If we may paraphrase Robert Morton Nance, one generation had re-invented the Cornish identity, it was for another to make it walk.[92]

Notes and References (Chapter 11).

1. Philip Payton, *The Making of Modern Cornwall: Historical Experience and the Persistence of 'Difference'*, Dyllansow Truran, Redruth, 1992, Chapter Six.

2. John Murray and The Survey Committee, *Devon and Cornwall: A Preliminary Survey*, Wheaton, Exeter, 1947, p.175.

3. Murray et al., 1947, p.239.

4. Kenneth Brown and Bob Acton, *Exploring Cornish Mines*, Landfall Publications, Truro, 1994, p.88; for other material on Cornish mining in this period see D.B. Barton, *A History of Tin Mining and Smelting in Cornwall*, Bradford Barton, Truro, 1965, repub. Cornwall Books, 1989, Parts III and IV; John H.Trounson, *Historic Cornish Mining Scenes at Surface*, Bradford Barton, Truro, 1968; J.H. Trounson, *Mining in Cornwall: Volume One*, Moorland, Ashbourne, n.d. c1980; Cyril Noall, *The St Ives Mining District: Volume Two*, eds. Philip Payton and Leonard Truran, Dyllansow Truran, Redruth, 1993.

5. John Rowe, 'The Declining Years of Cornish Tin Mining', in Jeffery Porter (ed.), *Education and Labour in the South West*, University of Exeter, Exeter, 1975, p.67.

6. John Rowe, 'Cornish Mining Crisis in the 1920s', *Cornish Banner*, August 1986.

7. R.M. Barton, *A History of the Cornish China Clay Industry*, Bradford Barton, Truro, 1966.

8. See Murray et al., 1947.

9. Murray et al., 1947, p.192.

10. Leonard Truran, *Thomas Merritt: Twelve Cornish Carols*, Dyllansow Truran, Redruth, n.d; see also, Kenneth Pelmear, *Carols of Cornwall*, Dyllansow Truran, Redruth, 1982; R.H. Heath (ed.), *Cornish Carols*, Browsers Books, Falmouth, n.d.; Philip Payton, *Cornish Carols from Australia*, Dyllansow Truran, Redruth, 1984.

11. See Bernard Deacon and Philip Payton, 'Re-inventing Cornwall: Culture Change on the European Periphery', in Philip Payton (ed.), *Cornish Studies: One*, University of Exeter Press, Exeter, 1993.

12. A.L. Rowse, *A Cornish Childhood*, Jonathan Cape, London, 1942, Jack Clemo, *Confession of a Rebel*, Chatto and Windus, 1949.

13. Jack Clemo, 'The Clay Dump', in Denys Val Baker (ed.), *Cornish Short Stories*, Penguin, London, 1976, p.12.

14. Jack Clemo, *The Bouncing Hills*, Dyllansow Truran, Redruth, n.d., p.9.

15. K.C. Phillips, *A Glossory of Cornish Dialect*, Tabb House, Padstow, 1993, pp.1-2.

16. Henry Harris, *The Luck of Wheal Vor*, Truro, 1901; H.D. Lowry, *Wreckers and Methodists*, London, 1893.

17. Richard Preston, *End of Cornwall*, Jonathan Cape, London, 1937, p.95.

18. Preston, 1937, p.261.

19. Preston, 1937, p.411.

20. *West Briton*, 29 December 1921.

21. *West Briton*, 29 December 1921.

22. Sven Berlin, *Horizons*, 1943.

23. Murray et al., 1947, p.63.

24. Christopher Cook, *The Age of Alignment: Electoral Politics in Britain 1922-29*, Macmillan, London, 1975; Philip Payton, 'Labour Failure and Liberal Tenacity: Radical Politics and Cornish Political Culture, 1880-1939', in Philip Payton (ed.), *Cornish Studies: Two*, University of Exeter Press, Exeter, 1994.

25. E.K.G. Jaggard, 'Political Continuity and Change in Late Nineteenth-Century Cornwall', *Parliamentary History*, Vol.11, Part 2, 1992; Edwin Jaggard, 'Liberals and Conservatives in West Cornwall, 1832-1868', in Philip Payton (ed.), 1993.

26. L.L. Price, 'West Barbary', 1895, in Roger Burt (ed.), *Cornish Mining*, Newton Abbot, 1969, p.130.

27. Bernard Deacon, 'Conybeare Forever!', in Terry Knight (ed.), *Old Redruth: Original Studies of the Town's History*, Redruth Old Cornwall Society, Redruth, 1992.

28. *West Briton*, 24 September 1885

29. Deacon, 1992.

30. Bernard Deacon, 'Attempts at Unionism by Cornish Metal Miners in 1866', *Cornish Studies* 10, 1982; Bernard Deacon, 'Heroic Individualists? The Cornish Miners and the Five-Week Month 1872-74', *Cornish Studies*, 14, 1986.

31. Gillian Burke, 'The Cornish Miner and the Cornish Mining Industry 1870-1921', unpub.PhD, University of London, 1981, p.383.

32. Deacon, 1982.

33. Deacon, 1986.

34. Richard E. Lingenfelter, *The Hardrock Miners*, University of California, Berkeley, 1974, p.6.

35. Mel Davies, 'Collective Action and the Cornish Miner: An Early Repudiation of the "Individualistic" Thesis', in Philip Payton (ed.), *Cornish Studies: Three*, University of Exeter Press, Exeter, 1995.

36. *Cornish Post*, 27 September 1900.

37. *Cornubian*, 20 January 1906.

38. Stephen Koss, *Nonconformity in Modern British Politics*, London, 1975, p.11.

39. Garry Tregidga, 'The Survival of Cornish Liberalism, 1918-45', *Journal of the Royal Institution of Cornwall*, II, Vol.1, Part2, 1992.

40. Cited in Tregidga, 1992.

41. See Sarah Foot, *Isaac Foot: My Grandfather*, Bossiney Books, Bodmin, 1980.

42. *Cornish Guardian*, 3 March 1922.

43. A.L. Rowse, *A Man of the Thirties*, Weidenfeld and Nicolson, London, 1979, pp.55 and 91.

44. See Kenneth Phelps, *The Wormwood Cup: Thomas Hardy in Cornwall*, Lodenek Press, Padstow, 1975.

45. D.M. Thomas, *The Granite Kingdom: Poems of Cornwall*, Bradford Barton, Truro, 1970, pp.37-38.

46. Cited in A.L. Rowse, *The Cornish in America*, Macmillan, 1969, repub. Dyllansow Truran, Redruth, 1991, pp.255-256.

47. Rowse, 1969 and 1991, p.256.

48. See Anon, *Better Pubs in Cornwall*, Better Pubs Ltd., Crediton, 1979, p.49.

49. Cited in Brenda Maddox, *The Married Man: A Life of D.H. Lawrence*, Minerva, London, 1995, p.231.

50. D.H. Lawrence, *Kangaroo*, 1923, Penguin, London, 1975, p.263.

51. Lawrence, 1923 and 1975, p.272.

52. Ella Westland, 'The Passionate Periphery: Cornwall and Romantic Fiction', in Ian A. Bell (ed.), *Peripheral Visions: Images of Nationhood in Contemporary British Fiction*, University of Wales Press, Cardiff, 1995, p.167.

53. For a straightfoward, sympathetic treatment, see Judith Cook, *Daphne: A Portrait of Daphne du Maurier*, Bantam, London, 1991.

54. Caroline Fox, *Painting in Newlyn 1900-1930*, Newlyn Orion, Penzance, 1985; Michael Jacobs and Malcolm Warner, *Art in the West Country*, Phaidon Press, Oxford, 1980.

55. David Brown (ed.), *St Ives 1939-64*, Tate Gallery, London, 1985; Edward Mullins, *Alfred Wallis: Cornish Primitive Painter*, Macdonald, London, 1967; Marion Whybrow, *St Ives 1883-1993: Portrait of an Art Colony*, Antique Collectors' Club, Woodbridge, 1994.

56. Michael Williams, *People and Places in Cornwall*, Bossiney Books, Bodmin, 1985, pp.30-39.

57. Philip Payton and Paul Thornton, 'The Great Western Railway and the Cornish-Celtic Revival', in Philip Payton (ed.), 1995.

58. Roger Burdett Wilson, *Go Great Western: A History of GWR Publicity*, David and Charles, Newton Abbot, 1970, repub. 1987.

59. Beverly Cole and Richard Durak, *Railway Posters 1923-1947*, Science Museum, London, 1992, p.31.

60. Anon, *Through the Window*, Great Western Railway, London, 1924, repub. Peninsula Press, Newton Abbot, 1994, p.7.

61. S.P.B. Mais, *The Cornish Riviera*, Great Western Railway, London, 1924, 3rd ed., 1934, pp.3 and 9.

62. Alan Bennett, *Images of Cornwall*, Cheltenham, 1992, p.68.

63. R. Colls and P. Dodd (eds.), *Englishness: Politics and Culture 1880-1920*, Croom Helm, London, 1986, p.15.

64. Malcolm Chapman, *The Celts: The Construction of a Myth*, St Martins, London, 1992, p.214.

65. John Lowerson, 'Celtic Tourism: Some Recent Magnets', in Philip Payton (ed.), 1994.

66. Lowerson, 1994.

67. A.L. Rowse, *The Little Land of Cornwall*, Alan Sutton, Gloucester, 1986, p.264.

68. A.L. Rowse, *A Cornish Anthology*, 1968, repub. Macmillan, London, 1968, p.276.

69. A.L. Rowse, *Matthew Arnold: Poet and Prophet*, Thames and Hudson, London, 1976, p.12.

70. Arthur Quiller Couch, *Poems By Q*, Oxford University Press, London, 1929, p.96.

71. C.C. Vyvyan, *The Helford River*, n.d., repub. 1986, Dyllansow Truran, Redruth, 1986, p.18.

72. L.C. Duncombe Jewell, 'About Myself and the Cornish-Celtic Movement', *Candid Friend and Traveller*, 5 July 1902.

73. *Old Cornwall*, II:8, Winter 1934.

74. Henry Jenner, *A Handbook of the Cornish Language*, David Nutt, London, 1904.

75. *Old Cornwall*, II:8, Winter 1934.

76. *Old Cornwall*, I:3, April 1926.

77. *Old Cornwall*, II:2, Winter 1931.

78. *Old Cornwall*, II:4, Winter 1932.

79. A.S.D. Smith, *How to Learn Cornish*, Smith, Arundel, 1947, p.20.

80. *Old Cornwall*, II:11, Summer 1936.

81. See Tim Saunders, 'Cornish - Symbol and Substance', in Cathal O'Lain, *For a Celtic Future*, Celtic league, Dublin, 1984, p.256.

82. *Cornish Magazine*, Vol.1, 1895, p.236.

83. Mais, 1934, p.7.

84. Hugh Miners, *Gorseth Kernow: The First Fifty Years*, Gorseth Kernow, Penzance, 1978, p.13.

85. A.K. Hamilton Jenkin, *Cornwall and Its People*, 1945, repub. David and Charles, Newton Abbot, 1983, p.viii.

86. Bernard Walke, *Twenty Years at St Hilary*, 1935, repub. Anthony Mott, London, 1982, p.33.

87. Hamilton Jenkin, 1945 and 1983, pp.199-200.

88. A.L. Rowse, *Quiller Couch: A Portrait of 'Q'*, Methuen, London, 1988, p.199.

89. *People's Weekly*, 23 August 1924.

90. Thurston C. Peter, *A Compendium of the History and Geography of Cornwall*, Houlston, London, 1906, p.202.

91. *Old Cornwall*, Summer 1933.

92. What Nance actually wrote, referring to the language, was 'One generation has set Cornish on its feet. It is now for another to make it walk'. See P. Berrefrod Ellis, *The Cornish Language and Its Literature*, Routledge, London, 1974, p.176.

CHAPTER 12

Into the Next Millennia

CORNWALL

Into the Next Millennia

'Paradox' is a word that arises time and again to explain the complexity of Cornish history, and nowhere is its application more apt than in describing the period since the Second World War. These have been decades of rapid change, for Cornwall but also for Britain, Europe and the wider world. Phrases such as 'the global village' and 'globalisation' indicate a world of intimate international interaction, of mass mobility and mass communication, a world in which the march of Western culture has been in many areas an agency of apparent mass homogenisation. In the 1950s and 1960s, social theorists argued that this process would lead inevitably to more uniform societies, in which the sense of place and local culture was destined to disappear. In some respects these predictions have become true, with individuals living increasingly uniform lives, consuming similar or identical products and tele-visual messages, engaging in similar leisure pursuits.

At precisely the same time, however, there has been a reaction against this 'globalisation'. As individuals and societies have grown more similar, so the differences between them have somehow become more significant. Within the growing integration of the European Union, regions have become increasingly important as foci of economic, cultural and political activity, the apparent move towards European uniformity in fact revealing, even encouraging a vigorous pattern of territorial diversity. In the former Soviet bloc, the collapse of Soviet power swept away the veneer of homogeneity created by the Communist regimes to reveal a bewildering ethnic and territorial complexity. Further afield, Australian society, for example, has shifted from 'Anglo-Celtic' homogeneity towards a new 'multi-culturalism'.[1]

In Britain itself, such trends have been profound. Although once characterised by political scientists and social theorists as the most homogeneous of advanced Western states, an almost text-book example of the 'civic culture' that was supposed to exist in such societies, the United Kingdom has in recent decades exhibited the same diversity that has become apparent in other states. Not only did the Northern Ireland problem re-appear after almost fifty years at the back of the British political consciousness, but the Welsh and Scottish dimensions became more visible and more important. This was not just a question of limited nationalist successes in elections but involved a range of political, socio-economic and cultural behaviour where Wales and Scotland were increasingly at variance with England. Within England itself, there was growing recognition of disparities and differences, prompting a 'North-South debate' in which the historic contrasts between the North and South of England were seen to have been perpetuated into the post-Second World War era. Periodic proposals for devolution or regional government, together with two major upheavals in local government reform, emphasised both the inherent diversity within the United Kingdom and the uncertainties and difficulties experienced by successive British governments in responding to often conflicting demands from different parts of the 'UK estate'.[2]

Intriguingly, contemporary Cornwall has emerged as a microcosm, an exemplar of these wider processes. On the one hand, Cornwall has apparently received the full-force of modernity's homogeneity and globalisation. Only a few years ago it was a matter of pride for some people that Cornwall had neither a *Sainsbury's* nor a *Macdonald's*, but now both are firmly entrenched here. A frenzy of road-building has made Cornwall more accessible, facilitating car-born mass tourism and mass in-migration. The local media, much of it based across the Tamar, tells Cornish people that they live not in Cornwall but in the 'Westcountry' or the 'South West'. Nearly twenty-five years ago, Professor Charles Thomas warned:

> . . . that Cornwall is approaching some sort of internal social crisis. It is increasingly difficult to be Cornish. It is correspondingly important for those who are Cornish, and presumably value their identity, to stand up and be counted . . . If we do not succeed, this little land of ours will end up scarcely distinguishable from the Greater London Area, with undertones reminiscent of Blackpool or Skegness.[3]

Support Canadian and Cornish Fishermen, declare the stickers in scores of Cornish car-windows. At Newlyn the fishermen express similar sentiments, declaring solidarity with their Canadian colleagues in the face of perceived Spanish incursions.

A little over a decade later, a study by Dr Ron Perry seemed to confirm Professor Thomas' worst fears, with Dr Perry concluding sadly that

> . . . the picture that emerges from our study is of a Cornwall swamped by a flood of middle-class, middle-aged, middle-browed city dwellers who effectively imposed their standards on local society. Integration and assimilation was a one-way process—of 'urbanisation' rather than 'ruralisation'.[4]

On the other hand, however, there was considerable evidence of not merely the survival of a separate Cornish identity but of its enhancement in the face of rapid socio-economic change. Politically, not only had the post-war era seen the rise of a small but persistent and relatively successful nationalist movement, but what one may term 'anti-metroplitanism' had become an increasingly important component of political dialogue, reflected amongst other things in a distinctively Cornish pattern of electoral behaviour. The profusion of Canadian flags flown by Cornish fishing-boats at Newlyn, Mevagissey, Looe and elsewhere in protest against the British government's perceived failure to stand up in Europe for Cornish fishing rights, was an expression of anti-metropolitanism as well as an assertion of Cornishness. The determination to ensure that Cornwall was not 'partitioned' in the recent round of local government reform, was as much an expression of territorial identity and the right to collective self-government, as it was of a concern to achieve a system of local administration best suited to Cornwall's needs.

Socially, the impact of rapid socio-economic change disturbed the local network of employment opportunities and gender relations, encouraging the creation of an informal economy amongst the indigenous Cornish. Many young people had to rely on extended family networks to find employment and housing, Professor David Dunkerley and Claire Wallace noting in their study that many youngsters had to devise 'coping strategies' to come to terms with their socio-economic situations. This involved 'both formal and informal work practices, casualization and self-employment',

Shades of 1497 and 1549, if not 1688? *Trelawny's Army* in full-cry at Twickenham, following Cornwall's victory over Yorkshire in the rugby football championship in 1991.

with many young Cornish '. . . socialised into long hours, hard work and poor rewards'.[5] Herman Gilligan detected such characteristics in Padstow, where the indigenous Cornish were increasingly consigned to the council estates where they contrasted their own economic and political powerlessness with the better-equipped in-migrant population attracted by Padstow's reputation as a tourist resort. This, in turn, '. . . enhanced the cultural significance of what it meant to be 'local', and engendered an almost exaggerated sense of Padstonian communal solidarity'.[6] May Day was the opportunity to assert this identity, the 'Obby 'Oss a dramatic cultural icon unequalled anywhere in the repertoire of Cornish symbolism. As the *Souvenir Programme* of the fiercely Padstonian, fiercely Cornish 'Red 'Oss' puts it,

> The bones of every Padstow Boy are fired by the Hobbyhorse. As soon as a child is able to lisp its parent's name it will chant the glorious strains of our ancient Festival Song; and will usher in May's first merry morn, with 'The summer, and the Summer, and the May, O!' And shall we allow aliens and strangers to usurp our pleasures, and rob us of our birth right, that we have inherited from Mother to Daughter, from Father to Son? No we will not! 'Cala Me Bys Vyken'.[7]

On a wider stage, such sentiment was expressed in the behaviour of 'Trelawny's Army', the huge crowds (as many as 40,000 in 1991 and 1992—almost ten percent of Cornwall's population) which travelled to Twickenham on three occasions in the late 1980s and early 1990s to witness the Cornwall rugby football team perform in the County Championship finals. A giant pasty, a giant chough, even a hobbyhorse, combined with a profusion of St Piran's flags and black-and-gold jerseys to present unforgettable displays of Cornishness. In 1989 the *Independent* newspaper considered that 'Twenty thousand Cornishmen used the great ground for a statement, if not of Celtic nationhood, then at least of their distinct identity', while the *Guardian* thought that '. . . the lusty spirit of national independence is alive and flourishing in the undeclared Republic of Cornwall'.[8] In April 1992 the *Western Morning News* went further, exploring the motives of those rugby fans who 'carry the Cornish cause into the capital of foreign England', deciding that '. . . in the reorganisation of power in Britain that must surely come, Cornwall must keep its own identity and should have enhanced power'.[9]

The Blue Ribbon 'Oss has just made its dramatic appearance from the Institute in the centre of Padstow. The *teaser* is working hard.

Although the assertions of Cornishness inherent in the Padstow 'Obby 'Oss or Trelawny's Army (or other demonstrations, such as Camborne's Trevithick Day and the Helston Furry Dance) were in part the reaction of the indigenous Cornish to the pace and scope of socio-economic change, there was also evidence of a high level of assimilation of in-migrants. Many post-war incomers had acquired 'Cornish characteristics', whether consciously or unconsciously, while their off-spring were often proud of their Cornish birth and, of course, were subject to the same socio-economic conditions that socialised the children of more long-established families. Mary Buck found indicators amongst in-migrants which '. . . might be taken as the achievement of a fairly high level of assimilation into a Cornish community . . .'.[10] As Mary McArthur observed, '. . . unless the category of Cornish is submerged (which currently seems unlikely) it is possible that . . . the incomers of today will become (or produce) the Cornish of tomorrow'.[11] This, however, as Peter Mitchell observed, begged the thorny question:

> How do you define Cornish? Does it mean just people born in Cornwall, even if we widen this slightly to include those whose parents are resident in Cornwall but who were unlucky enough to be born in Plymouth? What is the status of people born in Cornwall, but to non-Cornish parents? A possibly much larger group who may or may not be defined as 'Cornish' are those of the diaspora, born of Cornish stock but at one or two generations removed from Cornwall. Cornish Associations world-wide bear witness that Cornish consciousness is not dependent on Cornish birth in a geographical sense.[12]

Indeed, the burgeoning 're-discovery' of Cornish identity within the diaspora, particularly in Australia and North America, was evidence that Cornishness was a function, not of accident of birth, but of ethnic consciousness. Just as those in Cornwall had sought to assert their Cornishness with renewed vigour, so the overseas Cornish—in their own reaction to globalisation, in their own search for roots in the multi-cultural maze of America or Australia—had remembered or acquired their Cornish credentials. Mary McArthur concluded that 'There is evidence of a sharpening of conscious ethnic identity among Cornish people' and explained that 'The Cornish are a named group or community, with a self-awareness (albeit of differing degrees) of a separate identity, being long established in a well-defined territory, and according to this definition do qualify for the label 'ethnic group' or 'ethnic community''.[13] She added, 'It could be argued that the Cornish culture is today indistinguishable from the wider English culture but even if this was agreed (which it is not), the degree of such differences are in any case immaterial'.[14] As she explained, 'It is perception of difference, the importance attached to what may objectively be very small variations, which is relevant . . . it is not the attribute that makes the group, but the group that makes the attribute, important'.[15]

Cornish traditions continue to be passed from one generation to the next. Here youngsters perform the Children's Dance at Helston Furry Day (8th May).

The experience of the Cornish since the Second World War, then, has mirrored that of other ethnic-territorial communities—in the United Kingdom and elsewhere. Despite the apparent evidence of homogenisation, even assimilation, in which it seemed that Cornwall was rapidly becoming more or less like anywhere else, the reality was that Cornwall had not only remained 'different' but was in fact asserting that difference with renewed vigour. It is interesting that, while insiders such as Charles Thomas and Ron Perry had bemoaned the demise of Cornish distinctiveness in the face of overwhelming socio-economic change, for outsiders it was often the resilience of Cornish identity that was remarkable. Thus Colin Rallings and Adrian Lee could note that '. . . the historical and cultural distinctiveness of Cornwall has been eroded less by the pressures of the late twentieth century than one might expect', and that politically there was '. . . a relatively strong sense of Cornish identity or Cornish consciousness, and a growing sense of anti-metropolitanism'.[16] Equally telling was the small minority of newspaper correspondents who, with calculated malevolence, responded to expressions of Cornish distinctiveness in angry retorts which insisted that Cornwall was no different to a Hants or Herts. Little did such correspondents realise that their vitriol itself bore witness to such distinctiveness; they protested too much.

To elucidate this intriguing paradox of sweeping change but persistent identity, it is necessary to review the complexity of socio-economic, cultural and political development since the Second World War. Although these were areas that were until recently sadly under-researched, there has been consistent progress of late, much of it reported in the series *Cornish Studies* and in the major compendium, *Cornwall Since The War*.[17] The latter examines in detail issues such as economic change (including the rise of 'opposition' economics), mining, tourism, demographic change, housing, the family, questions of territory and identity, political parties and elections, language revival, and literature. Published in 1993, it represents an extraordinary snap-shot of life in a far-flung European region in the final half-century of this millennium.

The Second World War itself appeared to herald changes in Cornish society, disturbing for a time the paralysis into which Cornwall had sunk. There was an influx of evacuees, workers in key occupations, Service personnel (including Americans in the build-up to D-Day), and—as the war drew to a close—Polish and Italian miners. Economically, the war provided a boost to manufacturing in Cornwall, especially in the Truro district where there were increases in shipbuilding, engineering, metalwork, woodwork, and textiles as a result of war demand. The impact was transitory, however, and by 1947 'Certain types of regional production which were inaugurated or expanded during the war will have been drastically restricted, or closed down'.[18] In particular, 'Firms evacuated to the region will return rather than stay . . .', while 'The stoppage of war contracts will appreciably curtail employment'.[19] The Exeter survey considered that 'The prospects for employment in tin-mining are not roseate', while Camborne-Redruth and Hayle were threatened by '. . . the decay of tin-mining, by contraction in the export of mining engineering and reduced activities in textiles and other mineral working'.[20]

From such a perspective, Cornwall seemed destined to return to the all-pervading paralysis that had characterised its socio-economic life in the half century and more before 1939. Indeed, the evidence of the early to mid 1960s suggested that this was in fact the case. Unemployment in the

Camborne-Redruth district was consistently two or three times the UK national average, while in early 1964 the unemployment rate in Falmouth was some 20 percent. Geoffrey Moorhouse pondered such statistics and concluded gloomily that 'Unmistakably Cornwall is in a fix'.[21] And, in a penetrating analysis which revealed the inherent spatial imbalance in post-war British economic development, he explained how in the apparent boom between 1952 and 1960, the South East of England—with 27 percent of Britain's population—had acquired 40 percent of the newly-created jobs in the UK as a whole. Cornwall was firmly excluded from this 'Golden Circle', as Moorhouse called. 'How many', he asked rhetorically, 'are aware that by far and away the highest rate of unemployment . . . is not to be found in the North-east or along Merseyside, but in Cornwall?'[22]

In response to the alarming territorial inequalities that were by then apparent, the Wilson (Labour) government of the mid 1960s expanded the provision of 'regional development' measures to try to shift the focus of economic activity from the 'overheating' South East to more far-flung parts of the United Kingdom. Earlier post-war governments had introduced such policies but it was in the Wilson period that regional development assumed its place in the forefront of governmental concern, becoming an article of faith for both Labour and Conservatives (at least until the Thatcher era), its aim being to '. . . seek to reduce or eliminate disparities between different geographical areas in incomes, industrial growth, migration, and, above all, unemployment'.[23] To achieve this, the strategy was to identify specific areas requiring assistance (normally on the basis of high unemployment rates) and then devise incentives for firms to move to those areas. Development Areas were thus set up in 1966, based on the 'standard regions' of the United Kingdom devised by the Wilson government (Cornwall was part of a highly amorphous South West also including Devon, Somerset, Dorset, Wiltshire and Gloucestershire). In 1967, Special Development Areas were introduced to deal with localities with especially acute problems, and in 1969 the further category of Intermediate Area was introduced.

Cornwall emerged from this blend of provisions as an area attracting considerable assistance. The Falmouth-Camborne district was, for the greater part of the 1960s, 1970s and early 1980s, a Special Development Area, while almost the whole of the rest of Cornwall was designated a Development Area. Practical evidence of the impact of regional development policy in Cornwall was manifested in the appearance of so-called Advanced Factory Units, units built with government assistance to house relocating firms. New industrial estates sprang up across Cornwall; by 1984 there were no fewer than 49 such estates. Dr Derek Spooner considered this to be 'a minor industrial revolution' and concluded that 'The changes that are taking place do not appear to be temporary, but are creating a genuine long term transformation of the regional economy'.[24]

The experience of the late 1960s and early 1970s, then, appeared to suggest that regional development policies had been successful in lifting Cornwall from its erstwhile paralysis, reversing once and for all the protracted decline of the past hundred years. However, this apparent success had occurred against the background of economic growth in the United Kingdom as a whole, with regional development policy the mechanism for siphoning-off some of this growth in the direction of Cornwall. When the oil price rises of the mid 1970s plunged the British and other Western economies into renewed recession, the parlous position of Cornwall and the illusory (even deleterious) impact of regional development policy were exposed. As D. Grafton and N. Bolton observed, even in the early 1970s, the growth in employment in Cornwall had not been matched by a reduction in the numbers of unemployed (a function of in-migration),[25] while in 1979 a government report *Unemployment in West Cornwall* noted that 'Unemployment in West Cornwall has in recent years been much higher than that experienced in most other parts of the country. Since 1974 . . . the position had worsened'.[26] In Cornwall as a whole there was a net decline in manufacturing jobs between 1976 and 1982, with 4,000 lost and only 2,000 created. Between 1976 and 1981 there was a loss of a further 1,000 jobs in extractive industries (mainly in china clay), and in 1981 there was the symbolic closure of the Rank Radio factory at Pool, near Redruth, the very first Advanced Factory Unit to have been opened in Cornwall.

To this gloomy picture in manufacturing and employment was added the fact that Cornwall had remained a low wage economy. Many of the lowest paid jobs were in the tourist and service sectors. Many were part-time, short-term or seasonal in nature, and many were filled by women who, in turn, were skewed towards the younger/older age ranges and had generally a history of irregular employment. Professor David Dunkerley and Dr Ingrid Faerdon found low aspirations and low expectations amongst such people, and observed:

> There exists a large pool of available labour that can be tapped and untapped at will. This labour force is generally willing to work for low wages and with minimal security. Its low expectations and low collectivism make for a very malleable group who, if dissatisfied, can easily be replaced by others from the pool. What exists is a profile of seasonal workers who are dependent on this form of employment, who have few means of escape from their situation, whose resignation to the situation derives directly from the situation but which, equally, leads to them colluding in their own exploited position.[27]

By the mid 1980s Derek Spooner's estimation of a permanent reversal of Cornwall's economic position was no longer credible. By 1989 the Plymouth Business School was drawing what it saw as a sharp distinction between Cornwall and the rest of the South West standard planning region. Thus while 'The South West Region . . . is regarded as prosperous by UK standards . . . Cornwall is one of the most economically depressed [areas] in the whole of the UK', a fact demonstrated in the presentation of major economic indicators from average gross weekly earnings to the growth of new businesses, in which 'Cornwall not surprisingly . . . comes last'.[28] However, Dr Spooner had been correct in suggesting that something profound had happened to the Cornish economy, for although it had not been brought (as he had imagined) to the same condition as that of the South East of England, it had acquired a new set of characteristics. Principal amongst these were the 'branch factory' phenomenon and mass in-migration (or 'counterurbanisation', as it was known).

Ronald Perry was able to show that 60 percent of manufacturing growth in the 1960s and 1970s was of the branch factory type, a phenomenon encouraged by regional development policies which had enticed large companies to set up outposts in areas such as Cornwall. Dr Perry went on to demonstrate that a further 50 percent of manufacturing in Cornwall was brought under outside control in this period, so that by the end of the

1970s a full three-quarters of Cornish manufacturing personnel was controlled from beyond the Tamar. Even Holmans, the former flagship of Cornish mining engineering, fell victim to this process, becoming part of an international corporation. Later, English Clays Lovering Pochin, by far the major employer in the china clay country, was to move its international headquarters from St Austell to Reading, outside London. Like Doreen Massey and others who had perceived in the branch factory phenomenon a 'spatial division of labour', in which regional economies exhibited features such as low wages and seasonal unemployment while top jobs and decision-making powers were located in the 'centre', Grafton and Bolton argued that Cornwall had become even more dependent on outside influences as a result of regional development policies.[29] In times of economic downturn, it was the branch factories that were the first to close. As Gyorgi Barta and Alan Dingsdale observed, the apparent increase in employment, infrastructure and standard of living in Cornwall had 'largely been achieved by the extension of a branch-plant network and not locally based initiative';[30] hence its fragility and transitory nature.

Significantly, the perception of an increasing standard of living and greater prosperity had been enhanced by the phenomenon of counter-urbanisation, the mass in-migration which from the late 1960s had halted the century-long process of population decline. Between 1961 and 1981 the population of Cornwall increased by an extraordinary 25 percent. Although the 1980s were a time of recession, the rate of in-migration continued, with exceptional peaks in 1983-84 and 1987-88 when annual net migration soared to over 8,000. The creation of the branch factory economy had encouraged in-migration, bringing in managers and key workers to establish the new plants. Perry considered that there was strong evidence that newcomers were taking the best jobs, and a survey in 1982 indicated that over one-third of skilled workers in Cornwall were in-migrants.[31] The South West Economic Planning Council (SWEPC), an arm of central government regional development policy, considered that population growth was a necessary accompaniment of socio-economic regeneration, and had also encouraged in-migration. Initially, 'Overspill' schemes had assisted the relocation of Londoners in places such as Bodmin, and later (as evidenced in Cornwall County Council's *West Cornwall Study* in 1970) the emphasis moved to the 'voluntary' (as opposed to planned) encouragement of in-migration. The *Structure Plan* produced by Cornwall County Council in 1980 echoed the conventional wisdom that economic recovery and population growth were inextricably entwined and would proceed hand-in-hand.

However, even as this strategy was being articulated, Cornwall's branch factory economy was already faltering. The continuing rise in population was met, therefore, by rising unemployment. One of the curiosities of this experience was that, despite the onset of recession in Britain as a whole, and despite the falling job opportunities in Cornwall, people kept coming. This indicated that, whatever the impact of branch factories and regional development policies, there were also extraneous factors at work. Dr Perry had identified strong environmental reasons for many relocations to Cornwall, with people anxious to 'escape the rat race' and to seek a quieter, saner 'small is beautiful' way of life. Some people sought the idyllic Cornwall that they remembered from care-free childhood holidays, others were more determinedly New Age in their philosophies. There were, of course, retirees amongst this wave of in-migrants but, as Dr Perry also showed, the greatest increases were in the working-age population. Between 1971 and 1981, for example, the 30-39 age group in Cornwall had increased by an incredible 40%. But many had come to Cornwall in search of life-style rather than jobs, contributing to what Perry called 'imported unemployment'.

An interesting commentary on this idealism was conveyed in a later study by Malcolm Williams and Eric Harrison.[32] They showed that although in-migrants were normally 'better-off' than the locals on arrival in Cornwall, ten years on their economic fortunes had often come to resemble those of the indigenous Cornish. Those who had come to Cornwall for professional reasons (to take up a job) had generally done well but those who had moved for life-style reasons (often selling a house or business in the process) were less successful in economic terms. In housing, similar trends were observable. As Carol Williams indicated, in general terms 'in-migrants' had an advantageous position in the Cornish housing market, especially if they had sold properties elsewhere before moving here, but that this advantage was eroded with the passage of time.[33] Be that as it may, in the mid to late 1980s there was real trauma in Cornwall as buoyant houses prices in London and the South East allowed prospective in-migrants to sell their homes there for handsome profits, facilitating a move to Cornwall which would still leave cash in the bank. As one property advertisement put it in August 1987, 'For the price of a poky flat or a boring semi, you could move to Cornwall, buy one of these super properties AND have a fistful of change'.[34] Although, as Perry had shown, in-migrants had shown a marked preference for 'attractive' areas such as the Lizard, Carbis Bay and Feock, one major estate agent admitted in December 1987 that, throughout Cornwall, local first-time buyers were 'almost getting squeezed out'[35] of the Cornish housing market.

Although the rapid and wide-ranging socio-economic changes of the post-war years had, to say the least, made life difficult for the indigenous Cornish, there were—from the perspective of the Cornish identity—two 'positive' outcomes. First of all, those changes had underlined and perpetuated Cornish 'difference'—despite the hopes of Spooner and the fears of Perry and Thomas, Cornwall had not become a carbon-copy of the South East of England. Secondly, in the manner identified by Mary McArthur, socio-economic change had led to a sharpening of Cornish ethnic identity. This, as we have seen already, was expressed culturally (not least in Trelawny's Army) but it also acquired a political edge, prompting critiques of existing socio-economic policies and offering alternative strategies.

As we saw in Chapter Eleven, the Cornish-Celtic Revival in the decades before the Second World War was de-politicised, eschewing notions of Celtic nationalism and failing to take advantage of the distinctive qualities of Cornish politics. In the years after 1945, however, the distinction between culture and politics became blurred as the Revivalists broadened their horizons. To begin with, the symbolism of the Revival—the kilt, the recently-invented tartan, St Piran's flag, the revived language, the Gorsedd—was increasingly potent, strongly suggestive (as it promoters had intended it to be) of separate identity, even separate nationhood. Such cultural assertion was inherently political, as those who in 1985 argued successfully for the flying of St Piran's cross at County Hall in Truro, no doubt realised. Such institutional acceptance was highly significant, signalling advance from the margins to the mainstream, demonstrating the authority that Cornish iconography could command. Even more political was the demand for a Cornish postage stamp, voiced periodically in the 1960s and 1970s by those who argued that—as regional stamps had now been issued for Scotland, Wales and Northern Ireland (and as the Isle of Man and Channel Islands had their own stamps anyway)—Cornwall should have its own set too. Although this campaign proved unsuccessful, the support that it was able to muster (including local MPs who were prepared to ask questions in the House of Commons) indicated that Cornish distinctiveness was acquiring an overtly political dimension.[36]

Revivalist literature and literary performance also acquired a more overtly political flavour. In 1950 a much-trumpeted public performance of an extract from *Beunans Meriasek* was described by a BBC commentator as 'nationalist' in ambience and presentation.[37] In the 1970s Donald R. Rawe, novelist, playwright and publisher, produced a string of modern plays which were uncompromisingly evocative of the medieval miracle play tradition, intentionally drawing a connection between it and contemporary Cornish culture. The opening speech of *The Trials of St Piran* had a powerful resonance:

> We meet at this Round, this Plen-an-Gwarry,
> This gathering place of Cornish men in times
> Past, present and future: an amphitheatre
> Where all the hopes of grace and fears of death,
> Hell's torments and the shining joys of heaven
> Are made apparent, by the actor's skill, to them
> Who watch the mysteries ordained by God.[38]

Critics decided that Donald Rawe was 'becoming synonymous with a Cornish National Theatre'.[39] John Hurst, however, doubted whether there was such a thing as a distinctively Cornish 'school' of literature. There were 'foreigners' such as E.V.Thompson (author of *Chase The Wind*) and Winston Graham (of *Poldark* fame), and native Cornish writers such as Charles Causley ('all Cornwall is knocking at my door'), who individually might strongly evoke Cornwall. But there was nothing to draw them together. Even D. M. Thomas who, according to Hurst, 'catches the texture of Cornish life unerringly', was '. . . too singular, too rooted in the pursuit of his own obsessions, to provide a recognisable voice for Cornwall'.[40] However, by the late 1980s and early 1990s the 'Cornish novel' had made a reappearance in the guise of strong contemporary writing from the pens of Roy Phillips, Myrna Combellack and Alan Kent.[41] Although still echoing elements of that fatalistic edge recognisable in early twentieth-century Cornish fiction, this new work demonstrated something like a unity of theme and purpose, suggesting that in the literary reaction to all the changes that had overtaken Cornwall since the war, there was perhaps a new coalescence—a Cornish school in the making. There was a similar trend observable in Cornish poetry, notably in the work of Bert Biscoe, Pol Hodge and Alan Kent, whose *Modern Cornish Poets* was a collection where 'Even the personal or domestic take on broader political or historical meaning . . . poetry must get its hands dirty if it is to take on the enemy and help preserve the Cornish culture'.[42] Kent's 'Boscawen Street' sums up many a Cornish attitude to Truro:

> From England they were,
> young and lovely with laughter on their shapely lips.
> The sun's soft kisses on them still

after the moistness left by the sea,
a delicate music my ears could not properly hear,
and I felt some kindness towards them in my heart -
I understand how difficult it is for them
to know a Cornishman's wishes.[43]

The impressive publishing house of *D. Bradford Barton* of Truro, which grew rapidly in the 1960s and 1970s, exemplified a particular kind of regional publishing, rooted in local subjects and exhibiting regional pride and regional distinctiveness. There was, however, in Donald Rawe's *Lodenek Press,* a more overt agenda aimed at creating a Cornish national publishing industry, a strategy pursued with even greater energy and determination by Leonard Truran in the astonishing growth of his *Dyllansow Truran* publishing house. From Cornish language to local history, *Dyllansow Truran* attracted well-known literary and academic names such as A.L.Rowse and Roger Burt, as well as assisting the work of numerous other writers on Cornish themes to at last see the light of day.

The Cornish language remained an important icon of Cornishness (in the 1990s, Cornwall County Council even adopted the motto *Onen hag Oll*—One and All—on its ubiquitous logo), although sadly the consensus of the inter-war and early post-war years had been lost by the 1980s. In the face of sustained criticism from academic Celticists, who questioned the means by which Robert Morton Nance had constructed his Unified Cornish, Cornish language enthusiasts looked again at their assumptions, aspirations and methodologies. Dr Ken George decided that revived Cornish should continue to be based on the Middle Cornish of the medieval Miracle Plays. However, he considered it important to discover how Cornish might actually have been pronounced in that period (c1500), and devised a complex computer program to assist him in the process of discovery. Having established that pronunciation (to his satisfaction at least) he set about devising a 'phonemic' orthography (spelling) which might accurately represent it. The resultant system was known as Kernewek Kemmyn (Common Cornish), and was adopted by the Cornish Language Board in 1987. However, this decision did not meet with universal approval and, from the being the umbrella body charged with the welfare of the language revival as a whole, the Cornish Language Board found itself recast as a pressure group advocating one particular form of revived Cornish.[44]

Other Cornish enthusiasts had been drawn to the work of Richard Gendall who, in contrast to both Robert Morton Nance and Ken George, had looked for his model for the future in the Cornish language as it was last spoken and written. Arguing that the accent and intonation of West Penwith today held important clues to how Cornish was pronounced in its Late stages, Gendall compared the contemporary pronunciation with that recorded by Edward Lhuyd during his visit to Cornwall c1700. He considered that there was a high degree of correlation between Lhuyd's findings and the modern speech of West Penwith, and argued that the historical proximity of Late Cornish made it especially attractive to contemporary learners. A Cornish Language Council was formed to foster this Modern Cornish (as Gendall and his supporters had dubbed it), establishing its own network of language classes and founding a magazine, *An Garrack*. Meanwhile, Ken George's Kernewek Kemmyn had attracted considerable criticism, not only from those who considered its hypothetical spelling an aesthetic disaster (for example, Camborne emerged from the linguistic mangle as Kammbronn) but from Celticists who expressed serious reservations with regard to George's methodology and findings. At the same time, advocates of Unified Cornish found strong support in the work of Dr N.J.A. Williams who insisted that, after all, the language revival was best developed from the work of Nance.[45] While all this was going on, language classes kept their collective heads down, avoiding the 'flak' as individuals strove to pick up a working knowledge of everyday Cornish:

Rigo whye gwellas an telly nehuer?	Did you see the telly last night?
Reeg angye doaz avare?	Did they come early?
Reeg an gathe eva an leath?	Did the cat drink the milk?
Reeg e perna keaz?	Did he buy any cheese?
Riga ve danen photo tha whye?	Did I send you a photo?[46]

Although this conflict and confusion caused uncertainty for potential learners and did not always show language enthusiasts in the best light, the fact that there was a language revival at all spoke volumes about the nature of modern Cornwall. Bernard Deacon, in defending the revival, considered that the so-called language debate between supporters of competing versions of the language was a symptom of postmodernist uncertainty, to be understood rather than condemned.[47] Professor Charles Thomas felt that, despite the criticisms of Celtic scholars,

> . . . the achievements of Henry Jenner, Robert Morton Nance, and their contemporaries, was the establishment of a sense of Cornishness, of national consciousness . . . had this overall Cornish Revival not been attempted, and accomplished, it would by now be quite impossible to construct the particular platform on which the linguistic, cultural, nationalistic, and environmental movements in Cornwall all perform.[48]

Elsewhere, notions of Celticity and Celtic identity were also leading to potential conflicts of interpretation, and to new avenues of expression. Denys Val Baker had claimed that '. . . you need be neither a Celt nor an artist to be aware of the strange and compelling powers embodied in Cornwall's granite body',[49] an intimation that Celtic *vibes* were by no means the exclusive property of the indigenous Cornish and could be experienced and expressed by anyone with the appropriate level of sensitivity and empathy. As Ronald Perry had discovered, many of those post-war in-migrants attracted to Cornwall had come in search of their personal Ranamins, to a greater or lesser degree New Age travellers intent on escaping the pressures of degenerate England. Their objective was often a hazy mixture of latter-day Celtic Christianity and Celtic neo-paganism. In one sense, even John Betjeman was part of this seductive process. He implored 'Oh good St Cadoc pray for me/Here in your cell beside the sea', and

> At 'Holy! Holy! Holy!' in the Mass
> King Brychan's sainted children crowded round,
> And past and present were enwrapped in one.[50]

The work of Paul Broadhurst and John Michell has done much to popularise the spirituality of place in present-day Cornwall.[51] Ancient stones are again the focus of pilgrimage and ritual (devotees gather for the

The Saints' Way between Padstow and Fowey, like St Michael's Way between Lelant and Marazion, is evidence of a renewed enthusiasm for 'Cornish Celticity' and pilgrimage routes.

summer solstice at the Hurlers), and holy wells are venerated as they were in ancient times—a visit to Madron or Sancreed, with their cluties and votive offerings, can be an arresting experience. A correspondent in the *Cornish Banner* caught something of the New Age, alternative life-style flavour inherent in such Celticity, writing 'My family and I were at the Newbury Bypass Trees protest . . . and almost everyone there admitted to being Celtic—it seems that the battle between the Celts and the Romans is far from over!'.[52] Or, as John Lowerson put it, 'In the spectrum of modern Celticism, Cornwall has come almost to represent a British Tibet; distant, valued by outsiders and threatened by an occupying power'.[53] Dr Lowerson also noted the appeal of such Celticity within a re-defining Cornish tourism. Although, as Dr Paul Thornton had shown, the tourist industry in Cornwall had been generally slow in responding to changes in what John Urry has called the 'tourist gaze' (the distinctive or unusual that draws visitors to a particular destination), there was nonetheless a discernible movement towards cultural and heritage tourism in the 1980s and 1990s.[54] However, this movement itself had its critics, John Lowerson warning that:

> When trekking in Nepal was opening up in the 1970s, a native Buddhist observed: 'Many people come: looking, looking, taking picture: Too many people. No good . . . Some people come, see. Good'. It might serve to describe the impact of the neo-Celtic tourist on Cornwall as it [Cornwall] tries to cope with an identity some of its residents have helped to create and a spiritual hunger which threatens its ascribed isolation.[55]

The issue, however, was not so much one of numbers (Cornwall had become long-since inured to the invasions of mass tourism) but of 'moral geography'—the ways in which a particular landscape might read, the cultural values it embodied and reflected, the senses of ownership it evoked, the contested limits of its usage and development. The establishment of New Age 'traveller' colonies in the 1980s and 1990s had in fact provoked confrontation with local communities across Cornwall, from Crowan to St Cleer, villagers expressing little sympathy for an alternative Celticism which seemed to threaten the normal rhythm of Cornish life. More formal modes of cultural and heritage tourism were also contentious, not least those which intended to conserve hitherto derelict mining landscapes as leisure and educational amenities. A survey by the Cornwall Archaeological Unit in 1990 identified the so-called 'mineral tramways' country around Camborne and Redruth as a suitable case for treatment, noting that 'By contrast with other parts of Britain, Cornwall has not exploited the tourist asset offered by its archaeological and historic sites', adding that 'The industrial and archaeological heritage of the county could and should be a valuable educational resource'.[56]

Madron holy well — object of veneration for the 'neo-Celtic tourist' with his or her subtle blend of Celtic Paganism and Celtic Christianity.

Various organisations were established to assist in such work. Although they secured the timely conservation of numerous engine houses which otherwise would shortly have fallen victim to the depredations of Cornish weather, as well as preserving and making more accessible an impressive array of industrial archaeological features, the sheer scope of their ambitions caused some alarm. A fear that a hitherto wild, dramatic, inherently Cornish landscape was being sanitised and anglicised, made safe and familiar for Home Counties refugees, was complemented by a more diffuse sense

Water-sports have become increasingly popular amongst tourists and Cornish alike, and Cornwall is an international venue for both surfing and gig-racing competitions. Here sailboards lie scattered on the beach at Marazion during the British National Windsurfing Championships.

that the Cornish were somehow losing control of their landscape, its resources and destiny. Adrian Spalding called for sensitive and careful treatment of Cornwall's metaliferrous mine sites, reminding observers that they were highly distinctive wildlife habitats as well as of archaeological importance.[57] Bert Biscoe wrote:

> I read their dead interpretations
> and leaf their glossy publications
> at tables in white wine and cheesy receptions
> where I fall silent, from anger
> and fear of archaeological revelation . . .
> a Cornishman in their clinking midst.[58]

That such issues of contemporary identity had become so highly politicised, indicated the extent to which industrial Cornwall had been rehabilitated in the estimation of the Cornish-Celtic Revivalists. To many of them, the industrial landscape now mattered enormously. In marked contrast to the pre-war Revivalists, the generation after the Second World War had proved readier to include the iconography of industrial Cornwall within their ideological embrace. A.K. Hamilton Jenkin's *The Cornish Miner*, first published as early as 1927, had anticipated this rehabilitation, but it developed apace after 1945. The foundation of the Cornish Engines Preservation Society and, later, the Trevithick Society, expressed both popular and academic interest in the nature of industrial Cornwall. John Rowe's *Cornwall in the Age of the Industrial Revolution*, published in 1953, put this interest on the wider academic map, as did the succession of books from the pen of D. Bradford Barton. The Revivalists themselves were happier to include Cornish boilers, Cornish engines, Cornish stamps, in their repertoire of Cornish symbolism, alongside Celtic crosses and miracle plays and newly-invented icons such as the Cornish tartan.[59]

This rehabilitation led, in turn, to a new synthesis of Revivalist and popular culture in Cornwall. At County Championship rugby matches, for

Sun, sea and sand at Summerleaze Beach, Bude, the traditional image of holiday-making in Cornwall.

Goin' up Camborne 'ill, Comin' down! Traction engines prepare for their grand parade through the centre of Camborne on Trevithick Day (the last Saturday in April), an opportunity to remember Richard Trevithick and to celebrate the engineering heritage of Cornwall in general and Camborne in particular.

example, traditional symbolism such as the wearing of black-and-gold or the singing of 'Trelawny' and 'Camborne Hill', increasingly co-existed alongside Revivalist symbols such as St Piran's flag and the use of the word 'Kernow' on caps and sweatshirts. A similar, increasingly unselfconscious synthesis was also observable at Camborne's annual Trevithick Day, where steam engines and male voice choirs co-existed quite happily with Breton folk dancers. This synthesis was important, because it represented a more self-confident marshalling of hitherto disparate symbols in the drive towards a more forceful assertion of Cornish identity. And this, in turn, reflected the Revivalists' increasing willingness to address the socio-economic condition of contemporary Cornwall, again in contrast to their pre-war predecessors who generally avoided such issues.

Indeed, this willingness to address contemporary issues underpinned the increasing politicisation of the Revival after 1945, manifested first of all in the foundation of Mebyon Kernow (Sons of Cornwall) in 1951. Although conceived initially as a pressure group rather than a political party, Mebyon Kernow was overtly political from the first, and amongst its earliest aims was the determination 'To maintain the Celtic character of Cornwall and its right to self-government in domestic affairs'.[60] And alongside the desire to foster Cornwall's history, language, literature and sport, was the development of an economic policy—articulated in 1968 in the document *What Cornishmen Can Do*.[61] Growth was impressive, and by 1970 Mebyon Kernow could boast 21 branches throughout Cornwall, with a membership of well over 3,000. The Launceston branch was 100 strong, and in the Falmouth and Camborne constituency Mebyon Kernow claimed to have some 1,000 members. Geoffrey Moorhouse observed that:

> The cold fact is . . . that where a home-rule movement arises, at the bottom of it is generally to be found some very real grievance. Though the activities of Mebyon Kernow may be inflated out of all proportion, and though they take themselves a sight too seriously, it would be a very stupid Englishman who didn't recognise that this extravaganza expresses a fundamental resentment shared by many Cornishmen outside the movement.[62]

As a pressure group, Mebyon Kernow cultivated links with local Members of Parliament. Two Liberal MPs, John Pardoe (North Cornwall) and Peter Bessell (Bodmin), actually joined Mebyon Kernow, as did David Mudd, who became Conservative MP for Falmouth and Camborne in 1970. However, the pressure group role was progressively eroded, not least in the 'Overspill' debate where Mebyon Kernow articulated Cornish opposition to the scheme and in local elections won several seats (including the St Day seat on Cornwall County Council). Encouraged by this success and, taking its cue from the successes enjoyed by Plaid Cymru (the Welsh nationalists) and the Scottish National Party, Mebyon Kernow decided that it would recast itself as a political party. In fact, the process of transformation was drawn-out, Mebyon Kernow not finally abandoning its pressure group pretensions until as late as 1976. However, it did contest the Falmouth and Camborne seat in 1970, where, surprisingly, its candidate achieved fewer than 1,000 votes. Ironically, the seat was won for the Conservatives by David Mudd, a local man and Mebyon Kernow member who had made much of his Cornish credentials. In the two 1974 elections Mebyon

Kernow decided not to contest Falmouth and Camborne, moving its sights to neighbouring Truro instead. Again results were disappointing, with fewer than 1,000 votes being achieved on either occasion, and again Mebyon Kernow's thunder had been stolen by a local man with a passionately Cornish agenda—this time David Penhaligon, who won the seat for the Liberals.[63]

In the mid 1970s, the devolution debate dominated British politics, the apparent possibility of devolutionary governments in Wales and Scotland lending a renewed credibility to Mebyon Kernow. In the general election of 1979, Mebyon Kernow contested Falmouth and Camborne, St Ives, and Bodmin, achieving an aggregate vote of 4,155, leaving the recently-formed Cornish Nationalist Party to suffer at the hands of Penhaligon in Truro, where it achieved just 227 votes. With the collapse of the devolution proposals, Mebyon Kernow shared subsequently in the declining fortunes of the Celtic nationalist parties, achieving a little over 500 votes apiece in the Falmouth and Camborne and St Ives constituencies in 1983. Thereafter, in 1987 and 1992, neither Mebyon Kernow nor the Cornish Nationalist Party put up general election candidates, signalling the general failure of their strategies to pierce the Parliamentary electoral process. In local elections, however, Mebyon Kernow was generally more successful. In 1985, at the nadir of its fortunes elsewhere, Mebyon Kernow won the Penzance South seat on Cornwall County Council, its successful candidate—Colin Lawry—establishing a strong local reputation and power base. He also secured a seat on Penwith District Council, a success emulated in the mid 1990s when Tom Tremewan and Loveday Jenkin won seats on Carrick and Kerrier District Councils, an indication that Mebyon Kernow could emerge as a credible force where it was prepared to field popular candidates with positive reputations as local activists.

Mebyon Kernow's ability to perform well, given the right conditions, was also demonstrated in the 1979 European Parliamentary Elections where, reflecting widespread indignation that Cornwall had not been allocated its own seat in the European Parliament, the Mebyon Kernow candidate (Richard Jenkin) achieved 10,205 votes. As political scientists noted at the time, this represented a very creditable 5.9 percent of the vote in the Cornwall and Plymouth constituency, but if the Cornish vote was desegregated from that of Plymouth—then the Mebyon Kernow share of the vote was an impressive ten percent.[64] The party had also achieved an aggregate of some 10,000 votes in the District Council elections of that year, leading its journal *Cornish Nation* to conclude that '. . . 1979 has proved to be . . . a superb start to MK's first serious attempt to achieve multi-level representation from Parish Councils to the European Parliament'.[65] In fact, 1979 proved to be not the beginning but rather the highpoint of Mebyon Kernow achievement, the party's experience in the 1980s and 1990s being one of general decline, punctuated by the odd individual success.

Inevitably, the move from pressure group to political party had fragmented Mebyon Kernow's support in the community as a whole, while its inability to break through (or even devise a coherent strategy) in the Parliamentary election arena had caused considerable frustration in nationalist circles. This explained the creation of the breakaway Cornish Nationalist Party in 1975. It also explained why some activists preferred to concentrate their efforts within the Cornish branch of the Celtic

League (a Pan-Celtic group intent on creating a Celtic Confederation), and why others were drawn to attempts in 1974 to restore Cornwall's ancient Stannary Parliament. Although the latter was studiously ignored by the establishment (a more compliant approach might have recognised that, constitutionally, the Stannary enthusiasts had a case), these latter-day Stannators convened themselves unilaterally as the Cornish Parliament. In the Poll Tax debacle of the 1980s, the Stannary Parliament played a distinctive role, persuading individuals throughout Cornwall (and the rest of Britain) that they might avoid the tax by becoming 'Cornish tinners'—which meant purchasing £1 shares in a notional Cornish tin mine. Although this activity helped bring notice of the Stannary Parliament to a wider international audience, it also precipitated a split in the Stannary movement itself, so that by 1993 there were two separate groups claiming to be the legitimate Cornish Stannary Parliament. Although critics found this quaintly Ruritanian, the fact remained that Cornwall County Council cited the existence of the Stannary Parliament in its submission to the Local Government Commission in 1994 as part of its attempt to emphasise the distinctiveness of Cornwall, a fact recognised by the Commission itself.[66]

Given the relative electoral failure of Mebyon Kernow, and the consequent fragmentation of the Cornish national movement, the temptation is to suggest that the politicisation of the Revival had had only a marginal affect upon Cornish politics as a whole. Such an assessment would be wrong. In fact, Cornish nationalism had made an important impact on Cornish political culture, as well as influencing the mainstream parties at a time when they too were responding to the effects of rapid socio-economic change and the new mood of anti-metropolitanism. Although the Labour Party had won its first Parliamentary seat in Cornwall in 1950, with the Tories seemingly making general progress elsewhere at the expense of the Liberals, Cornish politics was not about to make a belated attempt to join the general Labour-Conservative 'alignment'. Although without a seat in Cornwall for the entire 1950s and the early 1960s, the Liberals remained the effective opposition party in Cornwall. As Vernon Bogdanor has noted, Cornwall was one of the few areas where the Liberals remained highly active and contested a majority of seats at a time which represented the nadir of their fortunes elsewhere. In fact, in the early 1960s, when Liberal support was still in decline in Britain as a whole, there was something of a Liberal counter-attack within Cornwall. In the 1964 general election, Peter Bessell won Bodmin, and in 1966 Bessell held Bodmin and John Pardoe took North Cornwall. Both men were Mebyon Kernow members.

Labour lost its only Cornish seat in 1970, and thereafter the Liberals were confirmed in their position as the main opposition party in Cornwall. Bodmin had been lost to the Conservatives in 1970, to be regained for the Liberals in February 1974 and lost again in the October, while in North Cornwall Gerry Neale (the Tory) managed to mobilise the second-home vote and oust John Pardoe in 1979. Neale was in turn defeated in 1992 by Paul Tyler, who re-established North Cornwall as Liberal (or rather, Liberal Democrat) heartland. In the meantime, David Penhaligon had won Truro for the Liberals in February 1974, consolidating his position in the October and in 1979. Following his tragic and untimely death, he was replaced in Truro in a by-election in 1987 by Matthew Taylor, another Liberal (Democrat). Adrian Lee demonstrated that such electoral behaviour was highly distinctive when compared to ostensibly similar areas of rural England. This, in turn, represented not only continuity from the distinctive inter-war period but also the more recent impact of anti-metropolitanism in Cornwall.

In 1967 Peter Bessell and John Pardoe had declared that, '. . . the Cornish people have the same right to control their country, its economy and its political future, as the other Celtic peoples of Scotland and Wales'.[67]

The Liberals, in particular, with their historic reputation as the 'Cornish party', went out of their way to respond to the new anti-metropolitanism. Nowhere was this strategy more successful than in Truro constituency, from the time David Penhaligon won his seat in 1974 until his death in a car accident in December 1986. For example, he argued vigorously against the inclusion of Cornwall with Plymouth in the joint European Parliamentary Constituency:

> . . . this a sad day for Cornwall. It is the first time in any election that the boundary of Cornwall, which is sacrosanct and important, has been ignored. The boundary has been denied by what many people in Cornwall see as a London- based Parliament . . . Cornwall is a Celtic area . . . the Celts of Cornwall regard this a sad day in their history, for it is the day when their boundary was ignored and denied.[68]

After Penhaligon's death, the *Western Morning News* lamented the loss of '. . . the man who was regarded everywhere as the voice of Cornwall'.[69] His memorial service on BBC Radio Cornwall was listened to by an estimated 100,000 people.

The transformation in the 1980s from Liberals to Liberal Democrats was not without its effects, but a similar anti-metropolitanism was also evident in the language and activities of MPs Matthew Taylor and Paul Tyler. Although the Conservative Party, unlike the Liberals, had never cultivated a specifically Cornish identity, it was noticeable that those Tory MPs who were able to attract a high level of *ad hominen* support were those who were prepared to vigorously pursue local concerns. David Mudd in Falmouth-Camborne has been noted already; in South East Cornwall, Robert Hicks earned a similar reputation as a local man prepared to speak out (against his own party if necessary) on local issues. Even Labour was able to develop a Cornish hue, not least in Harold Hayman (another local man), Labour MP for Falmouth and Camborne from 1950 until his death in 1966.

The distinctive characteristics of Cornish electoral politics were also mirrored in local government, especially in Cornwall County Council. The Independent tradition endured more strongly in Cornwall than almost anywhere else (it was not until the 1993 county elections that the Liberal Democrats won overall control) and when party-political intervention did occur, the pattern of contestation that developed was itself highly distinctive. However, the real impact of the new anti-metropolitanism was often observed outside the party-political arena, especially in the emergence of 'opposition' economics and 'territorial' politics. The former grew from an increasing uneasiness amongst academics, businessmen and others, a feeling that the policies that had moulded the socio-economic condition of contemporary Cornwall were fundamentally wrong-headed. In the 1970s, organisations such as the Cornwall Conservation Forum and the Cornwall Industrial Development Association became increasingly critical of both UK national and local policies:

> If the view of Cornwall, as seen from London, is that of a colony whose raw materials and labour are to be exploited for the relative well-being of a non-productive bureaucracy, while at

Wind farms dominate the Cornish sky-line, a source of division amongst environmentalists who argue variously that these farms are either an imaginative application of alternative technology or blots on the landscape.

> the same time maintaining the appearance of raising regional incomes, then the regional policies of successive governments begins to make some sense . . . .[70]

In the 1980s, when the full impact of both the branch factory syndrome and counterurbanisation had become observable, the debate became more focused. A Cornish Social and Economic Research Group was formed to investigate those policies and forces that were shaping modern Cornwall, and in 1988 it published *Cornwall at the Crossroads*, a milestone document which informed debate at the highest levels. The Group contrasted the apparent success of 'development' in Cornwall—'marinas, luxury yachts, millionaires' playgrounds'—with the 'submerged Cornwall that refuses to go away' of homelessness, unemployment and low pay. In a perspective which at the time seemed novel, even revolutionary, but which less than a decade later had become almost a conventional wisdom, the Group argued that key assumptions about Cornwall had to be changed if progress was to be made. Instead of the traditional emphasis on 'weaknesses' (Cornwall as 'backward', 'too small', 'remote'), there should be an emphasis on strengths—not least Cornwall's strategic maritime location (which placed Cornwall in the centre of things, not on the edge) and its distinctive identity. The latter was seen as Cornwall's trump card, the means of winning attention in Europe and on the international stage, of marketing a positive, attractive image of Cornwall. The Group called for the establishment of a Cornish Development Agency, and demanded 'More power for Cornwall' for 'Only decentralisation of authority can enable us to realise our opportunities'.[71]

Hand in hand with such a perspective went the 'territorial' politics that had emerged since the war. As Mary McArthur, Bernard Deacon and Dr Alys Thomas had all noted, concern for the territorial identity and integrity of Cornwall had been a key feature of the new anti-metropolitanism.[72] This, in turn, it was argued, reflected the central importance of territory within the make-up of the Cornish identity. As Mary McArthur put it, it was '. . . the land of Cornwall itself which has proved to be a powerful focus of ethnic mobilisation'.[73] But, as Alys Thomas observed, such mobilisation was essentially reactive, so that although '. . . strong arguments are being made for the strength and persistence of a distinctive Cornish identity,

Cornwall's territorial status is under attack from several directions'.[74] In other words, assertions of Cornish territorial identity have generally occurred against the background of perceived threats to that identity.

For example, the role of Plymouth as an aspiring regional centre has been the cause of periodic anxiety in Cornwall. In 1946 a proposal to expand the limits of Plymouth into South East Cornwall was beaten off by Cornwall County Council, as it was twenty years later when it re-emerged in the guise of local government reform. When the Crowther-Kilbrandon Royal Commission on the Constitution reported in 1973, it recommended that greater emphasis should be put on Cornwall's status as a Duchy, and it also observed that 'What they [the Cornish] do want is recognition of the fact that Cornwall has a separate identity and that its traditional boundaries shall be respected'.[75] However, as noted above, this did not inform the process that led to the creation of European Parliamentary Constituencies (EPCs), with the decision to construct a joint Cornwall and Plymouth EPC proving decidedly unpopular. In 1988, when EPC boundaries were reviewed, there was widespread demand for a Cornwall-only EPC. Feock Parish Council explained that 'Cornwall is not part of England'. North Cornwall District Council added that '. . . to travel to Cornwall brings one beyond the bounds of the commonplace into practically another country', while Kerrier District Council insisted that '. . . Cornish culture is distinct from the rest of England and in dire need of special treatment on the same basis as other national groups within the European community'. Cornwall County Council summarised such sentiment, explaining that:

> Such feelings of loyalty are of a very different order from most counties in England. Indeed, Cornwall is almost an island with natural boundaries fixed by the coastline. It is largely isolated from the rest of the country. It has a strong separate identity with its own history, traditions, customs, language and (to some degree) law and institutions. Many of these attributes are firmly rooted in its Celtic past. It seems anomalous that such a community should not have its own separate voice in the European Parliament.[76]

County Hall in Truro, the seat of Cornwall's local administration. The Institute for Public Policy Research, said to have the ear of the Labour Party, has suggested that Cornwall should have its own regional self-government.

The continuing prosperity of busy Falmouth Docks demonstrates the diverse skills base of the Cornish workforce as well as the exciting potential of Cornwall's maritime location.

The bold, innovative architecture of the Tate St Ives exemplified a new mood of self-confidence in Cornwall in the 1990s.

Despite the strength and consistency of such arguments from Cornwall, it was not until 1993 that the EPC was substantially revised—when it became the Cornwall and West Plymouth EPC! That the achievement of a high European profile for Cornwall as a region was a significant priority for many informed Cornish people, was evidenced in the vigorously pro-European stance adopted by Cornwall County Council and a number of voluntary bodies, notably the Cornish Bureau for European Relations which established close liaisons with both the European Union and the Council of Europe, as well as various European regional organisations such as ECTARC—the European Centre for Traditional and Regional Cultures based at Llangollen. However, such activity was at odds with a wider European strategy based on the 'Devonwall' project, an agenda which sought to construct a regional entity based on Devon and Cornwall. In 1993 a bid by the British Government for substantial levels of European funding (so-called 'Objective 1' status) for Devon and Cornwall failed on the grounds of their relative prosperity, despite the fact that a disaggregated Cornwall was actually poorer than other regions—such as Merseyside and the Highlands and Islands of Scotland—which did qualify.[77] In other words, the Devonwall approach had made Cornwall 'statistically invisible' in Europe. According to critics of the Devonwall agenda, the failure of the Objective 1 bid was symptomatic of a wider disadvantage suffered by Cornwall as a result of institutional linkage to Devon.

Further concern for the territorial integrity of Cornwall was expressed during the Local Government review of 1994-95, when the perceived threat was the partition of Cornwall into two or three small unitary authorities. A *Campaign for Cornwall* was set up under the patronage of David Treffry, a former High Sheriff, to preserve the integrity of Cornwall and to lobby for a single unitary authority—a 'super county' that would lend Cornwall strong regional visibility in Britain and Europe. Although the single unitary goal was not achieved, the campaign to prevent partition was highly successful. In its own submission to the Local Government Commission, Cornwall County Council emphasised Cornwall's 'geographic, economic, historic, cultural and ethnic integrity',[78] while the Commission itself acknowledged that 'Cornwall's Celtic roots create a strong sense of identity . . . Some suggest that it has never been legally incorporated into shire England . . . it has its own flag and patron saint . . .'.[79]

The government's decision not to partition Cornwall (in contrast to neighbouring Devon and Dorset) was welcomed as a great victory. But as Alys Thomas noted wryly, '. . . populism is less easily mobilised against the pragmatic trend towards linkage with Devon at diverse levels, and it could be that this presents a longer term challenge to Cornwall's territorial identity'.[80] However, by the mid 1990s there was a growing recognition that regional assertion in Britain and Europe would require regional institutions. The successful campaign to create the Tate at St Ives had had a galvanising effect, visible evidence that it was possible to marshal the arguments and the resources to achieve major projects in Cornwall.[81] The success of the Hall for Cornwall campaign in Truro was a similar boost. A plan by the University of Exeter to create a University College for Cornwall at Penzance was yet another ambitious project, designed to enhance the intellectual infrastructure of Cornwall and to provide significant educational, economic and cultural opportunities. Similarly ambitious was the Eden Project, a scheme to construct a vast under-glass botanical garden in a disused china clay pit.

A modeller's impression conveys the breathtaking scope and ambition of the Eden Project.

The *In Pursuit of Excellence* initiative in the mid 1990s gave a business perspective to this new energy and self-confidence, drawing attention to Cornwall's locational strengths and revealing the opportunities that these offered. Sir John Banham, former Director-General of the Confederation of British Industry, demanded 'a combination of anger and ambition' in those concerned for the future of Cornwall. In 1995 in the annual 'Cornwall Lecture' organised by *In Pursuit of Excellence*, he also called for the creation of a Cornish Development Agency, a streamlined local organisation able to speak with a single voice. This call was echoed by other local business leaders, including Peter de Savary, and in June 1996 the Liberal Democrats announced their *Enterprise Cornwall*, an economic policy of which the central feature was the creation of a Cornish Development Agency.[82] In looking to Cornwall's role in the next century, Sir John Banham emphasised the complexities and challenges of an ever-increasing globalisation. The prospect, however, was a positive one, for 'The problems may be global, but the solutions for Cornwall lie in that very exclusivity that has previously set it apart'.[83]

Notes & References (Chapter 12).

1. For example, see Victoria Syme and Philip Payton, 'Eastern Europe: Economic Transition and Ethnic Tension', in Michael Pugh (ed.), *European Security: Towards 2000*, Manchester University Press, Manchester, 1992; and Philip Payton, 'Ethnic Consciousness', in Michael Foley (ed.), *Ideas That Shape Politics*, Manchester University Press, Manchester, 1994.

2. See Philip Payton, *The Making of Modern Cornwall: Historical Experience and the Persistence of 'Difference'*, Dyllansow Truran, Redruth, 1992, especially chapter 1; and Philip Payton, 'Inconvenient Peripheries: Ethnic Identity and the United Kingdom Estate - The Cases of Protestant Ulster and Cornwall', in Iain Hampsher-Monk and Jeffrey Stanyer, *Contemporary Political Studies 1996*, Political Studies Association of the UK, Belfast, 1996.

3. Charles Thomas, *The Importance of Being Cornish in Cornwall*, Institute of Cornish Studies, Redruth, 1973, p.13 and p.16.

4. Ronald Perry, with Ken Dean, Bryan Brown and David Shaw, *Counterurbanisation: International Case Studies of Socio-Economic Change in Rural Areas*, Geo Books, Norwich, 1986, p.71.

5. David Dunkerley and Claire Wallace, 'Young People and Employment in the South West', in Philip Payton (ed.), *Journal of Interdisciplinary Economics*, Vol.4, No3, 1992.

6. J. Herman Gilligan, 'The Rural Labour Process: A Case Study of a Cornish Town', in Tony Bradley and Philip Lowe (eds.), *Locality and Rurality: Economy and Society in Rural Regions*, Geo Books, Norwich, 1984.

7. *The Original Old 'Oss Souvenir Programme*, Padstow, 1996.

8. *Independent*, 3 April 1989. *Guardian*, 2 April 1989.

9. *Western Morning News*, 13 April 1992.

10. Mary Buck, Lyn Bryant and Malcolm Williams, *Housing and Households in Cornwall: A Pilot Study of Cornish Families*, University of Plymouth, Plymouth, 1991, p.51.

11. Mary McArthur, 'The Cornish: A Case Study in Ethnicity', unpub. MSc, University of Bristol, 1988, p.97.

12. Peter Mitchell, 'The Demographic Revolution', in Philip Payton (ed.), *Cornwall Since The War: The Contemporary History of a European Region*, Institute of Cornish Studies/Dyllansow Truran, Redruth, 1993, p.153.

13. McArthur, 1988, p.81.

14. McArthur, 1988, p.81.

15. McArthur, 1988, p.81.

16. Colin Rallings and Adrian Lee, 'Cornwall: The "Celtic Fringe" in English Politics', unpub. paper, ECPR Workshop Brussels, p.6 and p.8.

17. Payton, *War*, 1993; the series *Cornish Studies* is published by University of Exeter Press.

18. John Murray and The Survey Committee, *Devon and Cornwall: A Preliminary Survey*, Wheaton, Exeter, 1947, p.272.

19. Murray et al., p.273 and p.279.

20. Murray et al., p.279 and p.289.

21. Geoffrey Moorhouse, *Britain in the Sixties: The Other England*, Penguin, London, 1964, p.35.

22. Moorhouse, 1964, p.18.

23. J.R.Cable, 'Industry', in A.R.Prest and D.J.Coppock (eds.), *The UK Economy: A Manual of Applied Economics*, Weidenfeld and Nicolson, London, 1982, p.228.

24. D.J.Spooner, 'Industrial Movement and the Rural Periphery: The Case of Devon and Cornwall', *Regional Studies*, 6, 1971; D.J.Spooner, 'Some Qualitive Aspects of Industrial Movement in a Problem Region of the UK', *Town Planning Review*, 45, 1974.

25. D.Grafton and N.Bolton, 'Planning Policy and Economic Development in Devon and Cornwall 1945-84', in Peter Grapaios (ed.), *The Economy of Devon and Cornwall*, Plymouth Polytechnic, Plymouth, 1984, p.7.

26. R.McNabb, N.Woodward and J.Barry, *Unemployment in West Cornwall*, Department of Employment, London, 1979,p.1.

27. David Dunkerley and Ingrid Faerden, 'Aspects of Seasonal Unemployment in Devon and Cornwall', in Peter Gripaios (ed.), *The South West Economy*, Plymouth Business School, Plymouth, 1985, p.22.

28. Peter Grapaios and Consultancy South West, *The South West Economy: Trends and Prospects*, Plymouth Business School, Plymouth, 1989, p.1.

29. Doreen Massey, 'In What Sense a Regional Problem?', *Regional Studies*, 13, 1979; Grafton and Bolton, 1984.

30. Gyorgi Barta and Alan Dingsdale, 'Impacts of Changes in Industrial Company Organisation in Peripheral Regions: A Comparison of Hungary and the United Kingdom', in G.J.R.Linge (ed.), *Peripheralisation and Industrial Change: Impacts on Nations, Regions, Firms and People*, Croom Helm, London, 1988, p.182.

31. Perry et al., 1986, p.63; D.Nelson and D.Potter, *A Survey of Employees in the Manufacturing Sector in the South West*, Department of Industry, London, 1982.

32. Malcolm Williams and Eric Harrison, 'Movers and Stayers. A Comparison of Migratory and Non-Migratory Groups in Cornwall, 1981-1991', in Philip Payton (ed.), *Cornish Studies: Three*, University of Exeter Press, Exeter, 1995.

33. Carol Williams, 'Housing in Cornwall: A Two-Tier System?', in Payton (ed.), 1995.

34. *Private Eye*, 21 August 1987.

35. Bernard Deacon, Andrew George, Ronald Perry, *Cornwall at The Crossroads*, Cornish Social and Economic Research Group, Redruth, 1988, pp.133-148.

36. See Payton, 1992, especially chapter 10.

37. Denys Val Baker, *The Timeless Land: The Creative Spirit in Cornwall*, Adams and Dart, Bath, 1973, p.54.

38. Quoted in *Cornish Review*, 24, Summer 1973.

39. Paul Newman, 'The Plays of Donald R.Rawe', *Cornish Review*, 24, Summer 1973.

40. John Hurst, 'Literature in Cornwall', in Payton (ed.), 1993, p.305; ('all Cornwall is knocking at my door' is from Charles Causley's 'The Seasons in North Cornwall').

41. N.R.Phillips, *The Saffron Eaters*, Exeter, 1987; Myrna Combellack, *The Playing Place: A Cornish Round*, Dyllansow Truran, 1989; Alan M.Kent, *Clay*, Amigo Books, Launceston, 1991.

42. Alan M.Kent, Pol Hodge, Bert Biscoe, *Modern Cornish Poets*, Lyonesse Press, St Austell, 1995, p.iii.

43. Alan Kent, 'Boscawen Street', in Kent, Hodge, Biscoe, 1995, p.32.

44. Philip Payton and Bernard Deacon, 'The Ideology of Language Revival', in Payton (ed.), *War*, 1993.

45. Ken George, *The Pronunciation and Spelling of Revived Cornish*, Cornish language Board, Torpoint, 1986; Ken George, 'Which Base for Revived Cornish?', in Payton (ed.), 1995; R.M.M.Gendall, *A Student's Grammar of Modern Cornish*, Cornish Language Council, Menheniot, 1991; R.M.M.Gendall, *A Student's Dictionary of Modern Cornish, Part 1: English-Cornish*, Cornish Language Council, 1991; Charles Penglase, 'Authenticity in the Revival of Cornish', in Philip Payton (ed.), *Cornish Studies: Two*, University of Exeter Press, Exeter, 1994; N.J.A.Williams, *Cornish Today*, Kernewek dre Lyther, Sutton Coldfield, 1995; N.J.A.Williams, '"Linguistically Sound Principles": The Case Against Kernewek Kemmyn', in *Cornish Studies: Four*, University of Exeter Press, Exeter, 1996.

46. Neil Kennedy, *Cornish Notes For Beginners*, An Garrack, Penryn, 1995, 6.3.

47. Bernard Deacon, 'Language Revival and Language Debate: Modernity and Postmodernity', in Payton (ed.), 1996.

48. Thomas, 1973, p.9.

49. Val Baker, 1973, p.ix; see also Tim Scott, *The Cornish World of Denys Val Baker*, Ex libris Press, Bradford-on-Avon, 1994.

50. 'Saint Cadoc', in John Betjeman, *John Betjeman's Collected Poems*, John Murray, London, 4th ed. 1980, p.98; John Betjeman, *Summoned By Bells*, John Murray, London, 2nd ed., 1976, p.87.

51. For example, Paul Broadhurst, *Secret Shrines: In Search of the Holy Wells of Cornwall*, Pendragon Press, Launceston, 1991; John Michell, *The Earth Spirit*, Thames and Hudson, London, 1975.

52. *Cornish Banner*, 85, August 1996.

53. John Lowerson, 'Celtic Tourism - Some Recent Magnets', in Philip Payton (ed.), 1994.

54. Paul Thornton, 'Cornwall and Changes in the "Tourist Gaze"', in Payton (ed.), *Cornish Studies: One*, University of Exeter Press, Exeter, 1993; Paul Thornton, 'Tourism in Cornwall: Recent Research and Current Trends', in Payton (ed.), 1994.

55. Lowerson, 1994, citing G.Rowell, *Many People Come, Looking, Looking*, Seattle, 1980, frontispiece.

56. Adam Sharpe, John Smith, Lyn Jenkins, *Mineral Tramways Project*, Cornwall Archaeological Unit, Truro, 1990, p.31.

57. Adrian Spalding, 'The Importance of Metaliferous Mining Sites in Cornwall for Wildlife (with Special Reference to Insects)', in Payton (ed.), 1995.

58. Bert Biscoe, 'In the Valleys of the Tin', in Kent, Hodge, Biscoe, 1995, p.140.

59. Bernard Deacon and Philip Payton, 'Re-inventing Cornwall: Culture Change on the European Periphery', in Payton (ed.), 1993; see also Payton, 1992, pp.192-194 and pp.207-210.

60. Mebyon Kernow policy leaflet and membership form, n.d.; see also Richard and Ann Jenkin, *Cornwall: The Hidden Land*, West Country Publications, Bracknell, 1965.

61. *What Cornishmen Can Do!*, MK Publications, Redruth, 1969.

62. Moorhouse, 1964, pp.41-42.

63. See Payton, 1992, especially chapters 2, 9 and 10.

64. David Butler and David Marquand, *European Elections and British Politics*, Longman, London, 1981, p.133.

65. *Cornish Nation*, Summer 1979.

66. Cornwall County Council, *Cornwall - One and All: Submission to the Local Government Commission*, County Hall, Truro, 1994, p.13; Local Government Commission for England, *Final Recommendations on the Future Local Government of Cornwall*, HMSO, London, 1995, p.5.

67. *Western Morning News*, February 1967; for an analysis of the distinctive qualities of Cornish electoral politics, see Adrian Lee, 'Political Parties and Elections', in Payton (ed.), *War*, 1993; for the distinctive characteristics of Liberal contestation in Cornwall in the 1950s, see Vernon Bogdanor, *Liberal Party Politics*, Clarendon Press, Oxford, 1983, p.79.

68. *Hansard*, 1161-1162, 4 December 1978.

69. *Western Morning News*, 23 December 1986.

70. Cornwall Industrial Development Association, *The Economy of Cornwall*, CIDA, Truro, 1977, p.62.

71. Deacon, George, Perry, 1988, p.181.

72. McArthur, 1988, pp.66-67; Bernard Deacon, 'And Shall Trelawny Die? The Cornish Identity', in Payton (ed.), *War*, 1993; Alys Thomas, 'Cornwall's Territorial Dilemma: European Region or "Westcountry" Subregion?', in Payton (ed.), 1994; see also Philip Payton, 'Territory and Identity', in Payton (ed.), *War*, 1993.

73. McArthur, 1988, pp.66-67.

74. Thomas, 1994.

75. *The Report of the Royal Commission on the Constitution*, Cmnd.5460, HMSO, 1973, para.329.

76. Feock Parish Council, *Boundary Commission for England: European Parliament - Representations of the Parish Council*, 1988, p.1; North Cornwall District Council, *Boundary Commission for England: Public Inquiry into the European Parliamentary Constituencies of Cornwall and Plymouth and Devon*, 1988, p.1; Kerrier District Council, *Boundary Commission for England: 1988 Review of European Assembly Constituencies . . . Representations of the Kerrier District Council*, 1988, p.3; Cornwall County Council, *European Parliamentary Elections Act 1978: Representations to the Boundary Commission*, 1988, p.4.

77. Payton (ed.), *War*, pp.235-236; for a recent discussion of Cornwall's 'statistical invisibility' within the Devonwall model, see Judy Payne, *Interpreting the Index of Local Conditions: Relative Deprivation in Devon and Cornwall*, Universities of Exeter and Plymouth, Exeter/Plymouth, 1995.

78. Cornwall County Council, 1994, p.5.

79. Local Government Commission, 1995, p.5.

80. Thomas, 1984.

81. Janet Axten, *Gasworks to Gallery: The Story of Tate St Ives*, Axten and Orchard, St Ives, 1995.

82. Cornish Liberal Democrat Parliamentary Team, *Enterprise Cornwall: An Economic Plan by the Liberal Democrats*, 1996.

83. *Business Journal for Cornwall*, In Pursuit of Excellence, Redruth, 1996, p.2.

Acknowledgements

An enormous number of people has made this project possible. I am indebted first of all to Howard Alexander, my publisher in this venture, whose vision this book is and who asked me to write it. The editorial and production team at *Alexander Associates* — Maggie Campbell-Culver, Martin Frost and Judy Martin — also deserve similar thanks, not least for their patience in the face of my continual suggestions and changes, as does Christine Alexander who was the glue and co-ordinated some 1200 subscribers. At home, Jane, Brigid and Unity have shown similar patience. At work, my colleagues have also been supportive and helpful, especially my secretaries Elizabeth Jackson and Heather Oliver.

I am indebted to A. L. Rowse for his kind Foreword. Alan Kent helped extensively with the photograph captions, especially in the early chapters, and Roger Penhallurick offered helpful advice on minerals and mineralogy. Professor Charles Thomas and Nicholas Johnson readily responded to my various queries on archaeology and prehistory, and Mark Stoyle read and made many important suggestions on the medieval and early modern chapters. Meetings of the New Cornish Studies Forum have provided the opportunity to debate the complex characteristics of modern and contemporary Cornwall, and I am especially indebted to Bernard Deacon for his stimulating discussions and ideas over many years. Many others have shown enthusiasm for the project, and I am especially indebted to David Treffry for his unfailing encouragement. I would also like to thank the following photographers and others who have been involved in the project, including Paul Watts, Ian Davies, Angela Maynard, Dawn Runnells, Dennis Tilley, George Salisbury, The Lost Gardens of Heligan, The National Trust, Cornwall Tourist Board, Frank Gibson, Jim Mathews, Cornwall Archaeological Unit, *Western Morning News*, Connie Ellis, Colin Weeks, Mount Edgcumbe Joint Committee, Stuart Smith, Trevithick Trust, Bill Newby, Royal Institution of Cornwall, Paul Reid, Jerry Wierzan, Philip Hosken and *Cornish World.*

Finally,I should like to thank the many publishers and authors who have allowed me to draw from their works. Individual acknowledgements are referenced at the end of each chapter. Every effort has been made to discover owners of copyright, but if any omissions have occurred, apologies are offered in advance and any errors in this respect will be corrected in any future editions.

Philip Payton.

'Cornwall' Subscribers

Alexander Associates gratefully acknowledge the Subscribers, without whose support and enthusisiam this book would not have been published. The list is shown in order of receipt of the subscription.

Howard Alexander
Fowey 1996

Colin William Brewer	*Wadebridge*
Catherine Lorigan	*Reading, Berks*
Bob Acton	*Truro*
Shirley J Roach-Atkinson	*NSW Australia*
Bert Biscoe	*Truro*
Barbara Swiatek	*Slough, Middlesex*
Mrs M. Barrett	*Broxborne, Herts*
William J Curnow Jr.	*NJ USA*
Brian C. Olivey	*Fareham, Hants*
C.H. Beer	*Newquay*
Owen W.C. Cock	*Pinner, Middlesex*
Jon Mills	*Luton, Beds.*
Dr Preston P. Williams	*Mn. USA*
Canon & Mrs M.H. Fisher	*Newquay*
Keith A. Roper	*Bures, Suffolk*
Justin Brooke	*Marazion*
William A. Morris	*Hampstead, London*
David Woolf	*Petersham, Surrey*
J. H. Brock	*Helston*
John Blowey	*Camborne*
John & Gwen May	*Or. USA*
J.W.G. Smith	*Liskeard*
Janet Axten	*St Ives*
Jeffrey Stanyer	*Exeter University*
Mrs C. White	*Padstow*
Miss Kerenza Jones	*Watford, Herts.*
Dr D.P. Blight	*St Austell*
Mr J.F. Parsons	*Bournemouth, Dorset*
Merfyn Phillips	*Dyfed, Wales*
Richard Dawe	*Enfield, London.*
J.H. Pearce	*West Lothian, Scotland*
Moira Tangye	*Newquay*
Patricia Edwards	*Loughton, Essex*
Miss J.E. Foster	*Truro*
Mr & Mrs E.C. Folley	*Bude*
John N. Hathcock	*Va, USA*
C. Vink	*Amsterdam, Holland*
Kevin Verrant James	*Totton, Hants*
T.W. Tremewan	*Perranporth*
Anthony Miners	*Tottenham, London*
Mrs Mabel Tun Win	*Camborne*
Mr J.P. Agnew	*Falmouth*
Dr Edna Kingan	*St Mawes*
Mr Chris Dunkerley	*NSW Australia*
George E. Laity	*Truro*
Mrs M.J. Thomas	*Liskeard*
Ann Trevenen Jenkin	*Hayle*
Robert W. Edwards	*Loughton, Essex*
Mrs N. Lacey	*Gillingham, Kent*
P.R.R. Clynick	*Crewkerne, Somerset*
Bert L. Trerise	*Ca. USA*
George & Ruth Jurriaans	*Vic. Australia*
Rev Brian Coombes	*Bodmin*
Lorraine Kerr	*New Plymouth, N.Z.*
Kevin A. McCarthy	*NY USA*
John Bersin	*Liverpool*
Richard W. Bowden-Dan	*Greenwich, London*
Dr F.L. Harris	*Redruth*
Miss R.P. Hirst	*Lydney, Glos.*
Prof Mathew Spriggs	*ACT Australia*
Colin & Joan Rolfe	*Plymouth, Devon*
Paul Laity	*Penzance*
Prof. Anders Ahlqvist	*Finland*
John C Symons	*Wadebridge*
RJ Daniel	*Torpoint*
Dr Ronald Perry	*Truro*
Penny Smith	*Loughborough, Leics.*
G.R. Vine	*NSW Australia*
Michael Oliver	*Poland*
David Midlane	*Sherborne, Dorset*
David Proffitt	*West Looe*
Major P.B. Jelbert	*York, Yorkshire*
Patricia S. Radinoff	*NSW Australia*
Michael F. Huckins	*Queensland, Australia*
John Lawton	*Wrexham, Clwyd*
Eric R. Marsham	*NSW Australia*
Mr P.A. Thorne	*Penzance*
Derek Williams	*Oswestry, Shrops.*
Philip Flamank	*Chorleywood, Herts.*
Prof John Lawlor	*Marazion*
Jonathan M. Webb	*East Taphouse*
Prof Jeffrey D. Mason	*Ca. USA*
Graham Thorne	*Maldon, Essex*
Mr & Mrs I.E. Thorne	*Plymouth, Devon*
Rev Barry Kinsmen	*Padstow*
P.K.D. Tregurtha	*Plymouth, Devon*
Stephen Roose	*Milford, Surrey*
Vivian Hony	*Peterborough, Cambs.*
Graham Hony	*Peterborough, Cambs.*
Stephen Hony	*Peterborough, Cambs.*
Mary Guttridge	*Peterborough, Cambs.*
Clare Witts	*Peterborough, Cambs.*
Dr Evelyn L. Born	*Padstow*
Cornwall County Council	*Truro*
Christina Knight	*Hamilton, New Zealand*
Reg & Jackie Wapling	*Brentwood, Essex*
George Hicks	*Penrith, NSW Aust*
V.T. O'Brien	*NT Australia*
Barry Carter	*Oxford, Oxon*
Mr R.F. Arnold	*Malvern, Worcs.*
Christopher Pollard	*Truro*
Mary McArthur	*Penzance*
Diana P. Ball	*Camborne*
A.R. Killick	*Worcester Pk, Surrey*
L.W. Michell	*Isles of Scilly*
Alan Titchmarsh	*Alton, Hants.*
James Hodge	*Penzance*
Gage McKinney	*Ca. USA*
John Faull	*Ca. USA*
Jacqueline McKinney	*Ca. USA*
Dr Constance F. Brothers	*NC USA*
Dr Colin Podmore	*London*
Peter & Lesley Lane	*Liskeard*
Alastair Tinto	*Callington*
James Jewell	*Wi. USA*
Thomas J Keast	*Mt. USA*
W.H. Hayes AO	*Adelaide, S. Australia*
Mr & Mrs R. Pengelly	*Liskeard*
Cornish Ass. of Qld.	*Queensland, Australia*
Adrian & Akiko Treloar	*Queensland, Australia*
Derek, Sue, Emily & Jack Treloar	*St Erth*
R.J.R. (Reg) & Pat Treloar	*Reading, Berkshire*
Pamela G. Leslie	*Queensland, Australia*
Stephen Clarke	*Wakefield, W. Yorks*
Clifford G. Tonkin	*Hemel Hempstd, Herts.*
Ray & Gillian Millman	*Indooroopilly, Australia*
Linda & Bob Cooke	*King's Lynn, Norfolk*
Joy Jorgensen	*NSW Australia*
Christopher Pittard	*Stafford, Staffs.*
Mrs Ellen McDonald	*Queensland, Australia*
Cornish Ass. W. Australia	*Western Australia*
Keir Trevithick	*Penzance*
Mrs Yvonne Benney	*Bude*
Allan J Vial DFC OAM OPR	*Queensland, Australia*
Marea Mitchell & Robert Mackie	*NSW Australia*
Douglas & Joan Mitchell	*NSW Australia*
Les Mitchell	*NSW Australia*
Jill Mitchell	*NSW Australia*
Jen & Robert Newhouse	*NSW Australia*
Andy & Julie Mitchell	*NSW Australia*
Penzance Library	*Penzance*
Richard R. Hancock	*S. Australia*
C.N. Wiblin	*Salisbury, Wilts.*
Mary C. Siegle	*Mn. USA*
Mary A. Kirby	*Tx. USA*
Nancy R. Lord	*Tx. USA*
Delores King	*Tx. USA*

Mark Vincent	Northampton, Northants
Maureen Anne Vincent	Northampton, Northants
R.D. Jelbart	London
Dr Alan H. Clark	Ont. Canada
Hilaria Honess	Hayle
Prof Moss Madden	Birkenmead Merseyside
Stephen Hosking	Truro
Andrew Hawke	Aberystwyth, Dyfed
Ron Lake	Polruan-by-Fowey
Mrs Angela Thorne	NSW Australia
Lynne & Cliff Ash	Chelmsford, Essex
I. Prowse	NSW Australia
Peter Searle	Leeds, Yorks
Mrs J.P. Biscoe	Truro
Paul Hardwick	Farnborough, Hants
Richard G. Jenkin	Hayle
Peter J. Lowrey	London
Rachel Mullins	Truro
Pastor Tom Hill	Perth, Scotland
Terry & Lesley Trudgian	Peterborough, Cambs
Paul Trudgian	Peterborough, Cambs
Tony Hak	Bracknell, Berks.
Janet Moyse	Par
Dr A.C. Todd	Leamington Spa, Warks
Mr & Mrs G.W. Prettyman	Pentewan
Mrs E.M. Donnison	Polruan-by-Fowey
Bill Cowan	Polperro
R.R. & P. Curnow	Queensland, Australia
F.G. Dufty	Bath, Somerset
Mrs G. White	Boronia, Australia
R.A. Sells	Liverpool, Merseyside
Mrs B. Harris	Probus
John W Clarke	Launceston
Rev JM Davey	Saltash
William R. Jennings	Ca. USA
J.B. Turner	Warrington, Cheshire
Jane Whitman	Pa. USA
C.C.C. Celt	Pa. USA
Blackwell Group	Oxford, Oxon
P.B. Read	Camberley, Surrey
Mrs Chris Miller	Les Marronniers France
William Davy Thomas	Alberta, Canada
John H. Bennett	Ca. USA
Dr D.C. Gill	Walkerville, S. Australia
Mr G. Harry	Christchurch N.Zealand
Corn. Archaeological Unit	Truro
Tim Raymond	Fowey
Dr Howard B. Nyman	Fowey
Men-An-Tol Studio	Penzance
R. Rednall	Callington
Robert D. Oxnem	Wi. USA
Trudy Martin	Al. USA
Gill & David Heathcote	Manchester
Cornish Assoc. of Victoria	Victoria, Australia
Mr J. Godfrey	Chepstow, Gwent
Alan Pearson	Falmouth
Mrs M.D. Rowe	Wadebridge
George E. Ellis	Lng Gully Bendigo, Aus.
Madeleine Clarkson	Toronto, Canada

P. Richards	Camborne
Shirley Clemo	New Plymouth, N. Z.
Gerald Freemantle	Falmouth
Judy Locy	Chicago, USA
Neal McMahan	Ca. USA
Douglas Truran	Ma. USA
D.S. Payn	Mevagissey
Prof Richard J Snedden	Malvern, Australia
Anne Carnall	Tywardreath
Mrs S. Butler	Saltash
Antony & Jane Vincent	Codicote, Herts.
David Protheroe-Beynon	Codicote, Herts.
Susan Pallister	Tywardreath
John F. Taylor	Wadebridge
Frank H. Beer	Liskeard
Fay Heath	Bristol
Jane Hinkley	Dunedin, New Zealand
David Elsam	Weybridge, Surrey
Maxine A. Knight	Vic. Australia
Laurel Hewish	Vic. Australia
Glynis D. Hendrickson	Vic. Australia
Clara Porter	Wa. USA
Dick Porter	Wa. USA
Linda Carnahan	Ar. USA
Hazel Eddy Cox	Ar. USA
Irene & Tom Tuttle	Ca. USA
Mrs Ruth Evans	St Austell
L.H.G. Bailey	Torquay, Devon
Kevin & Judy Martin	Fowey
Mrs Helen Doe	Eydon, Northants
Sir Geoffrey & Lady Holland	St Ives
Penzance Library	Penzance
Mrs Jean Egan	Bristol
Mrs A.J. Windsor	Rickmansworth, Herts.
George Kestell	Bodmin
Tim Scott	Wokingham, Berks.
Jerry Wierzan	London
Max Salisbury	Stubbington, Hants.
Mr S.W.E. Johnson	Newport, Gwent
Mr R.D. Jenkin	Redruth
Edward Martin	Ipswich, Suffolk
Dr H. Murray Lang	Ontario, Canada
Rick Wood	Preston, Lancs.
Claudia Chilvers	Looe
Keith Lowe	Lwr. Kingswood, Surrey
Miss I.H.S. Shaw	Falmouth
Simon Leggett	Dublin, Ireland
Terence G. Johnson	Newport, Gwent
Judith Chamberlain	Ca. USA
Nigel Nethersole	Penzance
Robert M.L. Cook	Plymouth, Devon
Stephanie Rolling	St Austell
John Pollard	Baldock, Herts.
Mr D. Flynn	Reigate, Surrey
Mr Cyril Keast	Reigate, Surrey
Conan Trevenen Jenkin	Hayle
Mrs M.L. Francombe	Worthing, Sussex
John & Gwen May	Or. USA
Chas. H. Butt Jr.	Tx. USA

Ian Gallehawk	Larkfield, Kent
K.G. Piper	Liskeard
Mr T.C. Hicks	Looe
C.P. Beard	London
Mrs J. Masterman	Bude
Christopher J. Masterman	Farnham Royal, Bucks.
Margaret Morrish	Vic. Australia
Dr E.T.E. Richards	Penzance
Ian Hambling	Bristol
The Venerable T. Barfett	Truro
Mrs B.M. Andrews	Penzance
Mrs R. Mason	Hants.
T.D.B. Giles	St Austell
Mr B.J. Matyjaszek	London
Graham & Angela North	Bude
Cornish Forefathers Society	St Austell
Bridget Selman	Fowey
Mr & Mrs J.S. Trethewey	Bodmin
Rev T.K. Vivian	Bristol
Mrs M.C. Coleman	Herts.
Barbara J. Gardner-Bray	Ont. Canada
Mrs J.M. Gascoigne	Surrey
Mr & Mrs Peter Stethridge	Truro
Mr W.G. Luke	Redruth
Henry C. Blackwell	Camborne
H.G. Vanderwolfe	Bodmin
Dr P.B. Mikahop	Truro
Mr B.D. McDonald	Lostwithiel
George Heyworth	St Agnes
Mrs Anne Longley	Ashford, Kent
R.F. Cumings	Aylesbury, Bucks
Mrs C.E. Corin	St Ives
Mrs Jane Scott	Portscatho
Miss C.L. Wilson	Croydon, Surrey
K. Blewett	Woking, Surrey
Mrs J.M. Hosking	Wokingham, Berks.
Derek C. Gill	Petersfield, Hants.
Michael J. Martyn	Truro
Mrs B.M. Alexander	Honiton, Devon
Michael S. Crellin	Woodbridge, Suffolk
Susan Ashcroft	Nr Wigan, Lancs.
Mr J. Barlow	Padstow
Mr Cyril D. Hore	Ascot, Berks.
Mr Martin James	Swindon, Wilts.
Graham Busby	Cullompton, Devon
Mr I. Edmund Smith	Hartlepool, Tyneside
Dr Guy Bunker	Truro
Mrs M.M.D. Watson	Eastbourne, E. Sussex
D. Buggins	Brackley, Northants
Mr J.W. Eddy FRCS FRCOG	Colchester, Essex
Dr K.S. Hocking	Falmouth
Justin Brooke	Marazion
D. Penrose	Truro
Fred Woodley	Poole, Dorset
N.S. Linford	Kings Lynn, Norfolk
William J.B. Rowe	West Ewell, Surrey
Mrs M. Cook	Tavistock, Devon
Mr R. Fittock	Petersfield, Hants.
Jean Verso	Vic. Australia

Joan Elaine Wills	*Nelson, New Zealand*
Leslie McCune	*Ingatestone, Essex*
Mrs Jean Nunn	*Falmouth*
Mark Taylor	*London*
Mrs M.J. Greaves	*Tavistock, Devon*
Miss Veronica E. Murphy	*London*
Carol Ell-Oxnam	*Nelson, New Zealand*
Hilary C.I. Bolitho	*Ilminster, Somerset*
Peter Hendra	*Margate, Kent*
D.J.W. Sowell	*Chester-le-St.Co.Durham*
Harry C. Nash	*Bedford, Beds.*
Mrs F.P.D. Perkins	*Bristol*
Rev & Mrs Thomas Shaw	*Perranporth*
Elizabeth Hotten	*Hayes, Middlesex.*
Victor John Pascoe	*Louth, Lincolnshire.*
Mr & Mrs A.W. Groves	*Penryn*
J.G. Trethowan	*Helston*
Mrs Eva Smith	*Coppull Chorley, Lancs.*
Mrs A. Rickaton	*St Austell*
Joan Oxland	*Cardiff, Wales*
Mrs P. Malcolm	*Melksham, Wilts.*
P.H. Williams	*Epsom, Surrey*
Lawrence Kendall	*Ramsbottom, Lancs.*
Mr & Mrs D.O. King	*Plymstock, Devon*
Clive Eric Bowden	*Witney, Oxon.*
Mrs M. Dawe	*Camborne*
Andrew Burt	*Harlow, Essex*
Mr M.C. Crabb	*Cobham, Surrey*
Mrs V.J. Willson-Lloyd	*Ravenshead, Notts.*
Mr J. Saunders	*Redruth*
Mr L.N. Newton	*Walton-on-Thames, Su.*
Mr Simon P. Vage	*Penryn*
Mrs B. Mawderstone-Mackrill	*Truro*
Mr M.J. Daniells	*Skerton, Lancs.*
Mrs M.R. Sargent	*West Wickham, Kent*
Mrs A. Gambier	*Penryn*
Mr C.D. Reynolds	*Falmouth*
Mr J.G. Thomas	*Redruth*
J.C. Julian	*Redruth*
Sue & Jon Connibeer	*Par*
Mrs E.J. Hawke	*Par*
Miss Gwithiam M. Guy	*London*
G.R. Richards	*Wadebridge*
Prof R.N. Curnow	*Reading, Berks*
Mrs J.M. Rankin	*Camborne*
Mrs J. Holmes	*Hayle*
Geoffrey J. Blewett	*Beverley, E. Yorks.*
Mrs W.E.N. Cripps	*Southampton, Hants.*
Mrs J.M. Davis	*Falmouth*
Henry Hand	*Birmingham*
Miss M.A. Worsdell	*London*
Mrs Carolyn Wood	*London*
John H.B. Tonkin	*Cambridge, Cambs.*
Jennifer Paling	*Penzance*
Victor Taylor	*Manchester*
W.J. Trethowan	*London*
Mr Peter N. Maynard	*Shepperton, Middx.*
Mrs Roslyn C. Maynard	*Shepperton, Middx*
Chrisrtopher Humphries	*Launceston*
Mrs M.E. Attfield	*St Austell*
Roger Anderson	*Basingstoke, Hants*
Miss S. Benney	*Portsmouth, Hants.*
Joyce D. Doughty	*Southampton, Hants.*
Dr G.P.G. Rowe	*Birmingham*
Mrs Ruth Hodges	*Keynsham, Somerset*
Steve Havery	*Marazion*
The Rev Geoffrey Perry	*Truro*
The Rev M.B. Geach	*Truro*
Mrs F.M. Smith	*Hayle*
Dr Francis E. Dunston	*High Wycombe, Bucks.*
Mrs Kath Slatter	*High Wycombe, Bucks.*
Mrs L. Stickells	*Holsworthy, Devon*
Peter John Phillips	*Truro*
Mrs H.M. Medlen	*Liskeard*
Roger Teagle	*Truro*
Dr Margaret Bennett	*London*
Mrs M.J. Little	*Cardiff, Wales*
Mike Morrish	*Truro*
Mrs R.J. Dawe	*Wallington, Surrey*
Mr Leslie Jenkin	*Burnham-on-Sea, Som.*
Mrs S.L. Davies	*Plymouth, Devon*
Kenneth Lanyon Pascoe	*Truro*
Mr J.C. Carbis	*Stanton, Suffolk*
Miss E. Kornhardt	*Oxford*
Dr Graham Pascoe	*Muhldorf am Inn Germany*
Raymond H. Prynn	*Bad Nauheim, Germany*
John B. Mildren	*Vic. Australia*
Richard T.A. Bolitho	*Toronto, Canada*
Mary Gibbs	*Co. USA*
Edwin J. Trevorrow	*Bishp's Stortford, Herts.*
Rev. James A. Trevorrow	*Glasgow, Scotland*
Mrs Kathleen Penberthy	*Blackburn, Lancs.*
Mr K.M. Penberthy	*Blackburn, Lancs.*
Wesley Harry	*High Wycombe, Bucks.*
Brian W. Olver	*Warwick, Warks.*
Rev Canon Anthony Phillips	*Warwick, Warks.*
Alastair Quinnell	*Bodmin*
Pamela Quinnell	*Bodmin*
T.J. de Lange	*Rotorua, New Zealand*
Vancouver Cornish Assoc.	*Vancouver, Canada*
Charles S. Farr	*Bodinnick-by-Fowey*
Mr. K.R. Lovitt	*Camborne*
Robert Reynolds	*Wells, Somerset*
Mr Adrian Wilton	*Liskeard*
Mr A.J. Bannister	*Padstow*
Mr David J. Corney	*London*
Duncan Paul Mathews	*March, Cambs.*
Michael J. Tutty	*Congresbury, Somerset*
Mr J.J. Lanyon	*Plymstock, Devon*
Mrs Annette Fitzsimons	*Southampton, Hants.*
Mrs G.R. Jongkees	*Voorschoten, Holland*
John Muchmore	*Mitcham, Surrey*
Mrs B.J. Porter	*Seaford, E. Sussex*
Barry J. Northcott	*Launceston*
Mr Peter J. Barker	*Wareham, Dorset*
Mrs D. Donohue	*St Keverne*
Stephen Dungey	*Hayle*
Cordelia Harveys	*Milverton, Somerset*
Philip Ellery & Pippa Cooke	*St Columb Major*
Thomas W. Stephens	*Birchington, Kent*
P.E. Martin	*Harpenden, Herts.*
Mrs O. Rixon	*Watford, Herts.*
Mr K. Pool	*Cardiff, Wales*
C.V.M. Tripp	*St Austell*
California Cornish Cousins	*Ca. USA*
Viscount Falmouth	*Truro*
Mrs M.B. Croggon	*Grampound*
Mrs K.M. Harding	*Pelynt*
Marion Coombe	*Hayle*
A.M.J. Galsworthy	*Truro*
Nicholas & Sarah McMahon	*London*
David J. Rickard	*Trowbridge, Wiltshire*
Timothy Pullin	*London*
Frederick Jones	*Olney, Bucks.*
The Rev David Nash	*Falmouth*
P.A. Biddick	*Camborne*
Julian Hocking	*Fulham, London*
Hugh Hocking	*London*
Margaret Killick	*Bridlington E. Yorks.*
Clive Allen	*Co. Wexford, Ireland*
Betty & Jack Eggleton	*Vic. Australia*
J.S. Ellery	*Canterbury, N.Z.*
Dominic Peachey	*Mitcham, Surrey*
Christina Hopkinson	*Leighton Buzzard, Beds.*
Mrs V.M. Foden	*London*
E.N.S. Clyma	*Invercargill, New Zealand*
Mrs J.M. Bourne	*Beverley, E. Yorks.*
J.A. Meer	*Plymouth, Devon*
Mr Alan C. Sellwood	*ACT, Australia*
Mrs N. Colville	*Launceston*
Owen Tregaskis	*Cheltenham, Glos.*
John A. Reynolds	*London*
Francis C. Mathews	*Norwich, Norfolk*
Miss J.G. Symons	*Newquay*
William George Thorpe	*Formby, Yorkshire*
John Forsyth	*Lanteglos-by-Fowey*
Sir A. Molesworth-St Aubyn	*Bodmin*
A.W. Phillips	*W. Vancouver, Canada*
Mrs 'Bill' Glanville	*St Columb*
M.C. Morris	*Bournemouth, Dorset*
Mathew Barton	*Perranporth*
Mrs Ann Hughes	*Aberdeen, Scotland*
John Hawke	*Vic. Australia*
Charles Roscorla	*Kingston-on-Thames, Surrey*
J.S. Kendall	*Birmingham*
John Courts	*Perranporth*
John Sawle	*St Agnes*
Miss B. Walshaw	*Huddersfield, Yorks.*
Mr R.M. Bray	*Bristol*
Mr & Mrs I. Balls	*Bristol*
Jane Osborne-Fellows	*Truro*
John Marrack	*Co. USA*
Grant Grindley	*Truro*
Ian & Pauline Gray	*Ely, Cambridgeshire*
John Body	*Falmouth*
Mr J.M. Wakefield	*Camborne*
Steve Carter	*Ma. USA*

Lord St Levan	*Marazion*
R.F. White	*Truro*
Geoffrey Williams	*Exeter, Devon*
Walter Hicks	*Woodbridge, Suffolk*
Harry Poole	*Le Muy, France*
Peter W.B. Semmens	*York, Yorks.*
Mrs P.A. Cohen	*Portscatho*
Mr Frank Stevens	*Saltash*
Mr B.P. Carlyon	*St Helens, Merseyside*
D.P. Pascoe	*Leigh-on-Sea, Essex*
M. Elizabeth Solomon	*Camborne*
Mrs W.E. Boyle	*ACT Australia*
Mr E. Rockey	*Bristol*
Lillian Knight	*NSW Australia*
Commodore I.M. Burnside	*ACT Australia*
Robert S.G. Cook	*Truro*
Mrs A.S.G. Cook	*Truro*
Mrs Evelyn Hall	*Ca. USA*
A. Mooney	*Stowmarket, Suffolk*
M.R. Sagin	*Helston*
Mr & Mrs R.A. Manning	*Pukekohe, N.Zealand*
G. Doughty	*Truro*
Mrs T. Oatley	*Cherhill, Wiltshire*
Robert N. Christian	*Ca. USA*
Meleta McDiarmid	*Ca. USA*
Mr & Mrs R.J.C. Richards	*St Day*
William Berryman	*Stafford, Staffs.*
D. Brian Gripe	*Truro*
Mr B. Juliff	*Karratha, W. Australia*
K.J. Burrow	*Bideford, Devon*
Mrs Betsy Verrent-Harvey	*Levin, New Zealand*
David R. Painter	*Newquay*
Mrs K.A. Jones	*Lake Rotoma, N.Z.*
Mrs D. Miller	*Mt Nebo, Australia*
Mrs P. Dungan	*Kohimarama, N.Z.*
John C. Street	*Wi. USA*
A.J. Ogden	*Billington, Beds.*
Patrick & Felicity Hutton	*Launceston*
Eric Roy Best	*St Austell*
Mr Darrian Richard Gay	*Truro*
Veronica & Susan Rockley	*East Looe*
Mrs S. Allen	*Basingstoke, Hants.*
Mr R.R Newcombe	*Basingstoke, Hants.*
N.B. Berry	*Blockhouse Bay, N.Z.*
N.F. Merifield	*Faversham, Kent*
Mr J.C. Hockin	*Swanage, Dorset*
J. Hurr	*Portreath*
Mr & Mrs S.J. Parry	*Dobwalls*
Mary L Drury	*Mn. USA*
Glenice Jenkinson	*New Plymouth, N.Z.*
Dr Philip R. Trevail	*Redruth*
Christine McDermott	*Qld. Australia*
Mrs E. Evans	*Falmouth*
Ian R. Slade	*Falmouth*
Mr Shaun Williams	*Leamington Spa, Warks*
Ainsley Cocks	*Par*
Major D.H.V. Lobb	*Sydney, Australia*
Mr R.M. Appleby	*Plympton, Devon*
Margaret Bauer	*Bundaberg, Australia*

J.A. Elvins	*Mevagissey*
Patricia H. Polidor	*New York, USA*
James Deriman	*Morden, Surrey*
Bernice Wood	*New Plymouth, N.Z.*
Mr R.J. Allen	*Newquay*
Colin C. Harris	*St Agnes*
W. John Tonkin	*St Austell*
Miss M.L. Richards	*Plympton, Devon*
R. Woodbine	*Par*
Norman D. Nocol	*Ca. USA*
Humphry L. Davy	*BC Canada*
Diana Woolnough	*Bristol*
Mr R.O. Harris	*South Australia*
Alan & Janet Speight	*Bristol*
C. Raymond White	*Helston*
D.B. Mather	*St Austell*
Mrs E.L. Hodgson	*Ont. Canada*
Mrs J. Kinloch	*Qld. Australia*
Dr K.M. James	*Truro*
Mrs Sandra Twining	*Woodcroft, Australia*
Joan Vernon	*Chiltington, W. Sussex*
T.G. Treseder	*Barnstaple, Devon*
William Hughes	*NSW, Australia*
Mrs Mary K. Woods	*Grantham, Lincs.*
Carwyn W. Cullis	*Ontario, Canada*
Mr A.S. Briant	*Tasmania, Australia*
Mrs G. Wakeham	*NSW, Australia*
Kathleen Webb	*Leamington Spa, Warks*
Sir Richard Carew Pole	*Antony House, Torpoint*
Mr T.M. J. Trewhella	*Marazion*
Mrs Lily Trewhella	*Marazion*
Mr David May	*Peterborough*
B.V. Gilpin	*Vic. Australia*
Mr James C. Godden	*Bodmin*
Thom Kinsman	*Mi. USA*
Phillis L. Igoe	*Il. USA*
Mrs M.J. Riley	*Auckland, New Zealand*
Lois J. Gartley	*De. USA*
Henry M. Floyd	*Etobicoke, Canada*
Mrs Peggy L. Hanwell	*Norwich, Norfolk*
Mary E. Connell	*Wi. USA.*
Carole Kernick Baxter	*Qld. Australia*
Mrs Myra Davey	*Ont. Canada*
William E. Paul	*NC. USA*
R. Roy James	*Romsey, Hants*
Melanie Threadgold	*Romsey, Hants*
Mrs S. Berry	*Bristol*
Mr & Mrs H.F. Bond	*St Ives*
Mrs Murrey Dingle	*Bundaberg, Australia*
Mrs H. Trump	*St Austell*
Stephen Colwill	*Par*
Mrs Fred C. Boyce	*Wi. USA*
Michael G. Bickford	*Falmouth*
L.C. Hunt	*Truro*
Michael Chenoweth	*Al. USA*
Mrs S.M. Gilbert	*St Columb*
David S. Terrell	*BC. Canada*
J.H. Burnard	*Christchurch, Sussex*
Mr A.W. Nancarrow	*Bournemouth, Dorset*

Mrs J.J. Bruton	*Papakura, New Zealand*
Ken Pye	*Hatfield, Herts.*
William Lucas Harry	*Ca. USA*
J.A. Dadda	*Poole, Dorset*
Mrs Joyce P. Litt	*Salisbury, Wilts*
C.B. Dowsick	*Tx. USA*
Baron Hodge of Cavan	*Guernsey Channel Isles*
Peter J. Hoskin	*Canberra, Australia*
William Gartrell	*Md. USA*
Dr John Rowe	*Par*
Fred E. Pomeroy	*NY USA*
Gregory J. Forbes	*Vic. Australia*
Dr F.C. Chapman	*Sydney, Australia*
Phyllis D. Feemster	*Ca. USA*
Lt..Col. Fred A. Morley	*Vi. USA*
Donald L. Shiele	*Pa. USA*
Mrs A. Menhennet	*Beckenham, Kent*
Gordon William Usticke	*NY USA*
Russel Dale	*Vic. Australia*
V. Symons	*S. Australia*
E. West Whittaker Jr.	*Ca. USA*
Mr & Mrs M.E. Greenhalgh	*Redruth*
M. Robin Tchertoff	*Plouer, France*
Robert H. Lyle	*Va. USA*
Dunbar L. MacNemar	*Md. USA*
Mrs Joan Fortes	*Otahuhu, New Zealand*
Keith Hugh Dodd	*Wandi, W. Australia*
Mr & Mrs O. B. Reed	*Hemel Hempstd. Herts.*
Darcy Loop	*Mi. USA*
Mr W.D. Woolcock	*Rickmansworth, Herts.*
Ken Trevathan	*Otago, New Zealand*
Mrs Jan Westworth	*Vic. Australia*
Len & Carol Snell	*Ont. Canada*
John Rowe	*Plymstock, Devon*
J.B. Stevens	*Ca. USA*
Barbara D. Mankin	*Ca. USA*
Mrs L. Kuhn	*Qld. Australia*
Ron Bowman	*Ca. USA*
Sally W. Edwards	*NJ. USA*
Michael E. Laws	*Camberley, Surrey*
Mrs Clare Stephenson	*Cape Town, S.A.*
Roger M. Ede	*Newton Abbot, Devon*
Jeanne Seaton	*Fl. USA*
Mrs W.H. Scheer	*Fl. USA*
Mrs B.L. German	*St Just-in-Roseland*
Julian German	*Truro*
Mr G.A. Taylor	*Plymouth, Devon*
Pauline Mary Coppock	*Stockport, Cheshire*
Les Spear	*Bristol*
Bill Harris	*Porchfield, I.O.W.*
Gregg Maunder	*Yeoville, Somerset*
Mrs P.L. Longrigg	*Bath, Somerset*
Dr J.R. Barber	*Vic. Australia*
Richard Rosslyn Cheffers	*St Albans, Herts.*
Mr A.T. Visick	*Warwick, Warks.*
David Andrew Trewhella Uren	*Howick, Natal , S. Africa*
Eric & Joan Nicholls	*Boscastle*
Emily Gilbert	*Bodmin*
Philippa Gilbert	*Bodmin*

R. Gilbert	*Bodmin*
Mr J.N. Austin	*Penzance*
F.J. Pearson	*Caton, Lancs.*
Ms A. Wardell	*Trowbridge, Wilts.*
Mrs R.O. Morgan	*West Wickham, Kent*
Mr C.H. Phillips	*Chichester, W. Sussex*
Thomas Barr	*Mitcham, Surrey*
F.L. Brewer	*Wokingham, Berks.*
F. Brewer	*Mevagissey*
Mrs J. Howard	*Fowey*
Stephen Millard	*Truro*
Mr W.J. Apps	*Huntingdon, Cambs.*
John F. James	*London*
William Kent Wellington	*NJ. USA*
Vernon Varcoe	*Wa. USA*
Gary T. Spargo	*Az. USA*
Mrs Pamela Sandoe	*Turramurra, Australia*
Marjorie A. Emidy	*Wi. USA*
John Hockin	*NS. Canada*
Hilary Fowler	*Moreton-in-Marsh, Glos.*
D.W. Johns	*Plymstock, Devon*
Mrs A.M. D. Shaw	*Lutterworth, Leics.*
Mrs L.R. Leadbetter	*London*
W.R.R. Bruce	*Enfield, Middx.*
Ann L. Curnow	*Ca. USA*
Michael C. Williams	*Probus*
Peter Boaden	*Truro*
Mrs Mary Croll	*Truro*
Fareed Ahmad	*London*
Joan Wood	*Wetheringsett, Suffolk*
Duchy of Cornwall	*London*
Phil Rendle	*Penzance*
Mrs C.D. Thomas	*Truro*
Robert A. Letcher	*Totnes, Devon*
Loraine L. Bessant	*Knutsford, Cheshire*
Mr J.P. Shea	*Penzance*
David Hodder	*Cheseaux, Switzerland*
Jean F. Dalke	*Il. USA*
Edel Klara Andersen	*St Austell*
Ernest B. Hamley, CStJ.	*London*
Yvonne Bray	*Qld. Australia*
Hazel Smith	*Fowey*
Francis & Erla Jose	*Ont. Canada*
Janet Lloyd	*Trowbridge, Wilts.*
Lucile Novak	*NH. USA*
Yvonne Frankson	*Hampton, Middx.*
Rachel E.B. Trant	*Pelynt*
Noel Thomas	*Lanreath*
F.W. Salmon	*Dyfed, Wales*
Colin Roberts	*Stoke-on-Trent, Staffs.*
Mathew Roberts	*Stoke-on-Trent, Staffs.*
William Roberts	*Stoke-on-Trent, Staffs.*
Verna Tripconey	*Stoke-on-Trent, Staffs.*
C.T. Benford	*Truro*
B. Dunstan	*Wainui Beach, N. Z.*
Ewart W. Blackmore	*Ont. Canada*
R.C.M. Brewer	*Perranporth*
Susan L. Saunders	*Redruth*
Mr I. Doherty	*Falkland Isles,S.Atlantic*

Bennet Jones & Co.	*Fowey*
Alverne Bolitho	*Penzance*
Edward Bolitho	*Penzance*
Miss Joan H. Andrews	*Wellington, N.Z.*
Terry Moyle	*South Darenth, Kent*
Dan & Mary Jane Dingle	*B.C. Canada*
Andrew Thomas	*Bristol*
David Hocking	*St Austell*
Clyde Berriman	*Ca. USA*
Michael Earls	*London*
Miss M.A. Jones	*Cheltenham, Glocs.*
D.M. Cocking	*Bristol*
Mr F.R. Grigg	*Tregrehan Mills*
Alan Honey	*Bristol*
Ms Jean Richards Timmermeister	*Wa. USA*
Miss Elaine Gosby	*NSW Australia*
Elaine L. Comes	*N.C. USA*
Mrs E. Wallace	*Vic. Australia*
H. Layton Bray	*B.C. Canada*
Mr F.M. Mitchell	*Perranporth*
Mrs S. Ham	*Liskeard*
Mr R.J. Bray	*Wadebridge*
Cecil W. Skinner	*Ca. USA*
Miss P.F.A. Mildren	*Birmingham*
Micheál O'Laoire	*London*
Lindsay J. Dalley	*Vic. Australia*
Alderman Roger Keast	*Kenn, Devon*
Kenneth Wallis	*South Australia*
Mr M. Moyle	*Qld. Australia*
Mr Reginald C. Harris	*Alberta, Canada*
Lena Kuhbier	*Hamburg, Germany*
Sir Vernon Seccombe	*Saltash*
I.T. & L.W. Lindsey	*Milford, New Zealand*
Howard Ralph Seccombe	*ACT Australia*
M.G. Todd	*Moorland, Lincoln*
Mrs M.I. van der Veken	*Maniamo, Canada*
Jackie Marrone	*Co. USA*
Mrs Elizabeth Ayscough	*Sidney, Australia*
Mrs Patricia Daniel	*La. USA*
Wade R. H. Pascoe	*Az. USA*
Wyatt E.B. Pascoe	*Az. USA*
Stephen Dennis	*Salter Point W. Australia*
Mrs W. Nelda Murray	*Canada*
Graham Mitchell	*Pershore, Worcs.*
Mr C.P. Brown	*Truro*
Mr G.N. Roberts	*Newquay*
Rob Tremain	*Launceston*
Eunice Hill	*Ont. Canada*
M.E. Walker	*NSW, Australia*
Darrell R. Cocking	*Vic. Australia*
Ian W. Smith	*Chigwell, Essex*
Chris & Dave Braddon	*St Newlyn East*
Mrs S. Byrne	*Newquay*
Stewart Arthur Richards	*Malvern, Worcs.*
WA Genealogical Soc (Gascoyne)	*W. Australia*
W.H. Williams	*St Austell*
Mr C.E. Sampson	*St Austell*
Mark Crowther	*Ingeldorf, Luxembourg*
David Lloyd	*Newquay*

Jan Paull	*Ca. USA*
Pauline S.C. Duinker	*Ont. Canada*
Meryl Kallio	*Mi. USA*
Paul W. Stanton	*Mo. USA*
Winifred A. Dietzel	*Mi. USA*
Mr K. Treleven	*Colchester, Essex*
Jeremy Knowles	*Redruth*
Richard Berryman	*Co. USA*
Miss Merrium Clancy	*Ontario, Canada*
John Treleven	*London*
Allan Pascoe	*Ohio, USA*
Mrs C. J. Greville	*Broken Hill, Australia*
Jim Groves	*Ontario, Canada*
K. Mathews	*Victoria, Australia*
R.J. Tremayne	*Tasmania, Australia*
D. S. Rickard	*Ashburton New Zealand*
Prof Glanville Price	*Aberystwyth, Wales*
Mary Jane Benage	*Mi. USA*
Mr & Mrs William J. Thomas	*Mi. USA*
John T. Caddy	*Mn. USA*
Owen T. Caddy	*Mn. USA*
Marcella Daly	*Ca. USA*
Roskillys	*Helston*
J. L. Armstrong	*Blaydon-on-Tyne, T&W*
Phyllis Trevena	*NSW Australia*
Shane Trevena	*Australia*
Jonathan & Sheila Stephen	*Reading, Berks*
Ms Janet Anne Varcoe	*Ione, Ca. USA*
Mr William Kenneth Varcoe	*San Francisco, USA*
J. B. Walker	*Warwick, Warks.*
Dorothy J. Robinson	*Avoca, Vic. Australia*
Quinton D. L. White	*Christchurch, N.Z.*
James E. Cornwall	*Koeln, Germany*
Robert Wm Pascoe	*Az. USA*
Mrs S. Burley	*Stithians*
Mrs Sarah Greenaway	*Stratford-o-Avon, Warks*
Diane Spargo	*Fl. USA*
Elizabeth J Carson	*Or. USA*
Devon & Exeter Institution	*Exeter, Devon*
Trevor Cock	*Sidmouth, Devon*
Fiona Crichton	*Tx. USA*
Jon & Chel Bardell	*NSW Australia*
Mrs Glenda Cook	*Ontario, Canada*
Jeremy Rowett Johns	*Clifton-on-Teme, Worcs.*
Michael O'Connor	*Par*
Mrs Joan Bruce	*Hull, E. Yorkshire*
F. Carl Roberts	*St Austell*
Mr R. T. Brock	*Liskeard*
John Flamank Finlay	*Exeter, Devon*
J. R. Gilbert	*Fareham, Hants*
Michael O'Rell	*Ca. USA*
Lown Peter	*Lanchester, Durham*
T. F. Waters	*Camborne*
Darren Bond	*BC. Canada*
Mr G. R. H. Poxon	*Penryn*
Roger Sadler	*Stetchworth, Cambs.*
Michael Cock	*Penryn*
Mr S. M. Turk	*Camborne*
D. A. Humphries	*Auckland, New Zealand*

Dr Heather J. Hinkley	*Buckhurst Hill, Essex*
Mrs B. Jeffery	*BC., Canada*
Rhona L. Angove	*Wa. USA*
Helen M. Baker	*Denver, Co. USA*
G. N. Bollenback	*W.DC. USA*
Ian & Barbara Fraser	*Lostwithiel*
Lucille Opie	*Lostwithiel*
Dr John C. Wright	*Solihull, W. Midlands*
Dr Andrew Warner	*Truro*
Christopher Brown	*London*
Joan Tregarthen Huston	*Wa. USA*
Susan Greetham	*Faversham, Kent*
J. T. Meyer	*Helston*
John Hendry	*St Newlyn East*
Mrs V. Dyer	*Almeria, Spain*
Anne Hulme	*NSW Australia*
Mrs R. Kinnaird	*Roche*
Les Eastlake	*Newquay*
Thomas C. Gross	*Ct. USA*
Lois G. Powell	*Upholland, Lancs.*
Martin & Alison Oudeboon	*Zaandam, Holland*
Timothy Patrick Oudeboon	*Zaandam, Holland*
Clive & Susan Williams	*St Just*
Sam & Lisa Williams	*St Just*
William & Isabell Ellis	*St Just*
Mr W. J. Brewer	*Newquay*
Mrs Leila Carey	*NSW Australia*
Scott B. Haywood-Casley	*Md. USA*
Mr & Mrs B. & Mr M. Toft	*Bodmin*
R. F. Silverlock	*St Austell*
Rev. Tim Russ	*St Dennis*
Martin Courts	*St Dennis*
Mrs G. Courts	*St Dennis*
David Treffry	*Fowey*
Mrs D.J. Campbell	*W. Australia*
Dr William Rodney Sheaf	*Stockport*
William James Sheaf	*Saltash*
Mr E. D. Hosken	*Falmouth*
Donald E. Phillips	*Callington*
Mrs Pat Banks	*Western Australia*
Mrs Julie Boardman	*B.C. Canada*
Clive Britton & June Marke	*Bristol*
Mrs G. J. Bridge	*City Beach, W. Australia*
Anthony J. T. Rule	*Helston*
John B. Fawdry	*Devoran*
Mr Les Graham	*NSW Australia*
Introgem	*Hassocks, Sussex*
Ian H. A. Argall	*Huntingdon, Cambs.*
Richard Rowe	*Vic. Australia*
Robert Wright	*Ca. USA*
Mrs M. E. Philbey	*South Australia*
C. Swinson	*Pinner, Middx.*
Woodrow Thompson	*Maine, USA*
Mrs E. M. Robinson	*NSW Australia*
Catharine Perry	*Oxford*
J. N. Swiggs	*Par*
J. & R. Gendall	*Liskeard*
F.W. Rundle	*Beaconsfield, Bucks.*
Huw James	*Cardiff*

R. C. & J. Cater	*St Columb Minor*
Paul T. Barfett	*Colchester, Essex*
W. Michael L. Trethewey	*Grampound*
P. H. R. Harris	*South Croydon, Surrey*
Mr & Mrs B. R. M. Berryman	*Porthleven*
Peter & Roselle Lutey	*St Austell*
Jack & Phyllis Rowe	*St Austell*
David Old	*Padstow*
Justin P. Brooke	*Ca. USA*
Mr D. J. Eddy	*Helston*
Peter McCombe	*London*
Mr M. A. Evans	*Horsham, Sussex*
Barbara L. Jondahl	*Mn. USA*
Moira Ravenscroft	*Kalgoorlie, W. Australia*
Robert Edgar Simons	*Walton-on-Thames*
Mr W. Trenerry	*South Australia*
Mrs J. M. Yelland	*Bristol*
Felicity M. Gould	*Ca. USA*
The Rev W. B. Rowett	*Thames Ditton, Surrey*
Teri Couch	*Ohio, USA*
Chairman, Cornwall C. C.	*Truro*
Paul Tyler MP	*Callington*
Michael S. Nyquist	*Mbabane, Swaziland*
Ann R. Edwards	*Wi. USA*
Jeremy Noble	*London*
Mrs P. Meadon	*St Martin by Looe*
F. G. Isaac	*Swanley, Kent*
G. V. Coon	*Ashburton, Devon*
Mrs J. Meston	*NSW Australia*
James H. Bath	*NSW Australia*
Malcolm F. Waters	*Foxhole*
Paul Toman	*Guildford, Surrey*
R. T. Manaton	*Tring, Herts.*
Dr David Young	*Sidmouth, Devon*
Edward Pender	*Redhill, Surrey*
Robin & Louella Hanbury-Tenison	*Bodmin*
Robert O. Bond	*Md. USA*
S. Collins	*Leamington Spa Warks.*
Mrs Margaret Clow	*Cambridge N. Zealand*
Raleigh Trevelyan	*London*
F. A. S. Fierz	*London*
Graham E. Bool	*St Columb*
June Corotto	*Pa. USA*
Mr J. Wellington	*Lower Hutt, N. Zealand*
Roger Trewhella	*Cheltenham, Glocs.*
Mr. R. P. C. Pearce	*Durban, South Africa*
Lorna Jane Glover Wythers	*Thornton Heath, Surrey*
Miss H Hancock	*South Glamorgan*
Mrs P. C. Richards	*St Austell*
Mrs M. P. Alvarez-Buylia	*Guildford, Surrey*
Vaughan Lloyd Tregenza	*Penzance*
Renee Moresco	*Ca. USA*
Philip Cannon	*London*
M. J. Hill	*France*
J. K. Bennett	*Stevenage, Herts.*
F. E. Leese	*Looe*
Judith McCall	*Wi. USA*
Prof. R. L. Ison	*Milton Keynes*
Prof. Richard Bowden	*NSW Australia*

Sir David Willcocks CBE, MC	*Cambridge*
John Binding	*Wadebridge*
Mrs Sidwell M. Bulbeck	*Truro*
Mr Kenneth Selwood	*Truro*
A. R. Richard	*Wadebridge*
J. H. & Nancy Bates	*Wadebridge*
Joy Jorgensen	*NSW Australia*
Percy Whitford	*Datchet, Berks.*
B. S. Goudge Esq.	*St Austell*
Mr J. A. Beaden	*Heathfield, Sussex*
Dr Barry J. Hensen	*Ca. USA*
Angela Maynard	*Reading, Berks.*
Richard Gerrard	*New Malden, Surrey*
Burnley Moses	*Bodmin*
Lady Crawshaw	*Fowey*
Nancy Rudden	*Oxford*
Jonathan Sutherland Hooper	*St Tudy*
Jimmie L. Butt	*Tx. USA*
Christopher D. F. Uren	*Falmouth*
Mr Lendel Gum	*N.Y. USA*
Annette Hawkins	*Colne, Lancs.*
Margaret Wooder	*Port Isaac*
John Lush	*Delabole*
E. M. Marshall	*B.C. Canada*
Sir John Ellis	*Woodford Green, Essex*
Robin Fuller	*Padstow*
Stuart Avery	*Christchurch, N.Z.*
Mr D. J. Young	*Toowoomba, Australia*
Anne E. Hodge	*Inverurie, Scotland*
P. Dodds	*Polgooth*
John Polter	*Va. USA*
Douglas Gill	*Ca. USA*
Harry J. Stevenson	*Tx. USA*
David R. Nicholas	*NSW Australia*
Peter M. Williams	*Guildford, Surrey*
John R. Carter	*Torpoint*
Philip Marack Hosken	*Redruth*
Ann & Harry Barker	*Ca. USA*
Jean Haigh	*Padstow*
John Baxter	*Trebetherick*
John & Wendy Watts	*Bolventor*
Peter Mullins	*Bolventor*
Rose Mullins	*Bolventor*
M. J. Mitchell	*London*
Mrs I. A. Thomas	*Marazion*
Ronald G. Masters	*Padstow*
St Austell College	*St Austell*
Joyce Carne	*Helston*
Sir John Trelawny	*Hythe, Kent*
Ian M. Saltern	*Bude*
Miss Claire Tripconey	*Newquay*
Mrs Ruth Sampson	*Newquay*
Anthony Cardew	*Eversley, Hants.*
William M. Bowling	*Az. USA*
Fern Gundry Wills	*Az. USA*
Malcolm Ferrett	*St Neots, Cambs.*
Gordon Weaver	*Byfleet, Surrey*
Mrs Beatrice M. Rickard	*Wadebridge*
Mrs Lesley A. Pollack	*Halifax, Yorks.*

Major & Mrs R. B. A. Harrison	*Bodmin*
Corlyn Holbrook Adams	*Tx. USA*
I. L. E. Austin-Smith	*Camelford*
Mr A. G. H. Biddick	*Goonhavern*
Clarinda & Keith Truscott	*Bodmin*
Heather & Ivan Corbett	*Mount Hawke*
Peggy E. Nicholls	*Blackwater*
David & Mary Rees	*East Looe*
Canon & Mrs M. A. Bourdeaux	*Oxford*
Debra Berger	*Co. USA*
Craig Weatherhill	*Penzance*
Don & Myrtle Martin	*Fowey*
T. R. Samwell	*Fowey*
Hugh Miners F.R.S.A.	*Penzance*
R. Williams	*Uckfield, E. Sussex*
G.A.Bray	*Carlisle, Cumbria*
Bunney Pool	*BC, Canada*
Mrs M.J. Kirk	*Walsall, W. Midlands*
Terry & Eileen Harber	*Beaworthy, Devon*
D.H. Potter	*Newquay*
G.J. Paynter	*Barnstaple, Devon*
Daniel Rogerson	*Bodmin*
Tracy-Ann Jennings-McArdle	*Munster , Germany*
Harvey Saundercock	*NSW, Australia*
Janet E. A'Lee	*Gloucester, Glos.*
Norman Welch	*Taunton, Somerset*
Rev. Jean Marshall	*Launceston*
Cornish World	*Redruth*
Isobel Barker	*Plymouth, Devon*
Jane & Corey Rawlings	*Plymouth, Devon*
Ian & Kim Acworth	*Mass. USA*
Mrs Adelaide R. Johnson	*Ca, USA*
V. Hawthorn	*Fetcham*
Susan Harrison	*Bath, Somerset*
B. Oliver	*NSW, Australia*
K. Kendall	*Cowes, I.O.W.*
Elizabeth Hines	*N.C., USA*
Dr Tony Wise	*Welwyn, Herts*
Susan Brook	*Tx. USA*
Major P.E. Hills	*London*
E.H. Roberts	*Reading, Berks*
J. Best	*Par*
Mrs A. G. R. Best	*Par*
Pete Farmer	*Delabole*
Leonard B. Ward	*Bude*
Mrs Virginia Graham	*Hamilton, New Zealand*
J.S. & J.L. Tregurtha	*NSW, Australia*
Mr P. G. Freeman	*Fareham, Hants*
Marilyn Hacking	*Worsley,*
Ian Patrick	*Skipton, North Yorks.*
William D. Beney	*Uxbridge, Middlesex*
Catherine E. Merry	*Northampton, Northants*
Michael F. Collcutt	*Findon, Northants*
Suzan Yerkes Fox	*Pa, USA*
John Cecil Jenkin	*Golant*
Ronald F. Lambert	*Alton, Hants*
Richard Watts	*Harborne, Birmingham*
Roland Deighton	*Vic, USA*
Roy A. Dunstan	*NSW, Australia*
Mrs J.M. Latham	*Vic, Australia*
Willem-Jan Trijssenaar	*Rotterdam, Holland*
A. Pemberton	*Vic, Australia*
Biddy & Douglas Sill	*Launceston*
Mrs Pat Hosking	*Helston*
Miss Wendy Peek	*Wirral, Cheshire*
Mrs S. Covus	*St Austell*
John K. Lewis	*Liverpool*
Ann Williamson	*Porthtowan*
Alistair George Kernow	*Melbourne, Australia*
Colin Gordon Allen	*Godalming, Surrey*
C.R. Jewell	*Bude*
R.T. Basher	*Helston*
Keith D. Staite	*Redruth*
John Bray	*BC, Canada*
Peter Conyngham	*NSW, Australia*
Mrs Rosemary Pollard	*BC, Canada*
Helmut Gabler	*Germany*
Chloë Short	*Pinner, Middlesex*
Rebecca Stokes	*Auckland, New Zealand*
Priscilla Reinowski	*Louisianna, USA*
Raul Rogers Reinowski	*Louisianna, USA*
E. Sheen	*Par*
Mr & Mrs P Urch	*Brentwood, Middlesex*
Mr & Mrs G Ferrari	*Brentwood, Middlesex*
Shields Flynn	*Mass. USA*
David Collinge	*Lanivet*
Jason & Vron Wickett	*Launceston*
K.P. Reeves	*Littlehampton W Sussex*
Mrs Peggy Hodges	*Falmouth*
Mrs Nan Middleditch	*East Brighton, USA*
Dr. G.H. Hones	*Bath, Somerset*
Marie Heard	*Horley, Surrey*
Lt. Col. R.H. Collins OBE,MC	*Bodmin*
Mr P. J. Paul	*Vic, Australia*
Lone B. Samwell	*Fowey*
Mrs Anne C. Littleton	*Weybridge, Surrey*
Philip Cooper	*Bodmin*
Denis and Daphne Cooper	*Bodmin*
Mr & Mrs K. J. Bresser	*Shrewsbury, Shropshire*
Edith S. Watts	*Wi, USA*
Mrs Betty H. Stephens	*Colorado, USA*
Mrs E.M. Wilson	*Vic, USA*
M.E. & J.W. Carne	*Camborne*
Mrs E.A.M. St. Aubyn	*Ashtead, Surrey*
Mavis Gaudion	*Vic, Australia*
John H. Sloman	*Rock, Wadebridge*
D. W. Jewell	*St. Blazey Gate*
Bruce Burley	*Stratton*
Mark Roberts	*St. Teath, Bodmin*
Susan I. Pellowe	*Il, USA*
Laurence Hunt	*Swindon, Wiltshire*
Peter & Becky Cross	*Truro*
John M. Pencheon	*Bodmin*
Peter Michelmore	*London*
Mrs J.M. Connelly	*Worthing, W. Sussex*
Mrs Joyce Devine	*NY, USA*
Nancy Oster Heydt	*NJ, USA*
Colin Weeks	*St Ives*
D.M. Richards	*Milton Keynes, Bucks.*
Dr Lawrence Snell	*Selly Oak, Birmingham*
Maureen Alexandra Parsons	*Canvey Island, Essex*
Charles Watts	*Polruan*
Nellie & Jim	*Torrington, Devon*
Ruth & Derrick	*Milton Coombe, Devon*
H. Anthony Spiller	*Liskeard*
Mrs Enid Bandey	*Truro*
Steven Martin	*Launceston*
M.R. Bawden	*Twickenham, Middlesex*
David & Sian Harris	*Swansea, Wales*
Jason A. Wilson	*Tintagel*
Windsor B. Murley	*NY. USA*
John & Sharon Tyler	*Sydney, Australia*
Michael & Margot Hartley-Edwards	*Lostwithiel*
Dorothy A. Sweet	*Swindon, Wiltshire*
Miss E.M. Wey	*Falmouth*
A.J. Reed	*Truro*
Robert Baxter	*Devoran*
Mary Dudley Higham	*Ca. USA*
Mrs M. P. Evans	*Porthscatho*
Mrs Dawn Austin	*Portwrinkle*
A. J. P. Blackman	*Perranporth*
National Trust	*Cornwall*
Mrs Nancy Norrington	*NSW Australia*
Mr T. Ball	*Rock*
Mr I. W. Armstrong	*Camborne*
Mrs D. Smith	*Shortlanesend*
Robert Bulkeley	*Portmellon*
Alexander Wright	*N. Woodchester, Glos.*
Nicholas Wright	*N. Woodchester, Glos.*
Marilyn Liddicoat	*Truro*
Georgina Alexander	*Nailsworth, Glos.*
Dr Geoff Mathews	*Tx. USA*
Robert E. Roach MBE, JP	*NSW, Australia*

Index

E

F

G

H

I

J

K

L

M